B

Politics in Eastern Europe
1945–1992

George Schöpflin

BLACKWELL
Oxford UK & Cambridge USA

First published 1993
Reprinted 1994 (twice)

Blackwell Publishers
108 Cowley Road
Oxford   OX4 1JF
UK

238 Main Street
Cambridge, Massachusetts 02142
USA

British Library Cataloguing in Publication Data
A CIP catalogue record for this book is available from the British Library.

Library of Congress Cataloging-in-Publication Data
Schöpflin, George.
    Politics in Eastern Europe, 1945–1992/George Schöpflin.
        p.   cm.
    Includes bibliographical references and index.
    ISBN 0–631–14723–3 (alk. paper). – ISBN 0–631–14724–1 (pbk.: alk. paper)
1. Communism – Europe, Eastern – History.   2. Europe, Eastern – Politics and government – 1945–1989.   3. Post-communism – Europe, Eastern – History   I. Title.
HX240.7.A6S36   1993
320.947 – dc20   92–45695
                                                                                      CIP

Typeset in Garamond 10.5 on 12 pt by Best-set Typesetter Ltd
Printed in Great Britain by T.J. Press (Padstow) Ltd, Cornwall

This book is printed on acid-free paper

This book is dedicated to
the memory of
Hugh Seton-Watson
(1916–1984)

Contents

Acknowledgements

Several chapters or parts of chapters have seen the light of day in earlier versions. Chapter 1 has the same text as my piece with the same title in *Daedalus,* vol. 119 no. 1 (Winter 1990), pp. 55–90, which was subsequently reprinted in *Eastern Europe . . . Central Europe . . . Europe,* edited by Stephen Graubard (Boulder, CO: Westview, 1991). I am grateful for the kind permission of the American Academy of Arts and Sciences to reprint the text, but I have restored the British spellings and locutions of the original. Chapter 4 is an amended and extended version of the article 'Stalinism in Eastern Europe', published in *Survey,* vol. 30 no. 3 (no. 130, October 1988), pp. 124–47. Earlier versions of chapter 9 appeared in 'The End of Communism in Eastern Europe', *International Affairs,* vol. 66 no. 1 (January 1990), pp. 3–16, and in the third edition of Stephen White et al., *Communist and Post-Communist Political Systems* (London: Macmillan, 1990); the present version has been printed completely rewritten. Several passages from chapter 10 have been printed in various versions – *International Affairs, East European Politics and Societies* and *New Hungarian Quarterly;* the text here has been radically recast and rewritten.

Introduction

This book is not a work of history, at any rate not in the conventional sense. Rather, its aim is to offer a political analysis of a series of interconnected historical events. The emphasis, therefore, is on analysis and not on narrative. While narrative – the recounting of what happened – is not avoided entirely, it takes second place to my attempt to give these events their appropriate political, sociological, economic contexts in order to reconstruct the mechanisms which lie behind events and to explore how they may have influenced each other at levels below the surface. There are a number of excellent narrative accounts of post-war Eastern Europe, including François Fejtö's *A History of the People's Democracies since Stalin* (in my view, it is absolutely scandalous that this book should have been out of print in English for about a decade), Joseph Rothschild's *Return to Diversity* and J. F. Brown's *Eastern Europe and Communist Rule*. Finally Fejtö, together with Ewa Kulesza, published the third volume of his account of post-war Eastern Europe in French, *La fin des démocraties populaires*.

I have constructed my own – not especially original – periodization as a way of organizing the material in time. I deal first with the antecedent processes of history, concentrating on the uses of political power up to the years after the Second World War; I also deal with the communist legacy of the interwar period and the take-over. Stalinism is concentrated into a remarkably short time-frame – 1949 to 1953. De-Stalinization from 1953 to 1956 and the years between 1956 and 1961 are touched on only lightly, for at this time there were virtually no initiatives. The 1960s lasted from 1961 (the second de-Stalinization) to 1968 (the termination of the Czechoslovak reform programme). The

1970s began in 1968 and ended with the suppression of Solidarity in 1981; the 1980s then continued until 1989. This is followed by chapters on the collapse of communism and post-communism, an assessment of the major underlying currents in the attempts to establish democracy by the successor régimes.

Examining six countries requires particular solutions of space as well as of time and I have attempted to find these by being both conceptual and comparative. So what I have tried to do is to look at the sweep of events over fairly short periods of time in at least six – on occasion all eight – East European countries. There are problems with this approach, as I am well aware. There are enormous difficulties in comparing countries as diverse as Czechoslovakia and Albania, one a quintessentially Central European society, which has been close to the European mainstream, and the other for all practical purposes a Middle Eastern country that happens geographically to be in Europe. At the same time, I have largely avoided investigation of Yugoslavia and Albania, both of which bear some similarity to the East European mainstream, but are sufficiently different to require separate treatment, above all because in these countries the communist system had a degree of native legitimation that was lacking elsewhere.

The central thread linking the chapters is the question of legitimacy. The problem of how communist régimes established themselves can most clearly be understood through the prism of legitimation and, by the same token, the ever more desperate quest for legitimation marks these systems after the possibilities of qualitative reform were ruled out with the invasion of Czechoslovakia. The slow stultification that ensued eventually impacted on the self-legitimation of the rulers and ultimately this led to régime collapse.

There are pitfalls – perhaps pratfalls – in making generalizations as broadly as I do. To every generalization about Eastern Europe there is at least one exception, if not actually eight. There are points in this book where some readers will unquestionably feel that I am being superficial, that the particular proposition I am making is not applicable to the country with which they are most familiar. Yet I believe that my conceptual approach, especially if it is the underlying spirit that receives the reader's emphasis, for all its intellectual difficulties has benefits as well – obviously, otherwise I would not have adopted it.

In the first place, I feel that new light is cast on some historical processes by my having taken the sweep of events rather than looking at the fate of countries one by one. In particular, I would suggest that certain problems of causation become clear from this approach, notably the one I tackle in chapter 5, my attempt to explain why de-Stalinization led to upheavals only in some and not in all East

European countries. Then the post-war history of Eastern Europe actually cries out for a comparative approach, in as much as it was the scene of an unprecedented political, economic, cultural and social revolution imposed simultaneously on six countries, coupled with the two that adopted it through largely native revolutions. Using this as the base line, the slow but inexorable changes in the imposed or adopted systems can provide illuminating perspectives on how and why change occurs and can permit some progress in the direction of separating what was derived from the Soviet-type system, what was derived from native traditions and the interactions of the two. Naturally, an understanding of this is helpful in interpreting the political processes of the post-communist period.

The communist period in Central and Eastern Europe is also relevant to analyses of continuity and change, particularly post-revolutionary change. One of my propositions is that the region underwent a modernizing revolution imposed from the outside and carried out from above, with far-reaching consequences for access to power, social stratification, industrialization, organization and so on. The central difficulty as I see it is that these alien revolutions entirely failed to root themselves in local soil, overwhelmingly because the Soviet Union blocked any moves in this direction. The result was a slow but inexorable seeping away of legitimacy, even of the conditional support of the early years that the system received from a minority. Furthermore, my argument has something to say, at any rate indirectly, about the effectiveness of modernizing revolutions of the Stalinist type.

I must say something here about Hungary. Hungary is the country in the region that I know best, obviously, seeing that I was born there and speak the language fluently. However, this does not mean that I have tried in any way to invest Hungary with the role of a paradigm; rather I have tried to use it as a source of much information in giving me intimate insights into the functioning of the Soviet-type system and its suc-cessor. But at all times I have tried to be aware of the experience of other Central and Eastern Europe states and, when some of their experiences were not replicated in Hungary, I asked myself the question why in order to find illumination. It is to be hoped that the reader will not feel that a distortion, a *déformation professionelle* or *personelle* has been committed and that the book is too Hungarocentric. Having said this, it is only fair to add that every-one writes about the country they know best and then hopes that it approximates to the whole of the region. My hope is that have avoided the worst of this.

Finally, I have written this book using the concepts, categories, language and vocabulary of political science. I make no apologies for this, on the contrary. I firmly believe that the approach of too many reviewers is not only conventional in its rejection of specialization, especially when expressed in specialized language, but is actually intellectually lazy. Every area of human endeavour develops its own technical vocabulary, as it must do to achieve precision and to avoid constant repetition – these are the functions of jargon. It is a form of arrogance on the part of some reviewers to assume that they ought to be able to understand everything that is written about politics, pre-sumably because they themselves take part in political life. I do not imagine that they would expect to be able to understand a textbook of anatomy, although they too have a human body.

This book has been a long time in the making, for I began writing the first chapter in the mid-1980s. I make no claims to special pre-science about 1989, for I was as much taken by surprise as anyone else, though I had an intimation that extraordinary things were afoot after a visit to Hungary in December 1988 and I had been developing my ideas on political decay for about a decade. Looking back, I have no regrets at having delayed finishing the book, for this has fortui-tously given me a very different perspective to the one of the mid-1980s.

Various people have helped me with this book (some were a hindrance, I shall not name them). Having to teach Eastern Europe was, obviously, enormously useful in clarifying my ideas on an everyday basis to critical and, just as important, to bored audiences. I have benefited from the comments of various colleagues over the years at conferences and other such meetings where academics for-gather. Finally, I would like to give my very special thanks to Jo Blezard and Judy Dempsey for moral and practical support. All the faults, shortcomings, lacunae, stylistic infelicities, logical gaps, how-ever, are entirely mine.

1

The Political Traditions of Eastern Europe

Hamlet: *Do you see yonder cloud that's almost in the shape of a camel?*
Polonius: *By the mass, and 'tis like a camel indeed.*
Hamlet: *Methinks it is like a weasel.*
Polonius: *It is backed like a weasel.*
Hamlet: *Or like a whale?*
Polonius: *Very like a whale.*

Shakespeare, Hamlet, *III. ii. 401–6.*

The political traditions with which Eastern Europe entered the contemporary period can be generally characterized as backward. This backwardness manifested itself notably in the significantly different relationship between state and society to what had evolved in Western Europe, in attitudes towards modernity and the definitions of modernity, as well as the demands that modernization makes on any society. Modernity in the context of an emergent Eastern Europe, that is in the nineteenth century, comprised the aspiration for greater prosperity embodied in the visible symbols of the West at that time – industrialization in a word – and the growing complexity of social, economic and political transactions. In the political realm modernity also implied a measure of participation by society in the determination of political strategies in the broadest sense. With its prosperity the West also acquired power, something which in Eastern Europe was comparatively scarce. The scarcity existed at two levels: the ruling political systems, the empires of Prussia, Austria, Russia and Ottoman Turkey, were weak in relation to the West; while at the same time, East European societies were weak towards the empires.

The set of political values and institutions developed on the basis of pre-existing habits to meet the challenge of modernity were therefore aimed at catching up with the West and paradoxically this produced a set of polities which differed markedly from the original model. These differences, which were intensified by the further differences existing between individual East European polities and societies, have persisted to the present day and have done so quite independently of the Soviet-type systems introduced into the area after 1948. This chapter is basically concerned both to trace the distinctive qualities of Eastern Europe and to explore what changes have been effected by the communist revolutions, as well as to look at the workings of the system itself. In other words, it will look at both the political cultural and the systemic factors involved.

State and Society

The Western political tradition that eventually produced the European variant of modernity differed from that of Eastern Europe in a number of ways, albeit Eastern Europe did share some cultural and political traditions, however fitfully. The distinction here is between the Western tradition and the one that evolved in Russia, for in this regard Eastern Europe forms a transitional zone culturally, just as it does geographically. The salient factors of the Western political tradition in the context of this analysis – others are possible – are concerned with the conception, generation, legitimation and exercise of power. From the earliest period the West gradually evolved towards a position that power should be divided, that the different areas of power should be separated and that the ruler should not be absolute either in his power or in his legitimation.[1] The peculiarity of the Western pattern of development lay in the separation of religious and secular legitimation. The ruler claimed to rule in the name of a divine right to do so, but this did not absolve him from a certain duty to God. To this extent this feature of the Western political tradition was paralleled in other systems, but the radical distinction lay in the autonomy of the religious sphere and the power of the Church to enforce its claim to be the sole arbiter of religious legitimation.

The symbolic drama of Canossa illustrated this vividly. In no other historical tradition was it conceivable that that a powerful secular ruler like the Emperor Henry IV would undertake a penitent's pilgrimage, in

[1] This analysis owes much to Jenö Szücs, *Vázlat Európa három történeti régiójáról* (1983). A translation is in John Keane (ed.), *Civil Society and the State* (1988), pp. 291–332.

a hair shirt and with a rope around his neck, to expiate his politico-religious sins or, in power terms, to recognize the religious authority of Pope Gregory VII, whom he had unsuccessfully challenged.[2] The idea of the Tsar of Muscovy or the Byzantine emperor or the Ottoman Sultan performing an analogous penance is an inherent absurdity.[3]

The particular point to be stressed is the fragmentation of power, at the level of both thought and practice. Over the centuries in Western Europe institutions evolved roughly in accordance with this tradition, despite repeated breaches and derogations. But the fact that they were viewed as breaches indicates the strength of the underlying tradition; no ruler ever succeeded in capturing the high ground of absolutism in this respect, apart from limited periods of time. Thus feudalism reinforced the concepts of reciprocity and accountability. The feudal superior, however grand he might be, had certain obligations to his vassals, notably those of protection, which he was expected to discharge. If he failed in this, he could be held accountable according to a set of recognized rules, thereby permitting the emergence of legality, a set of autonomously enforceable rules not within the hands of the ruler.

The concept of a contract, which was embodied in the oath of fealty or in the commercial codes serving the growing urban trading centres of the Middle Ages, constituted a crucial element in underpinning reciprocity in this system of values. A further feature of the feudal contract deserves notice. The contracting parties took on certain obligations in consideration of some duty to be performed in the future, that is to say the privileges of feudal power were conditional on performance and could, in theory at least, be challenged for non-feasance. The existence of these mutually recognized rights and duties would not in itself have been enough to sustain the set of values encapsulated in them. To achieve this it was necessary to create autonomous organs of enforcement, a mutually respected tribunal, which regulated disputes without undue intervention from either involved party. Here again, the role of the Church and the canon law

---

[2] Canossa was only one of several such symbolic contests. Others included the humbling of Raymond, Count of Toulouse, at St Gilles du Gard, where he was whipped naked in front of the church in 1208 for his alleged involvement in the assassination of a Papal legate; see John James, *Medieval France* (1986). See also Victor Turner, *Dramas, Fields and Metaphors: Symbolic Action in Human Society* (1974).

[3] I have set out my views of the relationship between the European and Russian traditions in rather greater detail in my article 'Central Europe: Definitions Old and New', in George Schöpflin and Nancy Wood (eds), *In Search of Central Europe* (1989).

courts was essential, albeit secular courts were also of significance. The grudging acceptance by the ruler of the autonomy of the law and of the broader interest in a regular, predictable and relatively transparent system of legal administration came to constitute a further feature and a factor on which the Western tradition was based.

An equally important development was that the rivalry of the ruler and the Church made it possible for third parties to emerge with their own sources of power. Three of these spheres – commercial, scientific and urban – had very far-reaching consequences. The emergence of the commercial sphere took place in the teeth of Church opposition, given the Christian ban on usury (and thereby on interest) and at times that of secular rulers as well, who disliked the growing strength of money over which they had no control but on which they depended. Centrally, the growth of networks of trading centres allowed a Europe-wide system to withstand repeated assaults by both secular and religious power-holders.[4]

Of equal, if not greater, significance was the emancipation of a scientific sphere from the tutelage of the Church. This took longer. The Church was unquestionably the custodian of classical and other learning and its role in safeguarding these during the Dark Ages cannot be overestimated, but it regarded this as being within its own religious sphere, to be used for its own purposes. However, by the thirteenth century this had begun to change. The founding of universities, originally as institutions for cultivating learning in the religious sphere, was decisive. Although for a long time universities remained within the ambit of the church and were closely associated with religious learning, a shift took place through the rise of universities with a degree of their own autonomy. The pivot of this was the movement away from rote learning. It came to be accepted that knowledge was more than a set of facts, but – however uncomfortable this might have been – it involved speculative thought. Thus in the universities which were founded in several European centres (Bologna, Montpellier, Paris, Oxford) at about the same time, the norm became the investigation of phenomena and the exploration of the underlying causation, instead of the repetition of previously amassed information, by whatever criteria seemed appropriate, rather than those acceptable to the Church. This development was crucial, in as much as it legitimated the idea of change and innovation. The shift from rote to conceptualization gradually resulted in the claim to an autonomous scientific sphere through the secularization of learning. The

[4] William H. McNeill, *The Pursuit of Power* (1983).

implications of this were extremely serious. It eventually provided cognitive instruments for challenging all claims, all privilege, all power flows. At its heart was the secularized variant of the originally Christian concept that the present can and must always be transcended in the name of a better future. But it involved the translation of a religious eschatology into a secularized teleology, so it was applicable to political situations as well.

All this points to the centrality of autonomous thought and practice from the power of the ruler in the Western tradition. The ruler was constrained to recognize that he did not exercise absolute power over his subjects, who retained politically or economically important spheres of autonomous action. Despite repeated attempts by various rulers – religious as well as secular – to extinguish or suppress these spheres of autonomy, whether in the name of order or routine or unity or rationalization, these were never completely successful. Autonomy and the separation of spheres remained a crucial feature of Western patterns and subsequently became the foundation for the extension of liberties.

However, another aspect of this tradition deserves emphasis. It follows logically from the foregoing that the Western tradition included a concept of change, a state of affairs where relationships shifted and where the various political and economic actors moved autonomously. Indeed, built deeply into this tradition was the idea of improvement through transcendence, derived ultimately from Christian eschatology. The contrast here with the significantly more static empires of the East is clear, not least in the recognition of complexity as something not to be rejected but as a normal feature of life. The continuity of intellectual curiosity in the West was another noteworthy facet of this tradition. The Arab world, having begun with a great burst of intellectual activity following the rise of Islam, then settled into a static, unchanging order in which innovation was frowned on and knowledge was reiterated in an unchanging fashion.

The role of towns likewise demands special discussion. The concept of the autonomous city, one which is not necessarily directly subordinated to a ruler and which is self-regulating is, again, a Western development. The political and economic power built up by these cities, together with the particular concentration of specialized skills that only urban centres could provide and coupled with the autonomy of these skills, came to comprise an important element in this complex of contending centres of power. The idea of exchange and specialization, together with the uncontrolled character of these, fostered and strengthened the reciprocal and multilateral quality of power and the framework within which it was exercised.[5]

Two crucial techniques of government were developed on the basis of this tradition as a whole. The essential powers of the ruler that had to be controlled were those of money-raising and army-raising In both these areas, with greater or lesser success, the ruler was gradually prevented from exercising absolute power. In seventeenth-century England the clash between the King and Parliament centred precisely on this issue. In Holland, too, the power of the monarch was curtailed. In France it was precisely this conflict which finally led to the revolution of 1789. The idea that society should have some say over how the fruits of its labour should be used, through representation in a popularly elected assembly, had both religious and secular roots – many of the techniques of voting were developed in Church government and the word 'vote' originally meant 'prayer' – but by the modern period a politically significant section of society had come to insist that its existence, aims and aspirations did not depend on the ruler, but on the contrary the ruler should depend on it. Indeed, there is a strong argument to the effect that the modernizing revolution of the nineteenth century was concerned with the extension of full rights of participation in politics to all sections of society, albeit the practice of this may have been very much less than perfect.[6] The upshot of this pattern of development in the West was to create a political ethos in which the right to participate was tacitly accepted in theory, even if it was denied in practice, which had within it the possibility of reopening the question of full participation at some later date. The French demand for the summoning of the Estates General after well over a century of abeyance of royal absolutism illustrates this point. Equally, the intermediate institutions derived from long-established traditions of autonomy functioned reasonably effectively to represent the interests of society against the state and to provide a framework within which the growing complexity of modern life could find room for manoeuvre.

The East European Path

There was much in the history of Eastern Europe that overlapped with that of Western Europe and, to this extent, Eastern Europe is

[5] John A. Armstrong, *Nations before Nationalism* (1982); McNeill, *The Pursuit of Power.*
[6] István Bibó, 'Az európai társadalomfejlödés értelme', in *Összegyüjtött Munkái*, 2 (1982), pp. 560–636.

quintessentially a part of the broad pattern of shared experiences and values in the European arena. To a greater or lesser extent, especially in Central Europe, where Eastern Europe had adopted Western Christianity, these societies shared in aspects of feudalism, mediaeval Christian universalism, the Renaissance, the Reformation and Counter-Reformation and the Enlightenment. Yet each one of these was shared slightly differently, less intensively, less fully, with the result that East European participation in the European experience was only partial. Not every East European society shared all the features sketched here, or not to the same depth, but as a broad picture the model is viable; how far any one society took part was determined by geography and politics, with the two often reinforcing each other.[7] In practice, Eastern Europe constituted a transitional zone between the Western tradition of the division of power and the Eastern tradition of concentration of power. In Eastern Europe there were indeed elements of autonomy, but the role of the state was generally stronger than in the West The power of the ruler was, in fact, challenged, but these challenges were on the whole rebuffed, with the result that the power of society failed to develop and concentrations of autonomous power could not and did not emerge, or at any rate they could not attain the necessary critical mass.[8] Instead, the state emerged as far more dominant than in the West, whether in politics or in economics. The experience of foreign rule and the corresponding weakening or destruction of native institutions made a further contribution to the emergence of the dominant state. The degree of dependence – smaller under the Habsburgs, greater in the Ottoman Empire – thus affected both the extent of native political experience and the survival of native political traditions, usually in an attenuated and distorted form.

The central principles of reciprocity and autonomy of law, while not entirely non-existent, were weak, sometimes to the point of invisibility. In Central Europe some acceptance of reciprocity by rulers and ruled – the nobility as represented by the estates – ensured a fitful survival of the principle in both Bohemia and Hungary; in Poland, the ruler was maintained in a position of complete weakness and concentrations of the nobility exercised power without any regard for society. In all these cases, the imperial overlordship and experience of imperially generated industrialization, i.e. a political-military-

---

[7] This is not to deny the impact of economics and the subordination of East and Central Europe to Western markets, as proposed by Immanuel Wallerstein, *The Modern World System*, 2 vols. (1974–80), but I would argue that the economic dependency of the area was only one factor among several in this respect.

[8] I would argue that Eastern absolutism was not as homogeneous as Perry Anderson describes it in *Lineages of the Absolutist State* (1974).

administrative reform based on foreign models and imperial (not local) interests, ensured the continued pre-eminence of state power in the area. This complex constituted the origins of étatism.

Particularly noteworthy in this connection was the doctrine of the discretionary power of the state. The concept is an extension of the principle of the royal prerogative, that the ruler has the right to take action in any area of politics unless he is expressly prevented from doing so by law or custom. This principle enabled the state to retain and promote *its* autonomy in the crucial fields of taxation and military organization. Society was too weak to exercise control over these areas, whereby it could not sustain its autonomy *vis-à-vis* the state. Where conflict between state and society did erupt, the state proved strong enough to hold off challenges. In the long term this precluded the emergence of parliamentary sovereignty in the nineteenth and twentieth centuries, even when elections were held under rules of universal suffrage – as in the pre–1914 Austrian Reichsrat – because these assemblies lacked control over certain key areas of state activity. By way of illustration, in 1914 Austria declared war without any form of parliamentary sanction and, throughout the 1900–39 period, governments in Eastern Europe did not lose elections. There were only two exceptions (Hungary in 1905–6 and Bulgaria in 1932),[9] both resulting from divisions in the ruling élite rather than having anything to do with the popular will. The state, using its control of the administrative machinery, was generally able to 'make' elections in its favour; it was only when the élite was divided and state power was used ineffectively that governments could change.

The enduring features of this system included an unmistakable element of façade politics. This had two aspects. On the one hand it involved a measure of outward and occasionally genuine respect for constitutional proprieties. The need to avoid opprobrium abroad for some particularly outrageous action, and thus the weight of international opinion, was another factor in this complex.[10] Hence some real autonomy could and did exist

On many occasions the courts delivered politically uninfluenced verdicts, the press could and did print criticism of the state, and interest protection organizations, like trade unions, could work for the benefit of their members. On the other hand, the system was equally evidently guided by the power élite, which tended to regard constitutional and

[9] Peter Sugar, 'An Underrated Event: the Hungarian Constitutional Crisis of 1905–06', *East European Quarterly,* 15 no. 3 (1981), pp. 281–306; and Nissan Oren, *Bulgarian Communism: the Road to Power 1934–1944* (1971).

[10] Pressure from France and Britain on the avowedly anti-Semitic Cuza-Goga government in Romania in 1937–8 was an example; see Joseph Rothschild, *East Central Europe between the Two World Wars* (1974), pp. 309–11.

legal procedures as an inconvenience and a façade, behind which it was free to defend its positions and interests unhindered by other forces. An external appearance of an institutional framework to provide for mass participation in politics existed, but in real terms political participation remained the privilege of the élite. Reciprocity of rights was largely limited to what the élite was prepared to concede at any one time. The political rights accorded to individuals in this system were few, although usage and practice could make it difficult to retract some long-established custom. In the main, these were restricted to near-ritualistic participation in elections and certain limited welfare provisions, like a few years of education. Participation by instruments of press criticism, strikes, political opposition already presupposed a measure of group organization which the state could not suppress entirely. In all, these systems could be termed hegemonial. The state exercised a paramountcy over society that the latter could do little to modify; by the same token, the state never claimed a monopoly of power for itself. Reluctantly or otherwise, it permitted the continued existence of areas of political, economic, social, religious, and other spheres of autonomy, preferably inchoate and unpoliticized. This was something else that would disappear in the post-war revolution.

The backwardness of Eastern Europe *vis-à-vis* Western Europe, both real and perceived, had further ramifications for political development. From the outset of the modern period, the late Enlightenment to the middle of the nineteenth century, East European élites took Western Europe as their criterion of modernity. It was immediately obvious that the task facing East European societies was to effect modernization, but the definition of this and the means to this end were not so obvious. Indeed, the East European élites tended to oversimplify the task by assuming that political and economic development to West European levels could be achieved quickly by the practice of adopting West European political forms regardless of their local appropriateness. Often, it seemed, East European élites were content with the introduction of West European institutions into their own polities pro forma and were unable or unwilling to appreciate the generations of development in values and attitudes that lay behind particular Western political technologies.

The crux of this problem lay in the existence of comparatively strong autonomous spheres and centres of power in Western Europe, on which a new 'modern' political system relying on civil society could be based, whereas these were weak to non-existent in Eastern Europe.[11] This led to a situation in which the functions performed by

[11] Andrew C. János, *The Politics of Backwardness in Hungary 1825–1945* (1982); see especially his introduction.

14   *The Political Traditions of Eastern Europe*

these autonomous centres had to be performed by some other agency. In Eastern Europe there was only one – the state. Thus from the outset the East European modernizers were involved in a contradiction, that of having to construct civil society from above. In the event this proved impossible, not surprisingly. Whenever society moved to fulfil the role that modernity assigned to it, the state proved unwilling to relinquish the power it had assumed to carry through modernization. Society, it would be argued, was not yet ready for this and would continue to need the pre-eminence of the state to protect it against itself or external enemies.

At the same time, the state as agent of change proved quite unable to make the far-reaching transformation needed for modernization, at least in the perceived sense. Most of all, a modernizing revolution from above – for this was what the East European élites were aspiring to in the second half of the nineteenth century – was by definition ill-suited to provide for the ever-increasing complexity entailed in modernity. Whether in the sphere of institutions or of social groups or even of theory, state-promoted modernization tends to work towards models of simplicity and the predictability that makes for easier administration; it shuns complexity or even rejects it, as some theories of populism and nationalism did. So in this one particularly important respect, modernizing states in Eastern Europe tended to underestimate the difficulty of promoting economic growth from above and of establishing an entrepreneurial class that would act continuously to maintain expansion.

There were a number of strands in this failure. First, although some state bureaucrats did have a vision of economic modernity copied from Western Europe, their primary concern was generally the well-being of the state machinery itself and their own standard of living as compared with that of the counterparts in the West. Hence more investment was channelled into military-strategic purposes or into consumption by the bureaucracy itself than could be supported by the local economies. This had further repercussions. A job in the bureaucracy became a coveted meal-ticket in itself rather than for the ostensible goal of rational administration and, if employment by the state could provide almost permanent security, then inevitably the state attracted many of the most talented to its service. This effectively drained off not just intellectual talent, for there would hardly have been any other employer for the possessors of technical knowledge at this stage of development, but it also sucked in any potential entrepreneurial talent and ensured that such persons could avoid the dangers of risk-taking, like bankruptcy.

For the members of the élite service in the bureaucracy offered another enormous advantage – a way out of the economic decline resulting from inefficient agrarian methods, while at the same time providing them with a form of employment in which their traditional values of hierarchy could be conserved. In some instances, notably in Poland where entry into the bureaucracy was less straightforward seeing that these were alien (Russian or German; there was no problem with entering the Austrian bureaucracy), the professions played the role of a functional equivalent.[12] Thus the old élite did not suffer disintegration as a result of economic changes, as it generally did in the West, but survived the crisis only marginally transformed in its habits and attitudes. An anti-entrepreneurial ethos was strengthened thereby and the emergence of a social group which could have been the foundation of political autonomy was blocked. Politics, therefore, offered a vista of glittering prizes at a lower personal cost than independent economic activity and, what is more, these were available without any serious checks on how power was acquired and whether or not it was used for personal gain. This ensured that the ethos of the élite would continue to penetrate politics, the state, the structure of institutions and attitudes towards economic activity as something not quite desirable.

In this last category a further phenomenon deserves notice – the hostility to 'modern' entrepreneurial types of money-making among the nobility, which viewed the handling of money with disfavour. Although the management of estates had a long tradition among the nobility, risk-taking was spurned, not least because of the exemption from taxation enjoyed as a feudal privilege. Particularly in the polities where the native nobility was sizeable (Poland, Hungary, Croatia, Romania), a tendency arose to attract an ethnically alien group to undertake the task of economic development. This perpetuated a perception of enterprise as somehow alien and as something in which the political élite did not engage. Furthermore, the political values represented by the entrepreneurial class, including a recognition of growing complexity, a commitment to institutions reflecting greater choice and the autonomy of spheres and thus to pluralism, likewise tended to be viewed with suspicion, not least because any substantial move in this direction would have provided for wider access to political choice. Thereby the élite's control of power would have been diminished. In all, this combination of factors ensured that the state would retain its dominance over society and that the political class which benefited from this arrangement would have no incentive to transform matters by introducing meaningful reform in the direction of

[12] Joseph Obrebski, *The Changing Peasantry of Eastern Europe* (1976).

redistributing power. On the contrary, the élite legitimated its attitudes by arguing that the state was the source of modernity and progress, while society was backward.

In the other polities of Eastern Europe (the South Slav lands and, for that matter, Greece) the situation was not substantially different, except for the absence of a native aristocracy. In their place had arisen a patrician-military-mercantile élite with very similar values, regarding the state as a source of private benefit and considering this as the embodiment of modernization.[13]

Only in the Czech lands of Bohemia and Moravia did anything like a native entrepreneurial class succeed in achieving a political position commensurate with its economic strength and in creating political structures corresponding roughly to the growing complexity of social life, even although this aspiration was partly blocked by the imperial power (Austria) and ethno-national rivalry with the Germans of the area. But even with its much wider social base, politics in the Czech lands were not fully democratic in the strict sense of the word. Before 1914 the practice of politics was indelibly marked by the Habsburg experience of discretionary power and the areas of power reserved to the state. In the interwar period Czechoslovak politics were unquestionably pluralistic and a very wide range of interests was able to participate in the political process. Parliamentary sovereignty, however, was not the reality of the system and global strategy was determined by the various interpenetrating Czech élites (political, administrative, economic, commercial, trade union, military), as articulated through the *petka*, the group of five parties permanently in office and guided by the presidency.[14] In all, the Czech experience suggests that even with patterns of development close to those of the West, especially industrialization and the existence of a native entrepreneurial class, these do not in themselves guarantee the evolution of a Western-style political system; they did, on the other hand, make Czechoslovak politics substantially more open and flexible than other East European polities.

The City

In West European development a key role in the evolution of autonomous organization and power was played by the existence of a

---

[13] John Lampe and Marvin Jackson, *Balkan Economic History 1550–1950* (1982).
[14] Victor S. Mamatey and Radomir Luza, *A History of the Czechoslovak Republic 1914–1948* (1973).

fairly dense network of towns. The West European town was a unique phenomenon in a number of ways, most significantly in its ability to develop autonomously of the ruler and the Church and to create specific political techniques intended to safeguard the basis of this autonomy, namely trade. The legal sphere and the emergence of various legal codes with the function of underpinning the reciprocity of contracting parties were crucial contributions to a relatively open tradition of politics. The practice of municipal government had a similar function. Most important, however, was the existence of the city as a forum of continuous exchanges, economic and social, in which transactions of growing complexity could be played out. The rules governing this complexity had to strike a balance between predictability and routine on the one hand and flexibility and change on the other. To these factors may be added the role played by towns in the development of political identities and concepts of citizenship.[15]

It is a matter of some controversy whether in this area of development Eastern Europe was always different from the West or whether it diverged from the Western pattern as a result of foreign conquest. For the purposes of tracing the emergence of an East European political tradition this disagreement is less important; it is more significant that by the eighteenth century the area was characterized by a dearth of urbanization. There were very few cities of any size in Eastern Europe and those that did exist lacked the economic and political autonomy, the commitment to interaction and innovation found in the West. There were no significant trading centres or urban settlements with any serious claim to political autonomy. The urban settlements of the area were either bureaucratic agglomerations – the seat of the administration – or garrison towns or static, introverted settlements clinging to commercial privileges and basing their existence on commodities of declining value and exceptional rights demanded by conservative guilds, unable to cope with the new technologies of the West.

Vienna serves as an instance of the first type. It lost its autonomy in 1621 and thereafter it was quintessentially the seat of the Habsburg administration and owed its position primarily to this, with the result that its citizenry was dependent on the the imperial court and state for its employment to a disproportionate degree until relatively well into the nineteenth century.[16] Timisoara (Temeschwar, Temesvár) was an

---

[15] Armstrong, *Nations before Nationalism*.
[16] Donald J. Olsen, *The City as a Work of Art: London, Paris, Vienna* (1986), pp. 58–81.

instance of a garrison town founded in the Banate to act as a bulwark against the Ottoman Empire; non-military activities tended to be subordinated to the needs of the garrison until the nineteenth century. Dubrovnik (Ragusa) or Brasov (Kronstadt, Brassó) illustrate the third category; in these towns a patrician élite clung to its liberties, remained frozen in time and was unable to respond to the challenge of new trade patterns.

The nineteenth century saw some changes in this dispensation and towns did begin to grow, but this growth was uneven and seldom accompanied by the rise of a conscious and confident bourgeoisie prepared to fight for equal access to political power. On the contrary, towns tended to remain dependent on the state which fostered their growth and sought to use them as instruments of their own, to extend greater discipline over the population and to infuse the people with loyalty to the ideals of the state. Hence the city in Eastern Europe could not act either to integrate urban and rural areas – the gap between town and country was significantly wider than in the West – or to develop new political ideas and identities. The cities that did grow up in the nineteenth century tended to acquire a certain alien quality in the minds of the bulk of the population; they were all but colonial intrusions in the countryside. Only towards the end of the imperial period did cities like Vienna, Prague, Budapest or Lwów (Lemberg) begin to function as centres of political, economic and social exchange, important for the integration of rural populations into a wider political consciousness, though even then their role as centres of autonomy was somewhat limited.

These two factors were to an extent interdependent. If Budapest had to serve as the centre of ethnic integration – the melting-pot in which Slavs, Germans, Romanians and Jews turned into (cultural) Hungarians with the encouragement of the state – then it proved difficult for either old or new members of the political community to develop claims to political autonomy, as these were resisted by the élite and popular aspirations were diverted into regarding the political structure primarily in national rather than economic or social terms. In Prague the ethnic conflict between Czechs and Germans, which resulted in a victory for the former by the end of the nineteenth century, tended to promote ethnic considerations above all others for both communities.[17]

---

[17] Gary B. Cohen, *The Politics of Ethnic Survival: Germans in Prague 1861–1914* (1981).

The Bureaucracy

The end of World War I saw the establishment of a network of relatively small states in Eastern Europe.[18] They were all endowed with theoretically democratic constitutions and they all based their existence on the national principle, the principle of national self-determination. Their weakness was widely recognized and fully documented in the context of international affairs. Internally they had to cope with all the problems of establishing and managing new state structures, usually on the basis of limited political experience and with socially and ethnically disparate populations. This last had one vital consequence. The failure of either social or ethnic integration into a single relatively homogeneous civil society also represented the failure of these new states to develop a single public opinion which could exercise control over the political sphere. The political élites had neither the instruments nor the interest to overcome this segmentation, despite a great deal of rhetoric to the contrary. Consequently the political élites retained their hegemony and remained the pre-eminent political class.

The make-up of the political bureaucracy varied somewhat from polity to polity and owed something of its composition and values to the emergence and previous history of that polity. Thus in Poland, Hungary, Romania and Croatia (Bosnia also falls into this category) the neo-feudal character of the political élite was dominant, with the colonization of the state administration by a gentry class (*szlachta*, boyars) having values similar to the way in which they ran their estates. Despite lip-service to land reform – Romania instituted a very radical reform, much of which remained on paper – the power of the landed aristocracy was only marginally affected, whether it drew its power from the land or not, and it continued to use the political resources of the state for its own purposes. The landowning or formerly landowning élite was intimately connected with the military, which it controlled and supplied with senior officers; naturally, the same stratum provided many, though not all, senior officials of state and local administration. Below the landowning stratum came the gentry, which had been largely obliged to abandon its uneconomic landholdings, but was unwilling to give up its nobiliary values to the extent of participating in trade. This sizeable group moved into the

[18] Strictly speaking, the Baltic states also fall into this category, but I shall not be dealing with them, in as much as they are outside my politically determined definition of Eastern Europe.

state administration at the middle levels and lent particularly the Polish and Hungarian administrative machinery their peculiarly neo-feudal character. Although recruitment from the peasantry was not unknown, it was still rare and tended to affect the wealthiest stratum of peasants, which could afford education for its sons.

The financial élite was separate from the political élite, though not wholly so. In Hungary this élite was overwhelmingly Jewish, assimilated by this time to Hungarian language and culture, but regarded as not quite fully-fledged members of the national community. The gentry-bureaucracy had successfully imposed its concepts and political values on the commercial-financial aristocracy, despite the fact that these were very much at variance with the logic and apparent interests of this entrepreneurial class. In Romania the financial élite was small and weak and tended to be dependent on external, Western patrons; it too was heavily Jewish and was far less assimilated than in Hungary. Its political strength was negligible, except for the international leverage it exercised through Western opinion, which then served only to underline its alienness from the Romanian majority. In Poland the situation was similar, except that a native entrepreneurial class, based primarily on the population of former Prussian Poland, had begun to emerge and to compete with a Jewish entrepreneurial class that it regarded as alien.

In the Balkans (Yugoslavia, Bulgaria) the bureaucracy was run by an analogous group, though without landed aristocratic antecedents, for the native aristocracies had been eliminated by centuries of Ottoman rule. They had come to power in the nineteenth century and seized control of the state machinery. Entrepreneurial activity was in any case limited and the economy was heavily dependent on the state, founded on backward agriculture. In Albania there was no state administration to speak of and tribal structures, based notably on the Muslim clans of the north, dominated society.

In Czechoslovakia there existed a somewhat different constellation, with a relatively well-functioning administration and considerable autonomy of the law. Nevertheless there was no qualitative difference, in as much as there was no full integration of society and politics was mostly a Czech preserve. This greatly weakened the constitution and cohesiveness of the Czechoslovak polity, for it operated as a civil society by and large for the Czechs only. There were, of course, numerous non-Czech participants in the political process and as beneficiaries of the political system, but only the Czechs were fully integrated into it. The Czech bureaucracy was recruited from and generally lived by the norms it had learned in Austria-Hungary; within the Czech national community, it functioned rationally and effectively, but for non-Czechs attitudes to the system were not so straightforward. These varied from regarding it with favour for its respect of the formal rules of democracy to deep distrust as a semi-colonial régime.

What was common to all these polities was the institution of the government party operating in a pseudo-parliamentary system. The government party, which was subjected to some electoral choice, was for all practical purposes an emanation of the bureaucracy. The bureaucracy oversaw its successes at elections, regarded it as a political dependency and exchanged its personnel at will. An illustration of this was the way in which prime ministers emerged from the political élite and then proceeded to 'elect' a new parliament to serve them. It is noteworthy, on the other hand, that East European parliaments were not monolithic; the élite did not seek to control the entire electorate, only so much of it as would give it uncontested control over public politics. This accounted for the continued existence of opposition parties of both right and left, often quite radical, and resulted in such apparent paradoxes as the presence of Social Democrats in the Hungarian parliament in 1944, in the centre of occupied Europe. In effect, the hegemonial system operated with a degree of flexibility, in that it accepted a wider range of options than its communist successors were to do.

The instruments of control used by the bureaucracy varied from outright fraud to intimidation. In some electoral districts opposition voters would be prevented from registering their votes; opposition parties might be suddenly banned; politicians might be temporarily arrested; phoney parties might be floated to confuse a particular section of the electorate; or the franchise might be seriously restricted.[19] Open terror was rare and, indeed, it was rarely needed. Electorates were either docile or prevented from voting or their votes proved irrelevant. While elections were held in Yugoslavia the Croatian Peasant Party dominated the Croatian electorate, but this electoral strength could never be translated into political power.

Other aspects of élite politics also deserve notice. Political parties frequently tended to be personal coteries united by loyalty to an individual rather than a political programme or ideology. This meant that clientilism was a key feature of the political order, regulated by a system of rewards and sanctions within the élite and from the élite downwards. It also meant that the make-up of parties could be labile, the composition of their personnel could change and individuals could

[19] Antal Garamvölgyi, 'Magyarország – Nógrádból nézve', *Uj Látóhatár,* 28 nos. 1–2 (1975), pp. 101–8; Anthony Polonsky, *Politics in Independent Poland 1921–1939* (1972).

readily transfer their ostensible political loyalties – ostensible because in reality personal links proved to be more significant than 'ideological' ones. The consequence of this was that political commitments could be relatively weak and politicians appeared to be opportunistic and unscrupulous. Again, the system was devised as much for the personal benefit and security of its participants as for the polity as a whole, to put it charitably. It is worth noting than an analogous uncertainty characterized popular support as well, particularly where peasant voters were concerned, so that parties would rise and disappear with bewildering speed.

A further aspect of the personal nature of politics in Eastern Europe is the role played by tight networks of informal influence, which sometimes resembled secret societies. Groups of individuals who had undergone some particularly intense shared personal experience, especially if concentrated in time, would attribute unique significance to that experience and elevate it to a level of loyalty higher than all others. This loyalty would then cut across lines of political interest and individuals on very different points of the political spectrum would participate in such networks. The Czech legionnaires, those who had taken part in the epic journey across Siberia, were an example of a network of this kind; in this case they ensured that the newly created Czechoslovak army would be dominated by ex-legionnaires and that former Austro-Hungarian officers, who for whatever reason had not been members of the legion, would play a lesser role regardless of professional competence. The Hungarian Etelköz Alliance, a group of anti-communist and anti-Semitic officers who provided the shock troops for the White Terror of 1919–20, were another example. So was the Crna Ruka, the Serbian Black Hand. Examples of greater or lesser significance could be found in every East European country.

Integration

Reference has already been made to the failure of East European polities to effect political integration in the interwar period. Integration operates on two levels: social and national. It implies that the overwhelming majority of society accepts the constitutional and political framework, together with broad, imprecisely defined goals of political and social development within the state. Both in terms of their historical legacies and their actual problems, East European polities found integration an extremely complex and ultimately insuperable task. In the first place, national integration was virtually impossible to achieve. The new frontiers left substantial national minorities or created multinational states, in which distinctive national subcultures with clearly divergent political objectives complicated matters. It is theoretically possible that an appropriate political and institutional framework could have integrated some or all of these minorities over a period of time, but that would have required the national majorities to make greater concessions to minorities than the former found possible or prudent or desirable. The pattern is well illustrated by the fate of Czechoslovakia, which failed to retain the loyalty of non-Czech minorities to the state in 1938. A genuinely integrated polity would not have disintegrated in this fashion, for its constituent member groups would have regarded loyalty to the state as of a higher order than any other.

After the Paris Peace Settlement, Czechoslovak spokesmen made promises to the effect that democracy would safeguard the rights of the non-Czech minorities and that the country would become a kind of 'Eastern Switzerland'.[20] The political implications – as distinct from the legal ones – of this promise to the minorities were that the new state would draw equally on all the national political traditions and cultures included within the new frontiers and that no one nation would enjoy pre-eminence. In fact, from the outset the dominant Czech élites had a different conception of the constitution of the state. It was to be a polity in which there would be legal equality for all, but politically the Czechs would have the constitutive core function, so that Czechoslovakia would be primarily a Czech state. This did not result in the exclusion of the non-Czech population from the political process but it certainly did create a political disequilibrium. The symbolic enactment of this was the failure to ensure the presence of any representatives of the large German minority at the Constitutional Assembly. The eventual consequences of this approach entailed the inability of the Czechs to effect genuine integration, to command the overriding loyalty of the non-Czechs or to feel secure that all the citizens of the state had an equal commitment to it. Therefore, when the state came under overwhelming pressure from abroad, from Nazi Germany, the Czechs suddenly woke up to the weakness of their position and concluded that they had no alternative but to capitulate to the demands of the minorities, in spite of enjoying certain military advantages both at home and abroad. The collapse of 1938 was as much the function of the loss of Czechs' self-confidence through the sudden recognition that only they actually wanted Czechoslovakia to remain as one entity as it was of Nazi German pressure.[21]

[20] J.W. Brügel, *Czechoslovakia before Munich* (1973) pp. 47–9.
[21] Walter Kolarz, *Myths and Realities in Eastern Europe* (1946).

Social integration existed in an analogous fashion and proved just as elusive. Here the problem was that various different social strata in the East European polities might have been cohesive within themselves – though even that is a somewhat doubtful proposition – but they lacked any overall commitment to the state and any sense of participating in the same political venture. The political élite, the peasantry, the workers, the bourgeoisie and other middle strata all tended to lead politically disparate lives guided by significantly different values and to have no well-defined communication with each other. In a word, these polities had to cope with the problem of both ethno-national segmentation and social fragmentation.

Social mobility was low to very low, with the consequences of relative weakness in the structure of the state – analogous to ethno-national segmentation – a higher reliance on coercion or the threat of it than is compatible with political consensus, low levels of loyalty and thus legitimacy. At this point ethno-national and social cleavages could coincide. It was an obvious choice for these weakly grounded semi-authoritarian or fully dictatorial régimes of the interwar period to seek to build loyalty to the state by the promotion of nationalism. To some extent this was successful, but it raised two problems. In the first place, it left open or exacerbated the issue of the national cleavage. Reliance on the national ideology of one ethno-national community frequently brought that community into conflict with another, as national ideologies tended to be incompatible and concerned with mutually exclusive goals, defined in terms of territory or people. Second, nationalism as a political doctrine provided answers to very few questions of political organization and the distribution of power. It created strong identities and a sense of belonging to the state for members of the dominant group, but said next to nothing about political structures, the resolution of conflicts of interests, the allocation of resources and values, participation and representation, i.e. the day-to-day problems of political, economic and social life. If anything, by stressing a transcendental vision of politics, in which implicitly all members of the nation shared a near identical view of the political elements of nationhood, nationalism came close to denying the need for intermediate institutions between the state and the individual, the state and society. The comparative vagueness of the nationalist message, together with its emotional intensity, produced a somewhat contradictory result. East European nations in the interwar period reached a fairly high state of national consciousness of their political identities as members of a nation and as to those excluded as non-members. At one and the same time the implicit promise of equality and justice, encapsulated in the nationalist message, was left unfulfilled, with inevitable frustration and resentment at the social-political closures enforced against society by its rulers.[22]

Social Classes: the Peasantry

The composition and values of the political élites of Eastern Europe have already been discussed in detail and need little further analysis at this point. Although there was considerable inequality within some East European societies, e.g. with respect to landholding, even where there were no latifundia or where they were restricted in number, no corresponding political equality ensued. In other words, the correlation between wealth and political pre-eminence was not direct. Bulgaria, for instance, had an egalitarian landholding structure: 63.1 per cent of all landholdings were between 0 and 5 hectares and only 0.4 per cent held over 30 hectares (1934 figures).[23] In spite of this and in spite of the existence of a fairly well organized peasant party, Bulgarian politics was controlled by a bureaucratic military élite which did not differ significantly from its counterparts in other East European countries.[24] The explanation for this state of affairs has to be sought in the character of the élite, its sense of ruling rightfully and the benefits to be gained from membership (in the terms discussed above), as well as from the difficulties of translating peasant aspirations into political realities and sustaining them organizationally.

One of the key factors helping to explain the survival of the bureaucracy in the face of formidable mass challenges in the aftermath of the First World War – a proposition valid for the entire area, not just Bulgaria – was the political experience and skills of bureaucracy. The corresponding inexperience of its opponents complemented this. The former understood how politics and power were to be managed, how people could be manipulated and how opponents could be bought off. This last factor was of particular significance in relation to post-1918 peasant parties, the leaders of which were extremely readily co-opted into the system.

[22] Ferenc Erdei, 'A magyar társadalom a két háború között', *Valóság*, 9 no. 4 (1974), pp. 25–53; Jozo Tomasevich, *Peasants, Politics and Economic Change in Yugoslavia* (1955); Anthony Smith, *The Ethnic Origins of Nations* (1986).

[23] Rothschild, *East Central Europe*, p. 334.

[24] Nicos P. Mouzelis, 'Greek and Bulgarian Peasants: Aspects of their Socio-Political Situation during the Inter War Period', in *Modern Greece, Facets of Underdevelopment* (1978), pp. 89–104.

The whole of the peasantry in Eastern Europe was marked by a deeply internalized set of values derived from centuries of tradition and contemporary structural constraints. The peasant was characterized by living in relatively small, insular communities, with strict ascriptive value systems. This generated a suspicion of the outside world, of strangers with different and inexplicable behaviour patterns. Within these communities there tended to exist clear-cut hierarchies which were perceived as unchanging and unchangeable. Overall, the peasant lived in a world marked primarily by the seasons, by a lack of functional specialization, by low levels of technology and little incentive to improve on this, and by a kind of negative egalitarianism that sought to equalize downwards (thereby fettering improvement through initiative). This system was stable, within the long cycles of upward and downward movement of agricultural prices, and self-reproducing. Crucially, peasant values concerning futurity and thus the feasibility of effecting change were governed by existential security; and that, in turn, was a matter of the reliability of the harvest. In much of Eastern Europe large numbers of peasants lived at or below subsistence level, so that their faith in the future was low. This value was inevitably carried over into the political realm and fed the sense of deference, helplessness and suspicion with which much of the peasantry treated the outside world. Correspondingly, it continuously aggravated a quest for security, which was seen as reachable either through the acquisition of land or escape through upward mobility. Neither was a ready option. The peasant lacked the surplus capital either to buy land or to buy education for his children. This self-reproducing system, therefore, was a vicious circle, which at the same time appeared to be the norm, so that the slow encroachment of the market by the late nineteenth century – which destroyed the system – was felt to be a severe threat, especially as its dynamics were not really understood.

This raises the entire question of peasant values, aspirations and attitudes to politics. Broadly speaking, the peasantry could be divided into three socio-economic categories, each with its own set of attitudinal responses to politics. The first and smallest was the entrepreneurial agriculturist, who farmed a comparatively sizeable landholding and responded to the market and to market conditions. In this category attitudes to the state were relatively relaxed. There was some understanding of how politics operated, how interests could be validated, how peasant interest organizations (like cooperatives) should function and how much could be expected from politics. Those in this category might not have had any particular love for politics, but equally they did not treat the political game as alien and undesirable. Significant sections of the peasantry in the Czech lands and Slovenia, as well as a rather smaller proportion in Poland and Hungary,[25] notably those fairly close to the urban concentrations to which they could sell their produce, fell into this category. They had begun to make the shift from patrimonial to commodity production where their output had an assured market. They responded quickly to changing circumstances and understood the importance of investment. This category was the most efficient and thus the most prosperous agricultural producer. After the communist take-over they bore the brunt of the anti-kulak campaigns.

The second category was the medium peasant, who had some knowledge of the outside world, but remained deeply suspicious of it. In this category the market was accepted to some extent, but at the same time it was regarded as a manipulation by the state against the peasant. On occasion those in this category took part in commodity production and at other times they withdrew into subsistence, discouraged by the tough discipline of the market and responsibility, for which they had neither the preparation nor the economic strength. The political focus of this category was the state and it sought to achieve its ends by means of peasant politics and parties. On the other hand, it continued to view the state and politics as alien, the preserve of 'them', a group which was socially and sometimes even ethnically different. Thus this category tended to look backwards towards the old village community and the values of that community, often nostalgically, as an idealized vision of society where there was order and predictability, even while the community itself was disintegrating and ceasing to be effective as a social and political unit.

The third and much the largest category was the one to which the term 'peasant' was customarily applied. These people were either landless or dwarf-holders, almost entirely outside commodity production, whose world view was bounded by the village and the seasons and whose experience of the state left them suspicious and hostile. Their contact with the state was through the tax-gatherer, the gendarme and the recruiting officer, all of them regarded as agents of the alien, parasitical 'city' that siphoned off the fruits of peasant labour, in consequence of which the peasant remained poor and exploited. There was a deep-level set of values in this urban–rural dichotomy. It included the honest peasant against the deceitful townee; virtue against vice; generosity against meanness; authenticity against duplicity and so on.

The political ideas of this category were strongly influenced and

---

[25] István Márkus, *Nagykörös* (1979).

reinforced by religious concepts, particularly that of salvation. Its perception of change was heavily conditioned by its understanding of change in the religious context, its dominant experience of a world outside the village commune, in other words, Christian salvation. This lent peasant politics a certain flavour of messianic expectations. Those in this category had a rather weak commitment to organization and to sustained, incremental action, as well having a low sense of personal responsibility or expectation of being able to effect changes. Their attitude towards the outside world, the money-using economy and everything that was seen as different was fundamentally hostile. This was the world of *Gemeinschaft,* the traditional community of status, ascription and static lifestyles, already under threat from the dynamism of the modern *Gesellschaft* with its constant challenge of change and personal choice, but resisting with all that it could muster.

The First World War had a considerable impact on these values and wrought certain changes on peasant politics, albeit without effecting any fundamental transformation.[26] In the first place the peasant was able to observe the importance of food production to the wartime economy and of his own role in this process, contributing to a rise in self-confidence. In this period the agricultural-industrial terms of exchange favoured the former, again boosting self-perceptions. Then, as soldiers, very large numbers of peasants who had previously lived in static village communities, suddenly underwent mobilization and enormously expanded their store of personal experience and thereby their criteria for judging their own status. The difference between the rigid discipline of peacetime soldiering as conscripts and of wartime combat was sufficient to explain why military service before the war had failed to make much impact on the peasant way of life.

Wartime political propaganda and the learning process undergone by the peasantry, as evidenced, for example, by the growing number of desertions during the war, which by 1918 had reached 100,000 in Croatia-Slavonia alone,[27] all helped to modify attitudes and fuel rising expectations. In particular, stronger peasant self-confidence was unquestionably channelled into the newly emergent peasant parties, which had the welfare of the peasantry as their central objective. At the same time, the impact of these parties proved to be limited because the old political establishments had nowhere been conquered, only temporarily defeated; because the political systems had been created by the élite which therefore knew how to operate its levers; and because peasant politicians proved not just inexperienced but also

---

[26] Tomasevich, *Peasants, Politics and Economic Change,* p. 230.
[27] Ibid., pp. 230–2.

incapable of resisting co-option through the lure of power. This inexperience, which peasant leaders to an extent recognized, resulted in peasant parties relying on a section of the intelligentsia for guidance through the maze of politics and representation in the political game. In consequence, peasant experience of politics remained limited and, indeed, there was little in peasant values to predispose the peasantry to adapt to an alien, urban style of power dealing. Hence peasant values remained coloured by the messianism inherited from the past and reinforced by the frustrations of the present, and by hostility to sustained organization, cooperation with outsiders, all of which combined to undermine the impact of the spasmodic irruption of the peasantry into politics.

The Intelligentsia

The intelligentsia developed in Eastern Europe as a very specific social and political group, with features which differed markedly from its counterparts in the West. In this context, the working definition of 'intellectual' used here is someone involved in the generation of values, ideas, alternatives and critiques of the present, whereas the intelligentsia, the bearers of technical knowledge, is involved in the administration of these values and ideas. The political role of the intelligentsia has generally been perceived as oppositional shading off into revolutionary, indeed, members of the intelligentsia are often regarded (and regard themselves) as the quintessence of opposition and as a substitute for it. This is particularly the picture in the context of nationhood and national consciousness. This assessment of the intelligentsia, however, is only a part of the picture and the other part, the conformist, is just as valid and significant as its nonconformist opposite number. The peculiar position of the intellectual and the intelligentsia in Eastern Europe can be derived from the general underdevelopment of the area and the continuation of the salient role played by this group is an indicator of the survival of political backwardness.[28]

Before the modern period the size of the intelligentsia was small. Its membership was to be found overwhelmingly in the Churches, the armed forces and the bureaucracies, but with the introduction of improved education and wider access to it the numbers increased. The problem was this: whereas in the West the newly emergent

---

[28] Zygmunt Bauman, 'Intellectuals in East-Central Europe: Continuity and Change', *East European Politics and Societies,* 1:2 (Spring 1987), pp. 162–86.

bourgeoisie could provide a political and economic medium for an equally autonomous and integrated intelligentsia, the absence or weakness of capitalist market development in the East restricted the options open to budding members of the intelligentsia. What is more, the survival of pre-modern political traditions channelled the intelligentsia into two relatively constricted areas. Their function was either to sustain the theological and teleological legitimation of the system or to provide it with the technological support necessary for the construction of modernity, as defined by the élite. Hence the rise of the ideologically committed, 'engaged' intellectual, whose origins are readily traced back to the Counter-Reformation. He placed his talents at the service of the political élite by creating the new ideology of nationalism or serving the ruling empires and creating an ideology of dynastic loyalty. Alternatively, there arose the pariah intellectual, who failed to find employment or status within the system and was forced to look for other sources of support, often in opposition to the system. The last group became the stereotype of the intellectual revolutionary, with a vested interest in the 'total' transformation of the system, and came to constitute an intellectual proletariat, not least in consequence of the overproduction of graduates towards the end of the nineteenth century.

The social origins of the intelligentsia also proved to be significant in ensuring the survival of certain political values not necessarily in tune with the pattern of development.[29] These roots varied somewhat from country to country in detail but not in essence. The churches provided a most important reservoir in training individuals and providing a channel of upward social mobility (Bohemia–Moravia, Serbia, Bulgaria). Elsewhere (Poland, Hungary, Croatia), the intelligentsia was in the first place recruited from the nobility and the socially and economically hard-pressed gentry. The latter had lost its livelihood, and to an extent its social status and function, in the nineteenth century, having proved incapable of meeting the challenge of competitive agriculture, and moved wholesale into towns, in order to look for employment in a form which it regarded as compatible with its status and values. The importance of military and legal occupations in this value system, which placed greater emphasis on birth and status than on achievement and merit, tended to bear out the validity of this conflation of old values and new careers.

At the centre of this complex of the identity of the intelligentsia was the value system of power. This remained in the hands of the

[29] Ágnes Losonczi, *Az életmód az időben, a tárgyakban és az értékekben* (1977); Miroslav Hroch, *Social Preconditions of National Revival in Europe* (1985),.; Obrebski, *The Changing Peasantry.*

traditional élite, which was hostile to the ideas of the intelligentsia when these represented a challenge to its power. Hence a kind of compromise was born. The intelligentsia, dependent as it was on the state, was accorded a subsidiary position in the hierarchy of power, allowed to exercise some of its intellectual functions – independent, non-status-bound knowledge – as long as this did nothing to damage control over power by the élite. This system of co-option, which relied heavily on the high value of traditional status deployed as an instrument of legitimation by the élite, lived on with minor modifications up to the Second World War and, arguably, was reproduced in the post-1960s compromise.

For a minority of intellectuals, however, this subsidiary status within the hierarchy of power, for all the benefits it conferred on them in the exercise of technical knowledge without serious constraints from public opinion, was insufficient. This minority was attracted by a radical vision of progress, in the name of which it sought to exercise its technical knowledge and committed itself to the service of intellectual objectives, often of a utopian or messianistic kind, rather than to immediate political goals. It lived in a utopian vision of the future and could readily subordinate its short-term technical rationality to the long-term aim. Radicalism of this kind was invariably oppositional, hostile to the existing order, attracted to power and, because it saw the future as a perfect society in which its own values would predominate, it tended to be dismissive of democratic values and the transactions of the market-place.

There is much in this value system resembling that of the peasantry. Many, though by no means all of its protagonists had peasant antecedents and, arguably, there was a carry-over from one value system to the other. The intellectual minority, frustrated and resentful in its sense of failure, went on to formulate the ideologies of left and right extremes which were in this sense and in this sense only united by a vision of total, radical change. Finally, the political significance of the radical minority should also be seen in its role of providing alternative conceptions of the future and strategies of development. In this respect the radical minority could contribute to establishing the limits of the debate and, to some extent, setting the agenda for the remainder of the intellectual community. However isolated these utopian and semi-utopian groups may have been, their wider political impact was not to be underestimated.

The Bourgeoisie

In Eastern Europe, given the weakness of towns and the inability of the area to compete with the developed West, no sizeable bourgeoisie –

an entrepreneurial class – emerged. The Czech lands constituted the sole exception and even there, the bourgeoisie was to a greater extent integrated into the politically determined ethos of the bureaucratic system than in polities further West, where autonomous economic values were pre-eminent. The Czech bourgeoisie was subordinated to the bureaucracy in a number of ways, although it was a more equal partner and had much greater power of its own *vis-à-vis* the bureaucracy than its counterparts in other East European polities. The nineteenth century saw the absorption of the surviving urban merchant class in Poland, Hungary and the Balkans and many of them gravitated towards the intelligentsia and adopted non-bourgeois values.

The relatively weak bourgeoisie that grew up with and was partly responsible for the economic expansion of the nineteenth and twentieth centuries was on the whole a new social group. Given that the traditional élite, with its anti-competitive, status-determined, nobiliary values – in the maintenance of which exemption from taxation played a not insignificant role – would not assume the dangers of risk-taking and the chance of losing status, wealth and power, the new bourgeoisie had to be recruited from elsewhere, in the main from low-status natives or immigrants. The ethno-social group that assumed the largest role in this process were the Jews emigrating into Eastern Europe from the Pale of Settlement in Galicia and Russia. Other ethnically different groups included Germans, Greeks and Armenians. Whereas in the West the entrepreneurial class tended to be well established and comparatively open, relying on agricultural prosperity for new capital and new entrepreneurs, the situation in Eastern Europe was quite different from the outset.

The central problem with entrusting economic development to an ethnically alien group was that both the group and its values tended to remain alien. Although many Jews sought to assimilate to the dominant local culture, few of them were fully accepted and, on the whole, they remained to a greater or lesser extent to one side of the national majority. While ethno-social segmentation of this kind might have been a standard feature of many traditional, static societies, in modern societies, with a steady expansion of the number of interactions and widening of choice and experience, segmentation could not easily be reconciled with the prevailing norms.

The lasting result of this order was that the entrepreneurial value system remained the ethos of a social segment, a kind of alien element intruded into or superimposed upon these societies. The alienness, whether of the system or of its representatives, never disappeared completely and the capitalist, whether Jewish or not, was regarded as different from the majority. Even in Hungary, where Jewish immigrants were closest to integration and indeed, were most fully assimilated in language, culture and customs, the foreignness remained. A peasant was reported as having remarked in the 1960s that there had been two Jews in his village; both kept shops, 'though one was a Jew only by his profession'.[30] This illustrates vividly the merger of the alienness of the two value systems. The alienness began to break down in the interwar period, as a native entrepreneurial class began to emerge, rather fitfully in some cases, only to discover that it had to compete with a group that it continued to regard as alien.

This state of affairs contributed materially to a deep-rooted, persistent hostility to entrepreneurial values of risk-taking, the market, competition, democracy, change – an attitude that was in any event a well-entrenched hangover from the traditional *Gemeinschaft*. It is in this sense that the East European bourgeoisie constituted a 'colony' of the West, not tied into the native socio-political fabric, in consequence of which it was incapable of performing the integrative function that it had carried out in the West. If anything, the bourgeoisie sought to assimilate to the neo-feudal values of political power and to the status of the élite, in the hope of gaining acceptance and access to a share of power. The structural weakness of the East European bourgeoisie, attributable in this sense to delayed modernization, contributed significantly to a corresponding weakness in the conceptions of modernity, attitudes to change and the institutions that would mediate between society and the state.

The Working Class

With the exception of the Czech lands and the areas later to constitute the German Democratic Republic, no East European polity had anything like a sizeable and politically conscious working class by the interwar period. The bulk of the population was still on the land and the economy had not expanded sufficiently to permit industrialization. No working class could emerge, except for pockets of manufacturing and extractive industry in Poland, Hungary and the Balkans (very limited in the last). Where one did exist, the level of technology tended to be low and relatively straightforward, e.g. food processing, textiles or construction. Indeed, the level of industrial production was well below the level of modernity in consumption practised by the élite. The industrial proletariat was, consequently, small and politically

[30] Zsolt Csalog, *Temető Összel* (1977), p. 43.

uninfluential. Its value system was characterized by this and also by the fact that most workers had only recently moved from peasant status, so that they tended to be quiescent in their political demands, even though they might be active in the pursuit of economic or welfare objectives. Their aspirations were articulated through trade unions and the social democratic parties which existed in the area.

Radicalism, especially radicalism of the left, was confined to a few geographically or occupationally distinct sectors. In Poland the Communist Party could rely on militancy in the Dabrowa basin, on the textile workers of Lódz and industrial workers in Warsaw. In Hungary the radical left gathered support from small groups of heavy metallurgical workers in Budapest, especially Csepel, the miners in the north and some seasonal workers.[31] In the Balkans even this limited degree of industrialization did not exist. The occupations which contributed most strongly to left-radicalism were mining, seasonal work and some other marginal categories. As these marginal categories increased in size in the depression of the 1930s radicalism increased correspondingly, but not automatically to the benefit of the left. The newly impoverished workers, especially those whose links with their peasant antecedents were recent, could just as easily gravitate to right radicalism, attracted by the slogans of nationalistic communalism and the rhetoric of sudden, all-encompassing change.

Economic activism, however, was another matter. Polish workers developed the technique of the occupation strike as a response to lockouts in the 1930s and, in 1936, 675,000 strikers took part in strikes in 22,016 factories, out of a total industrial working class of 830,000.[32] In Yugoslavia the working class was overwhelmingly peasant-worker in character, with working-class households drawing at least part of their incomes from the land and being to some extent enmeshed in peasant values. According to the 1931 census, 1.53 million workers plus dependants drew incomes from industry, including mining, out of a total population of 13.93 million. The bulk of Yugoslav industry was based on primary technology and the availability of raw materials. Of around 1800 factories, one-third were involved in processing food and agricultural products, another sixth in timber; had it not been for the number of workers employed in urban power plants those

[31] Jan B. de Weydenthal, *The Communists of Poland* (1978), p. 7; György Borsányi, 'Ezernyolcszáz kartoték a budapesti baloldalról', *Valóság*, 26 no. 8 (August, 1983), pp. 19–31.
[32] George Kolankiewicz, 'The Working Class', in David Lane and George Kolankiewicz (eds), *Social Groups in Polish Society* (1973), pp. 88–9; Jan Szczepanski, 'A munkásosztály összetételének változása', *A szociológus szemével* (1977), p. 19.

proportions would have been much higher. These workers could hardly constitute a foundation for working-class politics as it had developed in the West and, indeed, left-wing parties were marginal after the initial upsurge of the post-1918 era which had drawn its energies from peasant radicalism and war weariness.

The situation was somewhat different in the Czech lands and in what became the GDR. Here there was a sizeable and politically conscious working class, sections of which had a markedly militant tradition. In Czechoslovakia after the split in Social Democracy, the communists emerged stronger than the Social Democrats and remained a mass party, at least in terms of support, for the inter-war period. The situation was reversed in Germany, although there was strong support for left-radicalism in some of the areas that were brought together to form the GDR, i.e. Saxony and Saxony–Anhalt, as well as Berlin. In these two countries the contribution of the working class to politics was far from negligible.

The final point to note in connection with the working class in Eastern Europe is that its traditions had next to no impact on the post-war period. By one of those curious ironies of history that the area appears to specialize in, war and the communist revolution dispersed the old working class and replaced it with another, overwhelmingly new working class.[33] The industrial explosion of the communist era was sudden and extensive and the newly recruited workers from the land largely swamped the remnants of the pre-war workers. A large proportion of them had in any case found themselves the object of rapid, even over-rapid, upward social mobility, because they were regarded as trustworthy pillars of the new social order. There was, therefore, no far-reaching transmission of values from the pre-war to the post-war era, although there were localized exceptions to this.[34] The swamping effect was about as strong in Czechoslovakia and East Germany as it was in the other countries, where the working class was much smaller.[35] In Germany the dislocation caused by the war, the massive demographic shifts, including migration westwards, and the submergence of the Social Democrats resulted in a state of affairs

[33] See the argument in Walter Connor, *Socialism, Politics and Equality: Hierarchy and Change in Eastern Europe and the USSR* (1979).

[34] Witold Wirpsza, *Pole, wer bist du ?* (1972) argues this for Poznan, to the effect that the 1956 uprising was partly explained by the strength of working-class solidarity in the town. There is a good deal of evidence that Social Democrats played a major role during the Hungarian Revolution of the same year.

[35] On the histories of the Czechoslovak and German working classes, see William Griffith (ed.), *Communism in Europe*, vol. 2 (1966), pp. 157–276 and 43–154 respectively.

analogous to what was going on in the rest of the area, albeit it may not have been as deep-seated. Upward promotion accounted for much of the traditional working class in the Czech lands, as did the expulsion of the Sudeten Germans and the suppression of the Social Democrats. In all, then, war and the communist revolution came to be as much of a caesura for the proletariat, in whose name the communists launched their revolution, as it was for the rest of the population.

Conclusion

The Second World War constituted one of the great hinges of East European political development. It caused massive upheavals and deep-rooted changes in attitudes, which would have resulted in corresponding changes in the political structure even without the communist revolution.

The question of what kind of change and what kind of political structures would have emerged without the Soviet presence is, of course, unanswerable in strict terms; nevertheless answers to the question are not wholly irrelevant, because they can point towards an understanding of the East European tradition and value systems. Although based on guesswork, the answers would seem to suggest a major shift of power away from the beneficiaries of the *anciens régimes* and towards wider popular participation. This could well have seen the construction of particularly East European types of institutions, which would doubtless have been more étatist than those evolved in the West. A certain kind of collectivism or corporatism appears to be a near-ineradicable component of the reigning political ethos that informs the behaviour of some, though not all, of the population. This would not, as such, have excluded a measure of collective control over institutions, as the functioning of the *ad hoc* enterprise councils of the immediate post-1945 period in Czechoslovakia and Hungary testified.

Despite strong currents of radical populism, it is hard to see any solution of the peasant problem other than thoroughgoing industrialization, with all its attendant dislocation. The populist solution for land reform, peasant cooperation and the rest, never looked able to resolve the problem of rural overpopulation and would in any case have tended to conserve a rather anti-innovative system of values and agrarian economics. The old élites, while seriously undermined after 1945, were not destroyed (except in Poland and Yugoslavia) and could well have returned to politics to promote anti-modernizing values, but also to contribute political skills. These changes would have shifted Eastern Europe away from authoritarianism towards pluralism, though it is hard to see how they would have established democracy based on parliamentary sovereignty in the short term, even if this was by no means excluded over time. The development of Greece in the first two to three decades after the war is instructive in this respect.

The first half of the century in East Central Europe, then, saw the slow, fitful, halting construction of a modernization that was stopped and radically transformed by the communist revolution, with its own particular modernizing objectives, myths and utopias.

2

Communism in Eastern Europe
between the Wars

[Now do] ravens, crows and kites
Fly o'er our heads and downward look on us
As we were sickly prey.

Shakespeare, Julius Caesar, *V.i.84–6*

The Aftermath of War

The impact of war on society is generally to radicalize it and arouse expectations. A large number of individuals are subjected to major upheaval, to mobilization, to being transported to other areas of the world, to new types of discipline and to learning new skills. Hence when they return, they tend not to accept so readily the pre-existing state of their affairs and to be ready to press for change, especially political change. Whereas beforehand the bulk of society seems to accept the political order as natural and immutable, the experience of alternatives can awaken the hope that the individual's situation might be bettered along the lines seen elsewhere.

The Eastern Europe that experienced the First World War was backward and authoritarian. The bulk of the population was excluded from any significant control over political decision-making and tended to acquiesce in the old, established patterns of rule and deference. The war changed much of this, both through actual physical devastation and through mobilization. Fighting affected the lands of Poland, Serbia and Romania; the Balkans had already been shaken up by the two Balkan wars of 1912–14. The various imperial armies, together with the armed forces of the small independent states, called up enormous numbers of peasants and many of these found themselves victims of privation serving in entirely alien conditions. The home front too was put through the mangle, as industry and agriculture were increasingly brought under state control and the workforce placed under new rules of discipline. Food shortages began to affect several of the Austro–Hungarian towns, the populations of which increased with wartime expansion, by the last years of the war. Even the morale of the armed forces was beginning to crumble towards the end, as evidenced by the mutiny in the Austro–Hungarian navy at Cattaro in 1918. Correspondingly, by this period, militancy in the workforce began to rise. The target of this was rather diffuse, ranging from demands for peace to more traditional, organized unionism. The atmosphere was, if not combustible, certainly one where radicalism and radical solutions were gaining in attraction. This was the background against which the impact of the Russian Revolution has to be assessed.

While far from being the only trigger, the news of the Russian Revolution unquestionably acted as an encouragement to East Europeans to expect far-reaching political change. It suggested that the power of the political establishment was not as rock solid as it appeared and it made revolution a reality rather than a vague dream. The combination of events in Russia, war weariness and the mounting shortages of the last war years were, at the same time, coupled with another precondition for change. This was the loss of confidence on the part of the élite in the empires. The impact of defeat, the apparent inevitability of change and the breach in the habits of obedience to old patterns all pointed towards a deterioration in the morale of the old élite. The death of Franz Joseph in 1916 seemed to symbolize the passing of an era.

The subsequent changes in the territorial structure of Eastern Europe at the behest of the victors constituted, in this sense, the limits of revolutionary change tolerable to the newly dominant forces in Europe. Eastern Europe was to be transformed from its subject status to sovereign independence, the solution which Western Europe had found highly successful for itself and found equally acceptable as an export to the East. There were numerous willing buyers. The leaders of the newly independent states and those that aspired to independence recognized quickly that the Western formula would effectively guarantee their power against old or new challengers and many of them were genuinely convinced that independence would herald the new Jerusalem. There is no need to doubt or impugn the sincerity of the Czech or Polish or South Slav leaders in this regard. They believed that the end of empire and the adoption of Western-style constitutional government would produce Western-style democratic, stable and prosperous societies. In this, of course, they underestimated the difficulties of state formation and organization; indeed, they had become prisoners of their own nationalistic views of the world and saw politics overwhelmingly through the prism of nationhood, which they interpreted as necessarily leading to statehood.

For the population this was not enough. After the impact of war they wanted something more fundamental. Access to political power merely or mostly through the instrument of membership of a nation was far from satisfactory. It was at this point that the aspirations of the newly elevated élite and the semi-enfranchized masses diverged. The ideals of the élite were to lead Western-style political lives. The ideals of the mass of the population were decidely vaguer and less easily reconciled with what was on offer. Here the value system of the peasantry, which constituted much of the population, was directly relevant. Peasant values were inimical to complexity and saw change as a process to be achieved by something akin to salvation. These values had been formed in barely literate communities whose dominant, if not only, source of alternative ideas and visions of the future was the Bible and the Lives of the Saints.

With the end of the war and the semi-magical Russian Revolution, the millennium appeared to have arrived. Everything was to change for the better – of the peasant, that is – in terms of a simple, even primitive egalitarianism, in which all would be reduced to the same level of political privilege and, in a hazy kind of way, to the same level of technology. The anti-urbanism and anti-industrialism running through these radical peasant movements were palpable, as was the inability to come to terms with the market, the resulting suspicion of it and of the money-using economy. With a heave, all these parasites would be eliminated and peace and plenty would ensue. In areas where some concentrations of urban manufacturing existed, peasant radicalism was paralleled by working-class radicalism of a more familiar kind. What was common to both was the attraction exercised over them by the left.

The Role and Origins of the Radical Left

The left, for its part, had its own, variegated view of the situation. In the first place, it was mesmerized by the Russian Revolution and saw it as a model to be applied dogmatically and all but literally, regardless of local conditions. The idea that world revolution was imminent gained ground as mass unrest spread and the prestige of the Bolsheviks could hardly be higher. There was a tendency to identify all ruling élites with the Kerensky provisional government and to assume that they could all be as easily thrust aside as had happened in Russia. Secondly, the left's programme was firmly industrial and anti-peasant. The peasantry was regarded as a contradiction in the Marxian scheme of things, in as much as it was both an exploited class and a small-scale capitalist producer. From this standpoint the logical step was to eliminate the capitalist, property-owning characteristics of the peasantry, whereby it would assume proletarian qualities and be ready to make common cause with the urban working classes. This led the protagonists of Marxist revolution to misjudge the nature of peasant radicalism, to assume a superiority towards the rural population and to base their strategy on a fundamental misperception of their aspirations. The revolutionary potential of the situation was greatly overestimated. When combined with the first factor, the error eventually proved to be fatal.[1]

The various political forces which eventually came together to form communist parties had diverse origins. Strictly speaking, they could not be called 'communist' until after they had constituted themselves into a party of the Leninist type and were accepted as such by the Comintern, but for the sake of convenience the term will be used anachronistically. The three most significant currents, which were not mutually exclusive, were the old left-Social Democrats, those radicalized by political activity during the war and the returning prisoners of war who had lived through the Russian Revolution and had played an active part in it. Social Democracy in Eastern Europe had not been particularly strong before the war, hardly surprising in the light of its weak industrial base. Nevertheless, radical socialists did exist and drew their inspiration from Marx himself and from the writings of West European socialists. The German party had a strong influence, but so did the Russian party in the Balkans. In Austria–Hungary, naturally enough, the Austrian Social Democrats developed a strong and attractive tradition of their own. Several socialist movements before 1914 had split on left–right lines, notably those in Poland and Bulgaria. In the main, there was a close link between Social Democracy and the trade unions. However, the precursors of the communists, the Social Democratic left, tended to be impatient of the slow, incremental process of trade-union politics and were often strongly critical of the bureaucratization of the labour movement that ensued. The ranks of the Social Democratic left were swollen by radicals, anarchists and syndicalists.

[1] Milorad Drachkovitch and Branko Lazitch (eds), *The Comintern – Historical Highlights* (1966).

The anti-war radicals, predictably, gained in strength as the war drew on, but even in 1914 there was a small left-wing minority which stood out against the great tide of nationalism that called for war. Perhaps the most remarkable of these were the Serbian Socialists who refused to vote in favour of war credits even though Serbia was under direct threat of attack from Austria–Hungary. The third influential current was the returning prisoners of war from Russia. These were, of course, recruited only from among the armies of the states at war with Russia, primarily Austria–Hungary. They began returning to their homelands radicalized by their experiences, often having taken an active part in the Russian Revolution and in the ensuing fighting. Their exact numbers were uncertain, but their commitment was strong and enough of them had returned by November and December 1918 for them to have been able to act as the influential radical minority which represented the margin of revolutionary fervour. Above all, having been present at the birth of the Bolshevik state, they were endowed with a special legitimacy in the eyes of those who had missed out on this seminal experience. Also to the point were the contacts that some of them had made with the Russian Bolshevik leaders. Béla Kun, the leader of the Hungarian Soviet Republic, exemplified this third current most prominently.[2]

Finally, in connection with the origins of the East European communist parties and the antecedents of the communists themselves, a disproportionately large number of them were Jewish by descent. Many reasons have been offered to explain this phenomenon. Some of these relate to the impact of the Enlightenment on the closed world of Jewish settlements in the eighteenth century and the emergence of large numbers of Jews into a non-Jewish environment, only to find that anti-Semitism had not, as they expected, disappeared. This drew numbers of Jews into the socialist movements of the nineteenth century, which saw themselves as the legatees of the Enlightenment and of emancipation. Because Jews were generally banned from owning land and had been for centuries, their occupational concentration was urban and, for that reason, the impact of socialism on them was all the greater precisely because many of them were employed in manufacturing. Finally, there may well be one other explanation for why so many Jews in Eastern Europe were attracted to left-radicalism. In the nineteenth century, in virtually every East European country, Jews played a key role in entrepreneurialism and, given the limitations on other forms of economic activity open to them,

[2] Andrew C. Janos and William B. Slottman (eds), *Revolution in Perspective: Essays on the Hungarian Soviet Republic* (1971).

were for all practical purposes pre-eminent in spreading the money-using economy, in small and large-scale trading and in capital accumulation. The Jews who joined left-radical parties could, in many cases, have been reacting against the money-making ethos of the Jewish communities of the East European urban centres – a particular variant of the revolt of the sons against the fathers. The presence of this large number of Jews in East European communist parties had one other consequence. It gave rise to the stereotype of the 'Judaeo-Bolshevik', the Jewish radical who was determined to destroy putative Christian values. This stereotype contributed materially to the maintenance and even strengthening of anti-Semitism, encouraging right-wing regimes to associate Bolshevism with Jews as a way of trying to defuse the appeal of left-radicalism.

But this did not emerge until later. The period immediately after the First World War, roughly from 1917 to 1921, should be seen as one in which the likelihood of revolution and the possibility even of socialist revolution were strong. The dislocation, the vaulting expectations and the weakening of the old élites created a situation in which the redistribution of political power was high on the agenda. And for a brief time it looked as if this redistribution would be utopian, egalitarian and radical. The evidence for this, without the benefit of hindsight, was persuasive.[3]

The Hungarian Soviet Republic

The most thoroughgoing breach with the old order was the Hungarian Soviet Republic which lasted 133 days in 1919. The Hungarian Communists took power after the left-liberal government of Count Mihály Károlyi resigned in March 1919. The communists, who had actually been imprisoned by Károlyi, were released when he concluded that he would have to cede power to the Social Democrats, who quickly formed an alliance with the communists. But the crisis which forced Károlyi to resign already hid the seeds of a serious warning. He gave up office when the Entente powers ordered new demarcation lines for Hungary, ordering that the Hungarian government abandon yet more ethnically Hungarian territory to the successor states, Czechoslovakia and Romania. In other words, the change to communism was fostered by a national and not by a class

[3] The argument in this section has drawn on Joseph Rothschild, *East Central Europe between the Two World Wars* (1974); and Hugh Seton-Watson, *The Pattern of Communist Revolution: a History of World Communism*, 2nd edn (1960).

issue. This fusion of communism with nationalist impulses was characteristic of the moment; even if at the theoretical level the two ideologies are incompatible, they both appealed to the messianic, chiliastic mood and the incompatibility was ignored.

The Hungarian Soviet Republic was launched with a good deal of popular support. The bulk of the peasant population expected that the communists would introduce 'social justice' and 'revolution', a state of being in which everything would change for the better. The middle classes, on the other hand, gave the new rulers their conditional support because the communists promised to defend Hungary's territory against the Entente allies. The fact that the communists were doing this not on nationalist grounds, but on the classical Marxist argument that the larger a political unit the stronger its market will be, appeared to bother neither side in the first instance. But the confusion fairly quickly proved to be the communists' undoing, particularly when they set about destroying the various symbols of Hungarian nationhood. And as soon as they stopped trying to export the revolution, the middle classes withdrew their support. The communists' honeymoon with the peasantry was just as short-lived. Instead of embarking on land redistribution, the communists nationalized all landholdings over 100 acres, displayed general contempt for the peasantry and expected to move rapidly to collectivized agriculture. It was not a popular move as far as the peasantry was concerned. When the interventionist Romanian armies moved into Hungary, the Soviet Republic collapsed.[4]

This short-lived wave of mass support surged throughout Eastern Europe at this time. In Yugoslavia the communists called for strikes with considerable success to protest against Entente intervention in Hungary in July 1919. In the voting for the Constituent Assembly in November 1919 they emerged as the fourth largest party; their showing in local elections in 1920 was strong in many towns and they actually won the municipal elections in Belgrade. However, this electoral strength was deceptive and also illusory. It was concentrated not in the few industrialized areas, but in the backward rural districts, notably Montenegro. The vote reflected a protest vote, the revolutionary expectations of the peasantry and its sympathy for Russia, a crucial factor in the Pravoslav, traditionally pro-Russian south of the country. As the Social Democrat opponents of the communists pointed out, the latter were appealing not to the proletariat but to 'motley

[4] Andrew C. Janos, *The Politics of Backwardness in Hungary 1825–1945* (1982), especially pp. 195–8; Iván Völgyes (ed.), *Hungary in Revolution 1918–1919: Nine Essays* (1971).

malcontents'. This rural base of the party proved to be its weakness as well, for peasant values and expectations were inimical to the sustained organization and the underground activity that the Communist Party needed after the authorities drove it into illegality. The destruction of the party as an organized force proved relatively easy and, within a matter of months, the membership of the party was down from thousands to a few hundred. However, it should be added that the revolutionary upsurge of 1919–20 did live on as a memory and subsequently influenced parts of the Yugoslav countryside to view the Partisans with favour after 1941.[5]

Hungary and Yugoslavia represented the greatest successes of the communists in Eastern Europe at this time. But elsewhere too they made their mark. In Czechoslovakia, the only East European country where the party remained legal throughout the interwar period (until Munich), the communists emerged as the stronger faction after their split from the Social Democrats.[6] Even in Poland, where the communists had to contend with the twofold disadvantage of visceral anti-Russianism and the defeat of the Red Army by Poland in 1920, the traditionally radical areas of the country continued to give some support to the party.[7] In Romania, a backward country with a strongly anti-Russian tradition, there was a wave of strikes after the end of the war, though the communists – the maximalist wing of the Socialists – were only partly instrumental in fomenting the unrest and were unable to use it as a basis for extending their power. Harsh measures by the authorities were in part responsible. Still, in 1920 the Romanian Socialist Party counted a membership of around 140,000 and the influence of the left, which later split off to form the Communist Party, was far from negligible.[8]

The Bulgarian Upheaval

The situation in Bulgaria appeared peculiarly favourable to the communists. Not only was there a well-established Socialist Party, which had even undergone its own Bolshevik-Menshevik split into 'Narrows' and 'Broads', but the population was strongly pro-Russian;

[5] Ivan Avakumovic, *History of the Communist Party of Yugoslavia*, 2 vols (1964–7).
[6] Jacques Rupnik, *Histoire du parti communiste tchécoslovaque: des origines à la prise du pouvoir* (1981).
[7] M. K. Dziewanowski, *The Communist Party of Poland: an Outline of History*, 2nd edn (1976).
[8] Ghita Ionescu, *Communism in Rumania 1944–1962* (1964).

the country had been continuously at war since 1912; and unrest by the autumn of 1918 was widespread. In the 1919 and 1920 elections, the communists, gaining around a fifth of the vote, emerged as second in size only to Aleksandur Stamboliski's Agrarian Union. Yet when the old élite recovered in 1923 and removed Stamboliski, the communists stood idly by, insisting that the coup was no concern of theirs; roundly reproved for their misjudgement of the situation by Moscow, they launched an attempted coup of their own, which was a miserable failure. Here again, the communists' Marxist orthodoxy and the hypnotic effect of Russia in 1917 – the communists saw Stamboliski as the Bulgarian Kerensky and thought that he could easily be toppled by them – led to their defeat. They 'failed to understand this peasantist enthusiast and his movement, whose revolutionary militancy and chiliastic self-righteousness more than matched their own . . . and into whose mass support they were unable to make significant inroads'.[9]

The legacy of defeat had far-reaching consequences for communist attitudes and tactics in the period thereafter. They learned a number of lessons from it and these generally reinforced their own exclusivist, isolationist and messianic bent. They concluded that, in open political competition, their chances of success would be undermined, thanks to the immaturity of the population. The peasantry was evidently useless as an ally, because it did not behave as the tenets of Marx and Lenin had said it should. Indeed, the whole idea of mass activity, competing for votes and jostling for power in the open market-place of politics, was rejected as a bourgeois device to which communists had no need to subject themselves, given their possession of the Marxist key to the future. There is, incidentally, an odd echo of peasant messianism here, which likewise rejected political competition. The underlying currents of anti-capitalism evidently overlapped. They took much the same line towards other non-bourgeois parties, like the Social Democrats, whom the communists despised for their readiness to strike bargains with the old élites. The élites themselves were regarded not as political opponents but as enemies to be extirpated. The democratic slogans of the élites were not merely dismissed as window-dressing, but the very ideals and technologies of democracy – which had had their place in the writings of Marx – were consigned to the scrap-heap of history as instruments of bourgeois subjection which had no place in a proletarian utopia.

In all, their failure at mass politics led the communists virtually to welcome the ghetto of illegality into which the established régimes placed them. Illegality encouraged the communists to develop the

[9] Rothschild, *East Central Europe*, p. 339.

conspiratorial principle of rigid organization, centralized hierarchy, military discipline and cell structures; to distrust autonomous action; to favour 'entryism', the penetration of other, potentially friendly organizations like trade unions and the creation of front organizations; to promote the cultivation of the disciplined cadre party, the group of battle-hardened activists, professional revolutionaries ready to accept whatever instructions they received and to scorn recruitment on a large scale. Something of a fetish was also made of working-class recruits, even if intellectuals were disproportionately represented in the illegal parties. Both their ideology and their method of organized activity reinforced a propensity for authoritarianism and contempt for debate and discussion. They acquired a ruthlessness and a readiness to use any and all methods in their pursuit of the great objective.

These underground parties, as is common with similar ideologically motivated organizations, underwent a process of continuous doctrinal refinement, purges and restructuring. They fell prey to splits and counter-splits. Often they were penetrated by the police. Most significantly, their local weakness inevitably drove them further and further into the embraces of Moscow and to the jettisoning of whatever local socialist and Marxist traditions they may have had. Increasingly, under Comintern pressures, they adopted policies which had limited relevance to the countries in which they operated. That, in turn, tended to place communist parties entirely beyond the political pale and it was not difficult to depict them as nothing more than the unpatriotic agencies of Moscow, an alien, antagonistic state.

The Soviet Package

The experience of Sovietization was central to the evolution of communist parties in Eastern Europe. In many ways it was a most remarkable process of political development, especially in as much as it represented the 'colonization' of political organizations by the agency of a political culture largely alien in its traditions, aspirations, objectives and style. Sovietization, of course, was even more bizarre in the context of Western communist parties, like the German and the French, with their own powerful, autonomous, intellectual traditions. The idea that these parties would abandon the formulation of their own solutions in order to subordinate themselves to ones devised in Moscow would have struck most nineteenth-century socialists as absurd. That it happened was attributable to the failure of socialist ideas to prevent the war and the failure of the Social Democrats to overthrow the bourgeoisie in the aftermath of war. In these conditions the one successful socialist revolution acquired enormous prestige, even if it was in remote, non-industrial Russia. If these considerations applied to the confident, popularly based Western parties, they were far truer of the weaker East European communists, who really lacked the resources to withstand Sovietization (where they wanted to do so). And once locked into Soviet patterns, escape proved impossible. Where individuals sought to defy Moscow, they were expelled. Where parties were judged unsatisfactory, they were dissolved. And those non-Soviet communists who were unfortunate enough to have taken refuge in the Soviet Union found that the process of purge *à la Russe* affected them as much as the Soviet population, if not more so.

The essence of the Soviet package was the relatively speedy imposition of Leninist norms of organization and the unquestioning acceptance of the ideological paramountcy of Moscow in all questions. This, ironically, put an end to the *raison d'être* of the radical left as the formulator of alternative images and strategies of the future. There was only one socialist revolution, there was only one road to socialism, there was only one possible conceptualization of the goals and strategy of socialism – Moscow's. The definition of the 'socialist project', the meaning and content of socialism, was now firmly in the hands of the Soviet Union and the Soviet ideologists used this monopoly position as effectively as they could to drive out competitors from the market. The imperatives of Soviet-style socialism were insisted on by Moscow with the utmost stringency. There was no middle ground. Either one accepted the dictates of Moscow or one was an enemy, and enemies, in this canon, were to be destroyed as standing in the way of the march towards the radiant future.[10]

The origins of this Soviet concept are to be found, understandably, in Lenin's thought. Lenin was contemptuous of the ineffectiveness of the Second International in the face of the outbreak of war in 1914 and of the decision of too many socialists that they should support the war. Furthermore, he had his own strict recipe for the pursuit of revolutionary objectives – the tightly organized, clandestine party composed of dedicated revolutionaries – which had proved successful in the Russian case. At the centre of his conception was his insistence on stringent control and centralized organization, coupled with ideological purity as determined by Moscow, the successful centre of the world's first socialist revolution. These principles underlay the celebrated *Twenty-One Conditions* which the Comintern imposed on all communist parties.

[10] Henrik Vass (ed.), *Studies on the History of the Hungarian Working Class Movement 1867–1966* (1975).

The *Twenty-One Conditions*, in sum, provided the following. All communists were absolutely obliged to carry out its provisions, whether as individuals or in an organized fashion. Crucially, there was to be only one possible pattern of organization for communist parties. The leadership would take decisions and transmit these down a rigidly controlled hierarchy. Under the rules of party discipline, party members were obliged to carry out instructions from above without question. This was the organizational pattern which Lenin had developed for the struggle in the underground in Tsarist Russia.

Further, there must be a resolute struggle against all non-recognized ideologies of the left – reformism, pacifism, radicalism – in terms of both ideas and organization. Trade Unions must be captured from within by tightly organized groups of communists. Communist parliamentary groups are subordinate to the party's central committee and the party itself is subordinate to the Comintern. There must be a clandestine organization to parallel the open one, regardless of conditions in the country concerned. Communists must give their unconditional support to Soviet countries, i.e. the Soviet Union. All communist parties must undergo periodic purges to ensure ideological purity and they must accept the principle of democratic centralism, namely, that whatever the centre decides becomes binding on all lower-level party bodies. Finally, all Comintern directives were expressly declared binding on communist parties.

There were both advantages and disadvantages for the East European parties in this tight definition. Leninist organization and ideology gave them a strong sense of identity and a clarity of purpose uncontaminated by the requirements of day-to-day politics. Revolutionaries could feel secure that their commitment to the revolution was being safeguarded by the best possible institution yet created for this purpose – the vanguard party. Membership of the party had continuously to be earned and this reiterated trial by ordeal in itself reinforced the separate sense of identity that many communists welcomed. The party offered a separate way of life, with its own code of conduct, its own morality, its own symbols and its own language (or meta-language), all of which fostered the sense of differentiation and of being members of the elect. It made communists feel that their identities as political animals were enhanced and protected. This was all the more important given that so many of them were living with a sense of failure and frustration from having seen their high hopes of the upsurge fade away. It imbued them with a sense of rightfulness and a conviction that everyone was out of step except themselves, thanks to the insistence of the party on the transcendental validity of the Marxist claim. Regardless of what happened on a daily basis, history was on their side.

Sovietization was crucial in another respect as well. The various individuals who came together to form the communist parties had very different backgrounds and experiences. Many of them, as intellectuals, had a tendency to indulge in disputation and debate rather than being imbued with a commitment to action. From the standpoint of the political requirements of the period as defined by the Comintern, these were relatively dispensable qualities. Hence Sovietization was imposed on the radical left in order to weld together its disparate currents into a single, effective instrument of power.

Nor were the sense of discipline and conspiratorial organizational techniques unimportant in polities where the rule of law tended to be viewed as inapplicable to communists; where they were harassed mercilessly by the police; and where they enjoyed the suspicion of all other political forces on the grounds of being alien. The communists also benefited from the established élites' tendency to demonize them, to attribute all manner of evil to them and to brand them as the greatest enemies of the state. In the eyes of those who did not benefit from the system, this clarity of image endowed the communists with special qualities. If the holders of power regarded the communists as the enemy, then, on the principle of 'my enemy's enemy is my friend,' many victims of the system came to regard them with some covert admiration.

On the other hand, Sovietization (or Bolshevization) also had its disadvantages, ones which, in fact, were often the mirror image of the advantages. Political isolation may have had its allure in the 1920s while consolidation was the order of the day, but with the coming of the 1930s and the apparent success of revolution from the right, the communists began to look for allies, for a way out of the ghetto.

The Popular Front tactic was decided on by the Comintern at its Seventh Congress in 1935, but by then it was too late. The communists had been too successful in distancing themselves from the rest of the left and international developments – the Spanish Civil War, the Moscow trials – brought fresh evidence that, whatever they might say of themselves, communist parties were in reality nothing more than the agents of Soviet foreign policy and that Soviet reality was not necessarily identical with everyone's definition of the 'socialist project'. The sheer crassness of the Comintern in allowing the powerful German CP to stand by while Hitler destroyed the Social Democrats and then the communists in turn was regarded as the height of political folly. The Molotov–Ribbentrop pact was the final straw in this process.

The acceptance of Soviet codes of conduct and practice simply intensified this suspicion and strengthened the belief that communists could not be trusted because they were not part of the national political culture. Similarly, the subordination of local interests to Soviet ones merely exacerbated this.

The Fate of the Parties

Sovietization was the speediest where communist parties were weakest. Those parties – all but the Czechoslovak – which were forced into illegality developed a dependence on Moscow for support, materials, money which the Comintern fostered by every means possible. The stipulation of a continuous purge in the *Twenty-One Conditions* was fully applied to these parties, leaving only the most committed as members, even if this meant jettisoning a mass base. Throughout the interwar period the Polish party, the KPRP (Komunistyczna Partia Robotnicza Polski) later the KPP (Komunistyczna Partia Polski), was subjected to instructions and counter-instructions from Moscow, with the broad aim of bringing it under Soviet control and transforming it into an instrument of Soviet policy.[11]

The steps taken to achieve this included the shedding of the party's popular base, the subordination of its organizations to Moscow and then the destruction of Polish socialist traditions. By the end of 1921 the first stage had been largely completed: the KPRP had lost 80 per cent of its membership in the Dabrowa basin, 40 per cent in Warsaw and about 60 per cent in Lodz. The second and third stages took a little longer. Between 1922 and 1925 the KPRP sought to preserve some autonomy and took internationalism seriously, even going to the extent of disputing Comintern directives and arguing that it was best fitted to determine strategy for Poland. The result of this was that, in July 1924, the KPRP was strongly attacked by the Comintern for its 'disruptive activities'. What is more, the Polish party earned Stalin's undying dislike for having supported Trotsky in 1923. During these years the KPRP was controlled by its right wing, which pursued a cautious policy of cooperation with other left-wing forces and tactically accepted the Polish state.

In 1925 the Comintern intervened directly, dissolved the KPRP's

[11] Isaac Deutscher, 'The Tragedy of the Polish Communist Party', in *Marxism in Our Time* (1971), pp. 113–60; also Dziewanowski, *The Communist Party of Poland*, and Jan B. de Weydenthal, *The Communists of Poland: an Historical Outline* (1978) from which the figures are taken.

leadership, changed the name of the party to KPP (dropping the word 'Robotnicza' or 'Workers' from its name in order to bring it into line with other communist parties) and imposed a new left-radical leadership on it. This leadership engaged in a campaign of violence and terror, of 'revolutionary vigilance', leading to political bankruptcy and the imposition of a new leadership in 1925. Between 1926 and 1929 the KPP was in disarray, fragmented and drifting politically. Then the Comintern took over supervision of the party directly, installing a compliant left-minority leadership which ran it until its dissolution in 1938. The KPP was much distrusted in Moscow as awkward, troublesome, argumentative, as inexperienced in 'conspiracy' and on the ground that it was penetrated by the Polish police (a suspicion which was actually well founded). In the purges, thirty out of thirty-seven members and deputy members of the Central Committee were eliminated and in 1938, in circumstances which remain unclear, the KPP was itself dissolved. This was followed by a Comintern campaign to extirpate all organized Polish communist activity at home and abroad. There was no organized Polish party until 1941, when slowly the Soviet Union allowed it to re-emerge, but strictly under Soviet control.

Like the KPP, the Czechoslovak party also put up a struggle before yielding to complete Bolshevization. It looked back to a strong tradition within Austro-Marxism and had its own ideas as to how the goal of communist revolution should be pursued. This was not at all acceptable to the Soviet Union and most of the 1920s was spent in bringing the KSC (Kommunisticka Strana Ceskoslovenska) under Comintern control. For a start, it took a surprisingly long time for the KSC actually to be accepted by the Comintern as a communist party. It applied to join only in 1921, only to be rejected in the first instance because the party leadership had been unwilling to unite with the communist organizations founded by the Germans of Czechoslovakia; and even when this hurdle was vaulted, the leadership was reluctant to accept the Comintern's directive that Czechs and Slovaks constituted separate nations. As late as 1925, 70 per cent of the KSC's membership was made up of ex-Social Democrats and it was clear enough to Moscow that a hankering after ideological autonomy made the KSC a less than wholly reliable organization. Indeed, in 1928 the KSC was openly criticized in the Comintern as 'the worst section of the International'.[12]

[12] Rupnik, *Histoire;* Zdenek Suda, *Zealots and Rebels: a History of the Ruling Communist Party of Czechoslovakia* (1980) and Paul E. Zinner, *Communist Strategy and Tactics in Czechoslovakia 1918–1948* (1963).

Gradually, with Comintern backing – in which the role of the Comintern delegate to Prague was highly significant – the old leadership of Bohumir Smeral was eased out and a group of younger apparatchiks took over. This latter group was to remain in power for two decades, in striking contrast to the lability of the Polish party leadership. In 1929, when the new group took over, Bolshevization was completed. The remnants of inner-party democracy disappeared and elected organs lost their control over the party bureaucracy. An extensive purge followed. And the membership of the party, which had been 350,000 strong in 1921 and 150,000 in 1928, fell to 30,000 in the spring of 1930. The KSC had been transformed from a mass into a cadre party, regardless of the political cost to its standing in Czechoslovakia. In one respect Czechoslovak communists escaped the fate of their counterparts in the other East European states. Because the party was legal, there were comparatively fewer of them in the Soviet Union and thereby they were not caught up in the purges to anything like the same extent. But from this stage until the 1960s, the KSC remained one of the most obedient parties from Moscow's standpoint.

If the Polish and Czechoslovak parties did put up something of a struggle for their autonomous traditions and the right to decide over their own tactics and strategy, this hardly applied with the same force to the other, much more weakly grounded East European CPs. The Hungarians, shattered by the disgrace of having been the only communist party to have been ousted from power after having controlled an entire country (a distinction it held until Grenada), came fairly easily under Soviet power. Hunted by the White Terror in the early 1920s, then by Admiral Horthy's fairly efficient political police, the groups of *émigrés* in Vienna and Moscow had little resistance to offer. By the 1930s the Hungarian party was reduced to perhaps 2000 activists and the head of the Budapest police boasted that he knew all of them personally. However, data published in Hungary imply that while the membership of the party may have been limited, the number of those who had at some point been active as communists was much higher. The social composition of the party in the 1930s was around three-quarters working class, with unskilled workers the largest group within this category, and 13.5 per cent were intellectuals.[13] In 1936, in circumstances still to be explained, the Hungarian party's organization was dissolved, though (unlike the KPP two years later) it remained in existence as a party. And many Hungarian communists, including Béla

---

[13] György Borsányi, 'Ezernyolcszáz kartoték a budapesti baloldalról', *Valóság*, 26 no. 9 (1983), pp. 19–31.

Kun, lost their lives in the purges in the Soviet Union. After receiving an infusion of new blood in 1938, when Hungary incorporated southern Slovakia following Munich, and taking in the ethnic Hungarian communists from the area, the Hungarian party lapsed into irrelevance. In 1943 the leaders of the illegal party ordered its dissolution, apparently misunderstanding the significance of the dissolution of the Comintern.[14]

The Romanian party was from the outset deeply divided over the country's national question. Because the Comintern strongly insisted that the party adhere to the slogan of 'national self-determination up to and including secession', not surprisingly it attracted much of its membership from among the non-Romanian nationalities. Indeed, several of its leaders in the interwar period were not ethnic Romanians at all, a source of some distress to the party after it embarked on a nationalist strategy in the 1960s. Its membership was small – it probably never exceeded 5000 – it was severely repressed by police and it took next to no part in the life of the country.

The Bulgarian party, after the failure of the ill-prepared September 1923 uprising, found itself severely criticized by the Comintern for its utter mishandling of the situation. The leadership of the party mostly took refuge in the Soviet Union, but a few remained behind and formed the militant group which undertook the bombing of Sofia Cathedral in 1925, in an attempt to destroy the country's political leaders. This resulted in renewed repression and a new wave of emigrants. There were possibly as many as 3000 Bulgarian communists who made their way to the Soviet Union and the party was clearly characterized by its twofold existence, in exile and at home. Both in exile and at home, left militants gained control of the party. Operating through cover organizations at home, Bulgarian communists demonstrated their continued popularity, which encouraged the left militants to go on the offensive again. Their power was broken only after the 1934 coup in Bulgaria, when the communists were subjected to severe repression again. This, coupled with the rightward switch in the Comintern, allowed the Comintern to assume final control over the remnants of the Bulgarian party. The lesson of Bulgaria was that, as far as the Comintern was concerned, the main target was not the ideological content of the communist party programmes, but the degree of autonomy which each party felt that it had to formulate such programmes; Comintern objectives were to minimize such autonomy. Yet despite the repeated purges and the

---

[14] Vass, *Studies*; Bennet Kovrig, *Communism in Hungary: from Kun to Kádár* (1979).

blood-letting in the Soviet Union, Bulgarian communism retained an element of tenacity and dogmatism that were to revive in the resistance during the war and after the communist take-over itself. In 1941 the party claimed a membership of 10,600 and a youth organization of 19,000; some 12,000 took an active part in the resistance. The legacy of the 'narrows' remained strong at this stage.[15]

The Yugoslav party, after the high-water mark of its success in the early 1920s, found itself grappling with the national question as the central issue that split it apart. The Comintern insisted that it espouse a policy of demanding the dismemberment of Yugoslavia according to national lines, purged its secretary-general and generally relegated it to the sidelines. Dismemberment was abandoned after the Comintern came to favour a Popular Front policy and it was only then that Yugoslav communism could begin to re-emerge from the shadows. In 1937 when Josip Broz (Tito), known at this time by his cover name 'Walter', was entrusted with the leadership of the party, there were serious plans to dissolve it entirely; apparently it was only Georgi Dimitrov's intervention that gave Tito a last chance to reunite what had been a notoriously divided and faction-ridden organization. Tito's role in the purge of Yugoslav exiles in the Soviet Union is unclear; he alone of the seven-man delegation that attended the Seventh Congress of the Comintern survived.[16]

Conclusion

The longer-term significance of the Soviet package only emerged after the war. The experience of complete subordination to Soviet codes of political behaviour was successful in creating determined, dedicated and ruthless cadre parties, which were reliable in spreading Soviet strategy. Even so, without the second opportunity of war and the dislocation resulting from it, the communists would not have had much opportunity to use their skills. The established élites were more than a match for the conspiratorial principle and the communists had little enough room for manoeuvre to reconstitute the mass base that they needed for effective political action. But the authoritarian attitudes they learned from the Comintern and their years in the Soviet Union, their ideological certainty, their rejection of debate and argument, their hostility to autonomous action, their contempt for views other than their own and their attitude of treating political

---

[15] Nissan Oren, *Bulgarian Communism: the Road to Power 1934–1944* (1971).
[16] Avakumovic, *History of the Communist Party of Yugoslavia.*

opponents as political enemies served them in good stead in their march for power and continued to inform them until well after their successful seizure of it.

3

The Communists on the Road to Power

Light thickens, and the crow
Makes wing to th' rooky wood;
Good things of day do begin to droop and drowse,
Whiles night's black agents to their preys do rouse.

Shakespeare, Macbeth, *III. iii. 4–6*

The paradox of how politically weak and isolated communist parties were able to take over Eastern Europe in a matter of only a few years and establish their total control over all aspects of life is usually explained by reference to the presence of the Red Army and the feebleness of the Western response to Soviet expansion after 1945. The summit meeting at Yalta is usually cited as the event which sealed the fate of Eastern Europe, where the Western powers acquiesced in Stalin's demands in exchange for unredeemable pledges of free elections. The problem with this interpretation is that while it properly focuses attention on Soviet actions and Western inaction, it largely ignores Eastern Europe itself and implies thereby that East Europeans watched helplessly as external forces decided their fate. In particular, it suggests that at no point did East Europeans have any choice over their futures, that their fate had been completely predetemined from the outset. This appears to be a considerable oversimplification of what actually happened and, equally seriously, negates any responsibility that East Europeans may have had for their acts of commission or omission in the period 1944–8.[1]

---

[1] There are two symposia which deal with communist take-overs on a country-by-country basis: Thomas T. Hammond (ed.), *The Anatomy of Communist Takeovers* (1975) and Martin McCauley (ed.), *Communist Power in Europe 1944–1949* (1977).

In essence, the argument to be put forward in this chapter is that while the communist seizure of power could not have been successful without the widespread use of Soviet force and communist chicanery, there were also structural weaknesses in Eastern Europe, as well as errors made by non-communist politicians, which made it much easier for the take-over to be effected. Rather than proceeding from the assumption that, once the Red Army had established the Soviet presence in Eastern Europe, the take-over was inevitable, the question will be put as to why so little resistance was encountered, why the non-communist forces, which represented the majority in Eastern Europe, were unable to develop stronger resistance to communist pressure. Equally, there was a minority which found the communist message attractive and responded to it positively. Finally, the argument will be made that the communist revolutions, far from occurring in polities where the old élite stood firm and confident, in reality took place in states which had already been through a revolution-like experience. This has far-reaching implications for the legitimizing claim made by the communists that they emerged victorious in a revolutionary situation by overthrowing the bourgeois or neo-feudal oppressors; on the contrary, this historic task had already been performed by the communists' arch-enemies and occasional allies, the radical right.

The argument, which had wide currency in Eastern Europe during the communist period, was that resistance was pointless, that Stalin had determined to establish not only Soviet power but also a Soviet-type system in the lands his armies had conquered. This, however, fails to meet the counter that choices, however restricted, were available to the non-communists and that Stalin, however ruthless and powerful he may have been, was not possessed of superhuman abilities. In particular, the argument does not offer a satisfactory explanation of the case of Czechoslovakia, from which the Red Army withdrew in 1945 and where the non-communists had considerable political strength and the room to deploy it. Nor does the standard argument meet the case of Finland, where despite numerous similarities to the countries where take-overs were successful, the communists were never able to mount an effective attempt to seize power. The thrust of the counter-argument will be to look at the way in which the take-overs have been interpreted and then to broaden the context in terms of both time and space.

The Stages of the Take-overs

Far and away the most influential interpretation of how the communists seized power in Eastern Europe is the one put forward by

Hugh Seton-Watson. He argues that take-overs took place in three stages: genuine coalition, façade coalition and monolithic bloc. In the first stage a number of centre and left-wing parties, like Agrarian Radicals and Social Democrats, compete for power with the communists, albeit under certain restrictions, notably the presence or proximity of the Soviet Union and the control of the Ministry of the Interior by the communists; this does inhibit opposition somewhat, but it may be regarded as a fairly free political system. In the second stage, non-communist parties are still found in the coalition, but they are no longer wholly independent actors and are controlled by the communists; opposition is less and less tolerated. In the final stage, the political system has been entirely centralized under communist power; if other parties have an existence this is merely a formality and no opposition of any kind, no autonomous action is permitted.[2]

This model is persuasive in that it creates order in what was a complex and confused situation. It offers a valuable way of comparing the process of the take-over in different countries, notably how fast it took place; and it properly emphasizes what took place within East European countries, without discounting the impact of international events. At the same time, the model can be extended backwards in time to provide a longer historical context to the take-overs and thereby to amplify its explanatory power. Furthermore, the three-stage model focuses on the processes of 'visible politics', the actions of communists in coalition, and does not always give due emphasis to what was happening to other institutions – the administration, the military, the police, the judiciary, trade unions, the press and the like. In this chapter an attempt will be made to extend Seton-Watson's model precisely in these directions and then to assess the various factors that helped or hindered the communists in their seizure of power, as well as in how they proceeded to legitimate that power.

The socio-cultural context in which the communists made their bid for power has already been set out in the first chapter and needs no amplification here. In summary, the argument turns on the proposition that the states and societies of Eastern Europe were only weakly integrated; that important segments of society had no commitment to the state; that civil society had not been firmly rooted anywhere; that political activity and thus political experience had become the preserve of the élite; that pluralism and competition for power, while not wholly absent, were severely restricted; that the population had become habituated to authoritarian and étatist practices; and that social control over the state was fragile. To these politico-cultural

[2] Hugh Seton-Watson, *The East European Revolution,* 3rd edn (1956), pp. 167ff. See also Charles Gati, *Hungary and the Soviet Bloc* (1986), pp. 73–99.

factors must be added the impact of the war itself. Indeed, the effect of the Second World War on Eastern Europe was so substantial and represented so deep a caesura that it must be regarded as constituting a fourth stage to be added to Seton-Watson's three.[3]

The events of the war for all practical purposes destroyed the old élites and gave the bid for power by the communists a far better chance of success, simply because the forces to resist them had either been swept away or largely undermined. This not only impinged on the old élites themselves, but considerably weakened the democratic centre and left as well, many of whose leaders were imprisoned or killed or forced into exile. In this respect much of the groundwork for the communist revolution had actually been carried out by the Germans and their wartime right-radical allies.

Just as during the First World War, the population had been radicalized by war; expectations of massive change, often of a messianistic nature, were widespread in 1944–5. There was an expectation that a new political order, based on a more equal distribution of power, would be created. The communists, given their ruthlessness, their discipline and organization, their determination not to be caught in the trap of 1917–21 and their record of un-compromising hostility to the *ancien régime*, coupled with the prestige they earned from their activities in the resistance and their association with the Soviet liberator, were strongly placed to benefit from this state of affairs. In essence, Central and Eastern Europe was the scene of a power vacuum and the communists proved to be the force best able to fill it.

The extent and depth of the caesura caused by the war has often tended to be underestimated as an explanatory factor in accounting for the take-overs. The figures for Poland, for example, are instructive. As a result of German and Soviet action, the whole of the interwar aristocracy was scattered; one-third of the intelligentsia perished; of the 1.2 million people living in Warsaw in 1939, 800,000 were killed in the fighting that year and in the uprisings of 1943 and 1944; and around one-third of the population was involved in an unparalleled demographic shift. Even if there had been no Soviet involvement, post-war Poland would have been very different from the pre-1939 order. A new intelligentsia would have arisen and it would have been recruited from the peasantry and the working class, regardless of what régime was in power. War damage was not merely physical. The destruction of plant, buildings and equipment was exacerbated by the

[3] I have argued this thesis at greater length in *Encounter,* 64 no. 2 (February 1985), pp. 65–9.

dislocation of individuals, the disruption of continuity of settlement and bonds of loyalty, the fragmentation of lives and social solidarities, the tearing up of roots and the inevitable disorientation of values that ensued. Ultimately, the whole moral order was opened to questioning.

The Polish capital was an extreme case. The Warsaw that was rebuilt after 1945 was very largely a new city as far as its population was concerned.[4] And the same applied to the newly incorporated Oder–Neisse territories, which had lost their German population and acquired a Polish one. Too many people regarded sheer survival and the re-establishment of a bearable way of life as their primary objective to allow long-term political activism to be comfortably sustained. In these circumstances it was not surprising that the dynamism of the communists proved highly effective and that the non-communists were unable to develop the self-confidence to match it.

The destruction of war in Yugoslavia was equally far-reaching, if not more so. The state that was created in 1918, weakened by internal dissension, disintegrated when it was attacked by Germany in 1941 and the old élite lost its power, whether to the Axis occupiers or to Axis allies like the Ustasa state (the NDH) in Croatia or the communist-led partisans. Four years of fighting left devastation and a legacy of violence which the communists were able to exploit by proclaiming an uncompromising struggle against the foreign invader, by insisting on an end to inter-ethnic massacres, as well as promising to satisfy peasant radicalism. The chasm was similarly deep in Hungary, in spite of the success of wartime governments in keeping the country unaffected by war until 1944. The Germans then occupied Hungary and, after Admiral Horthy attempted to sign a separate peace, they replaced him with the Arrow Cross Hungarian Nazi régime, even as the Red Army had entered Hungarian territory. This combination of a wholly illegitimate government and hostilities on Hungarian territory, together with the privations of the ten-week siege of Budapest, the incarceration of about 200,000 Jews in the newly established Budapest ghetto, the random slaughter, was successful in shattering the morale of one of the most confident of *anciens régimes*. The discontinuity resulting from war in the part of Germany that was to become the GDR is self-evident and needs no further discussion here.

To the actual physical damage caused by acts of war – bombs, shells, explosions – should be added the destruction of plant by the activities of the Soviet war machine. It is frequently overlooked that the Red Army occupied large areas of Central and Eastern Europe and,

[4] Joanna K. M. Hanson, *The Civilian Population and the Warsaw Uprising of 1944* (1982).

where it did so, it made use of the existing industrial base in a ruthless, slash-and-burn fashion. They expected maximum output from equipment, allowed no time for maintenance and repairs and treated what they found as spoils of war, resulting in confiscations and removals without compensation. This process not only left thousands without work when hostilities ceased because the existing plant and equipment were beyond repair, but their owners were financially ruined and demoralized, incapable of playing any political role. It is not suggested here that this was part of a deliberate policy, but as an unintended consequence of Soviet actions, it should be seen as a welcome windfall.[5]

Even where war damage and fighting were less destructive, there were good reasons for the difficulties encountered by the non-communists in marshalling their forces after the war. In Czechoslovakia the old élite had suffered a massive loss of self-confidence and prestige as a result of Munich and the subsequent dismemberment of the country. The demoralization of the war enhanced this, in as much as the upper and middle classes were fiercely repressed – 38,000 of them perished at the hands of the German occupiers – while for those who survived there was a difficult daily decision to make as to where survival ended and collaboration began. The state of demoralization in 1945 was far greater than was recognized at the time, for it was masked by the apparent re-emergence of political normality and continuity, with the revival of a multi-party coalition and the reinstatement of President Beneš in the Hradčany. The decay of the élite in Romania, as in Czechoslovakia, dated from before the outbreak of the war, but was accelerated by it. Between the wars the Romanian élite proved less and less capable of running the country until in 1938 King Carol installed a royal dictatorship. Two years later, he was forced to abdicate and then, after a failed uprising by the Iron Guard, Marshall Antonescu installed himself as ruler and remained in power until 1944, when a palace *putsch* by King Michael replaced him with an anti-Axis coalition including the communists. The problem for non-communist leaders, like Iuliu Maniu, was that they were more closely associated with the failures of the interwar period than their counterparts elsewhere, and their readiness to face the post-war period intellectually had been undermined. Their sense of this – implicitly if not explicitly – led them

---

[5] I have taken this insight from András B. Göllner, 'Foundations of Soviet Domination and Communist Political Power in Hungary', *The Hungarian Revolution Twenty Years After,* special issue of *Canadian-American Review of Hungarian Studies,* 3 no. 2 (Fall 1976), pp. 73–106.

to rely unduly (and, in the circumstances, vainly) on Western support. The discontinuity in Bulgaria was of somewhat longer standing, for it dated back to the failure of the 1931 electoral victory of the left and its complete ineffectiveness in power. This discredited the non-communist left, while the experience of war radicalized the communists who were in any case informed by a markedly intransigent tradition.

The negative example of Finland also requires discussion at this point. Finland was an Axis ally which had fought the Soviet Union for much of the war and lost considerable territory to it. What is more, Finnish society was deeply divided by the legacy of the Civil War of 1918 between the Reds and the Whites, so that the communists, despite their interwar illegality, enjoyed extensive popular support. The Soviet presence in post-war Finland was symbolized by control of Porkkala, a large base within half an hour's drive of Helsinki, and by the Allied Control Commission, which was largely run by the Soviet representative, Andrei Zhdanov. Yet despite these potential advantages, the communists never had any serious chance of mounting a take-over. The explanation lies in the fact that while Finland was defeated, it was not conquered. The Germans were expelled by Finnish forces and the Red Army was present on Finnish territory only in transit. The result of this was that the continuity of pre-war institutions was not damaged, the old élite retained its self-confidence and its control of politics and the communists' claim for the restructuring of politics – a purge of the civil service, land reform, nationalization, control of capital – was easily rebuffed.

Communist Tactics

None of these details is to be understood as signifying that the communist take-over was accomplished without any recourse to violence, coercion, falsification and other illegal or semi-legal means. Indeed, if the impact of war is to be regarded as the reverse side of the process, the communists' determined push for power was the obverse. It is a matter of debate as to whether the communists returned to the political arena in Eastern Europe with the intention of establishing a monopolistic Soviet-type system straightaway or whether they would have been satisfied with hegemony had it not been for Stalin's pressure on them. There is little doubt as to their intention of establishing themselves so firmly that they could never be dislodged again, but there were indications that some East European communists were ready to move cautiously, to accept the activities of some countervailing political forces and to take seriously the slogans of 'People's Democracy' as being different from the Soviet political order.

The intensity of communist pressure varied in time and place, in any event, and in this connection Soviet strategy was clearly of crucial significance. Broadly, Stalin was determined to secure Soviet positions in the Soviet zone of occupation in Germany and to achieve this he needed maximum communist strength in Poland. At the same time, he was equally determined to push his power as far southwards into the Balkans as circumstances would allow, which meant that the early bid for power by the Bulgarian communists would have had his backing. That put paid to any possibility that the Romanians might have much room for manoeuvre to create a pluralistic system. But as far as the geopolitical centre was concerned – Czechoslovakia, Hungary, also Austria (which was under four-power occupation until 1955), as well as Yugoslavia – policy towards these states appeared to be governed by somewhat different considerations. Here the speed of take-over was not of the essence, democratic forces were given an opportunity of re-establishing themselves – in Yugoslavia it was Stalin who was reining in Tito rather than the reverse – and the prospects for communist-cum-non-communist coalitions were not unreasonable, at least in the immediate aftermath of the war. There is evidence from the secret deliberations of the Hungarian communists in October 1944 in Moscow that they expected to face a much longer timetable for achieving full Sovietization than what actually occurred.[6] It is possible that if the communists in Eastern Europe had met stiffer resistance, and if the Western Allies had been ready to articulate their hostility to Stalin's plans more vigorously, a slower timetable might, indeed, have been employed.

Nevertheless, the communist bid for hegemonial – let alone monopoly – power was implemented in the way already described. These tactics essentially consisted of occupying the high ground wherever it existed. Wherever there was an institution with power the communists sought to ensure that they would, as far as possible, control it and 'control' in this context was to be interpreted as being to their advantage. This meant not only 'visible' politics, the determination of policies by the political parties, but also control of the administration that actually executed policies. Much the same applied to social bodies: either they were taken over or they were suppressed.

From the outset, therefore, the communist strategy was to capture institutions and to 'colonize' them, to staff them with individuals either genuinely loyal to the party or who could be blackmailed into

---

[6] Gati, *Hungary and the Soviet Bloc.*

reliability. Former members of right-radical parties were a particularly useful reservoir in the latter respect. They were exposed politically to charges of collaboration and, at the same time, many of them had genuine radical credentials, albeit of the wrong kind. Equally, the communists relied heavily on Jewish survivors of the Holocaust, whose reliability as anti-Nazis could not be questioned, and for many of whom commitment to the party was a legitimate way of righting old wrongs or a matter of advancement or even simply of idealism. Mass recruitment was a key aspect of communist tactics at this stage. Party memberships increased correspondingly. The Romanian party, which had perhaps 1,000 members in August 1944 grew to around a million in four years. The rate of increase, if not quite so spectacular elsewhere, was impressive just the same: the Czechoslovak party went from about 40,000 as the war ended to 2.67 million by October 1948; similarly, the Hungarian figures rose from about 2,000 in November 1944 to 884,000 in May 1948.

The dynamism of the communists showed itself in other respects as well. They proved highly active in relaunching war-shattered societies, re-establishing institutions, setting up local and national bodies to run the administration. The fact that in doing so they frequently used the opportunity to advance their interests by placing reliable cadres in positions of influence later turned out to be of considerable significance. At the time, in the immediate aftermath of the fighting, it earned them the gratitude of many and the grudging respect of their opponents. It did their prestige no harm. Often communists moved in hours after the Red Army had expelled the Germans from a particular locality to set up local administration. The standard pattern they followed was to ensure that control of the police was in their hands. Other political parties might be allowed to operate, but only with the sanction of the communists. They oversaw the distribution of food and other scarce goods and generally, as far as they could, they made themselves indispensable.

Throughout the administration the communists insisted strongly on collaboration between themselves and the other parties, but they interpreted this entirely in their own favour. In other words, they enforced a one-sided compromise. This left the non-communists in a difficult position. To an extent they had already undermined their autonomy by agreeing to a very close relationship with the communist parties, as a result of which potential competitors were weakened or eliminated. The refusal to allow the Czech Agrarians to re-establish themselves on charges of collaboration with the Germans proved to be helpful to non-communists, but it left them dependent as well and impeded any potential move towards democratic autonomy. In

Hungary the four-party coalition that governed after the elections of 1945, in which the Smallholders had gained an overall majority (57 per cent) evolved into a politically most curious beast – a government that contained its own opposition. Although the communists were in the minority, they were in many instances able to dictate to the Smallholders by their tactic of constantly discovering new enemies on the right within the ranks of the government. The latter was kept off balance and could never recover to launch an effective counter-offensive.

Overall, the communists made effective use of their *élan* in the immediate aftermath of the war. At a time when their competitors had yet to recover their balance, they were everywhere at the centre of things and successfully convinced sizeable sections of the population that theirs was the future. Their self-confidence was in itself a source of attraction and their ruthlessness and understanding of power helped them to persuade those might have been hesitant or neutral. In this respect their attitude to the national identities of these countries proved highly significant.

The Use and Abuse of Nationalism

Another area where the communist parties proved themselves skilful was in exploiting underlying or overt nationalist issues. Despite the theoretical incompatibility between communism and nationalism, the communist leaders understood that the national identities of these various societies could be usefully manipulated as a political resource. By stoking up the fires of nationalist disputes, they could make life difficult for their non-communist rivals and undermine attempts at cooperation. Alternatively, they could produce settlements from up their sleeves, as it were, and add to their popularity.

The relationship between Czechoslovakia and Hungary in the immediate aftermath of the war proved to be a good illustration of these processes. Southern Slovakia had been re-attached to Hungary in 1938, in the wake of the Munich agreement, and obviously reverted to Czechoslovakia afterwards. The Slovak authorities, with the concurrence of Prague, immediately set about settling accounts with the Hungarian minority. They were denied citizenship, many thousands of them were sent to perform forced labour in the Sudetenland (now vacated by the expelled Germans), while others, around 100,000, were expelled to Hungary. All this was accompanied by an anti-Hungarian campaign that was near racist in tone and style. The object of the exercise was to demonstrate to the Slovak population that the communists were the most effective guardians of the national interest. In the event, though, the non-communist parties were far more successful in the 1946 elections, at any rate as far as Slovakia was concerned.

The leaders of the campaign – Gustáv Husák, Laco Novomesky and others – did not enjoy their nationalist laurels for long. They were imprisoned, ironically, as bourgeois nationalists a few years later. On the Hungarian side the communists were just as vociferous and in 1948, after the communist take-overs had succeeded in both countries, they claimed that the cessation of the persecution of the minority was entirely due to their internationalism. There is a further irony in all this. Although there is no direct evidence for the following proposition, it seems highly likely that the Hungarian communists – Rákosi in particular – were deeply incensed by the Slovaks' anti-Hungarian campaign and were determined to get their own back. The denunciations of the Slovak communist leadership made by Rákosi, when he was putting pressure on Prague after 1949 to 'find the Czechoslovak Rajk', and the insistence that they be tried were almost certainly traceable to the earlier antagonism.[7]

The anti-German aspect of Polish, Czechoslovak and Yugoslav communism should not be underrrated. The motives were similar, to mobilize support for communism around a nationalist axis. But there was a further dimension to this. Whereas the number of Hungarians expelled was relatively small, the total number of Germans forced to leave Czechoslovakia was around 3 million and the entire Oder–Neisse territory in the newly reconstituted Poland had become a virtual *terra inoccupata*.[8] This gave the party an extraordinarily effective weapon in its struggle for power. These newly vacated territories were a superb opportunity for patronage and they were, for all practical purposes, treated as a communist colony, where the non-communist parties were unable to establish even a toe-hold. In the case of Yugoslavia, the areas left by the expelled Germans were handed over to mostly Serbian and Montenegrin settlers, from the very backward 'passive regions'. These settlers generally had Partisan sympathies and were a completely reliable element from the régime's point of view.[9]

The case of Romania illustrated another aspect of the use made of nationalism by communists, the relationship between an ethnic majority and an ethnic minority. The leadership of the large Hungarian

[7] Jiri Pelikan (ed.), *The Czechoslovak Political Trials 1950–1954* (1971).
[8] Z. Anthony Kruszewski, *The Oder-Neisse Boundary and Poland's Modernization: the Socioeconomic and Political Impact* (1972).
[9] G. C. Paikert, *The Danube Swabians* (1967).

minority in Transylvania had been effectively captured by the left, largely as a result of the reattachment of northern Transylvania to Hungary during the war and the failure of the Horthy system at the end of it. The Hungarians, therefore, lined up with the Romanian left in the expectation that the new communist régime would deliver the fair and equitable treatment that the interwar royal government had failed to do. Indeed, there are grounds for arguing that the role played by the minority in helping the communists come to power in 1945–6 exceeded the capability of the minority and represented an over-large presence in Romanian politics as a whole. There was, in fact, something questionable about 2 million Hungarians helping to decide the fate of ten times as many Romanians. Once again, ironies came to the fore. Once in power, the Romanian communist party was rapidly Romanianized and the ethnic Hungarians found themselves in a far weaker position than they had anticipated. Indeed, the fairly reasonable treatment they received in the form of cultural and educational institutions was regarded by the party as a threat to its power and these were subsequently the primary target for re-integration, a process that took until the end of the 1950s. In other words, having taken the Marxist credentials of the Romanian communists seriously, the Hungarians discovered that in reality they were, after all, Romanians first and internationalists second, so that the help they given them in seizing power did them precious little good in communist eyes, even while it earned them the undying distrust of the anti-communist majority.

Popular Radicalism

Reference has already been made to the expectations of radical change in sections of the population at the end of the war. The implications of this phenomenon deserve further investigation. In the first place, it should be made quite clear that this radicalism was not committed to the communists from the outset; on the contrary, it was far less focused than that. The substance of this radicalism should be traced back to the nature of peasant belief systems explored in the previous chapter and, at the same time, to the legacy of the right-wing radicalism of the interwar period. There is a certain tendency nowadays to concentrate on the 'right-wing' quality of right-radical movements and to ignore their 'radical' credentials, something attributable presumably to the general feeling that radicalism is the exclusive preserve of the left.[10]

---

[10] Mihály Vajda, *Fascism as a Mass Movement* (1976); Peter F. Sugar (ed.), *Native Fascism in the Successor States 1918–1945* (1971).

The salient characteristic of these Central and Eastern European right-radical movements, however, was precisely their radicalism, their determination to destroy the existing structure of power and wealth and to create something fundamentally new in their place. The implication of this situation for the post-war period was that there existed a sizeable section of society which was ready to think in radical categories, for whom the root-and-branch extirpation of the old élite was welcome and who were fully prepared to respond to the language of total transformation used by the communists.

On the other hand, this should not be interpreted to mean that all these radicals were looking for the communist solution. A minority was clearly ready to work for the communist utopia and to use any and all methods to bring it about. The hard left believed in the Stalinist message of industrialization and internationalism, to be achieved in the fastest and, if necessary, toughest way possible, but the hard left did not begin to constitute a majority anywhere. Even in the Czech lands they probably did not exceed a quarter of the population.[11] The reality of the situation was that there were strong radical currents, but they lacked a political focus, structure or organization. The communists alone were in a position to provide these.

The argument put forward by Charles Gati supports most of these propositions for Hungary. He estimates that something of the order of half the Hungarian vote in 1945 could be considered as being in favour of radical rather than orderly, procedural change. The whole of the communist vote (17 per cent), around half the Social Democratic vote (9 per cent), all of the National Peasant Party vote (7 per cent) and the poor peasant section of the Smallholders' support (say 19 per cent) would fall into this category.[12] While there is no reason to doubt these estimates as broad currents, they should not be thought to have clearly defined predictive value. The meaning of these statistical estimates is

[11] Martin Myant, *Socialism and Democracy in Czechoslovakia, 1945–1948* (1981); Jon Bloomfield, *Passive Revolution: Politics and the Czechoslovak Working Class, 1945–1948* (1979) and Karel Kaplan, *The Short March: the Communist Takeover in Czechoslovakia 1945–1948* (1987) have different emphases and conclusions, but all agree that a significant section of the Czech working class was supportive of much of the content of the communist programme, notably the state control of the economy and an irreversible working-class input into politics. Thus Kaplan notes: 'Even the political parties that considered themselves non-socialist . . . were for social reforms that were not contrary to socialism and even resembled it. The majority of persons prominent in public life and in the cultural sphere also felt that the future of the country lay in socialism,' p. 34. François Fejtö, *Le Coup de Prague 1948* (1976) also offers some valuable insights.

[12] Gati, *Hungary and the Soviet Bloc*, especially pp. 67–71.

that there was, indeed, radicalism in Hungary, but there was no agreement over what kind of radicalism, how far it should go, what should happen to private property, should the market be abolished in its entirety and so on. Above all, it should be understood that the bulk of Hungarian opinion was relatively unsophisticated and politically inexperienced. The consequence of this state of affairs was that the communists, the most dynamic and most articulate political group, were able to capture this radicalism by their rhetoric and constant emphasis on the acceleration of reform, and to use the radicalism so controlled as a basis for demanding further change.

The fate of the agrarian radicals was particularly poignant in this respect. They gravitated towards the communists in the belief that they would gain a better deal for the poor peasantry from them rather than the 'bourgeois' parties. In the event, they could not have been more wrong. While the future of the peasantry was gloomy in all scenarios – the land simply could not support the rural population it was supposed to under agrarian plans – the evolutionary programmes of the non-communists would almost certainly have resulted in less brutal treatment for the peasantry than the forced collectivization under Stalinism.[13]

The Non-Communists

In a perspective of nearly half a century the non-communists of Central and Eastern Europe present a rather sorry sight. In the immediate aftermath of the take-over they were generally perceived as the heroic victims of overwhelming force, but this view is no longer tenable in its unamended form. They were, indeed, victims, but they contributed to their own marginalization wittingly and, far more extensively, unwittingly. Any fair-minded interpretation of the communists' opponents will see them as people of goodwill, often genuinely concerned to establish democracy as understood in the West, but lacking political skills and too uncertain to possess the determination to face down the communists. Crucially, they did not have any sense of the political space at their disposal, what their limits were, how far they could go before encountering an immovable object.

They tended to see the Soviet occupation as a definitive and incalculable constraint, in the face of which they were helpless. Their limits were, in fact, frequently circumscribed and it may be that the

[13] Olga Narkiewicz, *The Green Flag: Polish Populist Politics 1867–1970* (1976); Gyula Borbándi, *Der ungarische Populismus* (1976).

final outcome of Soviet domination and the imposition of the Soviet-type system would not have been different if they had followed another strategy. Nevertheless, the flaws of the non-communist opposition made the communists' task easier than it might have been and unquestionably contributed to the triumphalism of the 1950s, the sense that a revolution really had taken place and that the communists had earned their monopoly power. This conclusion had important implications for communist legitimation and self-legitimation.

The task faced by the communists was made much easier by the destruction of war, but there was more to it than that. The war not only eliminated the old élite or undermined its morale, it also weakened the not especially strong democratic forces as well. Obviously, it was not in the interests of the Nazis and their allies that democratic politicians should be free to act under their régimes, so they were systematically killed, deported or forced into exile. Those who survived did so with the burden of knowing that moderation had failed them, that against the revolutionary *élan* and ruthlessness of the Nazis, they were powerless. When confronted by a similar attitude on the part of the communists, they were helpless precisely because they already lived under the sign of failure.

Furthermore, the Nazi past cast a long shadow. This was not merely the case in terms of potential blackmail – all non-communists had to find a kind of alibi as to what they were doing under Nazi occupation, for in the communist mind-set everyone was guilty – but even when they were accepted as temporary allies by the communists, they could be forever blackmailed by the threat of 'reaction'. The communists were very adept in disarming the Social Democrats in particular by claiming that a given course of action or support for a given policy of which they disapproved would help 'the reactionaries'. Seeing that the Nazis had been eliminated only a very short time before, this was a risk that the non-communists simply could not assess. At no point were they able to say to their opponents that, as a matter of fact, there was no danger from 'reaction' at all. Nor were they able to see that their own domestic 'reactionaries' had been defeated politically and often enough eliminated physically.

Further, the non-communists constructed their political perceptions in terms of the West. They had entirely exaggerated ideas of what the West could and would do for them. They were captivated by the democratic glamour of the West and believed that their companions in the shared ideological commitment thought as they did, that one helped like-minded people in politics. They had a worm's-eye view of world politics and had no conception of the complexities of the cold war as these impinged on them. Consequently, they tended to formulate their strategies in a spirit of cooperation with the communists in the belief that this was what the West approved of, and lacked the internal and external independence of mind and morale to use what little space was available to them.

The democrats in Central and Eastern Europe were also encouraged in their attitudes by the general reluctance on the part of the West to face up to the implications of the Stalin phenomenon, particularly on the part of Roosevelt. The signals reaching the areas now in the Soviet sphere of influence were by and large those of Western ignorance or inability to do very much. The information that large tracts of the region had, for all practical purposes, already been written off by the Moscow Agreements of October 1944, the so-called percentage agreements, was unknown, but the general passivity of the West was an enigma, from which the Central and Eastern European democrats failed to draw the right conclusion. Or when they did, it demoralized them because of their unrealistic expectations of Western backing.

The reflected glory of the Soviet Union's triumph in the Second World War and its high prestige as liberator was undoubtedly helpful to the communists, to which a lingering element of Pan-Slavism can be added, at least in the case of Czechoslovakia and the Orthodox societies of the Balkans. Power in its raw form – military victory – likewise attracted sections of the population, which expected to be able to revenge itself on their previous rulers for the centuries of humiliations and servitude that they had had to endure, a theme deliberately played on by the communists, by gaining access to that power.

Finally, a word is necessary here about the nature of Soviet intentions towards Central and Eastern Europe. Until the archives of the Kremlin are fully explored, anything written on this topic has to include some guesswork, but a distinction can be made between guesswork based on the record and a kind which seeks to explore some ideological proposition. There is enough evidence to indicate that Stalin's war aims were to extend Soviet power to the extent that this was feasible, and that where he encountered strong resistance, he would retract. Where, however, Soviet power was established, a communist system would be established too. As reported by Milovan Djilas, Stalin said, 'whoever occupies a territory also imposes on it his own social system;'[14] a precept that Stalin certainly followed in the areas the Soviet forces occupied under the Molotov–Ribbentrop pact in 1939–41.

If one seeks to apply the principle drawn from this proposition to

[14] Milovan Djilas, *Conversations with Stalin* (1962), p. 114.

post-war Central and Eastern Europe one is still left with a question. What precisely did 'system' mean in this context ? Did it mean that the Soviet-type system, as developed in the Soviet Union, would be imposed down to the last nut or rivet, or would there would be some room for local variation and discretion? This question was only answered definitively after the Tito–Stalin split of 1948. Until then there was some ground for hoping that, while the communists were certainly looking for a hegemonial position, they might be prepared to share some power with non-communists.

Effectively, this is the idea that underlies the belief that 'People's Democracy' was something more than a device, a façade behind which the communists concealed their true intentions. It is difficult to be dogmatic about issues of this kind, essentially because the relationship between intentions and actions is always more vague, more contingent, more haphazard than it appears with hindsight. In the quest for a pattern one is inclined to overestimate the nexus between what individuals hoped for and what they actually did. In reality, a role was invariably played by chance, accident, igorance and incompetence, and the communists were especially effective in exploiting the opportunities provided by these gaps in the fabric. But this does not actually prove that they intended to seize monopoly power from the outset.

The implications are considerable. If communist objectives were less than monopoly then a separate East European road to communism enters the realm of possible options, one which might have spared the area some of its worst Stalinist experiences and, indeed, one that might have acquired genuine roots. Be that as it may, it is worth stressing that, regardless of communist intentions, they helped to foster an illusion that the total imitation of the Soviet Union was not necessarily on the agenda and this certainly strengthened their credentials among those who were sympathetic but not wholly committed to Soviet-style communism.

From the opposite perspective, whether the communist goal was monopoly or hegemony was inherently bad news. It implied that come what may, the communists would never cede a centimetre of power and that, regardless of the popular wishes, the communists would be there for the foreseeable future. This was a real issue, not a hypothetical one. By the winter of 1947 the Communist Party of Czechoslovakia, which had a pre-eminent position in the coalition, was running into unpopularity, something that opinion polls confirmed. In the event of elections the communists would lose some of what they gained in 1946. At least a part of the explanation of the coup of February 1948 lies in the unthinkability for the communists that they might cede power merely because the electorate had changed its mind. For communists their access to power was permanent and irreversible – after all, they had embarked on a socialist revolution and, according to their ideological tenets, history could not be reversed.

Conclusion

Overall, the successful communist take-over should be seen as having been based on an interplay of international and domestic factors, in which the communists never lost the initiative. The Soviet Union was well placed to repel support for its opponents from the West – the way in which Poland and Czechoslovakia were obliged to reject the Marshall Plan was one instance – and provided logistical and moral support for the Central and Eastern European communists on their home ground. But the most vital contribution made by the Kremlin was to be found in the ideological certainty that it lent the Central and Eastern European parties and in the organizational discipline that made it possible for them to carry through their strategy. Above all, communism was demonstrated to be a superb instrument for the seizure of power through the isolation and paralysing of all possible alternatives, until a sufficient number of people either believed or complied with the communists' claim that theirs was the future. For those who remained obdurate, the fear of death or worse was the deterrent.

Yet in a sense the very success of the communists in seizing monopoly power contained dangers that were eventually to undermine it. Precisely by eliminating alternatives, the communist ideology destroyed the feedback and self-correcting mechanisms that might have prevented the system from the rigidity with which it shortly came to be afflicted. The triumph and triumphalism of the early years acted as blinkers, which cut the communist rulers off from understanding the processes that were leading the system into a cul-de-sac. Once legitimation and power were elevated into ideological categories, communism entered an area where mounting problems could find no solution, because they could not be perceived. In that respect the victory of the communist ideology eventually proved its undoing.

4

Stalinism

We had fed the heart on fantasies
The heart's grown brutal from the fare;
More substance in our enmities
Than in our love.

W. B. Yeats, Meditations in
Time of Civil War.

For the whole of Eastern Europe Stalinism has been the central forma-
tive experience since the war, the benchmark against which all subsequent developments must be measured. Stalinism must, therefore,
be understood in all its different manifestations and at all its different
levels. Its extraordinary quality derives in the first place from its
breathtaking political scope. It is hard to muster a precedent for the
experiment conducted by the Soviet Union in eight wholly alien and
culturally rather diverse polities over such a short period of time. It is
this concentration of time and the compression of the process involved
that gave Eastern Europe's experience of Stalinism its second striking
quality. The third was the breadth, depth and intensity of the process.
All institutions, all organizations, all forms of communal activity, all
individuals were expected to conform to a predetermined set of norms
or suffer the consequences for failing to do so. It was in this sense that
Stalinism represented an attempt at totalitarian control, although even
at its height it was nowhere successful in actually establishing the total
penetration of individuals, their motives and activities. It was successful only in as much as it was able to exact conformity to a set
pattern of behaviour as far as the majority was concerned.

Stalinism functioned at a variety of levels – in ideology, institutions,
structures, the exercise of power, its impact on social groups and

society as a whole. At its centre was a proposition derived from Stalin's transformation of Marxism–Leninism, to the effect that this ideology represented perfection – the distillation of all human wisdom in its final form – by which these societies were marching towards a secular utopia. It was perfect, it was claimed, because it was rational in all respects and in all its manifestations. The advantage of this proposition was that it inherently excluded the possibility of all argument over alternatives, different strategies, policies and their implementation – it is, after all, logically impossible to disagree with perfection.

Consequently disagreement or debate was antagonistic, hostile activity or thought, therefore open to punitive counteraction. The implications of the ideology of perfection are very far-reaching and the way in which it was applied sought to extend it as far as possible. If Marxism–Leninism is perfect, then it is capable of providing the answers to questions not just of politics and economics, but also of technology or the natural sciences or any other branch of human knowledge. Conversely, what Stalinism declared to be a non-existent or reactionary area of human knowledge could simply be discarded. In this way it was logical to assert that there could exist a Marxist–Leninist way of building a bridge or performing an appendectomy or catching fish. In other words, one is dealing here with political reductionism of epochal proportions.

No activity, however apolitical it might appear, can escape the purview of the ideology because, by its own definition, everything is political and capable of being understood only through politics. It follows from this, too, that there could be no political neutrality. Neither individuals nor groups could stand back and say, as it were, 'we neither approve nor disapprove of the system; we are apolitical.' The political system driven by the ideology had to insist that everyone should be seen to give it his or her overt and continuous support, otherwise he or she was a potential doubter. How can perfection be doubted ?

Again, the ideology of perfection logically established itself as omniscient. There could by definition be no problems to which there was no solution. And should the solutions derived from the ideology fail, then this failure could not be attributed to the ideology but to its antagonists, the proponents of other ideologies, all of which were hostile. Consequently, the system excluded the possibility of error. If something went wrong, as it often did, someone was responsible. There could be no such phenomena as accident, chance or an honest mistake. All actions were invested with political purposiveness and all were categorized as 'progressive' or 'reactionary'. By the same token, criticism could not exist autonomously of the ideology, but had to be integrated into its imperatives. Only the criticism actually permitted or rather, more properly, directed by the political authority could find expression.

The political structure constructed by the criteria of this ideology was strictly hierarchical, disciplined and regimented. At its centre was Stalin himself. His will was the supreme political (and all other) imperative. On Stalin depended the individual East European party leaders, the party politburos, the central committees and members. The East European parties, acting as ever on directives from above, controlled all state and social institutions, which they permeated with the new body of thought. Parallel structures of control existed via the Soviet advisors strategically placed in all East European countries (Yugoslavia being the exception); they were particularly active in the instruments of coercion – the secret police and the military.[1] Thus in Poland, of the twenty departments in the Ministry of Security, eight were headed by Soviet advisors and at least five more departmental heads had worked for the NKVD or the Soviet armed forces.[2] In this way an identity of both form and content was imposed on Eastern Europe. What was also noteworthy was the remarkable concentration of power demanded by the system. While it would be an exaggeration to claim that all Stalin had to do was to press a button and simultaneously in every East European state there would be an identical response, nonetheless the degree of homogeneity imposed on the area and the extension of Soviet norms were very far-reaching indeed. At the time, when viewed from the outside, the appearance of identity was complete. It was only later that it emerged that conformity to externals did not automatically transform content, although it did not leave content unaffected.

The central proposition of the Stalinist experiment – the ideology of perfection – sought, therefore, to construct a total system from which both feedback and self-limitation were excluded as harmful and damaging. This was inherent in the nature of the project, for evidently there cannot be any feedback, any communication between rulers and ruled, where the rulers already are in possession of both past and future. In reality, of course, government without feedback creates enormous and insoluble problems for the rulers, in as much as it sets up tensions between the objectives of the state and the aspirations of

[1] Karel Kaplan, *Political Persecution in Czechoslovakia 1948–1972* (1983), p. 17 gives details for Czechoslovakia. These can be regarded as having been paralleled throughout Eastern Europe.
[2] Zbigniew K. Brzezinski, *The Soviet Bloc: Unity and Conflict,* 2nd edn (1967), pp. 120–1.

society. The latter can be overruled for a while, but ultimately the wishes of society will distort the workings of the system, even while the system has no cognitive instruments for decoding these as anything other than hostile conspiracy. The moral codes of society are partly destroyed and partly distorted, but they are never entirely transformed in the way that the Stalinists expected.

Self-limitation is likewise alien to perfection, for identical reasons. There is no logical need for a government to accept limits to its power when everything that it does is in any case perfect. Unfortunately, this proposition can be led back to a prior, tacit assumption that people are perfect or perfectible, which is manifestly not the case, with consequences both for the corruption of power and the strategies of compensation for powerlessness adopted by individuals. The use of mass terror was, therefore, the logical outcome of the tacit premise. It marked communism indelibly, with important consequences for the longer-term viability of the system.

Utopias and Futures

The system also proved highly detrimental to the development of society as a body capable of responding to initiatives and ready to participate in the projects of its rulers. Stalinism was completely destructive of social autonomy, a process with far-reaching consequences for subsequent periods. The imposition of a totalizing system, legitimated in terms of perfection, managed by convinced utopians and backed up by terror, resulted in the elimination of much of what makes a society a society, as distinct from an agglomeration of individuals. Autonomies and solidarities, terms of trust, codes of interpersonal behaviour, the rules governing micro-level transactions were shattered.

The destruction was not restricted to organizations, but was aimed at values as well. Any system of values not approved of by the party, all rationalities not conforming to Stalin's whims, any attempt by individuals to exercise their judgement autonomously were met with condign punishment. What applied to individuals applied even more to organized groups. Nascent civil society was smothered and then eradicated in the course of the Stalinist project. With it went the alternative value systems, competing currents, differing attempts to give answers to existential or ontological problems and eventually the whole idea of diversity, that decisions were formulated not by one single, overarching, hierarchical set of concepts, but untidily, through diversity and debate.

The elevation of Marxism–Leninism to be the sole source of ideals, values, inspiration and organizing principles was highly destructive of patterns of interchange in society, politics and economics. Not only did this severely narrow the range of options and thus potential solutions, but it pushed these systems towards a synthetic dynamism veiling stagnation. Intellectually these systems were inert. The insistence on one and only one 'correct' solution was a manifest absurdity. It led ineluctably to dogmatism. At the same time it also established a sterile Marxist/anti-Marxist dichotomy, which was to characterize these systems until the 1980s.

All these proved to have inflicted lasting damage, making regeneration difficult and leaving these systems vulnerable to normlessness. Centrally, the official ideology was incapable of infusing the bulk of the population with inspiration and could not become the source of values for them, once it was clear that Marxism–Leninism had become paralysed. The system, its ideology and its rulers had become frozen. In effect, the pre-existing systems had been destroyed and nothing lasting was put in their place.

The proposition that no solution is final, that all arrangements are subject to transcendence, is evidently anti-utopian in its implication, for it signifies that while utopia plays a pivotal role in structuring futurities, no actual political (economic, social, legal, aesthetic, etc.) order can ever be accepted as the utopia itself. In this respect Europe, as the heir of the Judaeo–Hellenic–Christian tradition, is the exception and is quite irreconcilable with, say, Islam. The European tradition, of which these societies were a part, is open to change, to questioning and criticism, and promotes a restlessness, an ongoing quest, a process of cognitive growth.[3] This is often profoundly uncomfortable and deeply subversive of the established order. It implies that nothing is fixed forever, but all things are in a state of flux. *Panta rhei.*

The political project, therefore, has been to construct an institutional order to cope with this, to establish systems that will provide stability and yet not exclude change. Both are there, both are demanded, both needed. Attempts in the past to foreclose, to declare that utopia has been achieved, have failed. Centrally they have failed not merely because they have in some way, the aetiology of which is obscure, failed to reach their stated goal, but because a proclaimed utopia excludes hope, and that in turn destroys the meaning of the past, making social life unbearable. The point is made by Dante;[4] 'You

---

[3] Ernest Gellner, *Plough, Sword and Book* (1988).
[4] 'Però comprender puoi che tutta morte/fia nostra conoscenza da quel punto,/ che del futuro fia chiusa la porta.' Cited by George Steiner, *In Bluebeard's Castle* (1971), p. 60.

must understand, therefore, that all our knowledge shall be a dead thing from the moment on when the door of the future is shut.'

During the communist period Eastern Europe struggled with the precise task of reopening the door of the future. Stalinism sought, and for a while seemed to succeed in the imposition of a declaratory utopia on the area, thereby proclaiming that no further change was necessary. A minority may even have believed that they were living in this utopia – even as late as 1968 Georg Lukács could say, 'the worst socialism is better than the best capitalism.' (Luckily he died before he could see the Pol Pot model of socialism in action.) But the majority understood from the outset that the system they now had to live with cut right across their individually formulated (and culturally derived) visions of the future.[5] They were subjected to powerlessness in the name of a utopia they neither wanted nor believed in and they responded, wherever possible, by trying to recover power. Because the utopia was not a utopia, but at best a highly imperfect system, at worst a kakotopia, it was always marked by interstices through which individuals could seek to construct alternative futures for themselves, though under highly disadvantageous conditions, on a short-term basis.[6] This exacted a terrible price in terms of the moral order, its cohesiveness, persuasiveness and meaning.[7]

The Purpose of Stalinism

The purpose of Stalinism is open to several possible interpretations. It could be regarded as the creation of socialism by the export of Soviet-style revolutionary communism to areas which had lagged behind the Soviet Union by reason of the travails of capitalism. Alternatively, the imposition of Stalinism on Eastern Europe can be seen in terms of pure *Realpolitik*. Stalin devised a new model of securing his wartime conquests and his Western glacis, by exporting a revolution of a type identical to the one developed in the Soviet Union. This was done by creating a political system that could exist only through dependence on the Soviet Union and by which the new rulers of Eastern Europe would give their loyalty to Stalin or else be swept from power. A third view is to regard the Soviet conquest of Eastern Europe as a new variant of the age-old Russian drive to the West or simply as a function

[5] Lukács interview in *Kortárs*, July 1968. See also the interview with Julia Minc, in Teresa Torańska, *Oni: Stalin's Polish Puppets* (1986), pp. 15–29.
[6] Leszek Kolakowski, 'Theses on Hope and Hopelessness', *Survey*, 1974.
[7] László Bogár, *A fejlödés ára* (1983).

of Stalin's power mania. All these interpretations contain elements of validity. However, it will be argued here that the political development of Eastern Europe since the war is best understood by interpreting Stalinism as a highly contradictory and even counter-productive modernizing revolution. The proposition here is that an analysis of the interplay between the traditional norms of political development and those of Stalinism constitutes the best explanation for subsequent patterns of development in the internal affairs of Eastern Europe.

Hence the definition of Stalinism adopted here is that it did amount to a modernizing revolution, but essentially one highly inappropriate to Eastern Europe and, paradoxically, its effect was as much to reverse or slow down the process of modernization already being experienced rather than to enhance the process. This proposition demands a definition of the modernity towards which modernization is supposedly leading. The concept of modernization is a notoriously elusive one, which, when boiled down to its essentials, often ends up looking suspiciously like the patterns developed in the United States or Western Europe. This need not mean, however, that the concept is made entirely useless by cultural bias. Rather, it demands a closer analysis of the relationship between the goals of modernity and the particular culture in which the process of modernization is taking place. This implies that each culture, however defined, has its own more or less autonomous model of modernity and these may well be closely influenced by the example (positive or negative) of other 'modernities'. If the United States variant of modernity is taken as one example, it is evident that this has been highly influential throughout the world; but this does not mean that by its mere existence it invalidates other modernities. In the same way, there are British, French, German and, by extension, East European models of modernity.[8]

The specific problem with the Stalinist model of industrialization lay in a number of broad areas. In the first place, Stalin for his own reasons, contingent on the particular military and technological needs of the Soviet Union in the 1930s, took a set of economic targets and methods and declared these to be the immanent truths of socialism. This served its purpose in that it helped Soviet society to live with the trauma of industrialization and to endure the privations Stalin required of it, but these targets had limited relevance to the needs of Eastern Europe after 1945. Eastern Europe had already embarked on a process of industrialization to a greater or lesser degree and was on the way to becoming a more complex social, economic and political organism.

---

[8] The concept of modernization has generated a major debate. See inter alia Cyril E. Black (ed.), *Comparative Modernization: a Reader* (1976)

Second, the Soviet model was heavily determined by specifically Soviet conditions like easy access to apparently unlimited quantities of raw materials (energy, iron ore, labour) and by the utterly different spatial relationships there. In respect of population density, Eastern Europe was much more like Western Europe than Russia. Furthermore, the particular targets selected by Stalin as 'socialist industrialization' tended to rely on relatively simple technologies of manufacture and extraction. Plan targets could be expressed in straightforward, comprehensible terms, viz. so many tons of coal or steel, and the level of skills required for their production was commensurate with those of the Soviet labour force of the time. Conditions in Eastern Europe, especially in Central Europe, were very different and the Soviet model of first-stage heavy industrialization had little to recommend it. By and large, Eastern Europe did not need a steel-manufacturing capacity or, at the next stage, heavy chemicals capacity, but its economic strategies would have been much better served by an emphasis on light industry, processing and the tertiary sector. The whole process of the imposition of the Stalinist model was further distorted by a contingent factor, the fear of imminent war between East and West. This war scare, which spilled over into hysteria at times (e.g. the Korean war), was also used as a justification for constructing heavy industry, particularly heavy metallurgy, to serve the needs of the military capability.

Third, the Soviet model was characterized by a very specific and again contingent model of egalitarianism. In essence, it postulated that the heavy industrial worker, above all the male worker in heavy metallurgy, constituted a kind of ideal proletarian and that all other social categories should be homogenized until their members came to resemble him. To this end the party adopted a strictly exclusive and one-dimensional concept of equality, from which not only were members of the former ruling élites, the bourgeoisie and other middle strata excluded, but so were most peasants – anyone farming any land at all independently – and to an extent even other workers, like craftsmen or those deemed 'lumpenproletarian', the weakest sections of the urban poor.[9]

The East European Response

The East European model was backward by the criteria of Western Europe (though ahead of, say, the Middle East by the same criteria and, for that matter, by the East Europeans' own criteria). The determinants

[9] Csaba Gombár, *A politika parttalan világa* (1986), pp. 35ff.

of the East European model must, therefore, be sought in both autonomous East European patterns and in how East Europeans perceived the West. As far as Eastern Europe was concerned Western patterns of change, complexity and choice were valid, albeit these were never as intensively propagated as in the West.

East European aspirations after 1945 were varied and this variety, which was to be found among polities and within them, was in itself the potential guarantor of a complex pattern of modernization. Different social groups had different interests and sought to articulate them in different ways. Whether this variety contained sufficient centripetal force to have permitted the establishment of political systems with the capability of surviving the strains of modernization is another matter and the precedents were not good. Nevertheless, there is no doubt whatever that the Stalinist model was unacceptable to the great majority.

This was so essentially for three reasons. In the first place, the Soviet model was recognized for what it was – an enforced rehomogenization of politics.[10] Whatever their shortcomings, East European political systems had begun to develop increasingly complex institutions, which allowed for conflicts of interests and some open debate (with whatever limitations) with greater latitude than that permitted by the Soviet-type model. The East European system as it emerged after 1945 (even if there were enormous variations) looked as if it would move towards greater rather than lesser complexity and choice. In this connection, the imposition of Stalinism represented a major step backwards towards a simpler, less demanding system, in which individual and group choices were almost wholly eliminated and decisions were imposed on society from above.

Obviously the degree to which individual East European societies pursued this aim of creating institutions to match complexity varied considerably from country to country. Albania, say, was a largely undifferentiated society in terms of function; people's roles were determined not so much by what they did, but by birth into one or other kinship network. In Czechoslovakia or East Germany, on the other hand, roles were defined much less by status (ascription) and much more by function. An individual at one and the same time could and did play a wide variety of roles and have a wide variety of interests, some of them mutually contradictory. He or she could simultaneously be a producer and a consumer; or someone looking for higher wages

---

[10] Béla Pokol, 'Alternativ utak a politikai rendszer reformjára', *Valóság*, 29 no. 12 (December 1986), pp. 32–45. See also Ken Jowitt, *Revolutionary Breakthroughs and National Development: the Case of Romania 1944–1965* (1971).

(entailing the faster use of resources) and for better environmental conditions (demanding greater care for the environment); or someone sternly insisting on personal freedom from supervision by the state and insisting equally that the state do something to curb the activities of groups of which he or she disapproves.

The codes of conduct in society and politics, the criteria for determining issues and the methods of arbitration are, on the one hand, sufficiently varied to take account of this differentiation and, on the other, are wide enough to be acceptable enough to all major sections of the population to create a degree of integration which would keep the polity together. Stalinism attempted to replace this by establishing a single, homogenized, centrally directed set of imperatives, which sought to eliminate rather than reconcile these variations and this differentiation. The fact that this project could not succeed meant that Eastern Europe was left with a political system inappropriate to its patterns of social, economic and political development and trajectories of its future aspirations. Or, as Stalin put it to Gomulka, the Polish communist leader, it was like trying to put a saddle on a cow.

The Stalinist system attracted criticism from another quarter, to some extent related. For the majority of East Europeans it represented an alien political system and was resented as such. Whether this concerned the names of new institutions (like 'central committee' or 'politburo') or their actual functioning, they were felt to be 'not ours' and for that reason to be rejected. This process was exacerbated by the way in which many felt Stalinism to be illegitimate, as deriving not from the desires of society or a section of it, but from the naked exercise of Soviet power. This led to the rejection of Sovietization because it was Russian, bringing into play the traditional anti-Russian sentiments which characterized the national identities of several East European polities, notably Poland, Hungary, East Germany and Romania; anti-Russian feelings were rather weaker in Czechoslovakia, Bulgaria and Yugoslavia (in the last until 1948).

It is worth speculating, however, that Sovietization was rejected not merely because it was of Russian origin; in other words, if, say, an American political system had been imposed on Eastern Europe under similar conditions, it would have encountered an analogous response. Another factor in this complex was the speed of change and the appearance of its irreversibility, generating feelings of frustration and helplessness. The changes these societies underwent were pushed through at a breakneck pace and that in itself caused disorientation and rejection. Arguably change, particularly rapid change, invariably gives rise to difficulties of adjustment, but this is at the very least made easier if the direction and the speed of change are based on a measure of consent.

Much the same applied to the depth and extent of change. The remarkably far-reaching transformation effected by the Stalinist revolution – a term properly used in this context – had its impact on virtually every inhabitant of Eastern Europe. Whether in towns or in the countryside, old-established patterns were transformed and each individual was in some respect forced to come to terms with the new order. It was, after all, during the Stalinist period that electrification was completed or extended, the transport network was developed to stretch into the countryside and heavy industrialization was launched, using rural labour, thus giving the rural population access to mass communication. It was in this overall sense that the forcible adoption of Stalinism constituted a revolution, whether this revolution was legitimate in eyes of East Europeans or not. This was the dynamic aspect of Stalinism. Its static aspect was that once the process was supposedly completed – in a very short period of time – it would immediately have reached its final form. The consequence of this was to endow Stalinism, and to some extent all the successors of Stalinism, with an oddly unchanging, unmoving quality. There was a surface appearance of movement, but often underneath pre-existing patterns were simply frozen.

The Supporters of the System

While the majority of East Europeans, in so far as these propositions can be validated, were probably in some respect or other antagonistic to Stalinism, there was a minority which either supported it or was sympathetically neutral towards it or simply accepted it passively. Those who flocked into communist parties were not all simple time-servers or opportunists. Some of them were genuinely motivated by the idealism derived from their faith in creating a better world. They believed that by the application of rationality and endeavour – and its reverse, the elimination of other patterns of thought – they could create a new Jerusalem in short order. Their beliefs gave them a sense of certainty and an intolerance towards other opinions, but they also endowed them with the energy to perform the transformation and to impose the new system on a sullen population.

The supporters of the system included the genuine believers, the radicals of the left and also of the right from the pre-war era. They frequently overlapped with the beneficiaries of the new system, Milovan Djilas's New Class. These people, often of working-class or peasant background, were promoted into positions of power by the party as reliable on the grounds of their class origins and discovered the pleasures of the taste of power and the privileges that went with it.

This one-off promotion of a generation of such activists constituted a source of support for the system and was enormously influential both then and in later years in structuring the value system of society.

There was some support for the communist ideal from sections of the intelligentsia as well, at any rate in theory. For some, the attraction of unlimited power to plan a new society, to impose a 'rational' order, to create 'scientifically' devised projects for the benefit of all proved a heady mixture. The proposition that all the resources of society, which had lain dormant until then, could be mobilized in a new, gigantic and perfectly functioning enterprise was enormously attractive; so too was the scale on which planning was to take place. The 'romance of size', the idea that mankind could effect a major transformation of the material base by the application of human resources in a perfectly rational way, was highly seductive for a section of the intelligentsia, especially those involved in technology. In this connection, the old-established étatist tradition of Eastern Europe, the distrust of society as reactionary and the belief in the state as progressive, also played a role in generating support for the party. The attractions of the prospect of unlimited power never entirely faded away for this section of the intelligentsia and explained, at least partially, its persistence.[11]

A further source of stability for the new order was its indirect beneficiaries – the mobilized peasantry. Although for many of them the trauma of leaving the land was devastating, it was not a wholly negative experience. At first sight, therefore, it might appear contradictory that the uprooted peasants, who formed the bulk of the new working class and who could have been expected to respond to their new environment with hostility, did not do so completely. While they may have found their new fate disagreeable, for conditions were generally primitive and unpleasant in the mushrooming new industrial centres, and the provision of infrastructure (houses, main drainage, hospitals) lagged far behind social need, the industrial revolution in Eastern Europe was as harsh as in any other part of the world. Yet inasmuch as their yardstick of comparison was the village, where their horizons were limited and their standard of living appeared inescapably low, even the harshness of Soviet-type industrialization seemed preferable. Their standard of living was somewhat higher, wage packets were regular, access to collective consumption was superior

[11] Pavel Kohout, *Diary of a Counterrevolutionary* (1969). See also the discussions between Ernö Gerö, the then economic boss of Hungary, and the technocrats, concerning the regulation of the Danube in 1953. In this the latter argued in favour of the most grandiose projects and Gerö, rather ironically in view of his record, emerged as the moderating force. The full text appeared in *Beszélö*, no. 12 (1985); a partial translation was published in *East European Reporter,* 1 no. 3, (1985).

and the prestige gained from working in industry proved to be sufficient compensation for leaving the familiarity of the village. This did
not mean that their loyalty to the new order was firm and generally
their response to crises was volatile, but it did have the result that this
first generation of workers was by and large satisfied with the greater
economic choice it gained from the industrialization process and did
not look for direct political participation.

The Shape of the New Order

The new political order created by Stalin's epigoni in Eastern Europe
was given the name of monolithism. This concept was the political
reflection of the ideology of perfection and omniscience; it meant the
denial of the possibility of error and political neutrality. It was neatly
summed up in the slogan proclaimed by Hungary's Stalinist leader,
Mátyás Rákosi: 'He who is not with us – is against us!' It meant that the
party – the leader of the party in practice – had the right to absolute
and untrammelled power and required no further legitimation for this.
The monolithic system, however, retained the outward shape of other
political systems. The institutions of state and society – government,
parliament, local government, the judiciary, trade unions, professional
associations – were not abolished immediately, but were to function
exclusively under the guidance and direction of the party. The party
would determine strategy and the institutions would implement it. In
practice these two functions proved impossible to separate and the
party took over the day-to-day running of everything. The degree of
centralization that this involved was very high and, in consequence,
there was a steady increase in bureaucratization, over-regulation and
bureaucratic overload. The result was the growing difficulty of implementing plans.

Stalinism had one further aspect. Although Eastern Europe was
backward by West European criteria, nevertheless the idea of there
being separate public and private spheres did exist. While traditionally
the state in Eastern Europe did regulate much more of the private
sphere than in the West, it never sought to encompass it entirely. With
the advent of Stalinism, this changed. Stalinism sought to effect a total
merger of the public and private spheres – more correctly to submerge
the latter into the former – as a way of enhancing its claim to total
control. This even came to include the family, which, in common with
all other institutions, was expected to serve the goals of perfection and
the self-styled agent of perfection, the party. Indeed, as one commentator puts it: 'Stalinist society expected of its citizens extraordi-

narily far-reaching allegiance to the state.'[12] This was legitimized by the argument that the fellowship of man – the agent of which was the party – transcended all other loyalties, including loyalty to the family.

The imposition of monolithism on Eastern Europe had as its immediate result the liquidation of whatever institutions already existed or their absorption into the monolithic façade. In this way all existing institutions and the ways in which conflicts of interest were regulated – the outcome of many years of effort to create them – were submerged and transformed into transmission belts. A transmission belt is, essentially, an institution which supposedly carries out the task of the party. Other institutions were abolished.

An example of the first, an existing body which became a transmission belt, was the trade unions. In a communist system autonomous trade unions which genuinely attempted to represent the interests of their members were self-evidently superfluous. It was inconceivable that the worker could have any interests which could in any way cut across those of the party. After all, in a system of perfection, the party could logically insist that it simultaneously represented the interests of the employer, the worker and the functions of economic and social signalling performed in a capitalist society by the market (supply and demand). The party aggregated all interests and there could be no conflicts of interest; if these existed, they were antagonistic, the result of hostile conspiracies or the relics of the previous system, fit only to be eliminated by the severest measures. This approach completely ignored the fact that the interests of the workers and their employers were not identical and could not be made so. Attempts to enforce it resulted in a harsher exploitation of the workers than by the market, given that even with all its imperfections the market could offer the worker some protection against a rapacious employer.

An example of the second phenomenon – the complete abolition of institutions – was the liquidation of all political parties other than the Communist Party. In Hungary and Romania the non-communist parties were absorbed into the ruling party, on the argument that they were superfluous. There could be no interests requiring representation through a competing party system. In the other states (except Albania and Yugoslavia) the relics of older parties remained in being, but they were, predictably, no more than façades.

It follows that all autonomous action from below suffered the same

---

[12] Katerina Clark, 'Utopian Anthropology as a Context for Stalinist Literature', in Robert C. Tucker (ed.), *Stalinism: Essays in Historical Interpretation* (1977), pp. 180–98.

fate. There could be no pluralism and no bodies representing any view other than that laid down by the party. In this way, all the various institutions created for the articulation of this or that interest were suppressed and transformed into organs serving the leading role (the phrase used to describe the party's monopoly) of the party. The mass media, for example, became the party's advertising agency. They were used solely for the purpose of propagating whatever the party's view of the situation happened to be at that time. Any unsanctioned attempt at organization or the expression of opinions not acceptable by the party or even the failure to express opinions required by the party brought the instruments of coercion into play.

Society and polity, whether as individuals or as groups, were to be as far as possible wholly insulated from alternative and thus deviant values, whether these were pre-existing or non-Soviet. All unsanctioned values were to be extirpated and replaced by the new value system of Marxism–Leninism.

The Impact of Stalinism on Social Groups

To ensure the party's rule over societies where it was recognized that legitimacy – the sense of being accepted by the population as rightful – was weak, the party systematically engaged in a process of levelling down. It deliberately destroyed the bases, especially the economic bases, of social groups which it regarded as a potential source of autonomy. The hardest hit was the middle stratum, predictably, for this group – the survivors of the old élite, the remnants of the entrepreneurial class, some sections of the intelligentsia – was recognized by the party as likely to constitute the greatest obstacle to the exercise of its power. Various devices were used to this end. Salaries were equalized, so that the gap between white-collar and blue-collar wages virtually disappeared.[13]

In many cases members of the old élite were dispossessed of their property, either by actually being thrown out of their homes or by being obliged to share their dwellings. The savings of the middle stratum, which could have given them a certain immunity, were as far as possible eliminated by currency reforms, punitive taxation and other devices. This could not, of course, exhaust all their reserves, notably of valuables, but dealing on the black market – selling valu-

[13] Jaroslav Krejci, *Social Change and Social Stratification in Postwar Czechoslovakia* (1972) discusses levelling down in Czechoslovakia.

ables to make ends meet – was severely punished. The party was able to achieve this not just by the exercise of terror, but through its control of the state, which had for all practical purposes become the sole employer (which it very largely remained). This monopoly position gave it the power to dismiss individuals it regarded as 'unreliable' or 'class alien elements' and either to prevent them from working at all or to oblige them to do manual labour at the lowest end of the scale.

The Working Class

The working class as a whole did not do much better from the revolution made in its name, although certain sections of it unquestionably benefited. New wage categories were introduced and this placed some occupations well above others, regardless of the actual value of the work done; this meant that miners and metal-workers, regarded as the citadels of support for the party, were given high wages. Others, like printers, who had generally given their backing to Social Democracy, were treated in a less generous fashion. But what was much more important was that all categories of workers were obliged to work to new norms over which they had no control, for these were set by the party according to its requirements. Working conditions were frequently primitive and, with some variations from country to country, the standard of living fell during the Stalinist years, sometimes to below the pre-war level. Supervision in factories, draconian disciplinary measures, inadequate housing (often in hostels with minimal facilities) were backed up by severe penalties for 'sabotage'. Sabotage was essentially anything defined by the party as such. It was a classic example of a politically defined crime. Many thousands found themselves penalized arbitrarily in this fashion.

The Peasantry

The fate of the peasantry was similar, indeed, if anything it was worse because of the animosity in the Marxist legacy towards the peasant. Whereas the worker was at the very least the agent of the Marxian utopia, the peasant was doomed to disappearance anyway, so that no real harm would be done by giving history a bit of push in this respect. Had not Marx, after all, referred to the idiocy of rural life? Second, the peasant, by virtue of being an independent entrepreneur, on however small and inefficient a basis, acquired thereby a degree of autonomy which the party was determined to break. Perhaps most strikingly, the peasant, despite his poverty and low intellectual status, was master of his own timetable to a far greater degree than an industrial worker From the party's standpoint this situation was scandalous. The party launched its assault on the peasantry because it could not tolerate the countryside being exempt from its penetration of society. Third, the peasantry – at least in part – was to bear its part in the financing of industrialization, so that for a few years, supposedly, while the industrial base was being constructed, the peasant would have to work for a low return, in common with everyone else. And because the peasantry was notorious (in the party's eyes) for its conservatism, the only solution was to coerce it to produce. Finally, the party's vision of the future of the agricultural population was that it would in a rela- tively short period of time become identical to the urban population; there would be no difference between working on a farm and at a work-bench. The fact that industrial and agricultural labour inescap- ably require different approaches and that efficient agriculture de- mands a good deal of autonomous decision-making by the farmer was simply ignored by the party. This, too, could be interpreted as an aspect of the party's determination to homogenize and simplify proc- esses and diminish the number of interactions in society.

The means by which the party intended to achieve its goal was collectivization. This was not, in itself, necessarily undesirable. The small plots of land resulting from land reform were rather inefficient and starved of capital; the level of skill used by many peasants was low; and the tradition of subsistence farming rather than commodity production for the market was still strong. Some kind of cooperative agricultural production could have beneficial effects and before the war there had been a tradition of it, but it had been based on consent and not coercion.[14] The imposition of forcible collectivization in the 1950s, therefore, and notably the fact that those sent to carry it out were neither particularly refined in their methods nor knowledgeable about agriculture, resulted in chaos merging into catastrophe. Ignorant activists would order peasants to plant a particular crop, regardless of suitability,[15] and when the crop failed the peasant found himself penalized for criminal conspiracy. The net result of the party's agricul- tural and rural policy was to drive the peasantry into sullen passive resistance, to production for subsistence, and to instil a deep detes- tation of communist rule into the rural population, thereby reinforcing the age-old gap between the peasant and the state.

[14] A. Balawyder (ed.), *Cooperative Movements in Eastern Europe* (1980).
[15] This was the policy satirized by the Hungarian film *The Witness (A tanú)*, where a campaign with the inspiring title 'For the Hungarian Orange' is described.

Intelligentsia and Intellectuals

The relationship between the party and the intelligentsia was not quite as straightforward. Although at the ostensible level the party needed the intelligentsia even less than it did the workers and peasants, in reality this relationship was more complex. The ostensible superfluity of the intelligentsia derived from the party's claim to incorporate perfection. If the party already knew everything, then neither the intelligentsia (the possessors of specialized knowledge) nor the intellectuals (the creators of new values and alternative visions of the future) had any reason to exist in these terms.[16] In reality, of course, even the perfect party had need of doctors or engineers or teachers in order that – at least in what was supposedly a transitional period – the services they performed should be carried out. From the party's standpoint, however, the problem was that much of the intelligentsia was inherited from the old régime and was for that reason alone untrustworthy. Even worse, members of the intelligentsia, by virtue of their specialized knowledge, had it in their power to devise alternatives at variance from the party line, to argue with party directives on specialized grounds and generally to raise technical questions with political implications. If these dangers were unacceptable to the party, those raised by autonomous intellectuals were significantly greater. Intellectuals, whether cultural (like novelists, artists and the like) or scientific (like historians, economists, sociologists etc.), actually had as their *raison d'être* the portrayal and criticism of the present, the analysis of social reality as they saw it and the formulation of alternatives for the future. In this respect the very existence of autonomous intellectuals challenged the monopoly of the party.

The solution was to deprive both categories of their autonomy, as far as this could be achieved, and to enlist them by force, threat of force or incentives to serve the goals of the party. The new function of both was to act as yet another transmission-belt at the intellectual and scientific level. Their new task was to propagate the perfect world of the party's ideology, to sing its praises, to disguise its shortcomings, to encourage the population to work harder and to believe in the party's vision of the future. In a word, they would be apologists. They would act as one of the many instruments in the hands of the party with the role of socializing the population into acceptance of 'perfection'.

The first step in this direction was to suppress all lingering claims to autonomy. The second was to resocialize the new socializers them-

---

[16] György Konrád and Iván Szelényi, *The Intellectuals on the Road to Class Power* (1979). See also Michael Shafir, *Political Culture, Intellectual Dissent and Intellectual Consent: The Case of Rumania* (1978).

selves. To this end, both categories – members of the intelligentsia and intellectuals – were required to undergo a kind of conversion to the newly obligatory ideology and to be seen to do this publicly and continuously. They were obliged to attend Marxism–Leninism classes, to perform rituals demonstrating their loyalty to the system, to turn out at mass ceremonies organized by the régime and, most importantly, to learn and use the new language of politics, the language of Marxism–Leninism. The imposition of this language constituted an essential aspect of monolithism and, indeed, formed a vital instrument of political control for decades to come. It functioned as a repeated public expression of the pervasiveness of the system, it prevented the expression of alternatives, it stultified independent thought and in particular generated the belief that the power of the system was invincible.[17]

The Rituals of Stalinism

Every political system lives to some extent by rituals. Rituals, ceremonies, political liturgies, symbols serve a vital purpose in giving order to complex, possibly inexplicable phenomena; they celebrate the familiar and promote a sense of community; they also make it easier for communities to resolve some of the stresses associated with the process of change, especially rapid change; but above all, rituals are about political loyalty and the structuring of the relationship between rulers and ruled.[18] Every post-revolutionary régime tries either to capture the rituals of the one it has replaced or to abolish them and replace them with rituals of its own. This was very much the pattern pursued by the communists and there are examples of both processes. Hence in an act of conscious syncretism the Hungarian party promulgated the new 'socialist' constitution on 20 August, with the objective of undercutting the attraction of St Stephen's Day, the day of the Saint venerated as the founder of the Hungarian state. An illustration of how the communists actually took over old folk festivals and emptied them of their former content is narrated by Milan Kundera, who described what happened to the ancient rite of the Ride of the Kings, which had as its aim the celebration of the seasons and the reinforcement of

---

[17] Adam Michnik, 'Ce que nous voulons et ce que nous pouvons', *L'Alternative*, no. 8 (January–February, 1981), pp. 5–14.
[18] Murray Edelman, *Politics as Symbolic Action: Mass Arousal and Quiescence* (1971).

village communities in Moravia.[19] Self-evidently, village communities of this kind were unacceptable from the party's point of view, constituting centres of autonomous patterns of behaviour.

More important were the entirely new rituals instituted by the régime. The most obvious of these were the show trials, but these were far from having been the only such innovation. There were, for example, the mass parades, at which attendance was obligatory, although in theory it was entirely a matter of choice as to whether one went or not, except that failure to be present could entail sanctions. Enormous crowds were marshalled to celebrate events deemed positive by the party, like the 1 May anniversary – devised as a festival of the labour movement in the nineteenth century incidentally – or liberation anniversaries or simply demonstrations in favour of peace or merely to greet some visiting celebrity. The purpose of these parades was to create the external appearance of mass participation, to give the particular event weight by the sheer presence of numbers and to make the inevitability of compliance with régime objectives evident by demonstrating the party's ability to organize vast crowds.

Other rituals had analogous political objectives. Stakhanovism, as the campaigns of 'socialist emulation' were known after the Donbas miner, Stakhanov, who purportedly cut 102 tons of coal single-handedly in one shift,[20] had as its aim to show the superiority and exemplary quality of the Soviet proletarian, the encouragement of the East European workers to emulate these supposedly heroic feats and more prosaically to increase output. It is noteworthy that the supposed superiority of the Soviet worker over his East European counterpart did not incorporate any concept of mastery of higher technological skills. If anything, the content of the Stakhanovite myth was that of an untutored worker who achieved his feat intuitively and by physical strength.[21] Once a particular target had been reached, often by entirely spurious means, it became easier to raise the norm, the output demanded of each worker before he was paid his basic wage.

The cult of personality was, again, a newly introduced ritual. Its centre, naturally enough, was Stalin, but Stalin's cult was paralleled, if

[19] Milan Kundera describes the entire process of how this particular festival was taken over by the régime in his novel *The Joke* (1983); Josef Skvorecky recounts something similar regarding folklore and folk dancing in *The Engineer of Human Souls* (1985).
[20] Stakhanov achieved this because all other work at the mine was halted and because he was assisted by a team of auxiliaries who did the work which would normally have been done by the man at the coal face; see Geoffrey Hosking, *A History of the Soviet Union* (1985), p. 158.
[21] Katerina Clark, 'Utopian Anthropology'.

at a marginally less exalted level, by the cults of local leaders. The objective of promoting this cult was to reinforce the message that all truth stemmed from the single leader, that he had heroic, superhuman qualities incorporating wisdom, knowledge and control of the future, and that these transcended all pre-communist political liturgies, like the veneration of Tomas Masaryk in Czechoslovakia or the lingering regard for Pilsudski (to gather great strength in the 1980s) in Poland. The lengths to which communist personality cults were taken appear ludicrous in retrospect. Stalin was referred to in the most extraordinary terms as the fount of all human knowledge and so on.[22] The Hungarian periodical devoted to the natural sciences, *Élet és Tudomány,* stated: 'The teaching of Stalin embraces all the universal principles of nature in its smallest details. He solves all the practical problems of understanding natural science.'[23]

In every East European country (except, obviously, Yugoslavia), cities, mountain peaks, factories, boulevards and the like bore the Great Leader's name, as a kind of symbolic re-enactment of his ubiquity; the ever-present posters, to be found in all public places, bearing his likeness, together with those of Marx, Lenin and the local leader, had the same function. The odes to Stalin, praising him for his wisdom, sagacity, humanity, etc., however absurd and embarrassing they may sound today, were also part of the same pattern.

The glorification of the Soviet Union and of the Red Army, coupled with the constant reiteration of the aggressive hostility attributed to the West, had as their function the socialization of the population into a new set of loyalties and, equally, the breaking of older, often very deeply rooted attachments. This was regarded as all the more necessary given the currents of hostility to Russia and the bitter resentment generated by the behaviour of the liberating Red Army. Hence the constant emphasis on the sacrifice brought by the Soviet Union in liberating these countries from Axis occupation, which was real enough, but it omitted the other aspect of the Soviet enterprise, namely its own interest in defeating Nazi Germany. Also striking were the campaigns to show the Soviet Union as the source of all progress, knowledge and scientific invention. An entire pseudo-historical industry was established with the purpose of demonstrating that Russian or Soviet inventors had been the first to invent electricity, radio, the

[22] As far as is known, however, Stalin never had himself formally deified; that particular innovation was left to Nicolae Ceausescu in the 1970s, who allowed himself to be described in the press as our Romanian 'lay God'. (The distinction between a 'lay God' and a religious deity is unclear to me.)

[23] Quoted by Brzezinski, *The Soviet Bloc,* p. 115.

internal combustion engine and so on – possibly even the wheel was claimed as a Russian invention.

With this process went the wholesale rewriting of history. Whereas in pre-communist history writing, which was not without its distortions, of course, the existence of the nation and its glories formed the pivot of historical perspective, all this was now jettisoned. Kings and nobility were declared to have been an unmitigated curse, to have been nothing but parasites living on the backs of the toiling masses and, in general, the concept of the class struggle was projected backwards. The intellectual endeavour involved was relatively straightforward. Whereas until then the nobility was deemed to embody the exemplary virtues, now an undifferentiated, mythicized 'people' had taken over this role and all events were viewed through this prism. Where a particular event could be given a Russian connection, this was all the better. The practitioners of this industry could occasionally surpass themselves and actually add an obligatory but fictitious Russian figure to events, presumably to lend verisimilitude to an otherwise bald and unconvincing narrative. The 1784 rising of Romanian peasants in Transylvania, a genuine popular movement led by Horia, Closca and Crisan, three peasants, was furnished with a new, until then unknown leader, a Russian officer called Mikhail Popensky, who happened fortuitously to be on the spot to lend fraternal Russian assistance to the benighted Romanians.[24]

The Show Trials

The Stalinist institution that attracted the greatest attention, however, was the show trial. With the exception of Poland and the GDR, every East European country staged a major trial of a leading figure in the Communist Party and selected acolytes. The fascination which these trials – perhaps 'trials' would be more appropriate – have exercised over Western imagination derives in part from their conscious perversion of a key aspect of legality, the fair trial, which has rightly been regarded as a guarantee of freedom. Why, the question might be asked, did these states choose to liquidate their opponents by pursuing the form of a trial and thereby institute a ghastly mockery of a valued institution? The answer lies in the politicization of everything, including the administration of justice (a term which strictly speaking has no meaning under Stalinism). Second, the show trials had a symbolic function. They were a very high-profile enactment of the party's

[24] As related by Dionisie Ghermani, quoting *Istoria RPR* (1955).

claim to omniscience and omnipotence, not just in the past and the present, but projected forward into the future. By insisting on the veracity of charges which were patently absurd – the accusations of simultaneous Zionist, Cosmopolitan, Trotskyist, Imperialist, Capitalist motivations were manifestly ridiculous – the party was emphatically stating that all its enemies were identical and that it would deal with all of them in exactly the same way.

Third, the trials were a way of demonstrating the party's omniscience and ever-vigilance. If the accused in these trials could confess to having committed the most heinous crimes against the party, the people and the state and if it was the protector of the proletarian revolution, the watchful secret police, which uncovered (unmasked) these malefactors, clearly nothing could escape the party's eye. All resistance was, therefore, useless. The party knew everything, perhaps even before it had happened. Hence the cruel sophistry of 'objective' and 'subjective' guilt, that an individual may have been perfectly innocent when he committed a particular action – there was no *mens rea*, to use the technical term – but by the criterion of class justice, he had objectively committed an offence for which punishment would be exacted. Fourth, the trials should also be seen as a purification ceremony. The concepts of 'pure' and 'impure', that which is acceptable and that which is not, in socio-political terms are determined by an interaction between rulers and ruled.[25] In a post-revolutionary order, however, the new rulers are determined to impose their own views of impurity on society. In the Stalinist case what was noteworthy was how far-reaching the party's claim to determine the boundaries of pure and impure extended and the extremely elaborate way in which these were made manifest. What is also noteworthy about these Stalinist show trials is that they appear to have roots or analogues in Eastern Orthodox religious rites. Whereas in Western Christianity confession is a strictly private communion, in Orthodoxy there is a tradition of the public confession of sins. Finally, of course, the trials had a direct political objective, that of ridding the party of elements regarded as potentially untrustworthy or as potential rivals for the existing leadership (this aspect will be dealt with in greater detail below).

The Political Impact

The direct impact of Stalinism on East European politics has already been touched on in the context of the destruction of existing institu-

[25] Mary Douglas, 'Purity and Danger Revisited', *Times Literary Supplement*, 19 September 1980.

tions. The other side of the coin was the creation of new institutions and the formulation of new political, economic and social strategies. At the centre of the Stalinist concept of politics was a form of dynamism, which was both real and synthetic.[26] It was real in that very far-reaching changes were instituted, but it was also synthetic as far as the actual internalization of the new belief system by society was concerned. The result of Stalinist policies was, in practice, external compliance with the new codes of conduct rather than genuine acceptance of the tenets of Marxism–Leninism. Attendance at rituals, the mouthing of the obligatory slogans, the passive acceptance of the new order were sufficient in day-to-day terms. This was inevitable, given that the entire post-revolutionary panoply was at variance with the real aspirations of society.

The party sought to compensate for this by its endeavour to achieve the complete penetration of every aspect of life, to exercise its power in all spheres and to regulate all forms of behaviour in the expectation that a successful 'breakthrough' into the consciousness of society would be the end result. It embarked, therefore, on a very far-reaching campaign of controlling both the day-to-day lives of the population and their longer-term perceptions of the future by using the organization of the party to supervise all possible activity. In theory, of course, the role of the party was to devise the current strategy to be pursued, even while other bodies were actually responsible for implementing policy. This marked the beginning of one of the most characteristic features of Soviet-type systems, the elevation of the political sphere over all others and the consequent politicization – actual or potential – of all interactions in society. The autonomy of other spheres – economic, legal, aesthetic, etc. – which had their own autonomous criteria, was eliminated and subordinated to the supreme, politically determined goal. In practice, the party controlled all other institutions and ran policy down to the smallest detail of which it was capable. The party thereby enveloped the state and sought to draw all activity into itself. This was paralleled by the heightened tempo of activity in all spheres and the extraordinarily ambitious targets that were set up by national economic plans.

Every East European country began the construction of a vast, high-prestige project – steel mills being the favourite – and of other heavy industrial plant. The extraction of coal or other energy carriers, heavy engineering and similar projects accompanied this. The figures, even if they related to gross output and were thus virtually meaningless,

[26] Michael Shafir uses the term 'simulated change' in his book *Romania: Politics, Economics and Society – Political Stagnation and Simulated Change* (1985).

looked spectacular. Thus the Hungarian Second Five Year Plan (1950–4) originally intended to raise industrial output by 204 per cent; this was later raised to an unbelievable 380 per cent.[27] The underlying philosophy of this industrial expansion imitated Soviet precepts in their leaning towards autarky, despite the economic irrationality of forcing small countries into industrial self-reliance.

The political implications of this strategy of economic development were severalfold. Each East European country would henceforth be obliged to rely on its own resources and limit its exchanges either to the Soviet Union or pursue them under Soviet supervision. In this sense autarky could be regarded as the international equivalent of domestic atomization. Second, Soviet-type industrialization would have irreversible consequences, not only of tying Eastern Europe to Soviet supplies, but equally ensuring that a section of every East European country's industry would be locked into a client relationship with the Soviet partner, making it near impossible to use those resources for any other purposes. Third, the formulation of a strategy centered on heavy industry resulted in its perpetuation by the emergence of what might be called a heavy industry lobby, those who had grown up in the shadow of this particular pattern of industrialization; who regarded it as the most effective means of running an economy and thus wanted to extend it and were determined to defend it. This heavy industrial slanting of Soviet-type systems remained one of its most tenacious and ineradicable features, that continued to influence its development by using up excessive funds in terms of cost-effectiveness.[28] The task of dismantling the heavy industrial base proved to be one of the most daunting and intractable for the post-communist régimes.

Another significant aspect of this development with enduring consequences was to shift the nature of political discourse in Soviet-type systems towards an over-concentration on economics. There was a marked inclination in these systems nominally to discuss all issues as if they were economic, to perceive solutions to non-economic problems in economic terms and generally to use the prism of the economy as the determinant one. This was all the more ironical in the light of the politically determined reality of Soviet-type systems, but in fact did make a certain kind of sense. Inasmuch as the language of public discourse was heavily influenced by economics, it made political issues lacking an obvious economic aspect, like representation or accountability, that much more difficult to raise. The pseudo-scientific

[27] János Berecz, *Ellenforradalom tollal és fegyverrel,* 2nd edn (1981), p. 30.
[28] Ota Sik, *Czechoslovakia: the Bureaucratic Economy* (1972).

language introduced by Stalinism, by which all phenomena could notionally be reduced to statistics, was similarly perpetuated. This could give rise to a perception of inchoate issues as much clearer than they might be, and encourage a kind of dogmatism in the way in which problems were approached.

Soviet-type industrialization, furthermore, was irreversible inasmuch as it precluded certain economic options for the future. Once carried through, it would be costly, at the very least, to formulate an alternative strategy of industrialization based on, say, tertiary production. The creation of large industry was for all practical purposes something that could not be uncreated. This had its social repercussions as well. It led to the emergence of sections of the working class with a vested interest in the survival of these industries and in the avoidance of using purely economic criteria for their evaluation; equally, numbers of administrators would have a personal stake in keeping these industries going. In this respect, the Stalinist revolution constructed a stratum of its own beneficiaries, which remained committed to some variant of it.

Stalinism, in addition, spawned a massive new bureaucracy, again dependent on the party that set it up. The number of administrators in Poland, for example, increased from 172,000 before the war to 362,400 in 1955.[29] These bureaucrats had to justify their existence, to put it at its lowest, so that the state became markedly more intrusive. In this, it drew on the official ideology for justification, in as much as the distinction between the public and private spheres in practice was severely weakened and largely proclaimed to be abolished. At the same time the system spewed forth a continuous stream of decrees, directives, instructions, regulations, resolutions and the like, which intensified arbitrariness and undermined predictability. The objective was political, to serve the officially determined goals by whatever means were to hand. The power placed in the hands of the administrator over the individual was all but boundless; it was limited only by hierarchical constraints and fear of the superior's opinion.

Two further long-term aspects of Stalinism are worth a mention. First, there is the anti-agrarian bias of Stalinist strategy, something that had its roots in Marx and was perpetuated by his successors. Agriculture, as suggested earlier, was to be transformed into a branch of industry and the techniques appropriate to industry were imposed on it regardless. This is typical reductionism and it failed; agriculture

[29] Jan B. de Weydenthal, *The Communists of Poland: an Historical Outline* (1978), p. 62, quoting Brzezinski, *Soviet Bloc*, and Maria Turlejska, *Zapis pierwszej dekady 1945–1954*, p. 183.

functions according to its own rationalities which differ from those of industry. Attempts to force one into the mould of the other have proved to be misperceived. But, as this was not self-evident to those guided by Stalinism, agriculture suffered and remained, to some extent, a Cinderella in terms of status and value.

Second, the classical Marxist attitude towards nature and natural resources is to treat them as limitless and cost-free. Whether in Stalin's day or after, the constraints of nature were on the whole ignored as irrelevant, with far-reaching consequences for environmental damage, which had no meaningful place in Soviet-type political culture. This was undoubtedly coupled with the 'romance of size' discussed above. Linked to this was a certain propensity to treat issues in black-and-white, exclusive terms, to deny that issues might be too complex for ready-made solutions, to incline towards a certain intellectual arrogance, namely that the élite always knew better, that the demands of society were a pettifogging nuisance best ignored because the consumer (say) would come to his or her senses anyway. There was in the core of this a kind of exclusivism that rejects debate and compromise as superfluous, for ultimately the élite was, after all, in possession of the supreme rationality, was it not?

The Terror

The Terror is widely regarded as the most characteristic of all Stalinist innovations. Its purpose was to enforce compliance, to destroy all pre-existing values, to break down preconceptions and make it easier for the new revolutionary values to take root. Equally, the role of terror was to facilitate the politicization of the system by giving completely free rein to the power of the party through the destruction of competing institutions and the horizontal links that underlay them. The scope of terror was supposedly total. Not a single action escaped it in theory, even if in practice such perfection was never achieved. But in Hungary, in the twenty-eight months after 1 January 1950, some 850,000 persons were punished, mostly fined, by the police. In the three and a quarter years from 1950 onwards the courts looked at 650,000 cases and sentenced 387,000 persons; finally, during the four years 1952–5, some 1,136,434 persons were subjected to police investigation and of these 516,708 or 45 per cent were actually sentenced.[30] A significant part of those affected were peasants, caught up in the collectivization drive, but it must also have included workers sentenced for 'sabotage', i.e. failure to fulfil the norm. It is not clear if

---

[30] Berecz, *Ellenforradalom*, p. 29.

these figures include the 100,000 plus persons, members of the old middle classes, who were deported to the countryside from 1950 onwards. The Terror in Hungary encompassed at least a tenth of the population and probably not a single family was left untouched by it. The scope of the Terror may have been greater in Hungary than elsewhere, though the absence of anything like reliable figures makes comparisons difficult, but the objective was similar throughout Eastern Europe.

The effectiveness of terror is, however, less clear-cut. It can certainly enforce compliance with the letter of the law, but fear is not efficient in promoting loyalty. Rather, those affected will tend to take refuge in passivity, in obeying the minimum, in paying lip-service, but in reality not in any way internalizing the values of the revolutionary system. Indeed, the experience of putting a society through the mangle tends to promote 'immune reactions' on the part of those affected.[31] People are forced to come to terms with a sudden and harsh intervention in their lives by an external agency, the state, which not only acts with complete opacity, but is unpredictable and arbitrary, its actions at variance with its proclaimed goals. Hence, they lose their social bearings and will incline towards distrust of the newly promoted values, preferring instead to recall older concepts even when they had previously been opposed to them. The role of religion was a classical example of this. By the 1940s, to varying degrees, Eastern Europe was slowly moving towards secularization. The communist revolution, by declaring religion, together with all other value systems, to be impure, endowed religion with an attractiveness that it had begun to lose. In this sense the Stalinist revolution halted a particular secularizing trend and actually acted as an anti-secularizing force.

The Achievements of the Stalinist Revolution

Apologists for the Stalinist revolution will argue that although the cost was appalling in human terms, it did drag Eastern Europe into the twentieth century by modernizing it. This claim to have constructed 'modernity' needs severe modification if it is tenable at all. By concentrating all power into the political sphere and subjecting the area to an extraordinary reductionist squeeze, energies were concentrated and an industrial base of sorts was built. This historic achievement, which had eluded the communists' predecessors (Czechoslovakia and the GDR excepted), was reached without significant inputs of foreign

[31] László Bogár, *A fejlödés ára* (1983).

capital, other than Soviet know-how and technology. The Soviet-type approach to primitive capital accumulation, avoiding the supposed irrationality of the market, had worked, this line of argument would claim. Yet this claim is vulnerable on two grounds. In common with such 'forced marches through history' they are achieved at a price and the price went beyond human terms. It saddled Eastern Europe with an outdated, distorted economic structure that was too intimately bound up with the equally distorted political structure to make remedy possible. Indeed, whatever may have been the intention of the Stalinists – and there is no need to assume that they were without exception power-hungry monomaniacs – they actually succeeded in constructing a political system that was and remained until the end dedicated to concentrating power and ensuring that this was never seriously diluted.

The political agenda was firmly controlled by the élite that ran the polity through the all-encompassing party and subordinated all other imperatives to those of power. Other rationales were outlawed in Stalin's day, though they were permitted to return to the intellectual spectrum in the 1960s, but in effect only in a subordinate role. The equal competition of rationalities and the separation of different spheres (political, economic, legal, aesthetic, etc.), the characteristic feature of liberal democracies, were never permitted to re-emerge. This enracination of communist power and the construction of a political system to secure it constituted the most lasting joint legacy of the Stalinist revolution. Challenges to that system were fought off by the application of superior force in order to preserve the system or a recognizable variant of it. Yet there is much to be said for the argument, which will indeed constitute one of the underlying themes in the remainder of this book, that conflict over the redistribution of power was the central feature of East European politics ever after and that as long as communism lasted, each time a seemingly irreversible redistribution was made, the *status quo ante* was speedily restored.

5

De-Stalinization

But in the gross and scope of my opinion,
This bodes some strange eruption to our state

Shakespeare, Hamlet, *I. i. 166–7.*

How long Stalinism could have lasted without coming apart under the tremendous pressures it was generating is a hypothetical question. In all probability like all revolutions – even one imposed from outside and kept in motion by the will of one man – it would have lost some of its intensity and begun to move towards an equilibrium. The issue, however, was resolved by the death of Stalin on 5 March 1953. Stalin's death was not merely symbolic, but had direct repercussions on the way in which the communist system functioned. It began gradually to eat away at the extraordinary political homogeneity that he had imposed on the Soviet Union's new possessions in Eastern Europe and launched a slow transformation which produced very different outcomes in the different East European states. This immediately raises the question why. Why was it that in some countries the process of decompression, of easing some of the enormous pressures under which these systems were operating, resulted in upheaval, whereas in others it went ahead relatively smoothly? This chapter will also look at the problem of destabilization. What are the factors that bring about a state of affairs in which an apparently solidly established communist régime disintegrates almost overnight, something that was to be seen again in 1980 in Poland, in a rather different fashion, in Czechoslovakia in 1968 and definitively in 1989?

The easy and unsatisfactory answer to the first question is to argue from political culture, to assert that Poles and Hungarians were 'different', in the sense of possessing a greater commitment to, say, freedom than Czechs or Bulgarians. The value underlying this argument comes close to assuming an immanent national character that predisposes some peoples to positive values and condemns others to servitude. It is unconvincing and made to appear even more so by the developments of the 1960s, when it was the Czechs who showed the commitment to freedom and the Poles and Hungarians who remained passive. The answer to the question has to be sought elsewhere, in the interplay of different systemic factors, as well as those of political culture. For the purposes of this chapter, however, one not altogether precise assumption, which does not undermine the argument to follow, will be made about the situation in Eastern Europe at Stalin's death. This is that the impact of Stalinism was identical on the political systems of the entire area (minus Yugoslavia, of course). Stalin's homogenization is assumed to have produced systems which functioned in very similar ways, so much so that the impact of de-Stalinization was initially likewise very similar. From this it follows that the differences in outcome must be attributable to different choices made in the different East European states. This means that the process must be assessed across the entire area, on a comparative basis. The methodology to unravel the answer to the problem of de-Stalinization, therefore, will concentrate first on the global environment within which it started and then look at the various systemic factors within the different countries. 'Global environment' in this context refers to the decisions taken by the Soviet leadership.

The Soviet Impact

The first point here is that de-Stalinization was very like Stalinism in one central respect – it was imposed by the Kremlin on Eastern Europe without regard for the appropriateness of the de-Stalinization strategies employed by the Soviet leadership. It was simply assumed that what was good for the Soviet Union was good for Eastern Europe too. The underlying criterion, presumably, was derived from the mind-set of the Soviet leaders, the imperatives of Marxism–Leninism, that these states had the same political system, they suffered from the same problems and the same remedies would resolve these, and from the contingent needs of the day, the task of ruling the Soviet Union without Stalin. This imperative was underpinned by other cultural, great-power and military–strategic ones. It evidently never occurred to the Soviet leadership – a term which is in any case too homogeneous for the shifting coalitions within the Kremlin – that Eastern Europe was so different that the simplistic imposition of de-Stalinization as devised in Moscow might produce very different results. For a start, the fact that in 1953 the system was thirty-six years old in the Soviet Union but only five years old in Eastern Europe might have given the Kremlin food for thought.

It should be understood in mitigation that the Kremlin too was in uncharted waters. The new leadership of Beria, Malenkov, Khrushchev, Molotov, Kaganovich and the others had all grown up politically under Stalin. Their potential choices, their field of vision, their conception of a socialist future were severely limited by that experience. They had relatively few ideas of what the agenda of socialism and the strategy of rule might be without Stalin. They might have had their misgivings about what Stalin was attempting to do, though if they ever expressed these they would have ended up in Gulag in short order, but at least they had a clarity and certainty about what socialism was. Gradually, these certainties had to make way for the greater complexities of modernity. Stalin's industrialization, for all its anti-modernistic one-sidedness, did transform Soviet society into one which was incomparably more complex in some respects than the one he took over in the 1920s.

Furthermore, the system that Stalin left behind him was a native system in the Soviet Union, in that it had been constructed from an amalgam of traditional Russian and foreign elements. This meant that the remedies for the excesses of Stalinism grasped at by his successors had the advantage of being authentic within the political cultural framework. This was almost wholly absent from Eastern Europe, where the Stalinist revolution had been viewed as alien by all except a small minority of committed militants. This was bound to produce different outcomes to de-Stalinization in the Soviet Union and its dependent empire.

The combination of provincialism, uncertainty, arrogance and internal conflict, coupled with a definite ignorance about Eastern Europe, led the Soviet leadership to adopt a somewhat hand-to-mouth strategy for de-Stalinization in Eastern Europe – if, indeed, strategy is not too grand a word for the *ad hoc* improvisation that the Kremlin employed at this time. In reality it was never clear whether de-Stalinization was a process of moving away from the worst excesses of Stalin's rule, but otherwise like it, or whether it actually encapsulated a new vision of socialism, whether – in a word – it was a method or a goal. In the event it was a bit of both, with the latter vaguely implied by the former, which unquestionably predominated. Consequently, what follows in this chapter is necessarily more systematized, more coherent than the actual events appeared at the time. To sketch the global environment, I have constructed an intellectual framework for de-Stalinization which it probably never had. This should be understood, then, as a heuristic device, one with validity to make sense of the underlying patterns of causation.

The Death of Stalin

Four broad factors deriving from Soviet events or actions impinged on Eastern Europe in the years 1953 to 1956. The first of these was the death of Stalin. The repercussions of this, as already suggested, were far-reaching. A number of factors may be suggested in this connection. Self-evidently a political system constructed by one man around his will must change when biology takes a hand. This was even more the case when the man in question arrogated a near-divine role to himself and insisted that his system was perfect and, therefore, not subject to change. Stalin, having been the fountain-head of all wisdom, knowledge and power at the symbolic level, did after all die, despite the widespread feeling that gods, on the whole, are immortal. People wept in the streets, the party machines brought up to regard him as the sole source of inspiration were left helpless, the political leaderships of Eastern Europe had to come to terms with the novelty that a new leadership in the Kremlin might operate differently. But beyond all these relatively contingent factors was one that stood out over all the others in its implications. Stalin symbolized permanence and changelessness in himself. His death negated and disproved this. At the symbolic and affective levels, the unity of the Soviet system was opened to questioning. And, equally significantly, the appropriation of the socialist agenda, which Stalin had used for his own purposes, was ending. In this sense change within the system re-entered the realm of the possible. By the same token, Stalin's demise also upgraded the meaning of Tito's challenge to Stalin's monopoly of socialism, in that, with the possibility of reassessing the nature of socialism, alternatives – the sole alternative – could become a beacon of attraction. For the first time since the imposition of his system of rule on Eastern Europe, the possibility of doing something differently, of disagreement, of change returned, if not to the immediate political agenda, at any rate to the wider sense of future. And, indeed, for the first time since the imposition of Stalinism on Eastern Europe, the proposition that alternative versions of the future might exist began tentatively to play a role in people's minds.

The New Course

All that lay in the future. For the moment the post-Stalin leadership had to devise instruments for running the legacy. This was the New Course, a mixture of tactical and strategic initiatives. It involved diminution of the Terror, the release of vast numbers of prisoners from Gulag, the hesitant ending of mass arbitrary action, though without any thought of abandoning arbitrariness as such. Of key importance to the leadership was its own security. Two moves were taken to assure this. First, a tacit agreement was reached that the upper echelons of the élite were to be exempt from terror. Beria, who symbolized the terror as head of the secret police, was removed; his death was, again, as much a symbolic act, a signal that the power of the secret police would no longer be exercised without restraints. Second, no successor of Stalin's would ever be allowed to gather as much power as he had done. To this end collective leadership was instituted. The offices of party leader and prime minister were no longer to be held by one man. The party, which had withered under Stalin's rule, would be revived and reassume its proper Leninist vanguard role of acting as the central powerhouse of the system. To gain a measure of popular support the strategy of massive, unceasing capital accumulation would be checked. There would be some shift in emphasis from capital investment to the production of consumer goods and agriculture, which had been starved of capital, labour and skills under Stalin, would be given some resources.

Implicit in this was the recognition that Stalin's policy of relentless mobilization had reached the end of its usefulness. This had ramifications beyond the immediate easing of restrictions. It signalled that the agenda of socialism was no longer to be considered as absolutely fixed and, thereby, that debate – halting and hesitant – was again within the Soviet canon, as it had been until Stalin consolidated his power. This immediately raised the role of the intelligentsia in the Soviet system. Under Stalin this role had been fairly straightforward. The technical intelligentsia was to use its specialized knowledge to implement what the leader told it to do. If the task was to construct power stations, then that was what they had to do, without raising objections about technical difficulties, because these were objectively impossible and thus antagonistic. The creative intelligentsia's role was to justify the system, to devise the apologetics to legitimate the system and make the transformation palatable. The new situation brought changes in both these areas. The intelligentsia slowly came to understand that it was in a position to regain some of its true functions – the exercise of specialized knowledge by its own criteria and the exercise of criticism without reference to the day-to-day needs of the political leader. The worship of Stalin was no longer the acme of intellectual achievement.

This was a major change. The prospect of debate and discussion, even involving disagreement, slight though it might have been at the outset, returned to the system. And it also signified that the politically motivated charlatanry of men like the pseudo-geneticist Lysenko would be recognized as such. Specialized knowledge would no longer be judged exclusively by political criteria. In one crucial respect this had enormous implications. The ideology of perfection, the party's claim to possess the absolute monopoly of truth, the Manichaeism, the insistence that there was Soviet knowledge (which was positive) and bourgeois knowledge (which was negative) were being if not abandoned at least diluted. Eventually this process was to debouch into the political system too, at a much faster pace in Eastern Europe than in the Soviet Union.

The dilemma for the political leadership in respect of the intelligentsia was how much latitude should there be, how much discussion was useful, how much destructive. In reality this dilemma cannot be resolved in these terms, for this way of posing the question still revolves around the monopoly of the political sphere over the others. It would continue to mean that the political sphere retained a residual right to intervene in other spheres. But for the moment the change was qualitative, palpable and sufficient to trigger off a ferment. Inside the Soviet Union this could be contained, in Eastern Europe, less easily so.

One last point about the nature of change in Soviet-type systems is worth noting here. Time and again, power-holders have shown a consistent preference for personnel changes over institutional reform. Obviously it is easier to sack individuals than to transform structures. But it goes beyond this. By and large, Soviet-type systems have consistently come to regard dismissals as actually constituting structural change, as if to argue that new office-holders would make the system function better and thereby make the need for reform superfluous. There is nothing wrong with the system that new leaders cannot cure. There is a kind of logic in this. If one starts from the unstated assumption that the system is excellent, that it was merely the distortions of the 'personality cult' that caused it to malfunction, then one will have achieved legitimation through continuity, reassured the relics of the previous system and made a bid for power through symbols. The problem is that this method of proceeding can imprison innovative leaders within the system by precluding a wide range of choices. But there is no question that the post-Stalin leadership, insecure in its power as it was, opted repeatedly for this easier course. It remained a characteristic feature of the system thereafter, in Eastern Europe as well as in the Soviet Union.

The Return of Titoism

While the imposition of the New Course on Eastern Europe and its effects will be discussed presently, I want to continue the exploration of the repercussions of Soviet actions on Eastern Europe. The third of these was Khrushchev's reconciliation with Tito. In May–June 1955 Khrushchev travelled to Belgrade and accepted that the system that Tito had constructed in Yugoslavia was, after all, within the world socialist system, both ideologically and thence politically. The excommunication of Tito in 1948, his vilification as an imperialist lackey and Trotskyist agent, the condemnation of self-management as revisionist were forgiven and forgotten. Indeed, Khrushchev came about as close as any Soviet leader could to offering Tito an apology for what had happened. He could not quite put the blame on Stalin – the casting out of Stalin was still some months ahead – but he could and did hold Beria responsible.

The significance of this for Soviet–Yugoslav relations is another story, though not without its implications for the Soviet Union's relations with any of its East European allies. One of Tito's lieutenants, Svetozar Vukmanovic-Tempo, recounted in his memoirs how he listened to Khrushchev and, when he heard the Soviet leader's attempt to put the blame on Beria, could contain himself no longer and burst out, 'But how will we know that at some future date, there won't be another Beria, that once again you will condemn us as revisionists.' Khrushchev was speechless. 'You petty-bourgeois element,' he shouted. The meaning of this exchange is twofold. One, already mentioned, is the emphasis that Soviet-type systems place on personnel change as a substitute for structural change. The other is the contingent nature of Soviet initiatives and the impossibility of anchoring them in any institutional form. It was this latter lability that Tempo hit on and, by mentioning it aloud, infuriated Khrushchev.[1]

But Khrushchev's blundering had incalculable consequences for the entire legitimacy of the Soviet-type systems in all the East European states. The proposition was painfully simple. If there could be a Yugoslav road to socialism that was now no longer revisionist and excluded from the canon, why then could there not also be Polish and Hungarian and Czechoslovak roads as well? There could be no logical answer to this as long as the official ideology was being taken seriously.

[1] Svetozar Vukmanovic-Tempo, *Revolucija koja tece* (1971), vol. II, p. 233.

The actual institutions developed by Tito – self-management in industry – were of lesser significance than the acceptance by the Kremlin of his historic decision in 1948–9 to remain in power and to insist on being a communist, thereby challenging Stalin's monopoly of communism. It was this legitimation of a communist alternative to Stalinism that Khrushchev, wittingly or otherwise, triggered off by the Belgrade Declaration. The Soviet Union's long-standing claim to be the centre of world communism, to have the sole right to determine what constituted authentic socialism and what did not and to take action to suppress undesirable variants was, as it were, being given away. The potential for East European reformers to find their own roads to communism was, it appeared, acceptable. One point should be noted here. The reformers mentioned here were intellectuals inside the system. They continued to believe at this time that a communist system was viable and that the distortions imposed on the political systems were the outcome of Stalin's misconceptions or the megalomania of their own Stalinist rulers or of insufficient heed being paid to local variations which did not influence the thrust of the ideology.

This made life extremely difficult for the East European leaders who did not want change, who felt that the Stalinist system, to which they owed their power, was perfectly acceptable as it was, and not in need of any reform. It became practically impossible to defend the system in terms of ideology; instead it had to be defended in other terms, like those of power politics or foreign threat or pragmatically, saying that the situation was not yet ripe for change. This conflict was the seed-bed of reform communism, which lived roughly from 1953 to 1968. Its end was still many years ahead, but the failure to take up the challenge in any real as distinct from propagandistic sense (e.g. 'Our system is the best because it is the best') was to have the long-term outcome of voiding the content of Marxism–Leninism entirely. The clash over Titoism was the first step in that direction.

There was a final aspect of Khrushchev's reconciliation with Tito that was also to create major problems for the East European leaders. Almost without exception, the leaders in power had taken a highly active part in the vilification of Tito in 1948–9 and, indeed, they were all (the GDR excepted) involved in the plans to invade Yugoslavia.[2] Rákosi in Hungary and Chervenkov in Bulgaria were particularly exposed in this respect. Indeed, Tito demanded their political heads as his price for the reconciliation. But while it may have been highly embarrassing for these and other leaders to be told that Tito was not,

---

[2] Details in Béla Király, 'The Aborted Soviet Military Plans against Tito', in Wayne C. Vucinich (ed.), *At the Brink of War and Peace: the Tito-Stalin Split in Historic Perspective* (1982), pp. 273–88.

after all, a hireling of the Imperialist–Zionist–Trotskyist conspiracy – as they had trumpeted just a few years earlier – but a loyal communist, that could be shrugged off and, for what it was worth, blamed on Beria. The far more serious issue was that of the local communists executed as Titoists. If Tito was not an enemy, then those sentenced to death as Titoists were in the same category. So, the question was being covertly put, how come that Rajk and Kostov and Clementis and the others were executed for something that had not been criminal? And what of the people who had been responsible for their execution, what should be their responsibility? Rákosi had boasted a couple of years earlier that it had been his personal vigilance that had succeeded in unmasking Rajk, except that, as it turned out, there had been nothing to unmask. And what of the confessions that had been made in open court by these people? How had these been obtained, what had happened to the judicial process? In the countries where de-Stalinization produced upheaval, the struggle for their rehabilitation became a central focus for the political conflicts of the mid-1950s.

The Secret Speech

None of the three factors described so far, whether jointly or severally, would have been sufficient to destabilize any of the East European states, though Poland and Hungary had entered a ferment by the time of Khrushchev's fourth and final throw – the Secret Speech. On 26 February 1956, during a special secret session of the 20th Congress of the Communist Party of the Soviet Union, from which foreign delegates were excluded, Khrushchev denounced Stalin for having been a murderous despot. He accused the former wisest father of mankind of having been a tyrant who sent thousands of good communists to their deaths, who wrought untold damage on the Soviet Union and the ideological legacy of Lenin. Khrushchev's motives, as with the Belgrade Declaration, were primarily to be understood within the context of the struggle for power in the Soviet leadership. When he found himself blocked within the Praesidium and the Central Committee, he moved the conflict to the Congress and, though he enjoined secrecy, took his assault into a wider public arena. Within a very short space of time the news and the details of the Secret Speech were out.

Their effect in the political climate of Eastern Europe differed markedly from the more placid response of the Soviet Union. It spread uncertainty among the cadres and stirred the intellectuals to renewed questioning, especially in Poland and Hungary, but there were reverberations in Czechoslovakia and the GDR as well. It brought the question of the socialist agenda and what Stalin had done to it to the fore with greater urgency than ever. The ground on which criticism of local practices could be based was now incomparably stronger.

By contrast, the Stalinists and even conservatives within the élite who were not necessarily committed to all the tenets of Stalinism but looked for a quiet life, were dismayed. It was not enough for their chief ideological inspiration to have died just short of three years previously, but now it turned out that they had been in grievous error in having vested their faith in him at all. The denunciation of Stalin, for an instant at any rate, acted as a kind of threshold. Each and every individual wielding power had to confront the question of by what right he or she exercised power, what really was the ideology that he or she was serving. The legitimacy of the system as understood by those in power was at issue. In states where the questioning was already advanced this was a severe blow, and the local Stalinists were hard put to deal with it. But even where the system remained relatively stable, the leadership had to respond to a renewed ground swell of criticism and questioning. The morale of the ruling parties was badly shaken.

Two small additional points, not strictly related to any of the four previous categories but within the ambit of the Soviet impact, also played local roles in accelerating political upheaval. In the case of Poland the popular legitimacy of the system was severely burdened by the legacy of the past. This included the emergence of Poland as an independent state in defiance of the fledgling Soviet state in 1918, the Polish–Soviet war of 1919–20, the Soviet attack on Poland in 1939 and the Katyn massacre. These were taboo topics at this time, but there was one other issue that could be ventilated – the fate of the Polish party which had been dissolved at Stalin's orders in 1938.[3] On 19 February 1956, the CPSU, in the name of the now defunct Comintern, rehabilitated the KPP, accepted that its leaders had been killed unjustly and put the blame on the distortions of the 'cult of personality'. This undoubtedly encouraged Polish intellectuals to persist with further questioning.

A similar rehabilitation took place in 1956 affecting Hungary, though it was not the puzzling dissolution of the organizations of the KMP in 1936 that was involved, but the person of Béla Kun. Kun was now recognized as having been a faithful communist and it became possible to re-examine the fate of the 1919 Hungarian Soviet republic as well. However, this was much less significant for Hungarian opinion than an event that had taken place the previous year – the Austrian State Treaty and the Soviet Union's recognition of Austrian neutrality.

[3] See Jan B. de Weydenthal, *The Communists of Poland: an Historical Outline* (1978), p. 32.

This event had a considerable influence on some currents of Hungarian thought, for not only was Austria geographically close to Hungary, but its cultural proximity made it a very attractive model to emulate. If the idea of neutrality was acceptable for Austria, then why not for Hungary? And if Austria was neutral then why was it necessary for the Soviet Union to keep four Soviet divisions on Hungarian soil, seeing that the original justification for their presence had been to guarantee Soviet lines of communication to Austria? No answer to these questions was forthcoming, other than a flat rejection, but they were to resurface in October 1956.

The East European Framework

The impact of the Soviet environment on its own can be no more than an outline of the necessary explanation for what happened in Eastern Europe, but not sufficient to account for things falling out differently in different states. To reach some kind of answer developments within the various states have to be examined. Here again, four categories have been established as applicable to Eastern Europe as a whole and, as before, they should be regarded as heuristic.

The Unity of the Leadership

The first and most important of these categories was the state of the political leadership in each East European country. In simple terms, where the leadership was united in its determination to hold onto power at any cost and to suppress all popular or intellectual questioning, its chances of survival, with only a nod towards accommodation, were excellent. Concessions could be made, lip-service to reform and pious sentiments about the importance of change could be uttered and the system would remain untouched in its essentials. And, of considerable value to the Kremlin, stability would be sustained.

The maintenance of unity was no easy matter. It was threatened by the ambitions of different East European leaders; by the factional struggles in the Kremlin, where different factions had their established coteries of supporters in Eastern Europe; by the leadership's ability to retain the confidence of its supporters in the party, state and other *apparats*; by pressure for social autonomy from below, as articulated by intellectual criticism; and at the outer margin by the response of the population.

The price to be paid for failure to maintain this unity or at least the semblance of unity was very high. It created a gap in the system and through that gap, all sorts of social forces – the ones which had been suppressed though not destroyed by Stalin's atomization – could arise and re-emerge. Intellectuals would regain some of their autonomy and would reassess their political functions in the light of the new situation. And, if the gap were not plugged in time, the worst could happen and the leaders of the vanguard of the proletariat might actually be faced by the proletariat exercising its political will independently of its vanguard, a phenomenon of which Lenin and all who followed in his footsteps generally had a rather low opinion.

The response to these pressures was, for the most part, to batten down the hatches, institute repressive measures where necessary, and keep troublesome critics of the system as silent as possible. The leaderships mostly understood that they had to retain their cohesiveness or else fall apart completely. Not least, they all sensed that their popular legitimacy was weakly grounded, as demonstrated most clearly by the 1953 East German upsurge.

What led to disunity varied, but insofar as any general rule can be deduced, disunity arose where disagreement coalesced around personalities. There were three cases of this: Poland, Hungary and Bulgaria. In each one the existing leader (Bierut, Rákosi, Chervenkov) found himself threatened by the political danger of a potentially attractive alternative leader (Gomulka, Nagy and several possibles in Bulgaria) and the alternative leader had support inside the Politburo. Had matters remained confined to personalities, disarray could have been prevented. In effect, this was what happened in Bulgaria. It was otherwise in Poland and Hungary.

Understanding the different paths in Bulgaria on one hand and Poland and Hungary on the other is crucial in explaining why the latter two entered on a course that led to destabilization of the system (and worse in Hungary), but Bulgaria weathered the crisis intact as far as relations between rulers and ruled were concerned. The conflict between Chervenkov and his rivals was very deep and he appears to have earned the personal dislike of Khrushchev as well. It could have torn the Bulgarian leadership apart.

The key differential was that however deep the rivalries remained, the various competing leaders all agreed on the overriding need to keep the system intact, to abide by the Leninist rule of keeping their conflicts within the leadership and to refrain from mustering support outside their own ranks, and this included the lower levels of the *apparat*. Although the conflict obviously did involve political issues as well as personalities, these were secondary when viewed from the standpoint of power. No one in the leadership seriously believed in the desirability of popular participation, in greater autonomy for the economic sphere, in greater freedom of criticism for the intelligentsia. On the contrary, their disagreements were about relatively minor issues on the margins, like the pace of mobilization, the rate of investment in Sector A (heavy industry) as against agriculture and the like. This is not to imply that these issues were unimportant to Bulgarian society. The question of the terror and its diminution were self-evidently of great significance. All the same, for the great majority the system was a given and they did not have high expectations of making a positive input.

The Bulgarian intelligentsia was likewise quiescent. Some of this was cultural (in the broad sense), for it was composed of recent recruits from low-status backgrounds who felt they owed their loyalty to the régime. There was no great dissatisfaction at this stage with the politically determined nature of their functions because, for the time being, the intelligentsia largely accepted régime goals of high mobilization and discipline and were less concerned with questions of freedom, democracy and autonomy. Bulgaria's lower levels of economic development were without doubt a factor influencing this attitude. The essence of the difference was that the leadership did not break into open factions and make attempts to recruit support within the *apparat* and the intelligentsia; and without this opening, the latter remained acquiescent in the *status quo*.[4]

The towering personality of Chervenkov may also have been a factor in all this. He dominated Bulgarian politics in a single-handed way that recalled only Stalin and seemed to mesmerize his rivals. When the New Course was imposed on Bulgaria, however, Chervenkov made an error. It was still uncertain in January 1954, when he made his self-criticism, whether it would be the party or the state bureaucracy that would emerge as dominant; he opted for the latter. But his self-confidence was evidently unaffected, for he noted, with conscious or unconscious irony, 'the cult of personality is harmful even when it concerns exceptionally powerful and eminent personalities.'[5] The party was placed in the care of Todor Zhivkov, a minor *apparatchik* and protégé of Khrushchev's whom Chervenkov thought he could control. His real rival was Anton Yugov, a home communist. But there was no disagreement within this group about the distribution of power, only about who should wield it.

It was otherwise in Poland and Hungary and events in these two

---

[4] Nissan Oren, *Revolution Administered: Agrarianism and Communism in Bulgaria* (1973).
[5] Quoted by François Fejtö, *A History of the People's Democracies: Eastern Europe since Stalin* (1971), p. 29.

countries seemed at first sight to run in tandem in the years 1953–6, though they were to diverge at the end. In reality there were major differences throughout. The first of these lay in the personalities composing the leadership and their readiness to make even minimum concessions. While no one would ever fairly accuse Boleslaw Bierut, the Polish leader, of having been a liberal, he was several degrees more realistic than Mátyás Rákosi was in Hungary, at any rate in his recognition that some changes were unavoidable. The second difference in personalities was between the challengers for power. In Poland, Wladyslaw Gomulka had been purged in 1948 as a Titoist, but though arrested was never tried. Gomulka was at all times a rigid authoritarian, whose real difference of opinion with Stalin was not over issues but over power – who should run Poland. Imre Nagy, in Hungary, was a very different person, above all one who had not lost his capacity to innovate, to absorb new ideas. Rákosi had placed him in a subsidiary position.[6]

A third difference was fortuitous, though extremely important. A major problem in the course of de-Stalinization was how to retire the Stalinist leader. In Czechoslovakia the problem was solved by Gottwald's death from a chill he caught at Stalin's funeral. Elsewhere, the fates were less kind. In Poland, however, Bierut did die in April 1956 at the height of the pressure for change, apparently from the shock of the Secret Speech,[7] whereas in Hungary Rákosi clung on to power until finally ejected in July 1956, by which time tempers had begun seriously to fray. A new leader, like Edward Ochab in Poland, had less of a personal commitment to Stalinism and could ease tensions more readily.

All the same, by the spring and summer of 1956, the Polish leadership had begun to separate into two groups, generally referred to as the Natolin and Pulawy factions. The terms 'hard-liner' and 'liberal' have been applied, but it is hard to know what exactly is meant by these under any circumstances. The division between the two groups is better understood by reference to their different attitudes to the readmission of Gomulka to the leadership, to the speed and extent of rehabilitation, to popular demands and intellectual criticism and to the Jewish question. The Natolinists were inclined to be pro-Soviet and authoritarian, seeking to generate support for their positions by blaming Stalinism on the Jews, who had in fact been numerous in the Polish leadership during the Stalinist years. The Jewish question re-

---

[6] Imre Nagy, *On Communism: In Defence of the New Course* (1957).
[7] See the interview with Edward Ochab in Teresa Toranska, *Oni: Stalin's Polish Puppets* (1987).

peatedly played a submerged role in post-war Polish politics. It was seldom referred to explicitly – the 1968 events were an exception – but it coloured attitudes and underlay otherwise obscure loyalties.[8] The Soviet Union likewise used this issue and adopted a consistently anti-Jewish approach in cadre policies in Poland and elsewhere. The Pulawy group was far from having been inspired by democratization, but it was prepared to accede to some popular demands and preferred a less subservient relationship with the Soviet Union. Ochab and the newly appointed prime minister, Józef Cyrankiewicz, took up positions somewhere between the two.

While the see-saw in the Polish leadership swung back and forth, Polish society moved further ahead under its own steam, independently of the party. The mood was changing and it was this changing mood that found expression in the Poznan upheaval on 28 June 1956. Poznan was a profound shock and had consequences pointing in two different directions. For those in favour of change it meant that change was not moving fast enough and that without more change there could be real danger. For the authoritarians Poznan merely confirmed what they had always thought, that the population was unsound and that if it was given an inch it would take an ell. As for Moscow, it was deeply shaken and concentrated much of its effort on salvaging what it could. This had a further result; while concentrating on Poland it tended to neglect the equally unstable situation in Hungary.[9]

Thus while the unity of the Polish leadership between 1953 and 1956 was severely tested and clearly began to come apart towards the end, the Poles escaped the ham-fisted Soviet intervention in the composition of the leadership that the Hungarian party had to endure in 1953. On 13–14 June 1953, a large top-level delegation from the Hungarian leadership was summoned to Moscow. It included Rákosi and Nagy.[10] In the Kremlin they were read a curtain lecture by Beria, who instructed them to adopt the collective leadership at once and, with a good deal of personal offensiveness, told Rákosi to desist from the policies of high mobilization that had brought Hungary to the edge of ruin. Nagy became prime minister and, a little later, read the Central Committee a most powerful indictment of Rákosi and his associates, who were in the hall at the time, accusing them of unparty-like be-

[8] Michael Checinski, *Poland: Communism, Nationalism, Anti-Semitism* (1982).
[9] Ochab in Toranska, *Oni*, and Veljko Micunovic, *Moscow Diary* (1980), pp. 76–7 discuss Poznan and its consequences.
[10] Details in András Hegedüs, *Élet egy eszme árnyékában* (1985). See also the anonymous chronology of Hungarian history between 1953 and 1963, *1956: A forradalom kronológiája és bibliográfiája* (1990).

haviour.[11] This was the beginning of a deep fissure in the Hungarian party, which was to contribute materially to the eruption of the revolution in 1956.

Nagy, however, was never able to launch his reforms properly. He was unable to have his speech to the Central Committee published and Rákosi, with backing from the Kremlin, counter-attacked. Some changes were introduced, including a halt to collectivization, slowing down the pace of industrialization and the slow release of political prisoners. Nagy sought to use the government bureaucracy to effect change, but discovered that the party was countermanding much of what he was doing. The tug of war persisted until the early months of 1955, when Nagy suffered a minor heart attack, his patron in Moscow, Malenkov, fell and Rákosi had him thrown out of office. A few months later he was expelled from the party and disgraced, but the damage had been done. Enough of the intelligentsia had been inspired and enough of the *apparat*'s self-confidence shaken to make the situation more and more unstable. Khrushchev's secret speech burst like a bombshell in this milieu. Rákosi was still trying to reimpose Stalinism on a society quite unwilling to submit, and after the 20th Congress his position was virtually untenable. He was losing his authority and his grip on the party machine. The intellectuals had long before turned against him. Their lever was the rehabilitation of Rajk and in May 1956, after Rákosi had grudgingly accepted that perhaps, after all, Rajk might have been innocent, he was openly called on to resign. He held on and it was not until 18 July, during which time attitudes polarized, that Rákosi was sacked, and even at that it needed the presence of Mikoyan, the Kremlin's ubiquitous troubleshooter, to ensure his departure. But, personalities again, the Kremlin's choice of successor, Ernö Gerö, proved to be a disaster. Gerö was a man in the Rákosi mould, but he lacked even Rákosi's adeptness in wielding power. Gerö simply made a bad situation worse by encouraging more polarization. But division in the leadership, though extremely uncomfortable, did not necessarily lead to upheaval. To reach that state of affairs other elements were needed.

The Role of Intellectuals

Some mention of this problem has already been made, but the Polish and Hungarian evidence, with the negative Bulgarian evidence, clearly indicate that destabilization occurred expressly when the different

---

[11] The translation of Imre Nagy's Secret Speech, as it has come to be called, was published in *Labour Focus on Eastern Europe,* no. 3–4, 1982.

sections of the leadership began to muster support among intellectuals in order to legitimate their political strategies. Furthermore, some intellectuals, having again become involved in critical as distinct from apologetic activities, discovered that they enjoyed this and began to express criticism independently of the political sphere, beyond what the different contending factions might have wanted. It is worth stressing again that these activities were within a Marxist framework and that the non-Marxist majority remained outside the conflict. This implied that intellectuals were motivated by some broader goal, i.e. that Marxism was still capable of generating a ferment of ideas; the contrast was with Fascism, which would have been quite incapable of eliciting any equivalent revival, because it lacked a vision of the future to inspire in the way that Marxism still did.[12]

At the same time, the role of intellectuals extended some way beyond this. Intellectuals and the intelligentsia – as previously defined – maintained a good deal of control over communication and the language of public discourse. By insisting on a greater degree of autonomy for themselves they began to use language more freely too. Equally, they began to create their own definitions of the agenda, making their own choices of targets for criticism. In the course of flexing their muscles they began to discover the actual reality of what was happening in their countries, that these were far from being a socialist paradise, but miserable, backward states, where people lived in wretched conditions not that far above starvation level. This discovery was a considerable shock for those who did believe in it, precisely because it was in this area of basic material need that it was supposed to achieve its greatest successes.[13]

The conclusion they drew was that Stalinism was a distortion of true Marxism, that overt criticism of the reality of Soviet-type systems was essential to bring about change and that by criticizing they could influence the political sphere. This led them to ventilate something of the popular mood of dissatisfaction, the appalling conditions in which workers and peasants lived. They also tackled issues like the moral values behind Marxism, the historic role of the proletariat, censorship, the nature of socialist realism in aesthetics and the nature of power relations constructed under Stalinism.[14]

The confluence of intellectual criticism and popular dissatisfaction was a vital element in hastening the destabilization of the system. It

[12] See István Bibó, 'Political Breviary', *Cross Currents: a Yearbook of Central European Culture*, no. 3 (1984), pp. 7–20.
[13] Tibor Méray and Tamás Aczél, *The Revolt of the Mind* (1959) offers an excellent illustration of this process.
[14] Fejtö, *People's Democracies*, pp. 59–60.

began to reconstruct the social community that Stalinism had destroyed, it sought to reintegrate an atomized society as individuals discovered that their experiences were universal and that solidarity would make the holders of power hesitate. Conversely, it fostered the self-questioning of the *apparat* and the secret police. The élite could rule untroubled in its own mind most easily when society was completely atomized and nobody had the courage to ask awkward questions, when everybody complied. Now compliance was gradually being replaced by something else, a less unbalanced relationship between rulers and ruled.

The process of reawakening was slow and uneven in both Poland and Hungary. But as early as 1953 there were writers in both countries asking hard questions about the price that had been paid by the peasantry for industrialization and whether this price was compatible with Marxism–Leninism. A near-emblematic moment was the publication of Adam Wazyk's 'Poem for Adults' in 1955. Wazyk had been a long-standing Marxist intellectual, who had supported the Polish party unhesitatingly, until he was affected by the new atmosphere. The poem is a stark depiction of the contrast between the harshness of Polish reality and the promises of the Marxian utopia and a call to the party to live up to its historic responsibilities in these terms.[15]

Wazyk was not alone; he could indeed be said to have represented an entire generation, the one that had believed in the promise of Marxism, discovered with a shock after the death of Stalin that, as they saw it, it had been hijacked, and was now calling for a return to the genuine path. For some it was evidently the inspiration of revolution that was the motivating force. Fejtö quotes the Pole Andrzej Braun:[16]

> When I rejoined the revolutionary ranks [in 1956], I knew what I was doing. We were absolutely convinced not only of the righteousness of the cause, but even more of its splendour . . . A new socialist morality, a new aesthetics, new customs, a new man, a new world.

This was the romance of the revolution yet again, a belief that the false turning of 1948–9 could be reversed and true socialism could be founded. But while this may have been the underlying motivating force for Marxists, other concerns that actuated a greater number. For some it was simple humanism, that industrial workers were living as badly under the communist system as they had before the war or that

---

[15] A near complete text is to be found, in translation, in Flora Lewis, *The Polish Volcano* (1959), pp. 73–6. The Polish original was published in *Nowa Kultura*, 21 August 1955.
[16] Fejtö, *People's Democracies*, p. 58, from *Nowa Kultura*, 18 March 1956.

the treatment of the peasantry had been particularly callous. For others there was resentment at the privileges of the new élite. And for others still there was a feeling that Marxism ought to emancipate rather than enslave and that, somewhere along the line, freedom was lost. Freedom, of course, has long and distinguished antecedents in the battle honours of East European intellectuals.

This raises a political cultural rather than a systemic issue. It is a truism that East European intellectuals have traditionally seen themselves as a surrogate opposition, a permanent 'contestation' and have legitimated their claims to influence by reference to that tradition. At the same time, while this was perfectly accurate, there was more to it than straightforward self-serving interest articulation. This oppositional role was accepted to an extent by the societies in which it had grown up, in which intermediate institutions were weak and intellectuals were as good as forced into adopting political roles. In the 1950s, despite the growing complexity of these societies, the rehomogenization of Stalinism, the starkness of the issues, offered the intellectuals – in Poland and Hungary above all – a chance to play this role once more. Never again would the opportunity recur. By 1967–8 in Czechoslovakia the creative intellectuals were obliged to share the stage with the scientific and technological élite, and this was repeated in the very different context of 1989.

The crucial element in hastening the destabilization of the system from the standpoint of the élite was the collapse of the carefully crafted façade of homogeneity, of the myth of perfection in which no doubt was permitted to enter. Once debate and disagreement seeped into public discourse, the leadership and its supporting élite began to lose their sense of justification, their will to rule. This was a dangerous situation for them, given that their legitimation was very weakly grounded in the claim to have made a revolution that was generally seen as hostile, in having modernized the country but in a way that brought dreadful privation, and solipsistically by power itself, viz. that the party ruled because it ruled. When this last point was challenged the whole edifice disappeared. The social force that could issue that challenge was society itself and society, thanks to the preparatory work of reintegration by the intellectuals, was no longer as atomized as it had been only a few years before.

The Role of Society

Society on its own, in the form of strikes, riots, protests and the like could not effect serious changes in a Soviet-type system. This appears to have been the lesson of de-Stalinization and equally of subsequent challenges. But without some input from society, without some demonstration to the élite that its legitimacy had disappeared in the eyes of the population, stability could be safeguarded. The period immediately after the death of Stalin saw several popular upsurges, none of which was anything like powerful enough to break the will of the leadership and the élite. These included the Plovdiv tobacco workers' strike, the Plzen riots, the strike and sabotage wave in Hungary and, of course, the Poznan affair of 1956 in Poland. The most far-reaching of all was the uprising in East Berlin and East Germany in 1953.

The East German upheaval will have to serve as a paradigmatic case to explain why popular upheavals do not inherently have the power to bring down the régime. Many of the elements that were to emerge later in Hungary were present in the GDR in 1953. There were, indeed, divisions in the leadership. There was popular resentment. Matters began in 1952, when the East German leadership launched a policy of liquidating 'the remnants of capitalism' by nationalizing what was left of the private sector – mostly services – and proceeding with collectivization. This led to mounting dissatisfaction in the towns and a food shortage, so that in April 1953 Ulbricht asked the Soviet Union for food aid, but was told that he should modify his policies instead. Ulbricht refused and opted to intensify the tempo of 'socialist construction' by insisting that work norms be raised by 10 per cent. Attempts to implement this decree (28 May) encountered bitter hostility on the part of the workers. On 5 June the Soviet Union sought to intervene by demanding of Ulbricht that he backtrack, which he did, not least because he had learned that the Kremlin was casting about for an alternative leader. On 11 June he accepted publicly that mistakes would have to be corrected and the standard of living should be raised. But the higher work norms would stay.

This combination of forcing the pace and giving way turned out to be fatal, for it created the impression of hesitancy and uncertainty about the intentions of the leadership. On 16 June the construction workers in the Stalinallee – East Berlin's showpiece boulevard – downed tools and were rapidly joined by workers throughout East Berlin. The demands they raised mounted equally quickly and passed from economic ones, that lower work norms be restored, to political ones for free elections. The demonstrations continued into the next day and the Soviet military commander declared a state of emergency. Soviet units moved in and there was fighting. The demonstrations had spread to the entire country and were put down with great speed by the Red Army. Order was restored after two days.

The lessons of the East German uprising were numerous. Popular expectations could be aroused by hesitation and inconsistency on the part of the leadership and this could have far-reaching consequences for the readiness of society to act. Second, in politically determined systems, the step from non-political to political demands is a very short one. Third, the East German intellectuals remained silent and played no role in the events at all. This requires some explanation. Unlike all other East European states, German intellectuals had one unique choice – they could live in either a Marxist or a non-Marxist German state, so that they could choose without having to emigrate to an alien culture. Hence those that had opted for the former had a vested interest in maintaining the Marxist nature of the GDR, and this they defined in orthodox terms precisely because of the ever-present non-socialist alternative, West Germany. They saw the 1953 events not as a movement for democratization in the context of a redefined socialist agenda, but as the threat of capitalist restoration. They preferred to support the status quo, despite Bertolt Brecht's acid comment[17]

> Would it not be easier
> in this case for the government
> to dissolve the people
> and elect another?

Actually, while Brecht was just being ironical, he had probably unconsciously seized the essence of the Stalinist revolution, which was aimed precisely at 'dissolving' the people, by atomizing the population, destroying their mutual solidarities and linkages and thereby creating an entirely new population. When three years later a group of intellectuals sought to put forward ideas of a Marxist renewal, they were ignored by society, which had not forgotten the intellectuals' passivity. Fourth, the divisions in the East German leadership aroused expectations that could not be fulfilled, because while that leadership was hesitant, it had yet to lose its self-legitimation, its belief in its own rightness to rule. In general that loss comes about when it has been eroded by criticism from the intellectuals who have begun to formulate alternatives. Finally the Soviet Union was probably more prepared to use force in the GDR than in any other East European state for strategic reasons – East Germany's forward role against the West – so that any internal upheaval would be rapidly wound up, regardless of what the GDR leadership was doing.

The difference between the GDR in 1953 and Hungary in 1956 was far-reaching. The divisions in the Hungarian leadership went back much farther and were more deep-seated. The replacement of Rákosi

---

[17] Bertolt Brecht, 'The Solution', *Poems 1913–1956* (1976), p. 440.

by Gerö came too late to halt the slide, for the morale of the upper echelons of the party had begun to corrode. During the crucial months of July to October 1956 there was no one at the top who could rally the party faithful – *apparat* and membership – and give it enough of a sense of purpose under the new conditions to encourage it to rally round a new purposiveness. To make matters worse, the party was also losing the loyalty of its supporting intelligentsia, which began to sense that a more radical transformation was in the offing than the party could devise and, more frighteningly, that this could be more attractive than anything the party could offer.

Too many intellectuals, on the contrary, found a new sense of purpose and mission around a loosely constructed set of ideas which could be called, to use this perplexing and misleading term, 'national communism'.[18] The debates of the Petöfi Circle, the ideas expounded in *Irodalmi Ujság* and elsewhere would have taken Hungary a very long way from the Soviet-type system that it had been saddled with after 1949. The ceaseless criticism of the summer of 1956, coupled with the intellectual bankruptcy of the leadership, left the élite reeling. The situation was dangerously close to an explosion.

There were two events to provide the spark. On 6 October the ceremonial reinterment of László Rajk took place. This was a moment of pure political symbolism. Rajk, who had been the hard-headed Minister of the Interior of the immediate post-war years, was suddenly metamorphosed into the symbol of democracy and the victim of Stalinist terror. To underline the latter the date of the reinterment has to be understood. This was an anniversary deeply imbued with the meaning of revolution and liberation in the affective universe of Hungarians. On 6 October 1849 the leaders of the 1848 revolution, the Martyrs of Arad, were put to death by the Austrians, the alien tyrants of the time. No one could have failed to understand its significance. A crowd of 150,000 to 300,000 came to the same conclusion.

This proved to be the dress rehearsal, the moment when thousands of atomized individuals recognized that they were not alone and lost their fear of the system, the moment when the possibility of changing

---

[18] The term 'National Communism', for all the popularity that it has achieved in the literature, is an impossibility. If ever an ideology can be termed anti-national it is communism, so that the proposition that it could somehow become national and remain communist is simply risible. On the other hand the term has been invested with a vague meaning, that communism can be given a national colouring, in this case Hungarian; thus a system would be both Hungarian and communist, presumably acquiring Hungarian characteristics and overtones. What this would do to the quintessential internationalism of communism has never been satisfactorily explained.

the régime from below returned to the agenda. On 23 October an even greater crowd, this time with an explicitly political objective, as opposed to the implicitness of 6 October, took to the streets, to demand political freedom and democracy. The revolution had begun.[19]

Conclusion

There are few processes in the post-war history of Eastern Europe that exemplify the impact of cause and effect as clearly as de-Stalinization did. The Soviet Union, caught on the hop, launched a badly thought-out strategy, not reckoning with the consequences, and found itself with a major crisis on its hands in Eastern Europe. It reacted by returning to the use of force – reluctantly or otherwise – and thereby ensured that no rethinking of the agenda of Soviet-type politics would take place for thirty years.[20] The pattern that was to prompt the Kremlin to regard the Czechoslovak events of 1968 as a heresy and the predisposition to slide comfortably into the stagnation of the Brezhnev years was established in 1956.

The lessons of de-Stalinization were only partly understood by the Kremlin. Khrushchev did recognize that de-Stalinization was not in itself a strategy for change, but more the abandonment of certain methods of governance that had become untenable and utterly counterproductive. Some other formula had to be found, because the system had reached a cul-de-sac. At the same time, the Soviet leadership also concluded that uncontrolled change would automatically lead to quite unacceptable demands in Eastern Europe, which would threaten the Soviet Union's strategic and ideological interests there. Much the same moral was drawn from the upheavals in Poland and Hungary by the East European élites. The outcome was that reform, when it returned to the agenda, was pursued cautiously and ultimately ineffectively.

---

[19] The Hungarian Revolution has generated a huge literature, as well as its share of polemics. Among others, Bill Lomax, *Budapest 1956* (1976) and Ferenc Fehér and Agnes Heller, *Hungary 1956 Revisited: the Message of a Revolution a Quarter of a Century After* (1983) are the most thoughtful recent accounts. I have set out my own views on some of the issues in 'Domestic Politics', Karl-Detlev Groothusen (ed.), *Südosteuropa-Handbuch, Band V, Ungarn* (1987), pp. 67–106.
[20] Charles Gáti, *Hungary*, suggests that there were deep divisions in the Kremlin and a great deal of reluctance before the Red Army was committed.

6

The 1960s: Reform and Failure

[They are] the children of an idle brain
Begot of nothing but vain fantasy,
Which is as thin of substance as the air
And more inconstant than the wind.

Shakespeare, Romeo and Juliet,
I. iv. 97–100

The de-Stalinization of the 1950s ended in a massive and shameful failure. The Soviet-type systems of Eastern Europe were moving nowhere politically and, by the early 1960s, their economies were showing this too.[1] Yet at the beginning of the decade, there was considerable hope that some reform of both degree and kind could be introduced that would make these systems more effective in terms of matching system to popular aspirations and thereby move towards a more consensual basis of power with a Marxist–Leninist framework. In effect, the early 1960s saw an attempt – it proved to be the last – to introduce reform from above.

The limits of this were not made clear at the time, indeed they could not be, given that both the Soviet and the East European leaderships were still fumbling in the dark, looking for a new definition of ideology and system. The only firm guidelines were the negative ones learned from the 1956 Hungarian Revolution – the leading role of the party was sacrosanct and so was the relationship with the Soviet Union, but these offered very little in the way of positive indication as to what the content and quality of a Marxist–Leninist political order was supposed to be like. In a very real sense the parties were moving on the basis of trial and error.

[1] Tamás Bauer, *Tervgazdaság, beruházás, ciklusok* (1981).

The difficulties were always going to be considerable. In effect, any reformulation of the ideology and the system had to meet five conditions for any viable socialism to be established. The first of these conditions was perhaps the easiest – the new order would have to be derived from the original Marxian impulse and would have to make continuous reference to it. This was not entirely hopeless, given that both Marx and Lenin had published widely and that sacralizing texts could be found in the works of either to support whatever new initiatives were thought desirable. This was, after all, the period when the 'young Marx' was pitted against the 'old Marx' as a means of importing liberal ideas into official Marxism. The one innovation that was outside the range of possibilities was the abandonment of Marxism, because this would have contradicted one of the basic elements of party legitimation, namely that the party held power because it had made a Marxist revolution. This did restrict choices somewhat; for one, there could be no truck with a multi-party system – not that anyone was contemplating this anyway.

The second condition was that the new formulation of socialism would have to legitimate the political order. In other words, it would have to be a variant of socialism that was flexible and dynamic enough to attract people in order to introduce a consensual element into what had until then been an overwhelmingly non-consensual system. Third, the new order would have to find a delicate balance between the reciprocity of rulers and ruled and political monopoly. There would have to be a degree of reciprocity, one that was capable of development, both because this strengthened consensuality and also because it made rule easier if there was some feedback. On the other hand, too much of this, especially if it were to be institutionalized, would threaten the party's leading role and, indeed, point towards a multi-party system.

Fourth, the new variant would have to be simultaneously a guide to the day-by-day running of a polity and a guide to the future. These two were almost impossible to reconcile, because the demands of everyday politics stressed stability and convergence, whereas the formulation of strategies for the future emphasized criticism and change. Finally, following on from this, the variant would have to make adequate provision for a framework of stability and intellectual creativity; here too, the balancing problem looked insurmountable.

Despite these theoretical difficulties there was one major and irreversible innovation of enormous significance. At the 22nd Congress of the Soviet party (November–December 1961) Khrushchev abandoned the monolithic concept of power. The significance of the second de-Stalinization in the history of communist rule should not be underestimated. Indeed, it proved to be the sole attempt to effect a genuine change in the ideology and practice by which the system operated and the only one that was never reversed. This, the abandonment of monolithism, had far-reaching implications, not all of which came anywhere close to being realized in practice. Centrally, it made it possible for a ruling party to accept that conflicts of interests could and did exist in a communist polity, that these were not inherently hostile or pathological and that means would have to be found to articulate and resolve them.

In one way the entire history of communism in Eastern Europe after 1961 turned on how far, by what means and with what success the party could devise a political system that could articulate these conflicts. The party was effectively caught in a trap. If it allowed autonomous articulation of interests, with their own legitimacy and representation, it would erode its own political monopoly over time, as these areas of autonomy would undoubtedly expand and intensify. If, on the other hand, it blocked these conflicts, then the system would gradually seize up and decay. After the snuffing out of the Czechoslovak experiment the party had evidently opted for the latter course and would run the risk of stagnation and decay, though that was hardly clear at the time. In the 1960s, however, it looked as if the pattern of development was following the path of greater freedom of articulation.[2]

In so far as the party had a strategy, and this was much more implicit than explicit, its underlying thinking was that the ideology of Marxism-Leninism was sufficient to hold the party and system together, that with the disappearance of the bases of class antagonistic conflict, society was ready for a more open variant of socialism and, in any case, its monopoly of the instruments of coercion was more than enough to see off any serious challenges. What the party could not foresee was the collapse of Marxism-Leninism as a living body of ideas. But in the 1960s all the signals were pointing in the contrary direction.

This opened up remarkable though illusory vistas of a reform communism, capable of modernizing itself sufficiently to reach an equilibrium with the aspirations of society and thereby create a consensual basis for communism. The second de-Stalinization was, in fact, the last genuine, living attempt to redefine the communist agenda in a broadly consensual direction. It signified that Marxism-Leninism was a body of ideas, the categories of which could be used creatively for both policy-making and the strategy of socialist development, in

[2] Ghita Ionescu, *The Politics of the European Communist States* (1967).

which the classical ideals of equality, justice and plenty could be put into practice. It was a heady prospect and it gave the 1960s a hopeful quality that the area never enjoyed again under communist rule.[3]

It was probably these expectations that gave rise to the obscuring of an extremely important distinction in the political realm. The transformation of the system was entirely in the hands of the party, so that the changes were brought in from above. This meant that the distinction between 'reform', the improvement of the existing system, and 'democratization', the genuine redistribution of power, was never made clear. There were positive consequences to this. It was possible for reformers and democratizers – in the senses defined above – to establish a common front and to put pressure on the party in the name of 'rationalization', something that the party itself had to accept in terms of its own goal-rationality, as well as to campaign for wider sections of society to be given access to power.

This confusion characterized the Czechoslovak reform process virtually from the outset and would have had major consequences had the reform not been stopped short by the Soviet-led invasion. Thus the reform coalition could include technocrats interested in the removal of political criteria from their own areas of specialized knowledge as well as radical democrats, who wanted to see a wider popular participation. It should be understood, nevertheless, that all this was taking place in a 'socialist' framework – the content of socialism was in the process of being defined, hence the quotation marks – so that the question of introducing a multi-party system was never seriously placed on the agenda. Socialism, it seemed, was synonymous with a one-party system, which was perfectly logical given that the recognition of conflicts of interests was restricted to non-antagonistic (i.e. lacking class criteria) conflicts and that a multi-party system was regarded as characteristic of bourgeois politics, where class criteria operated. These, of course, had been ended by the socialist revolution.

This process of definition gave the 1960s their particular quality of appearing to be without constraints other than those already outlined. The Khrushchevian transformation of ideology had major consequences, however, for the structure of politics and the exercise of power. Evidently the party would retain its leading role, but the extent and meaning of this leading role were no longer something static and final, the automatic corollary of the ideology of perfection, but subject to debate and change. This meant that the Soviet-type systems would be much more difficult to run than before. Under perfection, there could be no discussion; now the party was engaged – very hesitantly,

---

[3] Pavel Tigrid, *Amère Révolution* (1977).

it is true – in real politics, opening itself to alternative ideas and critiques. Equally by abandoning monolithism the party took a step closer towards consensual rule, which raised the question of competing modes of legitimation. Under monolithism ideology was the sole instrument of legitimation; now the way was opened to other possibilities, especially to some form of popular legitimation.

The Khrushchevian turn recognized, in this sense, that ideology was not sufficient to establish consent and that each party would have to find its own particular mix of policies to assure this objective. It was assumed, of course, that all this movement could take place in a socialist framework and that the ideology would remain flexible enough to offer solutions for all situations. But without this major shift socialism would stagnate and popular energies would never be generated to make it work.

The Leading Role Redefined

The leading role of the party, then, was reformulated to allow for greater flexibility. The party would no longer be the sole actor in society, but would permit other bodies to acquire a degree of controlled autonomy – how far and in what way were of course contingent issues. Potentially the party could be separated from the state and its penetration of society would be diminished; eventually a range of institutions could operate, infused by the party's ideology, to express what was probably always conceived of as a rather narrow range of interests. Under this dispensation the role of the party would be simultaneously that of goal-setter and executor, of supreme initiator and arbiter between conflicting interests. Inevitably this would lead to confusion, all the more so because there were and could be no simple criteria for settling such disputes and equally because the arbitrary, totalizing political imperative of communist rule tended towards simplification, recentralization and unpredictability.

In the area of rule the role of the party would unquestionably become more complex, ideally to reflect the greater complexity that society was supposed to have reached by attaining socialism. In essence the party formally accepted that it no longer had the answer to everything, that there was no one single overarching rationality which provided the key to all problems, but in some fields, modes of thought were possible which were not subject to the political sphere. In theory this was simple enough, but in terms of governing it raised the question of where the limits now lay, what did properly belong to the political sphere – and therefore to the direct power of the party – and what should be determined by other criteria. This particular dilemma never was resolved, as a matter of fact. The boundaries of politics kept changing, depending on *ad hoc* circumstances, 'pragmatic' decisions (much praised in the West) and power relationships within the party, though this was not immediately evident.

The key contradiction faced by the party was to be found in the field of power and legitimation. The Soviet-type system was quintessentially a totalizing one, in which the political sphere sought to encompass all other spheres (economic, legal, aesthetic, etc.), hence a loss of legitimacy in any one sphere would have damaging consequences for political power. In other words, economic failure would have repercussions not just for the popularity of the leadership but for the legitimacy of the system itself. The party's room for manoeuvre, then, was limited. It wanted to open up the system while retaining full control over it, so that it sought greater openness but without the outcome of that openness – the customary dilemma of would be cake-havers and cake-eaters. The impossibility of resolving this without a radical shift in the distribution of power explained the party's nervousness towards debate and its readiness to interpret criticism as questioning the fundamentals of the system, for this inevitably raised the unanswerable question, by what right does the party rule? It was obliged, therefore, to maintain the full repressive apparatus of power while simultaneously attempting to make it function goal-rationally, all this while its own vision of 'socialism' was limited, fluid, uncertain and under competition from the alternative vision of the West. There was always the danger that, in defending socialism from its enemies, the party would reduce it to little more than its own power.[4]

Implications of the Redefinition

The strategy of moving towards partial consensuality had further consequences in the long term. Under Stalinism the nature of politics and power, in keeping with the homogenizing ideology, was simple and direct. The new strategy, however, looked consciously towards the greater complexity that had already existed before the communists seized power and was enhanced by the Stalinist industrializing revolution and the qualitative changes that were targeted in the 1960s.[5]

[4] Ferenc Fehér, Ágnes Heller, György Márkus, *Dictatorship over Needs* (1983), pp. 137ff.

[5] Radovan Richta chaired a commission on the scientific-technological revolution for the Central Committee of the Czechoslovak party. The findings of this commission were published as *Civilization at the Crossroads: Social and Human Implications of the Scientific and Technological Revolution* (1969).

The more complex society and economy that were emerging or re-emerging raised problems of their own. In the first place Stalinism, like any other closed system imposed and maintained by force, swept a range of issues under the carpet. Distortions, contradictions, bad decisions were ignored, but once the system was opened up to a degree of criticism, many of these problems were again exposed to view. Ironically, this made the strategy more difficult to sustain, because it was all too easy to argue that the reforms had caused the problems as distinct from allowing them to be perceived, and the opponents of reform did exactly that.[6]

Recognizing that the system was not static but dynamic, and that the political resources of the system were increasing through economic expansion and social change, brought another set of longer-term difficulties in its train. More resources gave the rulers better opportunities for co-opting certain social groups, but as this expansion progressed, society would look to greater access to power and its aspirations in the political realm would intensify. The party's strategy was overwhelmingly located in the economic sphere and it was most reluctant to cede more power than it thought necessary from time to time, sometimes less than that. This ultimately brought about a persistent conflict between rulers and ruled, not least because solutions that might have satisfied society in the 1960s would not do so a decade later as expectations rose and these proved to be as much political as economic.

Besides, greater complexity made running these systems – political, economic, social etc. – more difficult. Here the particular ethos of communism was unhelpful to the party. This ethos emphasized the finite completion of tasks as the end-product of policies, rather than seeing them as a parts of a process in which a myriad interactions were combined. This approach tended to mean that once a particular project was completed, no further maintenance or servicing would be required in the party's view, for these were non-productive sectors. Then the utopian legacy, with its insistence on a static, final concept of rule, undeniably worked against flexibility and adaptation, above all because there was always an alternative reference point encoded in the official ideology which ran counter to the new strategy.

It was also damaging in an even more insidious way. By making politics the private reserve of the party, skills in the exercise of power were never seriously developed, because they did not have to be. There were few internal political challenges, only external ones from society, and these were fairly easily met. In effect, communist politics were more to do with administration than political decision-making.

[6] Csaba Gombár, *Egy állampolgár gondolatai* (1984).

The true locus of power was hidden behind a complex web of bureau-cratic infighting, personal loyalties and specialized interests which were never tested against public criteria. This might not have mattered too much had the ruling ideology been sufficiently clear to give ad-equate guidance on day-to-day or year-to-year issues, though it is hard to conceive of any ideology being capable of this, but for Marxism-Leninism with its history of distortions, the simultaneous need to evolve a new variant of the ideology and to devise solutions to the new political challenges simply proved too much.

Finally, there was a longer-term challenge that the strategy of ex-panding economic and social benefits raised. The idea that the party would rule and society would consume was based on the dubious assumption that higher consumption would satisfy the population indefinitely. In the 1960s the wider choice in consumption was un-questionably well received, but this strategy set the party on a road from which it could never deviate without great cost. It had to compete with the West, which would always be the yardstick of comparison in consumption and, equally, it subtly undermined the socialist values of its ideology by stressing the individualism implicit in higher con-sumption and material goods. In this contest the party was bound to be the loser. The contest did not really materialize in the 1960s, of course, but strategy chosen at that time set the agenda for the future.

The pivot of the new system was the proposition that some means would have to be found for the articulation of conflicts of interest, but this still left an insoluble problem. Through what institutions were these conflicts to be expressed, how much control should the party have over them and by what criteria should it resolve them? If, say, a decision was taken that a country needed a chemicals plant rather than a new hospital, who would decide this and would it be possible to question this decision? Opportunities for the abuse of power, for distorting the ostensible rationality of economic planning by insisting on other political criteria, were endless and, crucially, the planning system failed to provide the kind of self-correcting mechanisms that are arrived at through the market, because the planning system was, like everything else, subject to the political sphere. The party theorists' answer to this dilemma was that the ideology of socialism, though no longer all-encompassing, was nevertheless so superior a guide to space and time that all such problems could easily be corrected.

Thus as long as the ideology remained intact, some kind of purposiveness and strategic direction could be sustained. Marxism–Leninism, however repressive it might have been, did lend socialism a coherence and offered the prospect of intellectual growth, even if only a minority actively supported it. The trouble was to come later, when the ideology was emptied of content. But in the early 1960s this was not a serious danger. In this way, the leading role of the party was to be retained in the name of an ideology that claimed to be superior to others, because it was the most rational and efficient and the party ruled as the possessor of this rationality. It would remain the sole political actor, retain its monopoly of setting the political agenda, establish future strategies and priorities and supervise the execution of policies.

All of this would take place on a partially inclusionary basis. Different groups of society would be given something of a role in the way in which power was exercised. They could not, of course, question monopoly power itself, but by being invited into this 'consultant' status, they could voice their views on improving the system – 'further perfecting' it, to use the entirely contradictory term that was a standard part of Marxist–Leninist-speak – and thereby express constructive criticism. The scope and range of debate were potentially greatly increased.

At the centre of the party's newly defined role, however, the problem of what to do with different interests that could now find expression raised a range of political questions to which only equivocal answers were given. What interest was the party supposed to represent? That of the whole of society, the societal interest, could be one answer, but how was it to be assessed on a day-to-day basis? How could priorities be determined between investment and consumption or employment and environment, for example? The formal goals of Marxism-Leninism – equality, social justice, plenty – had nothing to offer in this regard. Likewise, if the party abandoned monolithism, that would automatically mean that it accepted a degree of individual choice as legitimate. The epochal significance of this should not be underrated, for it was a major step in the direction of recognizing people as individuals rather than as objects of class interests and went some way towards restoring some power to society. But once again the questions arose. How far and in what ways could this individual choice be exercised, in the economy or in terms of social status? Would it lead to the introduction of 'rights', which imply the acceptance of an independent legal sphere and hence criteria outside the political control of the party? Did this signify some recognition of an active and autonomous citizenship? No intellectually coherent answers were forthcoming, only a kind of pragmatic response, to the effect that this choice would be largely restricted to consumption and social differentiation would be recognized.

Political Institutions

The shift also allowed for some tinkering with political institutions. Parliaments were given a slightly higher profile and attention was given to parliamentary procedure, in the hope that a little friendly criticism would make the government operate more effectively. Attempts were made to give elections at least the semblance of authenticity by encouraging a choice between candidates, though not, of course, between policies – everyone had to subscribe to the leading role. The press was encouraged to express some of the differentiation that was now recognized as being in existence and to uncover abuses of power, i.e. flaws in the working of the system, though whenever this criticism came too close to the fundamentals it was slapped down. There were also attempts to separate the party from the state. This was a perpetual difficulty. The party's role notionally was to formulate strategy and oversee the execution of policy, though without being involved in day-to-day implementation. In practice this distinction was extremely hard to maintain and whenever genuine power was involved the party, which was not a homogeneous body, would use whatever methods were to hand to ensure that no institution would gain meaningful access to power, thereby often usurping the functions of government.

Nor were matters any easier with respect to the representation of interests. While the existence of conflicts of interests was now accepted, how these were to find expression was not clarified. The party continued to believe that it could act as representative, agent, arbiter and aggregator. Some institutions, like the trade unions and other mass organizations, were indeed encouraged to play something of a role corresponding to their ostensible functions, but this was usually undermined by the *nomenklatura* system. In particular, no answer was ever found to the awkward problem of group interests. The representation and control of the individual interest was easy enough; the party represented the global social interest; but how were intermediate interests to be articulated? In a perfectly rational system this might not have mattered, but gradually it emerged that contradictions and conflicts did exist and that the party did not necessarily have the criteria for resolving them. Besides, these could not be expressed directly. If a particular interest group were to be allowed into the open and acquire a real relationship with its supporters, it would gradually have attained a legitimacy of its own, to be followed by demands for autonomy and an autonomous legitimacy, and it would be in a position to challenge the leading role, the party's monopoly of power. The solution was no solution. Group interests were recognized as a necessary evil with something like an *ad hoc* function, a solution that favoured covert politics and permitted certain favoured groups, like the heavy industry lobby, to distort the system to its advantage and build up a network of patronage and power.

The pretence that society was homogeneous was, naturally enough, given up, though here too what was to replace that absurd concept was less than clear. Under the classical Stalinist schema there were two classes – workers and peasants – and intellectuals constituted a separate stratum. This set of categories was manifestly quite incapable of explaining the realities of society as it had evolved under the impact of the Stalinist revolution on the East European pattern of develop-ment. The working class was far more complex than the simple, and simplistic, homogenizing definition suggested, and the peasantry was something other as well. But it took the abandonment of the Stalinist schema to bring this home and provide intellectual space for analysis of different forms of stratification.[7]

In the political realm, however, the move away from monolithism and the acceptance of differentiation made it feasible for the party to develop new modes of accommodation with different sections of society. This new dispensation remained in being until the end of communism, through it was reshaped in a variety of ways in the three decades or so that were left, thereby suggesting that it did indeed possess a degree of flexibility. In broad terms the party offered these different groups a kind of rough-and-ready unwritten social compact. These were not mutually enforceable, whether legally or politically, and their terms were at all times determined by the party defining its interests alone. Nevertheless, by the simple recognition that different social groups had different interests, the party tacitly accepted a degree of input into politics from below, something that had been wholly impossible under Stalinism.

Economic Reform

In concrete terms, the great undertaking of the 1960s was the economic reform projects launched in several of the East European states in the Soviet orbit – Poland and Romania were the exceptions – all of which tended to incorporate the words 'new' and 'economic' in their description. There were several reasons for this concentration on the economy. In the first place there was the practical reason already

[7] George Kolankiewicz, 'Changing Social Structure', in George Schöpflin (ed.), *The Soviet Union and Eastern Europe: a Handbook* (1986), pp. 497–505.

Table 6.1   *The growth of GNP as a percentage of annual growth*

	1951–1960	1961–1965	1966–1975
Bulgaria	10.9	6.6	8.2
Czechoslovakia	7.5	1.9	6.1
GDR	10.1	3.4	5.4
Hungary	5.8	4.1	6.6
Poland	7.6	6.2	7.8
Romania	10.4	9.2	9.4

Source: Tamás Bauer, 'The Second Economic Reform and Ownership Relations: Some Considerations for the Further Development of the New Economic Mechanism', *Eastern European Economics*, 22 no. 3–4 (Spring–Summer 1984), pp. 33–87.

signalled. The entire area was in a downward phase of an economic cycle and all these economies were showing falling growth rates (see table 6.1). This was a considerable shock after the quite unbelievably high rates of expansion in the 1950s. The high growth rates were widely adduced as living proof of the success of the system and had their place in systemic self-legitimation as well.

Second, the extensive resources used to fuel the Stalinist expansion – surplus labour from the countryside, as well as the investment inherited from the previous régime – were more or less exhausted. As a result, the economies experienced a contraction that took the communist leaderships by surprise, for they had had no experience of anything other than hell-for-leather growth. This development, however, had potentially serious consequences. It meant a slowing down of investment and would make it hard to keep promises of mounting consumption. And even more seriously, economic failure had far-reaching implications for communism as a system. A great deal of pride had been predicated on the success of the planned economy as the road to modernity and prosperity, something that was at least in part respected in the West too. In these circumstances the decline in growth rates was felt to be a comment on the viability of communism as such and it represented a possible opening for domestic critics of the system.

These factors constituted the practical and intellectual origins of the reform, but other factors were also involved. It was clear to the party from the outset, if not to the intellectual critics that the leaderships had to contend with, that economic reform would have political consequences and the party *apparat* had to make a delicate calculation. They had to find a way of relaunching the economy without incurring political costs. In the 1960s they were largely convinced that this equation could be made to balance. The emphasis was placed on improvements in the planning mechanism, giving enterprises greater latitude in taking their decisions without the planners' closest supervision, a reduction (or abolition) in the number of compulsory plan targets to simplify the planning process, and generally a somewhat more arms-length approach to the economic process.

This was partially accompanied by yet another attempt (the New Course saw the earliest) to switch from heavy industry towards consumer goods, from investment in machinery towards infrastructure and agriculture and, at the same time, to emphasize quality over quantity. This, if it had genuinely taken place, would have meant a major strategic shift in communist-type economics and would have helped substantially in keeping these economies open and competitive in global terms.

The limits of this process emerged sooner rather than later and were clear wherever the question of politics was brought to the agenda by the reforms themselves. The greater latitude in the economy automatically raised the issue of whether there would be any redistribution of power and, if so, how this would be structured. If enterprise managers were to have greater say over what the enterprise did, what would happen to the workers, who would protect their interests? Autonomous trade unions were unthinkable in what were still constituted as workers' states, so the party – by means of its *nomenklatura* control over the unions and managers – sought to do both, thereby hoping to prevent the economic reform from spilling over into the realm of political power. Thus it blocked the reforms from taking full effect. Even the Hungarian solution of giving unions the right to veto the collective contract,[8] a genuine attempt to square the circle and breathe life into interest representation, failed because the trade unions were too closely controlled by the party to act independently and actually to recognize that workers' rights should be overtly defended.

Elsewhere, as soon as the political implications of the reform sank in, projects were slowed down in economic as well as in political terms, as was the case in the GDR.[9] The audacious Bulgarian project, which emulated Czechoslovak and Hungarian schemes in abandoning compulsory plan targets, was never actually implemented, because of its implications for the power of the party and the erosion of the *nomenklatura* system.[10] These anti-reform attitudes, which were evi-

[8] William F. Robinson, *The Pattern of Reform in Hungary: a Political, Economic and Cultural Analysis* (1973).
[9] Details in Martin McCauley, *The German Democratic Republic since 1945* (1983), pp. 107–16.
[10] J. F. Brown, *Bulgaria under Communist Rule* (1970).

dent before 1968, were reinforced by the dismay with which the Czechoslovak experiment was viewed both by the anti-reformers themselves and equally by some reformers, who were concerned, rightly as it turned out, for their own reform projects. The rapid inroads into the doctrine of the leading role in Czechoslovakia became an object lesson on the dangers of economic reform becoming political and thereby unacceptable.

The New Relationship

There was much in the new relationship between rulers and ruled that was positive. In the context of everyday life the relaxation of terror perhaps took pride of place. The idea of a totally arbitrary power, able and willing to strike at anyone at any time may have its appeal for Jacobin revolutionaries, but it was utterly appalling for the rest of society, which wanted only to live with a degree of predictability and routine. The new dispensation accepted this, indeed over time made a virtue of it. At the heart of this was an acceptance by the party that a distinction existed between political crime and political error, some-thing that followed logically from the abandonment of monolithism. Equally, although the distinction was made, society was not accorded any autonomy. The party continued to arrogate to itself the right to intervene without any constraints. There was to be no independent legal sphere, free of political intervention by the ruler, but the ruler accepted that unbridled terror was no longer goal-rational in the light of the new modes of legitimation that the system had assumed.[11] In areas where political power was not directly touched, routinization could be introduced and a simulacrum of legality followed; this might apply when different parts of the system, like two enterprises, were in dispute. Problems arose only later, when it emerged that the party's insistence on its right to be both goal-setter and executor frequently conflicted and that, beyond a certain minimal level, it found itself both judge and jury in its own cause. In such situations political criteria tended to prevail and these were likely to be contingent on the current needs of power.

Likewise, it followed that while Marxism–Leninism retained an ideological monopoly, some areas of life could be freed of political criteria and determined by other rationalities. In concrete terms this meant that, for example, the natural sciences were now free to develop according to universal norms and the kind of nonsense that Lysenko introduced under Stalin's wing could be dropped. This was in many

[11] Ferenc Fehér, 'Kádárism as applied Khrushchevism', in R. F. Miller and Ferenc Fehér (eds), *Khrushchev and the Communist World* (1984), pp. 210–79.

ways a sophisticated move, for it allowed the party to draw on some of the more successful aspects of Western development, which it had previously denounced as 'pseudo-science' and to adopt them into Marxism–Leninism. 'Technology,' as it was once put to me, 'has no class content.'[12] The move, however, should be seen for what it was: a concession. In individual instances the party retained the right to intervene and impose its own version of rationality on the secular rationalities that it now by and large accepted. In the main this tended not to affect the natural sciences, unless they impinged on politics, which they sometimes did, as with the informational repercussions of cybernetics. For the most part, this withdrawal from certain areas allowed new energies to be mobilized, the technical intelligentsia to be attracted to the system and the foundations of scientific and technological revolution to be laid (or so it was hoped). On the other hand, matters were far more difficult with the social sciences and the arts, where the direct political implications of intellectual freedom were clearer and the potential for criticism of the party and its policies were unmistakable.

The shift away from monolithism also meant the end of the crude black-and-white view of the world that had been so rigidly enforced under Stalinism. Although the new ordering principle was far from having accepted the relativization of values and the full range of intermediate positions characteristic of the West, it was an enormous change at the level of theory in introducing the possibility of grey. It did genuinely mean the retraction of ideology and thus of immediate political power from certain areas of life. Crucially, it recognized that some ideas and activities could be neutral or at most open to politicization rather than being actually political. The significance of this was that neutrality was brought into the system, the individual did not have to adopt a political position on everything and, something of considerable relevance from the standpoint of the individual, compulsory participation in all manifestations of the system petered out. The militarization of society, the compulsory turn-outs at parades, the attempts to turn the family into a transmission-belt, the intense pressure at the workplace gradually fell into desuetude.[13]

The Party and the Individual

The new dispensation had considerable implications for the individual in other ways as well. Above all choice, having been banished under

---

[12] A Hungarian official in a private conversation in 1976.
[13] This transformation is vividly portrayed in the Polish film *Man of Marble*.

Stalin, now returned to the agenda of this newly defined socialism. For the time being the practical implications were restricted, for there was not that much from which choice could be made, but over time this changed. In the early stages, in the 1960s, choice was by and large confined to consumption, which carried with it the implication that different individuals would make different choices. This too was to have a longer-term significance that was only understood much later. In the first place it put these socialist systems on the same track as the West, in competition with it, with the consequences discussed above.

Second, it laid a new burden on the party, that of determining the range of choice, which once again raised the question of criteria. What was to be the balance between collective and individual consumption, between investment and consumption and so on? What was to happen to the problem of rising expectations? And how would the party deal with the day when there was no more to consume? There were no clear solutions to be derived from the official ideology. As far as the last of these questions was concerned, of course, the party would simply have denied that it was valid. After all, the new formula had been found and the socialist countries were embarked on a voyage of permanent plenty.

The third outcome of this was that it tended to emphasize a certain focus on the economy-centredness in these systems. This meant that, as the party kept politics firmly within its grasp, many issues tended to be articulated through the debate on the economy, which is feasible, but does ultimately distort both politics and economics, for there are certain essential political issues that can only be expressed through politics. Political power and how it is used are the most important of these.

Last, it was assumed that material consumption would be sufficient, that society would not generate any non-material aspirations, but would remain content with ever more enormous palaces and sumptuous apparel – bread and no real circuses. Perhaps this assumption was pardonable at the time it was made, not least because underneath it was another assumption, namely that socialism really was the most successful system in the world.

The acceptance of choice, however limited, also had implications for social stratification. It meant that the crude homogenization of the 1950s was slowly given up and differentiation was recognized, even if it was not overtly welcomed. Equality was still on the agenda, but it was no longer to be attained through the harsh levelling down employed during the Stalinist period. Indeed, whereas in the 1950s equality was conceived, as we have seen, in terms of the male manual worker using relatively low-level industrial technology, the road was open to a much more sophisticated conceptualization of equality, recognizing that different groups could make different inputs and still be equal. Thus differentiation of values, standards of living, attitudes, ways of life and incomes were all recognized as parts of socialist society and not necessarily disreputable relics of the past, but living realities that would remain in being for a long time to come.

The redefinition of the party's role and its future tasks had two further theoretical implications with important consequences. It admitted the possibility of error in a Soviet-type system and, equally, by diluting the criteria of legitimation away from absolute reliance on ideology, it brought the parties face-to-face with one of the most intractable issues of all – the management of the national identities of the people of whom they ruled.

As far as the admission of error was concerned, this followed logically from the abandonment of monolithism and allowed for an element of space, of pragmatic experimentation and an easing of the near-paranoid Stalinist attitude to human activity. It meant that as activities were no longer to be assessed by ideological criteria alone, there could be variations in opinion, the acceptance that some procedures were not purely 'law-governed' and thereby could have more than one outcome. This development at the theoretical level, then, was most significant in the medium term in permitting deviations from ideological stringency and ultimately in the corruption of the formal imperatives of the ideology. The gradual routinization of the system, the move towards individual initiatives, the possibility of leading a more normal, less regulated life could all be traced back to this outgrowth of the end of monolithism.

The Problem of Nationhood

If the question of error could be accommodated by the existing system with greater or lesser difficulty, the national identities of the peoples of the area posed a far greater problem. The core of the problem was this. In strictly theoretical terms Marxism, which insists that class is the ultimate determinant of all human activity, simply cannot be reconciled with nationalism, which argues that culture is the ultimate source. Despite the efforts of various Marxist writers, the Soviet-type systems had no real solution for what was, after all, a genuinely insoluble contradiction.

Stalin's answer was straightforward enough. Suppress national identities and substitute internationalism, which became a code for cultural Russification, rather as if the Soviet man was a Russian and

nothing else. With the Khrushchevian shift it was automatic that nationhood should return to the agenda. Here the parties had to be
extremely cautious. They may genuinely have believed that nationalism was a bourgeois device to mislead the proletariat and that sooner
rather than later the workers would realize that they really did have no
country, but for the moment – recognizing that the 1956 events in both
Poland and Hungary had been driven by nationalism – they would
have to deal with it circumspectly.

The new strategy, therefore, involved some recognition of national
identity, but as far as possible in areas where this did not matter
politically. Some concessions could be made, for example, in the way
in which history was presented and taught, but there could be no
question of giving free rein to nationhood. But the new dispensation
did create the possibility for the use or perhaps abuse of nationalism,
and several parties lived with this. In this sense reference to nationhood became a potential source of power in addition to Marxism–
Leninism and economic well-being, albeit a dangerous one. The more
a ruling Marxist–Leninist party, which derived some of its claim to
power from the proposition that it exercised power because it had
made a communist revolution, relied on nationhood, the more it
weakened its communist credentials. Beyond a certain threshold a
communist party could never be the authentic agent of the nation,
however hard the Romanian or the Slovak parties may have thought
otherwise.

In the 1960s this danger was remote. If anything, the contrary
appeared to be the case, and there was a widespread belief that
nationalism could be one of the instruments of democratization. This
was true only up to a point. Inasmuch as nationalism weakened the
centralized power of the party and undermined the loyalty and discipline based on Marxism–Leninism, it did point in the same direction as
democratization, but sooner or later these two diverged. Indeed, in
one sense there was a tacit, off-stage alliance between communists and
nationalists. The communists insisted that the process of nation-build-
ing was over and that existing nations could exist in an unchanged
(and, to be hoped, a diminishing) form. Ironically, this freezing of the
development of nationhood, as well as the centralization of power,
made it difficult for any challenge to nationhood to be mounted,
something which the nationalists regarded with favour. Thus national
unity and centralized power to some extent overlapped. It took
Nicolae Ceausescu to bring this to its logical conclusion in 1972, when
the Romanian Communist Party formally declared that it and it alone
was the fullest and most perfect embodiment of every aspiration of
Romanian nationhood.

Social Groups: Intellectuals and Intelligentsia

The deal offered the intellectuals was the most complex, understandably since they were the most sensitive and most needed social group from the party's viewpoint. What the party was looking for, the core of its strategy, was economic growth and political stability (this is more or less the aim of every régime in the second half of the twentieth century) and the energies of society, contributed on a consensual rather than coercive basis, had to be harnessed to attain this goal. In Soviet-type systems intellectuals were in any case endowed with a special role in legitimation. Communism was in many respects an intellectual and, obviously, an ideological construct and needed intellectuals to legitimate it. Under Stalinism this consisted of apologetics, but in the 1960s the party expected intellectuals to legitimate the system in real terms. This was still to take place through the medium of Soviet-type language, but a part of the legitimation was that positive criticism was welcome. The role of intellectuals in what was ultimately still an ideocratic system was inevitably crucial. They had to demonstrate that the system was effective, rational and offered the best future In the light of this, the party could no longer rely on coercing intellectuals, but had to create elements of consensus, through which the ideocratic legitimation would gain a degree of authenticity. It was awkward balancing act: too much autonomy and the intellectuals would go too far and delegitimate the system in the party's terms; too little and there would be no legitimation at all.

Here a further distinction became significant, the one between intellectuals and intelligentsia. To recapitulate, in broad terms, intellectuals can be defined as those who create values, generate new ideas by their critique of the present and construct alternative visions of the future. Members of the intelligentsia, on the other hand, administer those values, use their specialized knowledge and generally claim rather less of an autonomous role.

Evidently the latter pose far less of a political problem than the former. The intelligentsia could be integrated far more easily into a power system because their aspirations were more readily compatible with the new, more flexible aims of the party, and in one or two areas they overlapped. The efficient functioning of a system where political issues were secondary – the end of monolithism signalled precisely this depoliticization of certain areas – was without doubt an area where the technical intelligentsia could work together with the party, even if it maintained certain reservations about doing so.

Given that the party was the sole possible employer of the skills of the technical intelligentsia and, at the same time, that the party was prepared to retract its political criteria from certain areas of activity, there was sufficient space for the intelligentsia to take advantage of the situation. They would not have to ask themselves difficult questions about ultimate aims, the eschatology of communism, for the party had redefined the 'construction of socialism' in such broad terms that there was room enough for those with special skills to use these without subscribing fully to Marxism–Leninism, to work within the system for other motives, like patriotism. This process came to be known as the switch from 'red to expert'.

The arrangement was mutually beneficial. It allowed the intelligentsia to regain its status, to deploy its specialized knowledge without the sense of an all-pervasive political supervision that would distort the rationality of that knowledge and to engage its energies autonomously. It was irrelevant that that this autonomy was highly restricted and that, in the longer term, the technical intelligentsia would be compromised by its association with the party, most seriously in that it was gradually recognized that while a political switch had taken place in the direction of greater flexibility, whenever there was any serious question of trading off the rationality of power against that of technical knowledge, power would always win. In the early 1960s, in the aftermath of monolithism, this did not matter and what dominated was the feeling that the goals of the party and the intelligentsia coincided.

The party also gained. It was able to harness the skills of this group through a relatively low-cost manoeuvre – a bit of ideological redefinition, giving the intelligentsia access to the outer fringes of power and abandoning attempts at large-scale social engineering through constant upward and downward mobility. The status it guaranteed the intelligentsia was to prove hereditary and result in a blockage of social mobility. But the short-term gains were considerable. It allowed the party to promise higher growth and a steady improvement in the standard of living, which it could do in the belief that the skills of the intelligentsia offered this kind of guarantee. This indicated a continuing faith in the 'scientific' qualities of Marxism–Leninism, that growth, social change and the like were plannable and predictable, if only the party had access to the proper scientific instruments. The transformation also allowed the party access to a new form of stabilization and hope for a new type of legitimation, through economic well-being, which, it was hoped, would prove a valuable addition to ideological legitimation.

Furthermore, by giving the intelligentsia its new status, the Soviet-type systems of Eastern Europe could claim that they were committed to 'reform' and thereby gain support both from its own population and from the West. In this sense the intelligentsia was co-opted into the legitimating mechanisms of the power structure. Besides, the manoeuvre was useful in another respect. It helped to conceal the sleight of hand by which 'reform' was substituted for 'democratization'. Although communist propaganda used the words interchangeably, what was on offer was reform and not the introduction of democracy, entailing the redistribution of power. The task of the intelligentsia, put simply, was to make the system function at the everyday level, so that the party's claim to be the most rational and most effective ruler could be sustained.[14]

The Intellectuals and the Party

If the party's task with the intelligentsia was relatively straightforward and low-risk, the same could not be said of its relationship with intellectuals. The latter have a universal function of creating values and devising alternatives, as suggested above, but beyond that they had acquired a very special role in Eastern Europe. Intellectuals gained their modern role with the Enlightenment, when, for the first time, they could claim status through privileged access to rational, secular knowledge and thereby subject all phenomena to criticism, something that had previously been denied or hindered through the operation of religious or dynastic codes. In the West these intellectual claims came into conflict with the rival aspirations of the bourgeoisie, the state and, later on, the working class. Intellectuals had to make their voices heard in a relatively well-developed society, which was able to resist their all-encompassing claims.

This was not the case in the East, where both state and society were weaker, less complex and less able to resist intellectual pretensions, particularly after the encounter between intellectuals and nationalism. This proved to be an extraordinarily fruitful and useful relationship and through it intellectuals have effectively been endowed with a special status as the conscience of the nation, a surrogate opposition and shadow government, a social group with the right and duty to speak out on all matters and, as guardians of the language of public discourse, they could control much of the public agenda.[15] It should be understood, therefore, that intellectuals exercised a political function, not merely a cultural one.

---

[14] Thomas A. Baylis, *The Technical Intelligentsia and the East German Élite: Legitimacy and Social Change in Mature Communism* (1974).

[15] Zygmunt Bauman, 'Intellectuals in East-Central Europe: Continuity and Change', *Eastern European Politics and Societies,* 1 no. 2 (Spring 1987), pp. 162–86.

Crucially, the role of intellectuals in Eastern Europe was for all practical purposes legitimated in a near traditional fashion. They enjoyed a high status because they were perceived as representatives of an authentic national tradition and, in turn, they were in a position to legitimate ideas, strategies and policies. With the communist seizure of power this role was abruptly denied. Once in power, the new rulers had no need of external intellectual legitimation because their ideology already provided the answers to all questions. Indeed, the potential for trouble that intellectuals could cause led the party to clamp down on them very firmly. There was little for them to do other than sing hosannahs to Stalin and generally to act as a transmission-belt.

On the other hand, when monolithism was abandoned, the relationship between the party and the intellectuals changed. Now that there was a degree of political space – room for choice – within the system and the party was looking for consensuality, it recognized that it needed a measure of external legitimation. In the nature of the situation it was all but automatic for the party to try and enlist intellectuals. They still retained their high status and, at the same time, they were looking for a role in the system that went beyond apologetics and propaganda. This the party now offered them. The intellectuals could not, of course, enjoy full freedom to criticize, but within certain limits – always defined by the party – they were permitted some freedom to discuss the functioning of the system, though not its essentials. This ought to have ensured that the system would function more effectively and that new ideas, always subject to the leading role, could be debated, that the party would be able to use the energies of this social group without running any serious risk. Marxism–Leninism ruled, but was no longer the strait-jacket it had been in the 1950s.

All this was not entirely to the taste of all of the party membership and the middle levels of the *apparat*, which stood to lose power and influence as a result of the new arrangement. The bureaucratic interest was well entrenched and remained a dominant influence even on the most reform-minded party leaderships. Hence anti-reform currents could always find a political springboard from which to launch counter-offensives and could generally use adequate ideological camouflage as well. In this contest intellectuals and intelligentsia tended to have the better arguments, but the party *apparat* was politically more important to the leadership, with the long-term result that the intellectual argument was regularly ignored in favour of the dictates of power. The result, understandably, was that some intellectuals grew disenchanted and recognized that 'reform' was too hedged about with the politically determined nature of the system for their own rationalities to be fully implemented.

Still, in the 1960s this system worked reasonably, as its limits were being cautiously explored. It was understood that criticism was to take place within a broadly Marxist framework that could be expanded to encompass a much wider range of of ideas than before. As the decade progressed the limits were pushed outwards, but this still meant that a whole range of ideas and currents – existentialism, Roman Catholicism – were beyond the limit. On the whole the relationship worked, though there were numerous hitches, like examples of individuals who took the testing of the new limits to their logical conclusion and were rapped over the knuckles in consequence. As far as the party was concerned, the 'bases of Marxism–Leninism' could include anything it found inconvenient at that particular moment and this unpredictability and arbitrariness were eventually to undermine the relationship.

In retrospect, what is striking about the 1960s is that this was the last period when the conflict between intellectuals and party was relatively restrained, when the majority of intellectuals worked on the assumption that on balance, the trend of events was broadly towards greater openness, something that they desired both for themselves and for the wider population and that, in the fullness of time, somehow power would be redistributed and a new political order would be created. This assumption was very salient in Czechoslovakia, but it was also present in Hungary, where intellectuals were happy to make do with the new, wider limits offered by the Kádár régime. In the GDR and Romania the limits were significantly tighter – these were the only two countries where Solzhenitsyn's *Ivan Denisovitch,* a notable benchmark of freedom, was not published – but the general principle applied.[16] Still, even in Romania, intellectuals hoped Ceausescu's rule might bring greater tolerance.[17] Only in Poland were things different; here the period of openness had ended in 1959 and the 1960s were spent in a bleak and sterile confrontation under Gomulka's austere, anti-intellectual reign.

The Working Class

For the working class the reforms of the 1960s offered something different, yet equally welcome. Under the category 'constructing socialism' workers were offered a tacit deal. They were to enjoy a steady increase in the standard of living through both individual and

[16] Details in J. F. Brown, *The New Eastern Europe: the Khrushchev Era and After* (1966), p. 146.
[17] I remember myself that in 1966 *Le Monde* was, all too briefly, fairly freely available in Romania; I saw copies on sale in a back street in Cluj.

collective consumption; there would be various forms of welfare provision, like subsidized housing and cheap transport; the labour market would exist, thereby allowing workers a degree of choice over their places of work; and labour discipline would not be too tight; indeed, this was subsequently defined, informally, as the right 'not to work hard', together with near absolute job security. Against this, the party insisted absolutely on its sole right to involve itself in politics. All political initiatives, representation, participation, interest articulation were a part of the party's monopoly and would remain that way. This régime governing the relationship between the supposed workers' party and the actual workers was defined as the tacit social contract[18] and it did, in fact, provide a basis for stabilizing the systems for a while.

It did have its social bases as well. The bulk of the working class in Central and Eastern Europe – the Czech lands and East Germany were the exceptions – was the first generation. It had arrived in the urban areas during the massive recruitment of the Stalinist period and did so with deeply negative memories of rural deprivation. Their new urban existence, however barbarous when viewed by Western criteria, was seen by them as an improvement. For the first time in their lives these new workers were in receipt of a steady wage and understood that they would not go hungry in winter, that they would have enough light and shelter to survive, albeit in conditions of some brutalization. They attributed these benefits to the communist régimes and, therefore, were less inclined to question the uneven distribution of power.

This was enhanced by their political inexperience. Peasant attitudes towards politics were discussed in the first chapter and this was a reasonably accurate assessment of the new working class. They were physically in urban areas, but their values were those of the country-side – distrust of the state, ignorance, quiescence, no tradition of demanding rights, of acting as a citizen, of looking for interest representation, and preferring to find ways round regulations rather than seeing any benefit in them. When the party trumpeted forth its slogans about the rule of the proletariat, this was to an extent believed.

These ex-peasant masses were further traumatized by their new work experience and discipline, above all by their loss of control over their timetables and the semi-military requirements of mass production. Only in very special circumstances could they be aroused against the régime, usually when they were led by much longer-established workers or were mobilized by nationalism. Consequently, all the party

---

[18] Antonin Liehm, 'The New Social Contract and the Parallel Polity', in Jane Curry (ed.), *Dissent in Eastern Europe* (1983), pp. 173–81.

had to do to retain their loyalty was to provide them with tolerable living and working conditions and make vague promises of an ever better future. This arrangement worked quite successfully as long as there was enough to redistribute, which presupposed a growing economy, and second, until the new generation which took all these benefits for granted would come to maturity.[19]

The Peasantry

The deal made with the rural population was even more straightforward than that with the workers. Its basis was the completion of collectivization throughout the area except for Poland (and, of course, Yugoslavia) by 1961. This had a number of consequences for the political system. The peasantry and agriculture were now inside the political game and it became possible to argue in favour of agricultural investment without the risk of being howled down as a supporter of the reactionary peasantry. Collectivized peasants were politically and ideologically acceptable in a way that private peasants were not. Through this it became feasible to divert some resources and investment into agriculture and to neutralize the countryside politically. Given that many of the most active and politically most troublesome elements of the rural population had already left for the towns – the agricultural population was ageing steadily – this proved not to be especially difficult. Essentially, the peasantry was offered a relatively acceptable option, that of being left alone to produce, with a minimum of interference. The peasantry was hardly likely to disturb the power of the party anyway. This part of deal proved to be quite significant already in the 1960s, because it allowed party leaderships to make provision for the adequate food supplies that were to form part of the bargain they made with the urban workers. The proof of the viability of this party-peasantry deal could be observed in the Czechoslovak reform process of 1968, when there was not a single demand calling for decollectivization, implying that on the whole the peasantry was content with the situation.

Types of Reform

The following list includes a typology of party strategies, illustrating the various options chosen by the various parties at different times:

[19] Jan Triska and Charles Gati (eds), *Blue-Collar Workers in Eastern Europe* (1981); Walter Connor, *Socialism, Politics and Equality: Hierarchy and Change in Eastern Europe and the USSR* (1979).

- reform of the economic system, competition of interests, possibility of some structural change (Poland 1956–9, Hungary 1961–72, 1979–89)
- reform of the economic system only (GDR 1961–8)
- proposed reforms torpedoed (Bulgaria 1961–8, Romania 1968–71)
- no reform, reliance on central control and on nationalism (Romania 1961–8, 1971–89)
- complete restructuring of politics, radical shift towards democratization (Czechoslovakia 1963–8)
- no reform, no change (Poland 1959–70)
- restricted changes, consumerism, rigidity (Hungary 1972–9, Poland 1970–80, GDR 1968–89, Czechoslovakia 1969–89)
- a standoff between society and its rulers, a weakened party, growing role for state and military, erosion of totalizing legitimation (Poland 1981–9)

The Czechoslovak Reform Project

What happened in Czechoslovakia between 1963 and 1969 can be regarded as the copybook illustration of Khrushchevian reform and its implications. Czechoslovakia had emerged from the 1950s virtually untouched by the changes that shook Poland and Hungary – indeed, it was satisfied that its suppression of all reform tendencies in 1956 was the correct policy – with the result that de-Stalinization had yet to be launched and the *nomenklatura* system existed on well-established foundations, with the leadership reluctant to consider the kinds of reforms that were being contemplated elsewhere. The leader of the party, Antonín Novotny, had full control over the system and was in no sense a reformer. Yet by 1968 a coalition of forces had come together inside and to some extent outside the party, removed him and, somewhat to its surprise perhaps, begun the Prague Spring.[20]

The first moves in this process came from intellectuals dissatisfied with the new 'socialist' constitution adopted in 1960, entirely without consultation. This questioning, encouraged by the second de-Stalinization of 1961, spread gradually to other intellectual circles, including party intellectuals, and was then reflected back on the party itself, thereby causing a widening of the debate. It is important to note

[20] There is a mass of literature on Czechoslovakia in the 1960s, especially H. Gordon Skilling, *Czechoslovakia's Interrupted Revolution* (1976); Vladimir Kusin, *Political Grouping in the Czechoslovak Reform Movement* (1972); Galia Golan, *The Czechoslovak Reform Movement: Communism in Crisis 1962–1968* (1971) and her *Reform Rule in Czechoslovakia: the Dubcek Era 1968–1969* (1973).

here that the main reason why this questioning had a dislocating effect was that the majority of the party still believed that Marxism–Leninism was an authentic and living body of ideas, by means of which a better system could be created; had they not believed in Marxism, then arguments with a Marxian premise would have fallen on infertile ground. The radical party reformers, who came eventually to demand the complete democratization of Czechoslovak life, had their origins in this process.

They were joined by the creative intellectuals, who had a twofold agenda: they demanded the right to be able to express their views freely and they wanted their views to be taken into account in the formulation of policy. Crucially they targeted censorship as an unacceptable phenomenon in a socialist state. In this respect they were evidently playing the traditional role of surrogate opposition and the articulation of public opinion. The range of views made public was both deep and wide and perhaps it is worth singling out those of Karel Kosík, the Marxist philosopher, who demonstrated that all ideological thinking was in some respects 'false'.[21] This was significant, because it permitted the still Marxist thought-world of the Czech intellectuals to be renewed, in that they could now make a clear distinction between ideological apologetics and genuine creative thought. The way was open for demands for a genuine, humanistic Marxism and the establishment of an 'authentic Marxism'. In a society where the dominant mode of thinking was heavily Marxist, this was a major development.[22]

The party did not share these views, however, and much of the 1963–8 period was spent in a sterile and increasingly antagonistic relationship, which culminated in the Writers' Union Congress of 1967, where stirring calls for freedom were made public.[23] This contributed to preparing the ground for what followed in the coming year.

On their own, probably none of these initiatives would have been sufficient to shake the system, but there was a coincidence of several dislocating processes. The downturn in the Czechoslovak economy experienced in the early 1960s – there was a negative growth rate in 1962, the first time that this phenomenon affected a communist country – seriously shook the confidence of the leadership and constrained it to look hard at the need for economic reform. This gradually involved the reform economists and, once the reforms got off the ground

[21] Kosík is discussed by Vladimir Kusin, *The Intellectual Origins of the Prague Spring* (1971) and Peter Hruby, *Fools and Heroes: the Changing Role of Communist Intellectuals in Czechoslovakia* (1980).

[22] Jacques Rupnik, 'The Roots of Czech Stalinism', in Raphael Samuel and Gareth Stedman Jones (eds), *Culture, Ideology and Politics* (1982), pp. 302–19.

[23] Dusan Hamsik, *Writers against Rulers* (1971).

after 1967, the enterprise managers too, who discovered that the party, alarmed by the loss of power resulting from the new system, was sabotaging reform by whatever means were available. This mobilized the technocrats in favour of a more and more radical variant of the reform and led them to the realization that there were political impediments to economic rationality.

Third, there was the Slovak question. Novotny greatly disliked the striving for greater Slovak autonomy in the 1960s and missed few opportunities to make his distaste public. This lost Novotny the potential support of the Slovak conservatives, his natural allies. The Slovak leadership under Alexander Dubček permitted various expressions of a separate Slovak culture, for example, through the 150th anniversary of the death of the nineteenth-century patriot Ludovit Stúr, and thereby lined up the Slovaks behind the campaign against 'Prague centralism'. This did not, of course, mean that the Slovak establishment had become converted to democratization, but all this nibbling away at the party's power contributed to undermining the leadership's self-confidence. The fact that this was an *ad hoc* alliance and that the aims of the Prague reformers and the Slovaks diverged widely was irrelevant at the time, though it was significant later in that it allowed Prague to buy off the Slovaks after the invasion.[24]

Fourth, there was wider public opinion. For much of the 1960s Czech opinion was relatively quiescent. Despite the tightening of belts following on the economic downturn in the early 1960s, the bulk of the population was not dissatisfied materially and was not inclined to be mobilized in the defence of non-material issues. This did not begin to change until the student demonstrations in Strahov in November 1967 were dispersed with some brutality by the police, a move that shocked many people. This too contributed to the atmosphere of expectancy that gripped the country by late 1967.

But before any change could take place, one further piece of the scaffolding had to be removed – Soviet support. East European leaders could generally rely on Soviet backing until the last moment, often well beyond what was actually goal-rational in terms of the Kremlin's interests.[25] In December 1967 Brezhnev arrived in Prague and more or less formally retracted the CPSU's defensive shield over Notvotny, probably as a retaliation for the protests that Novotny had been unwise

---

[24] See Golan, *The Czechoslovak Reform Movement,* and Eugene Steiner, *The Slovak Dilemma* (1973).

[25] Brezhnev's continuing support for Gierek up to 1980, well after the latter's support and ideas on what to do had begun to ebb, was another case in point.

enough to make public at the manner of Khrushchev's removal three years before.

The reformers were at this point joined together in an extemporary coalition, but there was little on which they were actually united other than Novotny's removal. There were those who wanted to remove Novotny on personal grounds only; the party centrists, who wanted to retain the leading role of the party but in a more relaxed manner; the technocrats, who wanted party power withdrawn from the running of the economy; the Slovaks, who wanted to diminish Prague centralism in favour of Bratislava centralism; and the democratizing intellectuals, a minority who were looking to effect massive shifts in the distribution of power.

With some difficulty they agreed on Alexander Dubček as Novotny's successor, but there any kind of agreement ended. The result of this was that the next two and a half months were spent in an internal party conflict, one which was increasingly going public as censorship eroded and issues were debated in the press, until in April 1968 the party issued the Action Programme. This was a remarkable document in many ways, most notable for its ambiguity.[26] It promised a complete transformation of the system, but subjected it to the leading role of the party, so that everything would depend on what kind of a party would remain in power in Czechoslovakia. This was never definitively resolved, but one of the main reasons for the invasion was the Kremlin's concern that the Extraordinary 13th Congress of the CPCS, scheduled for late August 1968, would elect a Central Committee utterly committed to a democratizing transformation, as a result of which it would no longer have been the kind of party that the Soviet Union would have wished to entrust with a leading role.

The system envisaged by the Prague Spring was, in fact, ambiguous and contradictory where its underlying principles were concerned. The institutional framework was essentially that of one-party pluralism, a curious hybrid that enjoyed an ephemeral revival under the rubric of 'constitutional communism' in the late 1980s.[27] There was to have been a full set of interest representation bodies, an autonomous government and judiciary and a free press, but no multi-party system. Elections would be held regularly, but all candidates would have endorsed the communist party. This was the central underlying prob-

---

[26] A full text of the Action Programme is to be found in Robin Alison Remington (ed.), *Winter in Prague* (1969), pp. 88–136.

[27] My own views are set out in George Schöpflin 'Reform in Eastern Europe', *Slovo*, 1 no. 1 (1988) pp. 1–5.

lem. Dubček had spoken of the communists having 'to earn their leading role', implying that the party would justify its monopoly in terms of consent. Very likely, there was a genuine and sincere assumption on the part of the radical reformers that 1948 had represented a final and irreversible commitment to socialism on the part of Czechoslovak opinion, so that the question of any ideology other than communism would never return to the agenda.

This was naïve. It simply the ducked the issue of what would happen if and when the party was perceived as having failed to earn its leading role. The assumption that the institutionalization of conflicts of interest would not produce the customary contest for resources and lead to competitive politics was ultimately untenable. Social autonomy, institutions with their own source of legitimacy, initiatives from below, 'uncontrolled' access to power, the entry of new political actors – these were all quite unacceptable from anything resembling the classical Leninist definition of communism. There was every likelihood that the inherent instability of one-party pluralism – at the moment when the question of consent returned to the agenda – would have resulted in either a return to coercion or an acceptance of multi-party politics. This was not a chance that Brezhnev was willing to take, hence the invasion.[28]

[28] This presumably was what Brezhnev meant in the exchange reported by Zdenek Mlynár when he insisted that Dubček 'did not understand'; see *Nightfrost in Prague: the End of Humane Socialism* (1980), especially pp. 240–1.

7

The 1970s: The Onset of Decay

> *But man, proud man,*
> *Dress'd in a little brief authority,*
> *Most ignorant of what he's most assured*
>
> Shakespeare's *Measure for Measure,*
> *II. ii. 117–19.*

The Soviet-led invasion of Czechoslovakia sent an unmistakable signal throughout the Soviet bloc. The limits of how far a party could go in rearranging its political system were much more tightly circumscribed had been thought. Whereas in the 1960s under Khrushchevism, as argued in the previous chapter, these limits were vague and concerned foreign policy issues like the alliance with the Soviet Union, the Brezhnev doctrine introduced new categories like 'creeping counter-revolution' and the insistence that the Kremlin had the right to 'defend the gains of socialism' whenever these were threatened in any communist country. The Soviet leadership would, of course, retain control over the definition of what constituted a threat.

Since no one wanted to be invaded by the Red Army, the leaderships drew in their horns and were obliged to listen more closely to their anti-reform lobbies, which was what many of them probably wanted anyway. These anti-reformers existed throughout the area and spoke for the *status quo*, the sections of the system that benefited from no change, like the increasingly dubious heavy industries of the past (steel, textiles), as well as those whose power would be limited by any further expansion of other rationalities, like economic criteria of supply and demand. The newly defined limits were a perfect justification for those who were satisfied with the situation as it was and allowed them to deflect demands for change by an argument somewhat more sophisticated than a blank *nyet*: 'well, we would love to introduce reform, but the Soviet Union would not like it.'

Once again, the definition of 'reform' became relevant, since the rhetoric, as distinct from the practice, of reform remained the stuff of communist politics in the 1970s, with the exception of Czechoslovakia, where the word itself was banned from public mention. Elsewhere leaders continued to talk about 'reform', in the belief that even simulated change[1] was better than no change in the eyes of those they wanted to impress – the West and sections of their own opinion. 'Reform' in the sense of redistributing power was, of course, off the agenda, but 'reform', meaning improvements to the existing system, could still be reconciled with the new Kremlin-generated limits.

Reform in this limited sense was the prospect for the 1970s and most leaderships embraced it at this verbal level. There was one major difficulty with this situation. The new limits, placing the party's political monopoly in the inner sanctum of politics, left society with no effective role in the system, except as passive objects of policy. As time moved on the popular desire for greater control over political decisions increased and the system was more and more out of touch with society's aspirations. Initially this did not matter and was, indeed, dismissed by a still self-confident party as a marginal issue. But gradually this exclusion of public opinion from politics reacted back on the self-legitimation of the leadership and impelled them to hand-to-mouth thinking, reducing their room for manoeuvre and political imagination. The December 1970 events in Poland ought to have been a warning that there were indeed limits to party power.

All this had other implications for the stability of the system. For all practical purposes, though this was hardly evident at the time, the system was moving into a crisis, in which the inability of existing institutions to fulfil their ostensible functions and provide an appropriate framework for the exercise of power was raising question marks over systemic viability. It should be added that this was an accelerating trend, in that societies do not stand still even if the institutional structure is obliged to.

A shrinking of the political horizon resulted in a restricted field for economic initiatives, which mattered because so much of the legitimacy of the system came to rest on economics, inevitably so once all means of political legitimation were excluded. The crux of the argument here is that, as society and technology became more complex, directives were not enough and the proper running of the economy

---

[1] The term, as previously noted, is Michael Shafir's, *Romania: Politics, Economics and Society* (1985).

needed the active participation of the population, in other words, their consent to being ruled in a particular way. This was not and could not be forthcoming except conditionally. Furthermore, as will be argued below, this narrowing of the limits freed the space within which an opposition movement, which wholly rejected the assumptions of the system, could establish a precarious existence.

The Decomposition of Ideology

What undoubtedly turned out to be the most momentous conse-quence of the Czechoslovak débâcle was that it undermined the ef-fectiveness of Marxism–Leninism as an ideology.[2] Whereas until 1968 it had been perfectly possible for individuals with a commitment to change to draw their ideas from the Marxist tradition, the Soviet in-vasion ended this. Apart from anything else, the Kremlin's decision to invade represented an insistence that Soviet Union intended to main-tain its monopoly over the limits of theory as well as practice and that these would be determined solely by Soviet criteria. Indeed, what had certainly troubled and alarmed the Soviet establishment was that the Prague reformers were introducing their radical ideas in the name of Marxism. It went down especially badly when, somewhat tactlessly perhaps, the Czech intellectuals patiently explained to their Soviet counterparts that they were 'rescuing' Marxism from the 'Asiatic de-formations' to which the Russian historical experience had subjected it, because the Czechs – by implication – were more European than the Russians. It made the latter see red, to coin a phrase.

These new limitations on the development of Marxist theory per-suaded many people that the whole thing was a sham, just a set of formulae, ritual incantations used with the aim of veiling the true nature of the system. This process, the decomposition of Marxism as a living body of ideas, had far-reaching implications for the system as a whole. In effect, it left the communist system of rule rudderless. De-cisions were still taken, of course, but they lacked an overall purposiveness, something which might have been beneficial in terms of pragmatism,[3] but was destructive in a system that still claimed overtly to be non-pragmatic. Attempting to adjust to a teleology that

[2] Leszek Kolakowski, 'Theses on Hope and Hopelessness', *Survey*, 17 no. 3 (80), (Summer 1971), pp. 37–52, and his 'Ideology in Eastern Europe', in Milorad Drachkovitch (ed.), *East Central Europe: Yesterday≈Today≈Tomorrow* (1982), pp. 4—54.

[3] Milan Simecka, *The Restoration of Order: the Normalization of Czechoslovakia* (1984), especially pp. 119ff.

fewer and fewer people accepted as real created a gap between the formal and substantive that reacted back onto a whole range of activities, both theoretical and concrete, including legitimation and economic planning.

The new order was thus affected by a very difficult contradiction – it claimed totalizing power in the name of a totalizing ideology which fewer and fewer people took seriously. Inevitably, over time, this stripped the nature of legitimation down to power alone and, once this happened, the ideological veil could be relatively easily pierced. This did not mean, of course, that those in power had no belief in any long-term objective – it is probably impossible to sustain any political system that attempts to subsist exclusively on power – but these aims were only tangentially related to Marxism–Leninism. They were guided by ideas of stability, prosperity, a vague perhaps sentimental ouvrierism (more honoured in the breach than in the observance)[4] and above all by the élite's insistence on its monopoly of power. Here too there was a gap, a space in which ideas and actions not sanctioned by the rulers could be launched.

This raises the question of why these parties maintained the official ideology at all, why did they not simply abandon it and construct something new, something maybe still drawing on the socialist tradition, but no longer encumbered by the dead weight of Marxism–Leninism. The difficulty with this course of action was that it would have led directly into the Czechoslovak cul-de-sac and would have been squelched by the Soviet Union. But even if the Kremlin had given the East European parties enough latitude for them to have pursued this course, it would still have been political suicide to embark on it. The problem was this. These parties claimed monopoly power on a variety of grounds, but one of them was that they ruled now because at some point in the past they had made a successful Marxist revolution. The moment Marxism is abandoned, this revolutionary legitimation falls, leaving the parties seriously exposed to challengers claiming power on other grounds.

The parties were effectively caught in a trap of origins. They claimed to rule in the name of the Marxist revolution by which they had initially seized power and this was neither negotiable nor convertible to any other kind of power, one legitimated by elections, for example. Nor could it be bargained in any way, for any attempt to argue that the initial revolutionary impulse was no longer valid would immediately question the entire basis of the régime.

---

[4] Attempts to legitimate the system in Hungary frequently resorted to manipulative rumour. In the 1970s one of the stories thus circulated had it that Kádár was in the habit of declaring, 'If I were a worker, I wouldn't want to belong to Kádár's party.'

It was this imperative that precluded Tito from abandoning the communist nature of the Yugoslav system after the break with Stalin in 1948. The Yugoslav communists were in power because they had made a communist revolution, which, as far as they were concerned, was irreversible. Any deviation from this would have laid them open to challenges from other political forces. Consequently Tito had no alternative but to embark on his epochal challenge to Stalin and to insist that the Soviet Union did not, after all, have a monopoly over the communist future. This rule of reference to revolutionary origins remained in effect throughout the four decades of communism and it was noteworthy that in Hungary the breakthrough towards collapse came in February 1989, when the party admitted that the events of 1956 were no longer to be considered as having been a counter-revolution but a popular uprising.

Finally, the trap of origins had a further outcome that came into play once ideological legitimation declined through decomposition. The rulers of Soviet-type countries found themselves with what was a false identity. They claimed to rule in the name of the proletariat and insisted that the working class was in power, when in reality the system was one of bureaucratic oligarchy. The tension between the two would arise when the working class in the genuine sense demanded representation or sought to gain access to power. In these moments the élite was left without an answer, not just in the eyes of those demanding changes, but just as significantly in their own. This decline in self-legitimation was one of the most serious consequences of ideological decay and was, of course, crucial to what happened in Poland in 1980.[5]

This explained the rigid adherence to Marxism–Leninism and the corresponding meta-language as the sole medium of public discourse and communication. Yet at the same time, this meta-language was also a cage. In the 1970s the ruling parties had no option but to persist with a language of public discourse that had only ritualistic significance. This might not have mattered if it had to be used only for liturgical purposes; unfortunately for the party, public business had to be conducted in it, whatever the difficulties and awkwardnesses in communication. The outcome of this was the unreal and ambiguous quality of public pronouncements in the communist world, in which there was only one certainty – the power of the party. As long as public discourse was expressed in the meta-language, the security of the régime was not in doubt, but because the meta–language was inflexible and an

---

[5] The concept of 'false identity' was used in this sense by Manès Sperber, cited in 'Die legitime moralische Grenze in der Politik: ein Gespräch mit Milovan Djilas', *Kontinent,* 11 no. 3 (no. 34), (July–August–September 1985), pp. 42–51.

obstacle to effective communication, it hampered the party in its quest for the best policy. In this respect, the continued use of the Marxist–Leninist façade contributed to undermining the goal-rationality of the system, the very rationality on which the party was now seeking to base some of its legitimacy.

In another sense this façade was a kind of security blanket, a reassurance for the régime, the supporters of which understood that the maintenance of the system depended on the strict observance of the ritual. There was a vivid illustration of what happened when the language was breached in Poland in the summer of 1980, when the Gierek régime came increasingly under pressure from the wave of strikes in July–August. In Soviet-type systems there could be no strikes. Strikes could only exist in class-antagonistic societies, i.e. capitalism. At worst, there might be 'unauthorized stoppages of labour', so that when the Polish media began to refer to 'strikes', as they did from mid-August onwards, everyone could understand that the régime was faced with a grave crisis. From the standpoint of society the obligatory use of Marxist–Leninist-speak was a perpetual reminder that the system remained well entrenched and could not be overthrown. In an ideocratic system, the rulers had to maintain the appearance of unanimity; anything less would have been a signal of something amiss. As Kolakowski put it, 'Admitting a weakness makes it worse. Obvious lies uttered aloud with impunity are excellent proofs of the health of the system.'[6] Václav Havel's example of the greengrocer, who displays a notice proclaiming 'Workers of the World Unite!' in order to signal that he is not challenging the régime, also illustrates this clearly.[7]

In addition, keeping the Marxist–Leninist shell in being served other purposes. It served as an instrument of censorship in the sense that it kept out alternatives. What was especially poignant in this regard was that it could fulfil this function precisely because Marxism as a living body of ideas had collapsed, and the language of the ideology had decomposed into a set of empty, ritualistic formulae. Had Marxism still been alive then real debates could have taken place, as they did in the 1960s, with the consequences demonstrated in Czechoslovakia. But even in Hungary, which strove hard to maintain an appearance of a reforming spirit, and where there was no question of any threat to the party's political monopoly, there was an ideological danger and this

---

[6] The quotation is from the Hoover Institution volume, see note 2, on p. 49.
[7] Václav Havel, 'The Power of the Powerless' in John Keane (ed.), *The Power of the Powerless: Citizens against the State in Central-Eastern Europe* (1985), pp. 23–96.

had to be eliminated by fiat – there was to be no meaningful discussion of Marxism as a source of alternative, unsanctioned ideas.[8]

When a meaningless meta-language is the obligatory language of public discourse, as Marxist–Leninist-speak became in the 1970s, it was next to impossible to formulate alternatives and thereby to challenge the party's view of the future in public. Hence the decomposition of Marxism–Leninism weakened the system in another way. It made it vulnerable to competition in the area where the party could least afford to tolerate rivalry – its claim to be a transcendental system. Once the party was forced accept that it was one possible philosophy among others and that Marxism–Leninism could be relativized, it was immediately open to claims and counter-claims from elsewhere.

In practice the programme of human rights, which the party unwittingly introduced into the area by signing the Helsinki Final Act, functioned in this way. For all practical purposes, human rights became a kind of logic bomb, for which the party had no remedy, because it insisted that certain activities had to be assessed by criteria outside the party's control.

Overall, however, while the insistence on the meta-language had its disadvantages for the rulers in terms of precluding change or even adjustment to changing realities, they had no alternative but to continue using it. Even as legitimation by ideology declined, other instruments were employed, of which economic legitimation looked the most promising, at least in the short term.

If legitimation by reference to utopia was largely discarded, what did the parties now use as their eschatology? Rather than claiming perfection, they argued that they had the right to rule because they were the most rational and most effective bodies in society. The claim to the monopoly of rationality had its roots in Marxism, the Enlightenment and ultimately in the entire set of Platonic currents of European thought. This implied that the party was above politics, that it was superior to popular control and, while no longer perfect exactly, it was still the embodiment of progress, while by implication society was, if not reactionary, certainly too backward to be entrusted with power. This was the essence of technocratic legitimation, the proposition that wise men possessed of special knowledge should rule over the ignorant masses. By the same token, effectiveness implied that the

[8] See György Márkus, 'Debates and Trends in Marxist Philosophy,' in Frantisek Silnitsky et al. (eds.), *Communism and Eastern Europe* (1979), pp. 104–32. This article, originally published in *Kortárs* in 1968, left the official spokesmen for the ideology paralysed. Their response was to ban further discussions of the kind that Márkus called for and in 1973 he and several others were effectively expelled from public life.

communist system of organization, administration and implementation was the best possible in the world and, in any case, would certainly produce a state of affairs that would demonstrably be welcome to the population.

The proposition in this connection followed directly from the introduction of economic legitimation before the invasion of Czechoslovakia, the party claiming a political monopoly for itself in exchange for securing the population a satisfactory and improving standard of living. As it turned out, this raised serious problems for the nature of communist rule, which could never be resolved and were ultimately to help in undermining the system. As Ernest Gellner has observed, it made the party's promises testable in this world rather than in the next, a situation that no transcendental legitimation could really afford for obvious reasons.[9]

Economic Legitimation

In effect, this shift to economic legitimation, a subset of the proposition that the party ruled because it was the most rational and most effective force in society, presented society with a potential counter-claim. If there was no economic improvement, if society could satisfy itself that there was an infringement of its consumption levels, it could take the initiative and indicate this to the party. This was a very dangerous weapon to place in the hands of society on the part of a body that claimed to rule by untestable criteria, all the more so in a system that also made reference to ruling in the name of the proletariat. A challenge of this nature appeared on the scene with the Polish events of December 1970 and what happened in Poland was to some extent indirectly applicable throughout the region.

This state of affairs left the system increasingly exposed to two sets of pressures. On the one hand, the communist economies would have to perform more than adequately to be able to sustain the rise in individual and collective consumption that the population now demanded; on the other, this would notionally require a workforce prepared to improve its productivity and participate in the system in a consensual fashion. As long as the party insisted on political monopoly, consensual rule was out of the question and, as argued above, the party was neither able nor willing to modify political monopoly.

Besides, basing one's political legitimacy on economic factors was a perilous course in another respect – it left the party dependent on

[9] Ernest Gellner, 'Islam and Marxism: some Comparisons', *International Affairs*, 67 no. 1 (January 1991), pp. 1–6.

processes it could not control. Much as it may have proclaimed the centrally planned economy to be the most rational and effective, reality lay elsewhere and the party understood this. This explained the so-called 'Western strategy' to which the communist states now turned, the opening of their economies to the West and soliciting large-scale Western investment as a means of modernizing their management and technology. Regardless of the historical irony of looking to capitalism to save communism, the difficulty with this strategy was that Soviet-type systems were now exposed to the vagaries of the global market to a serious extent, and when the West went into recession after the first oil shock of 1973 there was no easy remedy.

Nor was the reception of Western technology and investment as successful as it was originally assumed it would be. The tacit assumption had been that the transplantation of Western methods and equipment would produce much the same results as they had in the West, high levels of efficiency in other words. This reckoned without the cultural context within which technology operates, both educational and political. In Eastern Europe the culture of technology was much lower and the politico-economic system was similarly not designed to make the best use of such technology transfers. Indeed, in one sense new, more efficient ways of production were directly or indirectly threatening established interests, just as they were in the West, because they represented a different distribution of power. In the West, anti-innovative resistance of this kind could usually be broken down through the market or a combination of economic and political pressure, the latter being supported on a renewably consensual foundation, something which was not available to Soviet-type systems. Consequently the spread of technology was slower and it did not produce the high output expected of it.

Possibly the most crucial economic, as distinct from political, impediment to a more rational use of resources was to be found in the original sin of Soviet-type systems the initial strategy of overemphasis on heavy industry. Large-scale industry, requiring large-scale investment, was in a very real sense what communist economic strategy was about. This produced a clear and near immovable vested interest in the survival of these industries and the planning and investment structures that sustained them, a phenomenon accentuated when the heavy industry lobby could justify its constant demand for more investment by reference to military needs or exports to the Soviet Union.[10]

This heavy industrial lobby, which was influential throughout the

---

[10] Ota Sik, *The Bureaucratic Economy* (1972); Tibor Vámos, 'Iparpolitika és gazdaság: eredmények, gondok, távlatok', *Valóság*, 28 no. 6 (June 1985), pp. 28–38.

system as a key element of the communist establishment, successfully diverted sizeable funds from the Western investment credits that were entering these states in the 1970s. In effect, these countries underwent a second heavy industrialization, with emphasis on heavy chemicals as well as on the more traditional metallurgy, construction and energy generation. Some of it, a proportionately small but psychologically important part, was diverted into conspicuous consumption by the élite. The heavy industry lobby was determined to preserve its privileged position and it was in the interests of the party that it should do so, seeing that the two were extensively interdependent through various networks of power and patronage, and thanks to the support that the party understood it would receive from an economically unviable sector that would not survive in a system genuinely driven by supply and demand.

Similarly, the dysfunctions of the planning system now had much more direct political results than before. As long as the ideological legitimation was authentic and the role of economic legitimation was less salient, the poor record of the communist economic system – planning errors, large inventories, poor quality, low productivity and the non-satisfaction of consumer demand – was not overwhelmingly important. But now that the system relied on economic pacification to a much greater extent, these dysfunctions began to impact directly on the political system. The central problem was as before. The one-sided distribution of power and the ability of the élite to legitimate it in line with their own interests made projects for the rationalization of the economy unrealizable, just as they had, at the end of the day, in the 1960s. This double jeopardy of the system had far-reaching implications for the political stability of communism and eventually it was to contribute to to undermining it.

The story of the 1970s, then, was that the equation that traded off welfarism against depoliticization was beginning to come apart and it was unclear how and with what results this would take place. The party, for its part, recognized that any significant input from below would be fatal for the system and sought means of incorporating different sections of society by different means. The instruments established for the intelligentsia and intellectuals in the 1960s on the whole did not vary greatly. However, as far as the workers were concerned, in addition to welfarism, there was something of a campaign in the 1970s to recruit them into the party through a policy that came to be known as 'proletarization'. The thinking behind this was that the greater the number of workers in the party the more quiescent they would be, and quiescence was devoutly to be wished for after the December 1970 events in Poland had actually resulted in the ousting of the party leader, Wladyslaw Gomulka.

The success of proletarization was very partial. It may have kept some workers from doing anything very serious, but it is hard to imagine that party membership offered them any meaningful political satisfaction after the early stages. Only in Czechoslovakia was the situation different. Here the purge of approximately 500,000 supporters of the Prague Spring offered the Husák leadership a unique opportunity to exercise patronage, which it did to promote a new generation of working-class activists into the élite to fill the places of those who had been sacked. By and large, there were occasional strikes and stoppages in various places, but these very seldom spilled over into anything political, because the party understood that it would have to take urgent measures to prevent this.

The usual course of events was for workers in a particular workshop to nurse their grievance until one day they would down tools and demand remedies, which tended to include more money. The management in consultation with the local party secretary would offer them money in partial settlement and that would be the end of the matter. However, if this was not done for some reason, then tempers were readily frayed and the demands could quickly become political. The system was by and large quite successful in developing methods to take the sting out of potential or actual worker unrest. The instances that did spill over into something more substantial were cases of failure of crisis management, like the Polish strikes of 1976 or the Jiu Valley miners' strike of 1977.

The mechanisms of depoliticization were not unsuccessful. They established a kind of social quiescence and ensured that the power of the élite was not threatened by potential upsurges from below. The Polish case, where the Gierek régime was eventually swept away by such an upsurge, was the exception and was explained by factors peculiar to Poland (discussed below).

Legitimation by Nationhood

The legitimation problem was also tackled by continuing with the use of nationalism begun in the previous decade. There was no qualitative difference in the strategies developed before the invasion of Czechoslovakia, except for the factor already mentioned, that the decay of the effectiveness of Marxism–Leninism ineluctably raised the level and significance of nationhood, with all the attendant problems discussed in the previous chapter. Only in Romania did the use of nationalism as a source of power acquire new dimensions, for when Ceausescu

launched his renewed mobilization campaign in 1971, he also redefined the nature of nationhood under communism and tried to eliminate the contradiction between the two by arguing that it was under
the leadership of the Romanian communist party that the Romanian
nation finally reached its apotheosis, because communism resolved
the class antagonisms that had previously divided the nation.[11]

Elsewhere various concessions were made by the party to national
identity, for example, the use of symbols, the rewriting of history with
greater emphasis on national rather than class heroes and, where
relevant, an emphasis on national exclusiveness. So, for example,
among the first moves by Gierek's government were the replacement
of the portrait of the leader that hung obligatorily in every office by the
Polish eagle, and the decision to restore the Royal Palace in Warsaw,
a potent symbol of Polish statehood. Symptomatic of the more nation-
ally flavoured history was the gradual re-evaluation of the German past
under Honecker, so that Frederick the Great, previously condemned
as a proto-Nazi, gradually became an exemplar to the workers' and
peasants' state. Both Bulgaria and Romania began to place their ethno-
national minorities – Turks and Hungarians respectively – under severe pressure to denationalize themselves; the Bulgarians went to so
far as to insist that Turks adopt Slavic names and applied this even to
cemeteries.

This strategy intensified in the 1980s, as the economic option declined in effectiveness, and it was probably not quite as damaging in
the 1970s, but its longer-term contribution to the decay of the ideology
and the system was unavoidable, because it raised deep-level questions about the essential consistency of communist rule.

Social Decay

Decay in the ideology spread slowly, stealthily into other areas of
governance, something that was all the more significant in a system
that sought to be all-pervasive. In a very clear way the 1970s saw the
beginnings of the process that illustrated the underlying weakness of
political systems that sought to base their authority, purposiveness and
even deontology on a single teleology expressed in a compulsory
ideology. Once the ideology loses its power to compel, the remaining
parts of the thought-system and the power system begin to unravel
and affect every aspect of life. The concentration of all aspects of rule

[11] I have discussed this in George Schöpflin, 'The Ideology of Rumanian
Nationalism', *Survey*, 20 no. 2–3 (1974) pp. 77–104.

into the political sphere, which had seemed an advantage when the ideology still held firm, in as much as it made it simpler to concentrate the energies needed for the great Stalinist experiment, was now proving to be a grave drawback. Decay, then, became a feature of various facets of the Soviet-type system and the resultant gaps eventually made it possible for alternatives to be articulated.

Atomization

Social decay was manifested in two broad areas – atomization and the end of social mobility. Atomization was an instrument of party policy. In essence, the party had an interest in preventing society from coming together in any shape or form, for any development along these lines would potentially threaten the monopoly of power. To this end fairly high levels of coercion – force and the threat of force – were deployed to prevent social cohesion, unless it was taking place under the supervision of the party or the state. But matters went beyond this, in that the Stalinist transformation had very largely destroyed the unwritten rules by which social cohesion is maintained. In any society there is a set of codes which governs social behaviour; these are seldom made explicit, though they may from time to time be enacted into law.

The content of these tacit codes lays out what a community regards as right and wrong, what kind of behaviour elicits rewards and what sanctions, and determines the various boundaries that societies erect for their own purposes. The Stalinist revolution destroyed the high-prestige codes associated with the *anciens régimes*, but substituted nothing that was acceptable in their place, leaving a kind of void. When this destruction is very advanced the result is anomie or normlessness. The societies of Central and Eastern Europe were probably only partly affected by anomie, but the loss of any central source of authority was undoubtedly real and serious.

The confusion that resulted produced what have been called 'immune reactions'.[12] Society disliked much or in some cases all of the Stalinist and post-Stalinist political order, in particular its own powerlessness, and tried to find various ways of compensating for it. These resulted in a steep decline in public morality, in disregard for rules and regulations when this was feasible, and the generally widespread belief that political power was about exploitation and that it was unpredictable.

Societies where power is not distributed one-sidedly have the advantage over ones that are, to the extent that they enjoy a self-repairing

---

[12] László Bogár, *A fejlödés ára* (1983).

capability. Where pressure in an area distorts power distribution in favour of one interest, there will usually be some compensating mechanism whereby this can be recouped, at any rate partially. Soviet-type systems, which attempted to function with a minimum of feed-back, sought to dispense with this and thereby experienced another difficulty, namely the political system worked against these self-repairing capabilities. What society regarded as the 'normal' or 'preferred' ways of being and doing, with the broad aim of constructing and sustaining the community, were repeatedly contradicted by the political order, while attempts to reconcile the two were blocked.[13]

The consequence of this was a gap, which tended to increase in the 1970s for reasons discussed elsewhere in this chapter, between the formal structure of power, the real structure of power enjoyed by a minority, and the preferred structure of power in the eyes of a majority. In this context both the minority and the majority sought to maximize their power, which was in effect unregulated or only lamely regulated, by whatever means were possible. The politically determined char-acter of Soviet-type systems also prevented economic self-repairing mechanisms – supply meeting demand – from functioning, so that those affected felt themselves to be poorer economically and frustrated politically. To remedy this they would embark on a course of action that was at variance with the formal order and they legitimated it by arguing that the formal order was invalid. Thereby they invalidated in their own minds the formal, public order as a whole or large parts of it, though they might well have retained those parts they regarded as theirs, like the nation. But because there was no preferred regulation for this state of affairs, those active in this unrecognized world actually entered an unregulated jungle, in which most if not all of the com-munity underlying the formal order was at risk. And one of the first victims of this process was that the self-repairing mechanisms that fostered a sense of community were ignored or downgraded, because their role was conflated with the functioning of the formal order.[14]

Furthermore, there was little chance in this state of affairs for any social integration to come about. Just as before the war (see chapter 1), when the different sections of society were divided by very deep cleavages, so in a similar way these persisted in the 1970s and later. Apart from the impact of collectivization and the flight from the land, there had been very little change in the configuration of society. There

[13] The idea of self-repairing mechanisms is taken from Umberto Eco, *Faith in Fakes* [the paperback edition was entitled *Travels in Hyperreality*] (1986), pp. 178ff.
[14] Elemér Hankiss, *Társadalmi csapdák, diagnózisok*, 2nd edn (1983) and *Diagnózisok 2* (1986).

was, therefore, little communication between different social groups and even within groups divisions tended to be quite hard. Nor was there any correlation between social cleavages and political power. The remnants of the official ideology did, of course, make some movement towards the recognition of class differentiation, but other cleavages – ethnic, racial (e.g. Gypsies), religious, gender, territorial, age – had virtually no official existence.[15] The original drive towards homogenization could not entirely be abandoned. On the other hand, as the post-1968 order matured, there was increasing evidence that some sections of society were preparing to assert themselves in defiance of the official deployment of power.[16] Overall, however, the nature of communist rule ensured that society remained fragmented, that there was only a minimum of communication laterally between different social groups and that as far as possible power flows should go from the top down and thereby keep society divided.

Social Mobility

Social mobility turned out to be another area where the communist systems performed badly and were increasingly subject to greater rigidity. When they seized power the communists ejected the previous élite (or it had been depleted by war and exile) and replaced it with one owing loyalty to itself through the upward promotion of talented individuals of low-status backgrounds. This, as argued previously, was the pattern in the 1950s.

By the 1960s and 1970s the pattern had set and social mobility rates began to decline. What happened was that the newly promoted élite of the 1950s insisted that its children must remain in the élite. In Soviet-type systems there was for all practical purposes one major avenue of upward mobility – education. Channels which exist in the West, like making money, were not available in the communist world. Thus the new élite, in some cases – as in Hungary and Poland – bulked out by survivors of the old, monopolized the higher education system, leav-

<hr>

[15] Pavel Machonin's research was clearly based on conceptualizing stratification of this kind, but his book, *Ceskoslovenská spolecnost* [Czechoslovak Society] could only just be published in 1969 and it was completely uninfluential under the Husák régime; see V.V. Kusin, *The Intellectual Origins of the Prague Spring: the Development of Reformist Ideas in Czechoslovakia* (1971). In Hungary, when György Konrád and Iván Szelényi tried to suggest that there were serious social disadvantages resulting from 'underurbanisation', they were roundly condemned by the party; see their 'A késleltetett városfejlödés társadalmi konfliktusai', *Valóság*, 15 no. 12 (December 1971), pp. 19–35 and the official counter-attack by Éva Apró, 'Mi késleltette a magyar várossosfejlödést', *Társadalmi Szemle*, 27 no. 6 (June 1972), pp. 28–38.
[16] See chapter 10.

ing very little opportunity for the next generation of talented individuals of low status to make their way.

This had important consequences. It meant that the newly established working class, the ex-peasants, would have their life chances severely restricted, effectively being constrained to remain within the working class. These systems had unwittingly brought about a hereditary transmission of class status. This might not have mattered had the system been able to make provision for satisfying the aspirations of the brightest of the working class. As it was, they remained in the working class and were in a position to offer leadership to potential working-class political movements. The situation was particularly striking in Poland, where Solidarity was exactly a movement of this kind, because of Poland's unusually young demographic structure, with around 65 per cent of the population being under 34 years old in 1980. In Hungary the energies of these talented people were diverted into money-making through the secondary economy, while in Czechoslovakia, a second upward promotion did take place, with significant political consequences. In the GDR there is an impression that mobility was not quite as blocked as elsewhere, but in the absence of any data it is impossible to be sure.[17]

The broad outcome of this blocking of social mobility was to create a social configuration surprisingly like that of the nineteenth century or the interwar period. The middle strata, stratified internally as well, were well-to-do and quite separate from the less well-off, with different value systems, aspirations and tastes.[18] Not only were their life chances better in material terms, but they had much better access to political power as well. This had certain ramifications. It resulted, probably more indirectly than directly, in the growth of a sense of the uselessness of politics as something remote and unattainable, that political participation achieved nothing and it was better to stay away from it all. Naturally, this did not operate everywhere or all the time, but even in Poland, where there was an increasingly aware and mobilized working class, conscious of its success in having removed Gomulka, considerable numbers of workers – the least skilled and educated – fell into the broader Central and Eastern European pattern.[19]

---

[17] None of the literature that I have consulted discusses mobility in the GDR; Strmiska denies the existence of such data; see Pierre Kende and Zdenek Strmiska, *Equality and Inequality in Eastern Europe* (1987), p. 144.

[18] Ágnes Losonczi, *Az életmód az időben a tárgyakban és az értékekben* (1977).

[19] George Kolankiewicz, 'Employee Self-Management and Socialist Trade Unionism', in Jean Woodall (ed.), *Policy and Politics in Contemporary Poland: Reform. Failure and Crisis* (1982), pp. 129–47 and Jacques Rupnik, 'Dissent in

Élite Corruption

Corruption is a fluid concept and extremely difficult to define satis-factorily, but it can be identified in terms of major deviations from the professed norms of the system, in this instance from the ostensible and even the tacit ideology of the party. There are major problems in measuring the scale and scope of corruption and equally in assessing its impact. Nevertheless, despite these methodological problems, it is hard to doubt that with the decline in the effectiveness of Marxism–Leninism as a source of discipline and patterns to govern public be-haviour, coupled with the slow but perceptible easing of coercion, the Soviet-type systems began to experience growing corruption in the 1970s.

Steve Sampson distinguished three types of activity which could be defined as corrupt by being in breach of the ostensible regulative framework.[20] The first of these was benign, in as much as informalism helped the bureaucracy to reach its objectives by making it more flexible. The second was corruptive. Here the goals achieved differed from those stated, for example, through nepotism and embezzlement. This could create alternative social hierarchies and value systems. The organization, therefore, malfunctioned, but the system muddled through, though it was subjected to continuous transformation and the gap between the informal and the formal increased. In the functioning of communist bureaucracy crisis was in many respects the norm, in as much as the organizational mechanisms of communist management were crisis-orientated, the better to be able to justify intervention,[21] but the crisis was averted or diverted by distorting the formal pattern, something which was not acknowledged. By way of illustration, a situation could arise in which, instead of demanding that extra buses be put on, people would bribe the driver to take them on.

The third was explicitly system-threatening. When political legiti-macy declined, access to material goods was wholly inadequate, and corruption was insufficient to effect redistribution and reallocation, then the alternative could become a threat to the system and launch a ground swell aimed at cleaning it up, at making authenticity the public norm. It should be noted, finally, that all three can coexist at the same time and each activity can be any of the three simultaneously.

Poland, 1968–78', in Rudolf Tökés (ed.), *Opposition in Eastern Europe* (1979), pp. 60–112.

[20] Steve Sampson, 'The Informal Sector in Eastern Europe', *Telos,* no. 66 (Winter 1985–6), pp. 44–66.

[21] Maria Hirszowicz, *The Bureaucratic Leviathan: a Study in the Sociology of Communism* (1980).

Corruption tended to advance through all levels of the system and, while in some respects helping to make it operate more effectively in the short term, it undermined its overall logic and validity. All the same, the system did not grow corrupt evenly. Some countries became much more more corrupt than others and some sections of society participated much more actively in dubious practices than others.

The contrast between Poland and Hungary was instructive as far as the first of these propositions was concerned. There is ample evidence that during the 1970s the Polish élite grew more corrupt and more avaricious, probably because the opportunity for this presented itself at every turn and fairly rapidly acquired a dynamic of its own.[22] There is little doubt that the failure of the party leadership to impose any kind of meaningful discipline in this area was a contributory factor. A further possible explanation lies in the hypothesis that societies, or at any rate élites, which gain sudden access to what are perceived in the cultural context as unearned money, especially when large sums are involved, tend to lose any perspective in the culture of spending. The very large Western loans taken on by Poland without any serious domestic accounting or audit system, and with the sense that the criminal law did not apply to the *nomenklatura* because its provisions could always be countermanded by reference to political monopoly, fairly clearly played a role here.[23]

Corruption, especially in Poland but to an extent throughout the communist world, assumed political characteristics in another sense. Individuals in high positions were well placed to insist on favourite projects of their own for reasons of prestige or patronage, and simply ignored counter-arguments. In this way they would override the claims of other sectors of the economy and validate their own by political power. Corruption of this kind was especially striking because it could involve enormous outlays, like major investment projects without any rationale other than prestige. The Katowice steelworks, built for these reasons by Gierek, was described during the Solidarity period as 'the greatest swindle in the world'.[24] Anyone who opposed this project was simply removed from office and all objections were overruled. All the control mechanisms of the previous era evaporated

[22] Michael Vale (ed.), *Poland: the State of the Republic – Two Reports by the Experience and Future Discussion Group (DiP) Warsaw* (1981); Janine Wedel, *The Private Poland: An Anthropologist's Look at Everyday Life* (1986).

[23] There is an interesting parallel here with Iran at around the same time, where the sudden inrush of oil wealth destabilized the élite, which, in an already corruptible culture, lost all sense of restraint.

[24] *Zycie Warszawy*, 22 April 1981, cited by N. K., 'How Not to Build a Foundry', *Radio Free Europe Research*, 29 May 1981.

and a massive investment project was launched in the name of what can only be described as a fine example of a piece of political conspicuous consumption – an undertaking intended to satisfy the political whims of Gierek and his Silesian cronies.

In Hungary there was also enough corruption to call attention to the dubious nature of the system, but it never reached Polish heights (or depths). In the 1970s and 1980s the country was regularly abuzz with stories of party secretaries and enterprise managers who would use official funds for personal purposes.[25] But these stories shared one common feature, for the examples remained in the sphere of personal consumption and never spilled over into the political; the mechanisms that allowed the phenomenon to happen were political, but that was where matters ended.

Throughout the area the élite indulged itself and, indeed, encouraged other members of the élite to ignore the formal rules. The purpose of this was twofold. It created a network of mutual interests, a kind of currency for the transfer of power, and it made them all equally responsible for breaches of the rules. The practice was legitimated by the argument that the members of the élite put more into the communal stew-pot than others and were, therefore, entitled to take more out. There was no sense of public service in Soviet-type systems.[26] Furthermore, by establishing this shared basis of responsibility, the régime also gave itself an added control mechanism over the élite. Individuals knew that they were breaking rules, even if it was winked at or encouraged, but the rules continued to exist and on occasion they were enforced. From time to time individuals were singled out as the current scapegoats, as a warning that the two systems of norms co-existed, that if corruption was taking place it was, in common with everything else, at the discretion of the party.[27]

A further aspect of corruption was that it was almost automatically bound to arise at the interface between the official, socialist sector and the tolerated private economy. From the systemic viewpoint private enterprise was an anomaly, seen as temporary at best and lacking

[25] I recall an item from the Eleventh Congress of the HSWP in 1975, which I covered as a correspondent for the BBC, when one particular malefactor was accused of having had villas built for all his children out of enterprise funds and, when taxed with this, protested that he had only acted out of parental love, or so the Audit Commission's verbal report had it. The published and presumably slightly edited version left out 'parental love', but I remember it distinctly; see *A Magyar Szocialista Munkáspárt XI. kongresszusának jegyzökönyve* (1975), p. 134.

[26] The 'stew-pot' metaphor comes from Ferenc Karinthy, *Harminchárom* (1976).

[27] János Kenedi's *Do it Yourself: Hungary's Hidden Economy* (n.d., but early 1980s) is an excellent analysis of the complex networks of power and influence that grew up under the Kádár system.

ideological legitimacy. Hence the granting of licences, the permission for the continued functioning of a repair shop or restaurant or the availability of supplies was always subject to interference by officials, because there could be no true legal basis for such activity, even within the very limited definition of what constituted 'legal' in a Soviet-type system.

The Secondary Economy

The secondary economy evolved gradually in the 1970s and with varying impact in different countries. A certain range of economic activities outside the control of the state always existed, of course, but it was generally subjected to stringent penalties on charges of sabotage. What differentiated the secondary economy from its earlier counterparts was that the régime acquiesced in it, not officially but in practice, to the extent that it accepted that certain types of unregistered economic activities might be beneficial, at least in the short term. Naturally enough this raised other issues. As secondary economic activities moved from the area of prosecution to toleration, though without ever acquiring more than a minimum of recognition, they came to accepted by the population as well. The secondary economy came to include various activities, starting from selling the produce of the agricultural private plot and expanding into letting rooms to tourists, catering, repairs, services and small-scale manufacturing. It included the intelligentsia and even intellectuals, who were to take on consultancies and research work for the primary sector, although this was very much a phenomenon of the 1980s rather than the 1970s.

Types of activities, however unofficial, gradually acquire the quality of a custom over time. When this happened, the party found it increasingly costly to retract what was no doubt regarded as an *ad hoc* concession. It could always be done – that, after all, was the fate of NEP in the Soviet Union, but Central and Eastern Europe in the 1970s was not about to undergo a major mobilization.

The functions and outcomes of this shift, which was gradual and implicit, had several implications.[28] Part of the reason why the system acquiesced in what was difficult to justify ideologically was that it corrected the shortcomings in the socialist sector and introduced a flexibility for which the planning mechanism proved to be too rigid.

---

[28] I have looked at the secondary economy in greater detail; see George Schöpflin, 'Corruption, Informalism, Irregularity in Eastern Europe: a Political Analysis', *Südost-Europa,* 33 no. 7–8 (July–August 1984), pp. 389–401 and the literature cited there.

Once the shift to consumerism had taken place this was a logical move, given that the satisfaction of consumer demand had become, again implicitly, a primary target of régime strategy. Furthermore, activity in the secondary economy diverted energies from politics. It was preferable from the régime's point of view that enterprising individuals were active in the economy rather than trying to effect political change.

Third, the secondary economy was a useful instrument of labour mobilization. The original tacit contract with the working class allowed for rather low levels of labour productivity; in the secondary economy, where the labour market was much more authentic, individuals would work far harder. Then the output of the secondary economy satisfied demands that the primary economy could not and thereby promoted political stability. Such activity could maximize incomes at a time of austerity by encouraging people to exploit themselves. This promoted stabilization, again more in the 1980s than 1970s, at a time when the consumerist trade-off against depoliticization began to look rather threadbare.

On the other hand, the tacit encouragement of the secondary economy had negative consequences as well, in that it brought the official collectivist value system, still ostensibly a part of the legitimating ideology, even further into question. Furthermore, the spread of the secondary economy created new inequalities, because not everyone had equal access to these newly emerging markets. Those with skills to sell (like electricians or plumbers) or those with a locational advantage (like peasants with private plots near large towns) would benefit more than people lacking these (like miners).

Social differentiation also grew because those who did well under the secondary economy had nowhere to spend their money except on consumption, which inevitably became conspicuous consumption. Reinvestment was possible, as long as it was the entrepreneurs' own business that benefited, but this would simply raise the problem a few years down the line, as investment of this kind would improve the efficiency of the business and make bigger incomes possible. Investment in someone else's business raised the problem of a capital market, which a Soviet-type system could not accommodate for ideological and power political reasons.

Finally, throughout its existence the secondary economy struggled with an insoluble problem. In a socialist system economic initiatives of this kind could never be regarded as fully legitimate or legal; they would always have a somewhat furtive quality. This encouraged participants to go for rapid turnover and quick profits, in the belief that sooner rather than later the state would intervene and clamp down. It was only after the collapse of communism that the advantages of having tolerated a secondary economy became evident. In Hungary, where the Kádár régime accepted and even fostered the secondary economy, the bulk of the population gained some experience of the market and was, in consequence, far less anxious about its impact than, say, in Czechoslovakia, where the Husák régime maintained a much tighter control and regarded the entire phenomenon as illicit.

The 'Softness' of the State

Another aspect of decay was the declining effectiveness of the state and its agencies in their executive capacity. Just as the monopoly of rationality was in doubt, so was the claim to be the most efficient implementor of policies. In a wide and growing number of areas official policies and legislation were ignored, thereby gradually undermining the functioning of the system. Often, indeed, the system could operate only if some regulations were ignored, because of overlapping and contradictory rules. Political implementation, especially coercion, remained the tightest, but this was at a cost, as the rising budgets for ministries of the interior testified during the 1970s.[29] In many other fields this proved not to be the case.

The irony in this state of affairs was that Soviet-type systems had an image of being particularly 'hard'; they were perceived as being extremely well organized and fully capable of carrying out their tasks, whereas in reality they were becoming 'soft'. This softness had several facets. There were always, for example, strata of society who constituted an underclass, the poorest sections, who were below the welfare net and outside consumerism. Those below the poverty line were estimated at being around a third of the population in both Poland and Hungary; the figure may well have been rather lower in Czechoslovakia and the GDR and higher in Romania and Bulgaria. For them the institutions and structure of the system were irrelevant; if they encountered coercion they would ignore it, just as the coercive forces ignored them, given that they were not a political threat to the system. Alcoholism and other forms of deviance, increasing phenomena throughout the area, could be regarded as symptoms of this decay, and with economic contraction, coupled with hidden inflation, the welfare net was declining in effectiveness.

---

[29] See the table on p. 81 in George Schöpflin, 'The Political Structure of Eastern Europe as a Factor in Intra-bloc Relations, in Karen Dawisha and Philip Hanson, (eds), *Soviet-East European Dilemmas: Coercion, Competition and Consent* (1981), pp. 61–83.

Softness was manifested in other ways, with its origins in over-regulation. Just as Kornai[30] pointed towards the existence of softness in budget constraints, the same could be said for much of enterprise activity. The controls over what enterprises did, how well they fulfilled their targets, whether quality criteria were met, how, if at all, goods were priced and so on were increasingly overlooked. As the 1970s wore on this became a major problem with pollution, essentially because the state was both polluter and guardian of the environment and, in the light of its rationalist origins, it almost invariably favoured output over environmental damage, even when this created major public-health crises, as was the case in northern Bohemia or in Giurgiu (Romania). The rationale for over-regulation was that it permitted the authorities an added control mechanism over enterprises which might otherwise have made a bid for autonomy. If the regulations under which economic bodies operated were contradictory, then the discretionary power of the rulers would be strengthened, even at the cost of undermining the overall rationality of the system.

Opposition

The evolution of opposition began with two basic changes. The first of these was the recognition that with voiding ideology of real content, there was a gap between the system and reality, that the totalizing ideology would permit the creation of areas of space, which could be used to establish alternative modes of thought.[31] The second was the reception of human rights as that alternative mode, which was all the more effective for being formally recognized and sanctioned by the Helsinki Final Act, signed by all the communist countries, and for importing a referent that transcended the claims of Marxism–Leninism.

First a definition: there is a clear distinction to be made between opposition and dissent. Opposition means that there is a readiness to play a public role, to establish organizations which reject the leading role of the party and to create information networks; in other words, activity that would go beyond face-to-face contact and assume responsibility for acts beyond the individual's control. Dissent, on the other hand, was restricted to independent acts of defiance or dis-

---

[30] János Kornai, *A hiány,* 2nd edn (1982).

[31] The Kolakowski 'Theses' (see note 2) were quite explicit on this; his ideas were adopted as a kind of bible for the opposition, notably by Jacek Kuroń, 'Pour une plateforme unique de l'opposition', *Politique Aujourd'hui,* no. 3–4 (1997) and Adam Michnik, 'The New Evolutionism', in *Letters from Prison and Other Essays* (1985), pp. 135–48.

agreement, even if it was expressed overtly, say as a letter to the authorities, as long as that communication remained within official channels. The aims of opposition were, therefore, political, that is to say, to effect changes in the political sphere on a routinized basis, while dissent was not necessarily intended to set a precedent beyond the individual.

The basic preconditions for the emergence of opposition in the communist world were the collapse of ideology, as already outlined in this chapter, and the corresponding acceptance by Marxist intellectuals that they would have to abandon their claim to a monopoly of Marxism. The contrast between the early 1970s acts of opposition in Czechoslovakia, which were expressly a socialist opposition designed to take régime claims seriously, and Charter 77, which discarded the need for a Marxist basis, is clear and striking.[32]

Abandoning Marxism meant that these ex-Marxist critics of the system could make common cause with non-Marxists – human-rights activists, religious believers, supporters of alternative lifestyles and so on. Their common platform was human rights and democracy and they denied having an explicit political programme, indeed they generally denied being political at all. Charter 77, for example, was drafted as a legal and not as a political document.

In the narrow sense of party politics, challenging the power of the party directly, this was correct; but in the wider sense of offering an alternative the opposition was political, inasmuch as in a totalizing system any challenge of this nature has political implications. It essentially meant that a group of individuals rejected depoliticization and were taking on the party in the formulation of alternative strategies of the future by placing themselves outside the limits defined by the system. Their objectives were to compel the party to undertake a dialogue with society and to insist that it abide by its own formal legality, which would, of course, have undermined the system completely. This imported the idea of reconstructing civil society into the region and simultaneously brought with it the concept of self-limitation, both of which were to be influential during and after the collapse of communism.

Even if the opposition could not make major inroads into society as a whole, they could certainly influence the intellectuals. New discourses, which could not be ignored, were introduced into the system and compelled more cautious critics to pay heed. In a very real sense,

---

[32] Jirí Pelikán (ed.), *Socialist Opposition in Eastern Europe: the Czechoslovak Example* (1976) as contrasted with H. Gordon Skilling, *Charter 77 and Human Rights in Czechoslovakia* (1981).

by appearing on the scene, the opposition transformed the relationship between the loyal critics, the ones who would never question the bases of the system, and the régime by shifting the margin outwards. Although these loyalist régime critics, the para-opposition,[33] may not have welcomed the rise of the opposition – it posed difficult problems of conscience about the acceptable limits of cooperation – they recognized that a new situation had come into being and the margin of criticism had been widened as a result.

A politically determined system cannot suddenly recognize the autonomy of the legal sphere, the rule of law, without effectively writing itself out of the script. Likewise, a dialogue with society would have introduced feedback into a system that made a virtue of denying the need for feedback, so that neither proposition could make any headway in the face of determined régime hostility. Short of this, the opposition breached the information monopoly of the party, which was of considerable significance in systems relying on the appearance of unanimity.

This breach in the wall of censorship influenced other intellectuals and gradually legitimated the opposition in the eyes of the West, something that proved to be highly significant as an instrument of pressure on the régimes and a source of protection for the opposition. With the growing integration of the Central and Eastern Europe states into the world economic system through détente and the expansion of trade, communist leaders did not like to see themselves pilloried in the West as oppressors of human rights.

Lastly in this section, the launching of the opposition was a far-reaching challenge to régime legitimacy, in that it posited that alternatives were, after all, possible, that the ideas and language of the party did not have to enjoy a monopoly and that the Marxism–Leninism professed by the party was a sham which did not have to be taken seriously. The claim that human rights transcended Marxism–Leninism proved to be deeply destructive of official legitimacy and self-legitimation, because this, the proposition that there existed a set of ideas superior to the official doctrines, was something with which the régime just could not deal. This impact was strengthened by the ideocratic nature of Soviet-type systems. Just as their original legitimation had, at least in part, been an intellectual construct legitimated by intellectuals, so the new challenge went to the heart of legitimation and the régimes understood this.

---

[33] I first used this term in George Schöpflin, 'Opposition and Para-Opposition: Critical Currents in Hungary', in Rudolf Tökés (ed.), *Opposition in Eastern Europe* (1979), pp. 142–86.

Poland

There are two aspects of the Polish crisis of 1980 that deserve particular scrutiny – how the Gierek régime came to crumble and, once it had, what kind of society emerged from under the party monopoly. The collapse of the Gierek régime confirmed what might already have been suspected from Hungarian and Czechoslovak precedents, that communist leaderships require support from the bureaucracy, from the bulk of the intelligentsia and intellectuals, it should not become the target of mass popular antagonism and, above all, it must retain its self-legitimation. What was also striking about the 1980 débâcle was that the popular input – relatively unimportant in Czechoslovakia, though central in Hungary – was possibly the single most influential factor in the Polish case.

It is no exaggeration to suggest that Gierek was the architect of his own downfall; during his ten-year career he had had to make various choices and on most occasions he opted for a course that came to weaken his position. Take 1970, when he succeeded the dreary and authoritarian Gomulka as a direct consequence of the food price-rise demonstrations. Gierek arrived with a good deal of goodwill, but in a weaker position than his predecessor because, in order to buy social peace, he had had to withdraw the food-price increases that had triggered off the outburst in the first place.

In other words, the outcome of the December 1970–February 1971 period of instability was that political stability was equated with food-price stability. This was tantamount to accepting an external veto on a certain range of policy-making. Food prices would no longer be determined by supply and demand, but by political expediency. At the very least this should have put Gierek on his guard, made him aware of the need to keep open his channels of political communication and establish sources of legitimation other than stable prices and growing consumption. For the first months he kept up appearances, promising that he would never become as isolated as Gomulka had been. He made frequent visits to factories where a kind of 'consultation' would take place, with Gierek addressing workers' meetings. But this policy of responsiveness petered out fairly soon, essentially as he consolidated his position in the party by purging Gomulka's placemen.

He then chose to rely on a technocratic form of rule, including grandiose schemes for the future,[34] and on his Western strategy of

---

[34] Some of these, like his promises to provide decent housing for every Pole and to overhaul the education system, make pitiful reading today, as a classic missed opportunity. Details in R. F. Leslie et al., *The History of Poland since 1863* (1980), pp. 417–19.

taking on credits with which to modernize the Polish economy in the expectation that the loans would be paid off by the output of the now modernized economy. In the course of this he seemed entirely to have forgotten the hostage to fortune in the shape of the external veto by society. His reliance on technocracy, furthermore, was misplaced, for without political direction and supervision, the technocrats would simply spend for their own purposes. The other negative outcome of this reliance on technocratic government was its growing isolation from the population, and this was enhanced by the tax exemptions and other privileges granted to the members of the *nomenklatura*.[35] As the 1970s wore on the Polish élite behaved as if it knew everything and society was a nuisance.

In retrospect, the thoroughgoing lack of circumspection with which Gierek exercised power seems nearly unbelievable – he carefully alienated one group after another, until even the bureaucracy had no particular reason for supporting him. Every major social group found itself with strong reasons for dissociating itself from the system. The intellectuals, first of all, were activated by Gierek's decision to launch a reideologization campaign, culminating in the proposal to revise the constitution by including in it the leading role of the party and the indissoluble link with the Soviet Union in 1975.

In a Soviet-type system, it might be thought, society would simply accept this as yet another expression of façade politics, but this reckoned without the myth value of constitutions in the Polish tradition, the key point of reference being the great liberal constitution of 1791. A major protest was launched, with the Church weighing in as well. Once galvanized into action, the intellectuals persisted with the launching of KOR, the Committee for the Defence of the Workers (later KSS, Social Self-Protection Committee) and that expanded into a massive movement of opposition activity, which *inter alia* produced a flood of samizdat. The minor concessions that were made by Gierek could be counted a defeat. The alienation of the peasantry proved to be another major error, in that the agricultural sector, in despair at the constant depression of procurement prices and other forms of harassment, began to produce for subsistence only. This left Poland unable to feed itself.

Then, in 1976, the leadership decided that the gap between supply and demand required it to raise food prices. This was duly done and the response was immediate – protests, sit-in strikes and other expressions of working-class discontent. Within twenty-four hours the price increases were rescinded. This effectively left Gierek in an im-

[35] See Alexander Smolar, 'The Rich and the Powerful', in Abraham Brumberg (ed.), *Poland: Genesis of a Revolution* (1983), pp. 42–53.

possible situation. It was as if a government had been defeated at elections, but there was no mechanism for replacing it. He drifted without any real strategy after this, except coercion to keep control and continued imports, financed by Western loans, to keep himself afloat.

By the spring of 1980 Poland's debt-service ratio on a foreign indebtedness of 27 billion dollars was dangerously close to 100 per cent or default; the slightest shock would have been enough to unbalance the situation. In these circumstances Gierek had another go at increasing food prices and this triggered off the series of strikes that eventually debouched into the setting up of Solidarity.[36] To illustrate how out of touch Gierek was by this stage, in the middle of August, as the strike wave rolled on from enterprise to enterprise, he went off to the Soviet Union on holiday. Finally, the negotiations at the Lenin shipyards in Gdansk produced the agreement that directly denied the leading role, an enormous defeat for the party, and Gierek was obliged to step down by a bureaucracy that was afraid for its own future. Gierek had lost the last vestiges of support; his legitimation was at an end.

The Solidarity period of sixteen months was remarkable for demonstrating the nature of the values of Polish society. Possibly the most important of these was the sense of homogeneity in society and dichotomy between rulers and ruled, as if the confrontation between state and society was one between good and evil. The assumption that society was one and indivisible, not structured by cleavages, probably led the Solidarity leadership to overestimate its strength.

Other values to emerge included an insistence that society would not itself participate in power, but that those who did exercise power would be under tight control. Stringent election and recall procedures were introduced in enterprises and the horizontal movement sought to break the system of hierarchical power flows by which the party kept individual organizations in ignorance. Accountability for the past misdeeds of the party, notably how Poland came to find itself with a massive foreign debt, led to insistent demands for openness and an end to the party's monopoly of information.[37] The Solidarity programme, adopted at the organization's congress in the autumn of 1981,

---

[36] There is a wealth of literature on 1980–1, notably Kevin Ruane, *The Polish Challenge* (1982); Timothy Garton Ash, *The Polish Revolution: Solidarity 1980-1982* (1983); Jadwiga Staniszkis, *Poland's Self-Limiting Revolution* (1984); see also Anthony Kemp-Welch (ed. and trans.), *The Birth of Solidarity: the Gdansk Negotiations* (1983).

[37] George Kolankiewicz, 'The Politics of "Socialist Renewal"', in Jean Woodall (ed.), *Policy and Politics in Contemporary Poland: Reform, Failure and Crisis* (1982), pp. 56–75.

would have reduced the party to little more than Poland's representative in the Kremlin. The party would have been stripped of most of its functions, as the entire range of social and political institutions would have been freed of the *nomenklatura* system.

On the other hand, the homogenization had other consequences which proved to be less effective in terms of society's goals. There was a strong tendency to see events in moral terms, with everything done by Solidarity as positive and the actions of the party as negative, thereby reducing the chances of compromise. There was a low tolerance threshold of ambiguity and reluctance to relativize one's perspectives, together with elements of populism.[38]

From the party's standpoint the Solidarity months were disaster. The élite lost not only power, but also what remaining authority it possessed and was completely demoralized. The legitimacy of the Gierek system, not just Gierek's leadership, was at an end and could not be resuscitated. Hence when the counter-attack came it sought its legitimation in patriotism, order and the suggestion that it was the sole alternative to a Soviet invasion.[39]

The post-coup leadership of General Jaruzelski tried to establish an analogous centralization of power, though the system that he constructed was no longer governed by the rules of democratic centralism, in that it allowed a variety of unsupervised phenomena (samizdat, factory committees, discussion clubs, particularly on Church premises) to persist and it was ambiguous about its commitment to totalization as far as its legitimacy was concerned. The Jaruzelski system, however, was weaker than Gierek's, above all because it was quite unable to create a legitimation that would give it authority as well as power. That was to be its fatal inheritance during the 1980s.

---

[38] Staniszkis, *Poland's Self-Limiting Revolution.*
[39] Ryszard Kuklinski, 'The Suppression of Solidarity', in Robert Kostrzewa (ed.), *Between East and West: Writings from* Kultura (1990), pp. 72–98.

8

The 1980s: Towards Collapse

Corcyra fell into its component parts [because] the agreed upon currency of words for things was subjected to random barter.

Thucydides, The History of the Peloponnesian War, *3.82.4.*

In some respects the 1980s – the years between the introduction of martial law and the end of communism – are the most difficult to assess, at any rate from the foreshortened perspective of 1992. It is far too easy to fall into a historicist trap and assume that the collapse of communism was inevitable and then explore only those aspects of the decade that support the hypothesis of inevitable collapse. Western Sovietology failed to foresee the end of communism, it is true, so there is the added danger of self-justification in any approach of this kind. Yet at the same time, even if collapse was not predicted or predictable, the proposition that the communist systems of Eastern Europe were in serious trouble and the communist rulers of these countries were rapidly running out of political resources was argued, albeit by a minority of the profession and not always to the approbation of the majority. Analyses of the growing decay of communism were being made by the early part of the decade and this implies that concentration on this theme here is not purely a projection of the present on the past.

Indeed, many of the themes explored in the previous chapters can be extended forward into the 1980s and intensified, but this would not convey all the particularities of the period. Although many of the political, economic and social factors in the 1970s were looking decidedly negative for the communist systems, they did not at the time have an air of drifting without purposiveness other than power and coercion, whereas by the 1980s, despite the ideological bluster, this sense of rudderlessness was increasingly evident to the sensitive observer, whether inside or outside the system.

At the heart of the argument to be put forward in this chapter is the proposition that, with the decay of legitimation, communism was losing its authority and running into the danger of ruling through power stripped of any support. The loss of authority was far and away the most visible in Poland, where the aftermath of Solidarity left behind a generation of intellectual and working-class activists for whom the existing régime was completely inauthentic and who simply opted out of official structures wherever and whenever they could. The Polish stalemate was emblematic of the rest of the region by highlighting the systemic problems of communism in an especially acute form.

Legitimation was the single most significant, overarching problem facing the communist leaderships and systems. Perhaps for the first time since the take-over, the distinction between the two was no longer all that relevant. When one went the other would go too. Leadership conservatism had become the immediate real and symbolic obstacle to change. Noteworthy in this connection was the fact that not a single East European leader was changed in the 1980s (as defined). Leadership changes, with ramifications in patronage and new policies, were always rather feeble ways of making other political changes. A group of ageing, increasingly sclerotic leaders presided over a state of affairs that was degenerating from stability into stagnation and from stagnation into decomposition.

This decline also tended to weaken the device of attempting to link systemic legitimacy to leadership authority. It was always easier for an individual to build up authority, possibly even popularity for himself, as if to convey the message, 'Well, the system may have its shortcomings, but you can certainly trust me.' But as the system was increasingly unable to meet its part of the tacit compact of the 1960s and

Table 8.1 *Dates of succession, dates of birth and number of years in office.*

	Succeeded	Year of birth	Years in office
Nicolae Ceausescu	1965	1918	25
Erich Honecker	1971	1912	17
Gustáv Husák	1969	1909	19*
Wojciech Jaruzelski	1981	1923	8
János Kádár	1956	1912	31
Todor Zhivkov	1954	1911	35

* Husák was ousted from power at the end of 1987 and replaced by Milos Jakes, but this does not significantly alter the picture

as it sought to renegotiate this unilaterally, it became difficult for leaders to keep their distance from the political order over which, they presided. The unpopularity of the system began to rub off on the leaders, so that leadership authority became a wasting asset. Indeed, towards the end of the period, the pressure for the removal of the leader evolved into one of the focuses around which efforts to achieve change were concentrated, and removal was generally seen as a necessary condition for effecting transformation. The call to arms in the Hungarian opposition's document on change, 'Kádár must go,' issued in 1987 and entitled *Social Contract*, was the clearest illustration of this.[1]

Not that the chances of legitimation were superior to those in the 1970s. If anything, in one respect, the possibilities for buying support were poorer than before because an important resource had dried up – Western credits. The Polish fiasco caught the Western banking community unawares. There had been a vague belief that communist countries could not default and that, if they did find themselves in difficulties, the Soviet Union would bail them out.[2] In the case of Poland this turned out to be a mistake, but Bulgaria, which experienced repayment problems in the early 1980s, was tided over with Soviet support. Western strategy from this point on was threefold – no more lavish loans because these were not working; everything would be done to avoid formal rescheduling, because this looked bad; and where a country was especially agile loans would still be forthcoming, though without the enthusiasm that characterized the 1970s. East Germany and Hungary fell into the last category. Romania insisted on repaying every penny regardless of the cost to the Romanian population. Czechoslovakia remained aloof from the great credit bonanza and Bulgaria tried to limit its exposure. The result was that the expansionary vision of the 1970s, not unimportant in the quest for legitimation, was replaced by the rhetoric of belt-tightening and, what was worse, by a long-term perspective of austerity.

It was a serious blow to legitimation that the régimes abandoned their radiant future of catching up with the West and prosperity for all, and opted for a dreary survival strategy instead. It was rather as if the Gomulka years were now to be visited on the entire region. This switch to austerity was made all the worse as it became evident that the West, recovering from recessions induced by the oil shocks of the 1970s and early 1980s, was embarked on a new round of qualitative growth and technological change. Whereas in the 1960s the industrial-

[1] A partial text appeared in *East European Reporter*, 3 no. 1, pp. 54–8; the original Hungarian was published as a special number of *Beszélő*, June 1987.
[2] Charles Levinson, *Vodka-Cola* (1978).

ized Central European countries were ahead of the poorer Western states, by the 1980s this had been reversed, as Greece and Portugal were beginning to catch up and overtake the communist world, let alone Austria and Finland.

This was visibly brought home to the East Europeans through films, television and printed material. It was fascinating at the time how Western films conceived as criticism of capitalism were decoded for their local colour, the lavish settings, as a glimpse into an alien and rather unattainable world. Foreign travel and tourism enhanced this. As greater numbers of people, particularly from Poland and Hungary, visited the West, they began to understand that the whole of Western society had some access to prosperity. Psychologically this was quite devastating, because it meant that the majority of the population began to understand that there was nothing to be done with the communist system, except to get rid of it. In the Weberian sense, it had ceased to be exemplary.

While the gap between living standards seemed to be widening, the inability of régimes to generate more growth obliged them to cut back on their existing welfare provision, thereby further undermining the basis of the hoped-for stability targeted in the 1960s. Infrastructure was neglected and consumption stagnated. It was striking for anyone visiting these countries in the 1980s that the assortment of goods available hardly changed. This even applied to Hungary, the favourite of Western television producers forever looking for a communism that worked, despite the best efforts of the boutique owners of the secondary economy in the Váci utca.

In effect, the economic problem had not changed either. This had a number of components, of which two will be singled out here – the role of consent and the impact of the heavy industry lobby. The question of consent did not arise directly; by and large, the impression one had was of a docile workforce that went tranquilly about its business. This was largely true, to some extent even of Poland, where the impact of the Solidarity experience was still reverberating through the system, but where at the same time the overwhelming majority of the population carried on working. On the other hand, the work that was done was the minimum that one could get away with. The system was caught in another of the traps it had set for itself.

Because it could not introduce an element of consent it had to operate with hierarchical, coercive structures that set management and workers, them and us, in an adversarial relationship which effectively precluded efficient working and higher productivity.[3] Try as they

---

[3] Maria Hirszowicz, *Coercion and Control in Communist Society: the Visible Hand in a Command Economy* (1986).

might, the structure of the relationship prevented the economic planners and enterprise managers from transforming this, and the attitude
that persisted was summed up in the *bon mot* of the time, 'they pretend
to pay us and we pretend to work.' Once working in the secondary
economy gained ground, as it did in Hungary, the socialist sector could
not compete with the wages that workers could obtain in their spare
time, not least when they used their jobs in the primary sector to rest
from their labours in the other.

The effect of the heavy industry lobby was equally an impediment
to change. If any part of the system had a vested interest in its survival,
it was the industries of yesteryear, the leaders of which understood full
well that any economic reform worthy of the name would sweep them
to oblivion, for they were obviously taking far more from the system
than they were contributing to it through manufactures. The party,
management and workers all understood this.[4] There was simply no
way in which this arrangement could have been changed except by a
redistribution of power, for the heavy industry lobby inevitably became one of the most faithful supporters of the system and had to be
nourished by it, regardless of the cost.

The functioning of the heavy industry lobby points towards the
existence of a group of indirect beneficiaries of the communist system,
which was probably always wider than many people supposed,
though it nowhere constituted a majority, if a guess had to be made. In
addition to the heavy industry lobby and its clients, one should note
that many of the employees of the overstaffed bureaucracies preferred
the *status quo* to any change, not least because they felt that, even if
they were underpaid, they would find life even more difficult in a new
order. Often their qualifications were low and they drew esteem,
identity and power from their status, however frustrating their world
might be.[5] More significant in many ways were the direct beneficiaries,
like the members of the instruments of coercion (police, para-military,
armed forces) and party bureaucracy, who enjoyed special privileges,
liked favoured access to housing. At the higher levels, members of the
group lived very well indeed. They had immunity from any kind of

---

[4] In 1985 I remember talking to a Cracow taxi-driver whose services I had paid for
with 3 dollars for an afternoon; he told me that he had worked for twelve years at
the Lenin steelworks in Nowa Huta and that the workers there were fully aware
that the steel they produced cost six times the world price, but they did not care,
for until they gained some kind of political representation, they would carry on
taking disproportionately from the economy.

[5] Jiřina Siklová, 'Nacionalizmus Közép- és Kelet-Európában', *Valóság*, 35 no. 1
(January 1992), pp. 114–16 translated from *Frankfurter Allgemeine Zeitung*, 4
September 1991.

responsibility, but exercised considerable power and enjoyed a disproportionately high standard of living. These direct and indirect beneficiaries represented a secure basis for the continuation of communist rule.

To them should be added another social periphery, the politically and socially weak, those who had been traumatized by their life experiences and wanted to have nothing more to do with politics, as well as those who just accepted that whoever was in power was always right. This last attitude was particularly prevalent among those who had only recently left the land. The socially weak – the poorly educated, single mothers, the sick, the elderly, pensioners – simply accepted the rather low level of welfare provision made by the system and opted out.

These sources of support for the system were sufficient to let the party hold on to power, but they could do nothing to replenish its purposiveness. For short periods power alone is probably enough to infuse a political élite with the will to rule, but over time this will not work. Every régime, however repressive, seems to need some kind of wider goal – which may be future orientated or structured in terms of maintaining some aspect of the past, though usually combining elements of the two – to endow it with a reason for exercising power and lending it an identity. In the case of Soviet-type systems this problem became acute with the gradual voiding of its ideology and its barely noticeable replacement by the sentimental ouvrierism mentioned in the previous chapter and other vague claims.[6] Purposiveness may not matter so much with open systems that accept feedback through elections and other responses to public opinion, but evidently it was a key aspect for Soviet-type systems which sought to do without feedback.

The loss of the ideological impulse had a further outcome. For all practical purposes these systems became futureless, in that they suffered a draining of their perspectives, with a consequential narrowing of choices, both at the level of the concrete and at that of meaning. In effect there was less and less of a reason for these régimes to be in business at all. Horizons shrank and change was put on hold as the once dynamic, ideologically energized régimes vegetated. Indeed, communist countries in the 1980s were characterized by tedium; the better regulated they were the greater the boredom, necessarily be-

[6] During a conversation in 1986 with György Aczél, still a member of the Hungarian Politburo though no longer at the zenith of his career, he solemnly informed me that what the Hungarian Communist Party was doing was seeking to build 'democracy and socialism'. This seemed to have about as much meaning as wanting the weather to be good.

cause here individual or personal choice was most effectively penned in by coercion, regulation and other social control mechanisms. The GDR exemplified this most vividly; the population had next to nothing to do and spent its time putting itself to sleep by watching West German television.

Futurelessness had been imposed on the East European populations by Stalinism, as sketched in chapter 4; now internal and external conditions had, ironically, reproduced an analogous state of affairs for the heirs of the Stalinist revolution. With the future losing its meaning, the present increasingly declined in effectiveness as either binding or exemplary. And by the same token, the past too eroded as an instrument of legitimation. The loss of futurity automatically and inevitably reacted back on the present and past in this fashion. Possibly the central aspect of this gradual degeneration was that it had begun to eat into systemic self-legitimation.

Self-legitimation is dependent on purposiveness. A leadership which no longer feels that it is in power to achieve anything very much will be ill placed to resist challenges and this loss of purpose will be communicated downwards in the hierarchy, so that subordinates will draw their own conclusions as to the viability of the system of which they are the beneficiaries. The process of self-questioning will make the representatives of the system hesitant and less willing to apply rules with full rigour, thereby making yet more concessions. The sustaining myths of the system will be seen as hollow not merely by those who are supposed to be powerless and atomized, but by the power élite itself; as a corollary, they will be less determined to sustain atomization and deprivation of power. While demands for social autonomy will not be acceded to formally, they will be acquiesced in tacitly.

Patterns of behaviour, theoretically deviant and thus destructive, will be tolerated or overlooked, essentially because those who should enforce the rules do not feel that it is worth doing so. What is particularly noteworthy in this context is that a particular pattern of behaviour, established over a period of time, acquires a kind of justification, whether it is formally legal or not. A kind of customary right can be constructed in the interstices of the system, which then becomes too troublesome or too costly to claw back. In theory the formal rules of the system continue to apply, but it is widely understood that they will not be enforced. As these islands of customary behaviour proliferate, the effectiveness of the system diminishes correspondingly.

Society, then, enjoyed a kind of low-level re-empowerment. Various types of action which the system should have excluded or eliminated were tacitly redefined into acceptability. The most stringent constraint concerned the direct exercise of political power itself; as long as this was left untouched and unchallenged, a variety of activities could be carried on without serious restraints; only where the power and privileges of the élite were touched could sanctions be expected and these were necessarily unpredictable and arbitrary.

This unpredictability pointed towards a key problem area. Islands of empowerment did exist, but they were not subject to any ordering principle; they were not, indeed could not be regularized. Consequently the codes of behaviour governing these activities were various and arbitrary. There could be no ordering principle extracted from what would be acceptable to society and the islands of autonomous activity were too scattered, still too divided for integration to take place from below, not least because there could be no agreement as to which principles might serve as the integrator. Even in Poland where, as a result of the Solidarity experience, sections of the working class and intellectuals did succeed in coming together around a democratic platform, larger areas of society remained outside, uninterested.

Nationhood as a Surrogate

In reality there was only one principle around which integration could take place and this was contested – nationalism. The rulers sought to appropriate nationalism for their purposes, to appear as the agent of the nation and thereby to secure their power legitimately, but they had to narrow its confines and teleology to suit their aims. The nationalism that was on offer matched at best only a part of the aspirations of the nation. Official nationalism was too restricted for society, which had its own agendas – autonomy, access to power, the elimination of alien control. The outcome was predictable. Both sides were dissatisfied. The rulers could regularly invoke nationhood, but the response was not necessarily what they wanted – anti-Russian sentiments had to be suppressed, but they were implicit, for example, in the GDR's campaign to revive Prussia, with its echoes of the *Drang nach Osten* and other anti-Slavonic reverberations. Nor did this really help to sustain the régimes; at the end of the day, they knew or sensed that any identity between a communist party and society based on nationhood could be little more than coincidental and ephemeral, an *ad hoc* coalition. It could not become a reliable basis for legitimation, because someone else could always outflank a communist by being a more authentic and thus a better nationalist. The Croatian crisis of 1971 illustrated this very clearly, when attempts by the Tripalo leadership to generate support by posing as agents of the Croatian nation brought into being a challenge to the Croatian party's leading role from the spokesmen of real Croatian nationhood around the weekly journal *Hrvatski Tjednik.*[7]

However, society was also short-changed. Nationalism could certainly sustain an alternative, competing consciousness and thereby weaken the ruling ideology, as already described, but on its own it could never be the vehicle for an alternative programme. Nationhood in its ethnic dimension concerns identity rather than the distribution of power and when the two agendas – identity and power – are combined the outcome is confusion. Crucially, ethnic nationalism has nothing to say about the nature of the institutional system through which power is diffused or about the procedures needed to ensure the regularity and predictability that will eliminate arbitrariness.[8] Besides, when a régime pushed its nationalist campaigns to extremes, as Ceausescu did, this tended to void nationhood as such, for the nationalist slogans emanating from the top ceased to have any meaning. The popular attitude towards the régime remained negative, so anything propagated from above was tarred with the same brush. This state of affairs promoted an even greater confusion, with uncertainty about which elements of the national agenda were desirable and which were not.

The voiding of Marxism–Leninism and the steady drift towards the assumption of a nationalistically tinted ideology in the 1980s were to have important consequences for post-communism. The acceptance or possibly even the reception of nationhood as a viable category by communist parties left many of their members attuned to nationalist responses and, because their communist world-view was so enfeebled, they found it fairly easy to slide from one all-encompassing set of categories to another. The fact that the contents of the two ideologies were, at heart, completely at variance proved irrelevant, because it was not the content that mattered but the existence of an ideological-political ideal, which could offer a more or less respectable safe haven for those to be discredited by association with the previous system. Furthermore, while there is no direct evidence for the proposition that the slide from Marxism–Leninism towards nationalism was a proximate factor in inducing the collapse, it is hard to avoid the conclusion that it made it easier to live with the end of one system if an acceptable alternative was to hand. To this extent, the vacuum created by the voiding of Marxism–Leninism was partially filled by nationalism and that in turn was to facilitate the transformation.

---

[7] Dennison Rusinow, *The Yugoslav Experiment 1948–1974* (1977).
[8] Anthony D. Smith, *National Identity* (1991).

In one sense the entire communist project could be interpreted in terms of representation, agency and substitution. The party, by assuming that its ideas were derived from the iron laws of history, sought to unite the political aspirations and moral values of the whole of society, thereby claiming to represent its hopes for the future and to act as its agent. This kind of substitution greatly exceeded the representation undertaken by elected governments, necessarily so, given the ideologically determined nature of communist rule. Similarly, the claim was not feasible in terms of capacity and capability.

Hypothetically, had the ideology and the system constructed on the basis of it been uniformly successful, had the Soviet-type system actually satisfied popular aspirations, indeed – seeing that the aspirations were in part constructed by the party through the creation of an industrial working class in the name of which it justified its rule – had the party met the systemically generated expectations, as distinct from those which arose from the existence of the alternative, i.e. the West, communism might have been able to enracinate itself to a much greater extent. Under this scenario the substitution would have been more effective and the degree of acceptability might have been converted into legitimacy. As it was, the system could not cope with the conditional nature of legitimation, with the fact that legitimacy is not conferred on the ruled for ever, but must be renewed regularly.

The insight into the nature of Soviet-type systems of the Croatian political scientist, Zarko Puhovski, is also relevant in this connection.[9] The essence of Puhovski's argument is that the socialist project failed because it attempted to replace systems that were still viable, that were still capable of self-renewal and self-regeneration, and that in order to do so socialism had to create its own, alternative version of reality. By the 1980s these systems were less and less capable of sustaining this reality or intervening in it to further their own ends. But at the moment when comparison between this internally generated version of reality with the Western world was evident to the population, the Soviet-type systems disintegrated, because it was no longer seen as real.

Society and the Role of the State

It has been argued consistently in the foregoing that the official ideology was an empty shell by the 1970s and had no legitimating force, and that other instruments of legitimation were likewise losing their effectiveness. Two further points about economic legitimation require

[9] Zarko Puhovski, 'The End of the Socialist Construction of Reality', MS, 1990.

some discussion here. The changelessness of economic consumption has already been noted, but the gradual deterioration of infrastructure impinged on collective consumption, which then raised question marks about the remaining 'socialist' characteristics of the system. Transport, schools, hospitals declined and social welfare provision was less effective, primarily because the necessary support funds were inexorably gobbled up by the ever voracious loss-making heavy industry that was such a crucial political prop to the régimes. By the same token, environmental deterioration was ignored and the costs of ignoring this pollution were expressed in deteriorating public health. This deterioration did not in itself prompt the population to revolt, but it probably contributed to the growing sense of malaise that gripped most of the Central and Eastern Europe countries by the middle of the decade. The most striking sign of this malaise was the steady worsening of social health indicators – suicide, death from stress-related illness, alcoholism were all on the rise.

As bad as these trends were, and they were increasingly understood as such by a perceptive minority of Central and Eastern Europeans, they were made to appear far more negative by the technological transformation undergone by the West over the same period. The spread of computers and the revolution in information technology were simply not understood or, where they were, they were feared for the power that such a development would place in the hands of the individual. Towards the end of the decade it was beginning to be perceived that the gap was unbridgeable and that Central and Eastern Europe was fated to lag behind the West for the foreseeable future. The grandiose dream of a massive leap into modernity under the banner of rational socialism was an empty nightmare. The capability of these systems to gain any respect in their own eyes faded.

Much the same might be said about the functioning of the state. As overall political purposiveness faded and the will to keep the state machinery functioning with a reasonable degree of effectiveness declined, bureaucratic dominance became the pre-eminent mode of the 1980s. It was increasingly static, aimed at generating more bureaucracy, administering itself rather than its carrying out its formal functions and characterized by opacity and over-regulation. It was clearly paternalistic in spirit, even if its formal discourse was punctuated by denials of paternalism and the occasional insistence that state was not a universal provider. In any case, as already suggested, its capacity to deliver any quid pro quo declined, so that paternalism tended to slide into dominance. There was a continued denial of any reciprocity, implying that the low-level provision that was being made came from the generosity of the system, rather than from the surplus exacted from the population.[10]

The mode of rule by bureaucratic dominance also employed various forms of linguistic manipulation. It sought as far as possible to keep control of the language in its hands and to maintain society in a state of linguistic incompetence, so that individuals would be pre-empted from making demands on the system by their lack of understanding of the technical language and necessary procedures for dealing with the bureaucracy. This might be regarded as the bureaucratic counterpart to maintaining in being the empty shell of the ideological language. At the moment when society or a few members of it were able to break through this language, the entire apparatus of linguistic repression unravelled fairly quickly or could only be sustained by other means. It was noteworthy that during the 1980s samizdat spread fairly consistently throughout Poland and Hungary, albeit in far greater quantity in the former, but while Polish samizdat tended to try and slough off the bureaucratic language of the state and to convey its message *en clair,* as it were, the Hungarians, addressing an intellectual and political readership, employed a complex and convoluted language that the man in the street found very hard to follow.[11]

The Dilution of Democratic Centralism

Over and above these broad flaws, the system itself was inherently weaker and less capable than before of enforcing its will. It could still control the streets and attempts to demonstrate the symbolic weakness of the system by rallies could generally be dispersed by a judicious amount of force, certainly in the first part of the decade. The regular confrontations in Poland between workers and the detested riot police, the ZOMO, ended in a *de facto* victory for the latter. While the Jaruzelski régime was prepared to live with dissension behind closed doors and in factories, it would not tolerate the open and symbolic flouting of its power that the demonstrations represented. To that extent there remained a degree of safety for the régimes, but an internal canker proved more serious to their health – the erosion of the Leninist system of organization.

The original communist impulse had placed great emphasis on

[10] Ferenc Fehér, Ágnes Heller, György Márkus, *Dictatorship over Needs* (1983); see also Júlia Szalai, 'A szociálpolitika nyelve – amit kifejez és amit eltakar', *Medvetánc,* no. 4, 1984–no. 1, 1985, pp. 105–19.

[11] See various issues of *East European Reporter,* 1986–88, *passim.*

democratic centralism as an instrument of control essential for a minority intent on seizing and controlling power and as a way of providing an identity for the new rulers. We have seen how the initial stringency and then the ideological imperative were gradually loosened during the post-Stalin decades. By the 1980s, however, the structures of power were themselves diluted, thereby considerably transforming the nature of communist rule. The claim to a political monopoly was not abandoned, but the means of implementing it had become diversified.

The evidence by the mid-1980s was incontrovertible. In the case of Poland the Jaruzelski system could still be called communist by reason of the claim to monopoly and a vague, largely off-stage reference to Marxism–Leninism, but the system of power and control had become something very different from orthodox Leninism. Supreme power was in the hands of a group of around 200 generals, who ruled particularly through the Main Political Administration, the section of the party charged with supervision of the armed forces, through the instruments of coercion and the military-industrial complex. The state administration and the economic bureaucracies were separate, though obviously influenced by the former; and the communist party was yet another bureaucracy with nothing like the power and influence that it had enjoyed in the 1970s. This demotion was the direct consequence of the defeat that it had suffered at the hands of Solidarity in 1980.

In Hungary the central party apparatus was gradually losing its direct powers of intervention and appointment. The *nomenklatura* system, while not entirely in tatters, was nowhere near as effective as before. Partly as a result of the Kádár style of consultation and fudge, local party machines gained increasing power over local *nomenklaturas* and would not relinquish these to the centre. The centre could veto appointments, but its power to impose its nominees was weak. In the last decade and a half of the Kádár period only one county party secretary was appointed by the centre, in Kecskemét, and that was someone who had come from that particular county in the first place; all the others were local figures, whose elevation was rubber-stamped by Budapest.

In Romania Ceausescu had deliberately abandoned democratic centralism anyway and ruled through a complex system involving autarchy,[12] the appointment of family members and continuous rotation of cadres.[13] Besides, the Romanian party had long ceased to be a

[12] I am using this word in its proper sense, of 'rule by one person', which should be distinguished from 'autarky' meaning 'self-sufficiency'.
[13] Trond Gilberg, *Nationalism and Communism in Romania: the Rise and Fall of Ceausescu's Personal Dictatorship* (1990).

vanguard party and had come to include around a fifth of the entire adult population, indicating that its significance in the hierarchy of power was much diminished. In Czechoslovakia, where something approximating to a second communist take-over was effected in the 1970s, party organization remained tighter, but even there it slackened once the initial impetus of the great purge of the 1970s was over. By the 1980s a Leninist organization remained in place, but it was increasingly a matter of form rather than content and, as in Hungary, local cliques acquired greater power against the centre.[14] Only in the GDR was anything resembling the strict control and hierarchy envisaged by democratic centralism largely in place, though there too some deviations were occasionally registered.[15]

The state administration was likewise subject to analogous processes. Throughout the area there were constant references to bureaucratization, i.e. the growth of an uncontrolled bureaucracy acting in its own spcial interests rather than the ostensible goals it was supposed to serve. This is, of course, a universal phenomenon; the difference in the communist world was that the remedies were far more difficult to apply than in open societies. An assessment of the situation in Czechoslovakia should serve as a paradigmatic illustration of the problem. In 1969 the number of administrative workers in the country was reported as being 690,000. The tighter control of the period immediately following (1970–1), what has been called here the second take-over, reduced this by 65,000. However, the pressure in the opposite direction could not be stemmed, and by 1976 the number had risen to 787,575 and by 1981 to 817,271. The increase was occasioned by two factors. First was the constantly growing output of decrees, directives and guidelines by ministries and central offices, estimated as being between 2000 and 3000 a year. Second, the response from below was a flood of reports, forms and indicators. In 1975 mining industry enterprises had to work on 86 forms; by 1980 this had risen to 265. In other words, the system ran on paper, which probably nobody really had the time to digest, but the completion of forms and reports acted as justification for taking on more personnel, expanding bureaucratic empires and delaying decisions.[16]

If the structures of power were decidedly friable by this time, so was its ability to implement the wishes of the élite. There were a number of

[14] Milan Simecka, *The Restoration of Order* (1984).

[15] Sigrid Meuschel, *Legitimation under Parteiherrschaft in der DDR: zum Paradox und Revolution in der DDR 1945–1989* (1992), notes pp. 260–1 on the fears of a multiplicity of interests finding expression in the unity of the system.

[16] Data taken from P[rokop] M[achan], 'The Plague of Bureaucracy', *Radio Free Europe Research: Czechoslovakia*, 17 March 1982.

200 The 1980s: Towards Collapse

reasons for this, in addition to the weakening structures. First, the quality of the planners and of the state and economic bureaucracies was imperfect. While the qualifications of the personnel certainly improved when compared with the Stalinist years, the level of education and training at the middle and lower levels was indifferent at best, not least because many appointments were controlled by the *nomenklatura* and were made on grounds of political reliability. The emphasis was on reliability and acceptance of hierarchy, not originality and innovativeness. This was a problem that varied in its importance from country to country, but it was a reality throughout the area. The culture of these bureaucracies was far from Weber's legal-rationality. Information was restricted to virtually a need-to-know basis; it was supposed to be 'collective', meaning that there was nowhere for the buck to stop; and it promoted a mentality that is best described as a kind of flight from decision-making.[17]

Second, possibly more significantly, the Soviet-type system inherently sought to do too much and was attempting to do what it was doing from above, by means of rational construction, when it lacked the capacity and capability for achieving these goals. The planning process illustrated this most vividly. The original idea behind planning was that the market was anarchic and irrational, thus wasteful and inefficient, whereas by planning the economy all these negative phenomena could be eliminated. Thus was born the idea of total planning, where every transaction and interaction would be encompassed by the all-rational state. Even if this original idea was modified by the 1980s, the countries that retained central planning with compulsory plan targets continued with some explicit or implicit belief in plannability. In reality there were strict limits to plannability, those deriving from structure and from the ability of the planners. The structure of the plan, formally at any rate, demanded that it be hierarchical and that all its elements be in harmony, so that each and every interaction should work its way through the system without producing bottlenecks.[18] It was related that in the late 1970s the annual plan in Romania had some 10 million indicators; it was absolutely impossible for all these to be integrated in any systematic and rational way.

In concrete terms, if enterprise A wanted to acquire copper piping, then enterprise B, the manufacturer, should have that copper piping

[17] Sándor Erdélyi, 'Külkereskedelem – egy beruházó mérnök szemével', *Valóság,* 19, no. 1 (January 1977), pp. 50–60. This article described the situation in Hungary in the mid-1970s; there was no reason to assume that matters improved later; on the contrary.

[18] Teréz Laky, 'A recentralizálás rejtett mechanizmusai', *Valóság,* 23 no. 2 (February 1980), pp. 31–41.

instantly available. Life, as they say, is not like that and the pipes were seldom where they should be. But of course there was a knock-on effect, as enterprise A, in the absence of the pipes, could not fulfil its obligations to enterprise C and so on. In practice, the system survived on a series of patchwork arrangements, sometimes illegal, sometimes merely informal, that acted as a corrective to the plan. The broader consequence was that planning itself and the bodies entrusted with enforcing it became discredited. The shortages resulted in defensive behaviour by other enterprises, like hoarding, and also by consumers, who were deeply sceptical of official promises, which they knew would never be met, and therefore behaved 'irrationally' in market terms by buying whatever they could whenever they could, thereby adding to the distortions.

The under-qualified personnel, the excessive bureaucratic regulation and the under-financing produced an overall state of affairs that continued to exacerbate the softness of the system (as defined and discussed in the previous chapter), so that the ability to implement decisions, for the state actually to carry out what it said it was doing, was increasingly limited. Softness was least applicable to areas where political power was directly challenged, for here the instruments of coercion were prepared to enforce the will of the élite. Still, even in this area there were, to put it mildly, contradictions. During the trial of the murderers of Fr Jerzy Popieluszko, the popular pro-Solidarity priest in Poland, it emerged that the killers, members of the secret police, had difficulty in keeping up with their intended victim because his Volkswagen Golf was faster than their Polski Fiat.[19] Or, to put it another way, poor-quality equipment was impeding the work of the secret police. This is quite apart from the tale of amateurishness and incompetence that is so characteristic of the way in which the Polish secret policemen planned and executed the murder. In other areas of administration, however, the gathering softness was growing ever more evident and the trends noted in the last chapter can be extended and amplified.

There was one final, almost desperate throw by these régimes in their quest for legitimation – legitimation by power alone. This was a deceptively simple proposition: communist parties ruled because they ruled, by right of possessing power. The implication of this claim was that the systems had legitimately arrogated supreme power to themselves by their original revolution and no one could strip them of it, or else. The trouble was with the 'or else' and its undertone of readiness

[19] Roger Boyes and John Moody, *The Priest who had to Die: the Tragedy of Father Jerzy Popieluszko* (1986), pp. 142–3.

to use force. Despite the massive investment in coercion and the regular, symbolic flaunting of force – through ceremonies like Liberation Day (i.e. when the Red Army conquered the country), Armed Forces Day, Frontier Guards Day or even Secret Police Day – the reality lay elsewhere. As the self-doubt, the softness, the uncertainty, the lack of purposiveness advanced, the will to use force declined correspondingly. And crucially, the intellectual difficulty with legitimation by power was that, when that power was visibly challenged, the claim was by definition undermined. All it needed was for a sizeable number of people to follow Havel's call and to reject the system; or, as Lenin is supposed to have said somewhere, if the entire audience in a theatre sneezed simultaneously, the sets would collapse. By the end of the 1980s the communist systems looked dangerously like theatre sets, albeit few people recognized their weakness before their collapse.[20]

Patterns of Social Autonomy

With the decline in the will and ability of the régimes to fill the entirety of social, economic and political space, tentative steps were taken by society to expand its autonomy. Several different areas were carved out in this way, at times without much overlap. However, it should be stressed that, in the central area of political power, the régimes held firm and no form of political representation was established until after the communist parties conceded their own defeat. To this extent, the key feature identifying Soviet-type systems as a distinct political formation, the claim to a monopoly of power, initiative and organization, remained intact until the end. This also helps to explain the speed of the collapse. The moment that this last feature was gone the system could no longer exist.

The autonomy constructed by intellectuals in the interstices of the system[21] continued to expand, albeit very gradually and unevenly. This had two broad aspects. The technical intelligentsia had made a tacit deal with the system, that it would be permitted to use its specialist knowledge as long as this did not interfere with the party's monopoly of power. With the fraying of the edges of power the limits and rules of the game grew unclear, and this contributed to the frustration felt at political interference cutting across the lines of technical rationality. To

[20] One of the few who did was Zbigniew Brzezinski; see his *The Grand Failure: the Birth and Death of Communism in the Twentieth Century* (1989) and the text of his Hugh Seton-Watson Memorial Lecture, 'From Eastern Europe back to Central Europe', in *A Year in the Life of Glasnost* (1988).

[21] See the discussion in chapter 7.

this may be added that the technical intelligentsia was less and less enamoured of the failure of the system to match the West in development. A good illustration of these processes may be seen in the report prepared semi-officially by a group of Hungarian economists at the end of 1986, entitled *Turning Point and Reform,* which warned the party leadership that without far-reaching reform of the economic system involving greater marketization, the country's economy was headed for disaster. It underlined its argument by pointing out that the Pacific Rim countries had effectively overtaken the communist world in economic development and were outperforming it, even though they had started later and from a lower base-line. The implication was unavoidable: the Soviet-type system was an economic failure. This document was the most public (and publicized) critique, but there were less widely known analogues from the Institute of Forecasting in Prague and from Polish economists. In Bulgaria too a younger generation of technocrats had looked at the West and concluded that what it had to offer was far in advance of the Soviet model.

Society also sought to regain and expand its autonomy by engaging in a variety of economic activities, building on the patterns of expanded economic space discussed earlier. The private sector in agriculture (the household plot), with its complex parasitical relationship to the state, may never have been more than a simulacrum of private enterprise on the land in economic terms, but it undoubtedly helped to instil a more independent-minded attitude sociologically and to some extent even politically. The ancillary economic activities in towns – from repair work to consultancies – performed a similar function for sections of the urban population, from workers to intellectuals. For all practical purposes something like a twofold labour market was coming into being, in which some individuals could market their skills and thereby lessen their economic dependence on the state. This pattern was most advanced in Hungary, but there were parallels elsewhere.[22]

Several aspects of this process should be noted. First, there was the significance of time. As noted in the previous chapter (see page 192), any practice acquires a special quality if it has been unchallenged for a while, even if it is formally deviant in terms of the system. The possibility of greater economic autonomy gradually acquired the character of a customary right, not one that could be enforced, of course, but one that was politically too troublesome to disturb. In this way small sections of society further enhanced their independent-

---

[22] István Kemény, *Ouvriers hongrois 1956–1985* (1985) discusses some of these issues.

mindedness by regularly enjoying what began as a privilege, and this encouraged others to try their luck.

Access to economic autonomy strengthened the preparedness of those involved to ignore the bureaucracy and its myriad regulations or alternatively to simplify the situation by trading favours in exchange for ignoring the rules. This pattern, in turn, drew the bureaucracy, particularly at the local level, into expanding the networks of favours and patronage. Naturally, there were barriers which could not be breached – the formal power of the party was the most serious obstacle, but the status of key individuals in the power structure was also important – but on the whole there was little to impede the process of broadening the experience of society and weakening the system. Furthermore, in the secondary economy, norms had to be regarded as authentic. While dealing with the state, the individual felt that he was powerless and therefore permitted himself any and all deviations from the rules that he could effect successfully. In dealing with others in the secondary sector, the transactions were real and far more unmediated, so that some experience of operating with genuine codes of conduct was gained.

Not all of this was positive from the standpoint of greater autonomy. Obviously, access to economic autonomy was very partial, both economically and politically. Thus only those sections of private agriculture flourished which had both a product and a market. If a particular cultivator owned land at some distance from a town, it was almost useless to try and supply the urban market, because the distribution network was too under-capitalized and too personalized to permit him greater self-enrichment. The absence of capital mobility and the determination of the state to keep self-enrichment within the bounds of the family likewise militated against the widening of the process. The fact that infrastructure was starved of investment did not help either. Essentially any such expansion would too significantly undermine the power of the *nomenklatura* to protect its own positions.

Nevertheless by the late 1980s, with variations from country to country, middle levels of the bureaucracy were increasingly complaining at their loss of income and status as the newly prosperous were challenging the supporters of the system. At the same time this growing economic autonomy had other consequences. It provided an opportunity for the newly well-off to exercise patronage and to seek to change the existing patterns of social mobility in their favour. Architects, for example, were certainly benefiting in Hungary and Poland, as well as Yugoslavia, from the ambitions of those with money to build themselves elegant dwellings, frequently in themselves an expression of conspicuous consumption. The extraordinary new villas on the hills of Buda were not built solely for the party élite, but the new economic, professional and technical élite too.

The quite unbelievable amounts of money made by the medical profession throughout the area could only be spent in ways like this or in buying hard currency on the black market at whatever the going rate was. The relationship between all these groups and the state was complex, for the state both made their prosperity possible and constituted an impediment to the further growth of empowerment through unchecked economic and professional activity. Thus capital goods formally in state ownership were regularly used by workers in factories, with the benign neutrality of the management, but the possibility of emancipating this activity entirely was not feasible, for the reasons suggested above.

The problem of what to do with profits was never resolved in any of these countries. Formally the commitment to egalitarianism remained a kind of off-stage referent, although the rhetoric of the system had generally switched to denouncing those who regarded the state as a universal milch cow, something that was conveniently ignored by Western egalitarians, who continued to purvey their socialistic illusions about the Soviet-type system until the very end. The formal commitment did have a real consequence, however – it made it impossible to elaborate a socialist concept of 'just profit' and, as noted, blocked the emergence of a capital market ('the exploitation of man by man' rather than, it might be said, the exploitation of man by the state). In the absence of any guidelines on profit and likewise of a socialist concept of consumption, for these were essentially 'capitalist' phenomena, the fate of surplus earnings became arbitrary and unpredictable.

The only rule that was applied, albeit informally, was that such large sums should be spent invisibly as far as possible. Certainly, the sumptuous villas and holiday homes were tolerated, especially if they were built at the behest of the professional strata rather than well-to-do enterpreneurs, but the relics of austerity and egalitarianism made this toleration a reluctant one, which encouraged those able to afford it to spend their money as quickly as possible. After all, there was nothing worth saving for, was there? Besides, at the end of the day the *nomenklatura* preferred people to expend their energies on making money rather than indulging in political mischief. It was an uncomfortable state of affairs, with more or less constant tension between the formal and the real parts of the system, but it was the least bad option in the circumstances.

The growth of economic activity sketched here was much the most advanced in Hungary, where the Kádár régime effectively abandoned earlier attempts to maintain monopoly control of the economy and simply permitted society this form of re-empowerment; then it went on to claim credit for it, as a 'reform', something that its Western admirers readily swallowed, rather than recognizing the move as a failure of the system. In Poland, where the continued existence of private owner-ship in agriculture gave the country's economic structure a qualita-tively different look anyway, the second economic sector was not as developed and remained more parasitical on the state; on the other hand, the amount taken directly from the state through various corrupt deals exceeded that in Hungary, at a guess.

In Czechoslovakia control was tighter, but not impossibly so, and the régime ensured that the bureaucracy, professions and other élite groups had access to sufficient surplus income to permit the acquisi-tion of a weekend house, a car and other consumer durables. Sig-nificant sections of the working class similarly experienced a growth in their standard of living and the agricultural sector was too insignificant to matter. The situation was tighter still in Bulgaria, but again the élite enjoyed access to a variety of goods and badges of status. Romania was a greatest exception, thanks to Ceausescu's decision to squeeze consumption massively in his relentless pursuit of debt repayment. This generated extensive informal and corrupt behaviour, but it was focused on goods to be acquired from the state and not independently of it. Yugoslavia, of course, was in an entirely different category.[23] In all, the loosening of the system allowed sections of the population, varying in size according to the country, a route away from the all-enveloping paternalism of the party-state and the direction of greater individual choice and responsibility.

Civil Society

A much greater impact was made by the democratic opposition and its arguments in the 1980s. The mechanisms of the opposition sketched in the previous chapter were not significantly changed, except that the continued existence, and in some cases expansion, of opposition activity were in themselves noteworthy. However, the content of these arguments also deserves some analysis. The democratic opposition

[23] The following works are relevant: Janine Wedel, *The Private Poland* (1986); Ivan Volgyes (ed.), *Social Deviance in Eastern Europe* (1978), particularly Andrzej Korbonski, 'Social Deviance in Poland: the Case of the Private Sector', pp. 89–111; Georgi Markov, *The Truth that Killed* (1983); Peter Bell, *Peasants in Socialist Transition: Life in a Collectivized Hungarian Village* (1984); István R. Gábor and Péter Galasi, *A 'második' gazdaság* (1981).

argued its commitment to democracy on the grounds that it was seeking to re-establish civil society. This concept was left undefined, but it was broadly interpreted as the end of the party's political monopoly of organization, initiative and political thought and language. Correspondingly, atomized individuals would be emancipated and and society would be revitalized and transformed into groups of 'citizens', with the will and capacity to determine their own affairs without the tutelage of the infantilizing state.

As implied, this was to be a two-pronged process, intended to re-energize society politically and incapacitate the system. The latter proved to be far easier than the former, as it subsequently turned out. But the opposition's origins in measuring itself constantly against the all-embracing state and its desperate quest for intellectual and political space marked it indelibly. A Soviet-type system could only give rise to the kind of opposition that it did – one concerned with highly intellectual issues like 'space', 'dialogue' or 'authenticity', with the character of power and so on, rather than bread-and-butter issues like prices and wages. And because the Soviet-type system was quintessentially concerned with the concentration of power and the permeation of all spheres of society by politics, the opposition tended to develop an aversion to power as such, to reject it, together with the institutions for the control of power, and to place its faith in a qualitative re-evaluation of life, in which power would be so diffused that political life in the conventional sense would be unnecessary. This was the approach that came to be known as 'anti-politics'.[24]

If the central organizing experience of the democratic opposition was the totalizing state, the doctrine of human rights became the single most effective weapon in its armoury, one that wrought devastation in the intellectual coherence of the system. But human rights are not and never could be a political programme in themselves, only instruments for diluting the self-legitimation of a totalizing ideology that was running out of options.

To take the democratic opposition beyond human rights posed certain difficulties, not least because the doctrine represented a kind of lowest common denominator on which all its suppporters and sympathizers could agree. Nevertheless attempts were indeed made, and these varied considerably from group to group and from individual to individual. What was particularly striking in this connection, though this was far from having been emphasized at the time, was that in Poland, Czechoslovakia and Hungary, the three countries where the

[24] György Konrád, *Antipolitics* (1984).

opposition had established itself,[25] democracy was conceptualized in rather different ways.

In summary form, in the Czechoslovak opposition, the scene was dominated by Havel's rather idealistic approach. He posited a rather idealistic goal, in which individuals would assume responsibility for their social actions and in which, by implication, there would be no need or at best minimal need for institutions and interest aggregation. He envisaged a civil society of equal citizens coming together in autonomy and eschewing institutional organization, as that could never accurately reflect social reality, but would distort it through the requirement for an anonymous bureaucracy, accountable to no one, an opacity and thus the release of individuals from responsibility. In addition to idealism, Havel's project was marked by a strongly ethical and anti-utopian quality, directed as much against the West as communism, which postulated individuals behaving more than a little like members of democratic opposition.[26]

Adam Michnik shared the emphasis on ethical values as the means to inspire society and political action. He looked to a situation where reason would rule rather than ideology or passion; tolerance rather than intolerance; history would be a guide to action rather than a source of mystification; and civil society would be marked by a restoration of human dignity. Michnik's project would be achieved through the idea of social self-protection, society organizing itself from below in groups and coming together in community. There would be no vision of an ideal society, as that would lead to the imposition of terror – this parallels Havel's anti-utopianism – and equally there would be no doctrinal purity. Running through Michnik's writings is a deep suspicion of power, but no clarity on how power was to be structured and controlled, other than through ethical and humanistic values. 'The leading idea of Solidarity is to achieve a Self-Governing Republic and not to seize power,' he wrote.[27]

[25] There was also a slow shift from dissent to opposition in the GDR, to some extent under Czechoslovak influence, but principally under the impact of events, through the recognition that the problems being addressed by the East German opposition were not single issues, like disarmament, but derived from the essence of the system. However, it should be noted that this opposition never broke with socialism and tended to see itself as a kind of loyal opposition, had the régime permitted such a thing. *East European Reporter* published a number of documents which supported this proposition.

[26] Havel's ideas are widely available in a number of volumes, notably *The Power of the Powerless* (1985), *Disturbing the Peace* (1990) and *Open Letters: Selected Prose* (1991).

[27] Adam Michnik, *Letters from Prison and Other Essays* (1985); the quotation is on p. 90.

The Hungarians produced separate strands in their approach to the problem. György Konrád argued in favour of anti-politics, while János Kis took a more nuanced approach. Konrád's position was essentially that all power was undesirable, that individual autonomy and the freedom to think were needed to offset the exercise of power by the state. Anti-politics, he argued, concentrated on ignoring official hierarchies and on developing the small freedoms which already existed, with the eventual objective of pushing the state into the margins of life.[28]

Kis's thoughts were developed in response to the shock of the declaration of martial law in Poland and took the form of asking the question: what exactly are we in business for, if we can allow ourselves to be demoralized by an external event? His solution was that opposition meant more than merely issuing declarations and extending the influence of non-régime ideas in the intellectual world. To an extent the functioning of the system itself must be affected by the opposition, by demonstrations of civil courage, by standing up to middle- and low-level representatives of the system and insisting that formal regulations must be followed, that where the ostensible legislative framework offered openings these should be exploited. By the mid-1980s, however, Kis's ideas had moved on and he concluded that the strategy of using the system through involvement in it and ignoring it where appropriate had reached its limits. This was what lay behind the launching of the document entitled *Social Contract,* a call for the introduction of one-party democracy, which has also been described as 'constitutional communism'. The core of this idea was that both the party and society would accept a different distribution of power. The party would continue to rule – this was essential to satisfy the Soviet Union – and society, as represented in parliament, would oppose, while an independent legal system would act as the arbiter between the two.[29] There was no suggestion of the anti-institutional attitude of Havel in his thinking and his anti-utopianism was, perhaps, even more pronounced, in that the question was never really tackled directly. Kis looked to the establishment of a liberal democratic order in which there would be legal, procedural and institutional guarantees of freedom.

The effect of this broad current of ideas was less than its protagonists hoped and more than the systems could cope with. In no country

[28] Konrád, *Antipolitics.*
[29] János Kis, *Politics in Hungary: For a Democratic Alternative* (1989). See also Kis, *Vannak-e emberi jogaink?* (1987). My own own views of one-party pluralism are set out in George Schöpflin, 'Reform in Eastern Europe', *Slovo,* 1 no. 1 (198) pp. 1–5.

could the democratic opposition constrain the party-state to take much notice of it, let alone enter a dialogue. Nevertheless, the very existence of the opposition and the constant reminder that an alternative existed, not only for the West but at home as well, proved to be dislocating and disconcerting, above all because of the relationship between the demands of intellectual legitimation and the growing doubts, fed by systemic decline and the existence of an alternative paradigm, as far as pro-régime or neutral intellectuals were concerned. In Czechoslovakia, for example, by 1989, despite severe repression and a readiness on the part of the rulers to use high levels of force, there were many inside the system, not just members of the opposition, who were prepared to sign documents and protest against the régime's harshness. In Poland the situation was inherently different and the Jaruzelski leadership made only fitful attempts to regain the loyalty of much of the intellectually active population. And in Hungary, the extent to which alternative ideas had spread was shown by the 1985 elections, in which a fair number of independent candidates, with no connections to the democratic opposition, articulated ideas similar to those that had been published in samizdat.

The Impact of Perestroika

While the types and scope of autonomy claimed through nationalism have already been dealt with, in their negative as well as positive aspects, it is worth discussing the impact of Gorbachev's perestroika in the communist states of Central and Eastern Europe. Until Gorbachev's accession to power in 1985, especially under Brezhnev but also under his successors, the Soviet Union had become a completely conservative state, resolutely opposed to change. Indeed the Soviet conception of communism excluded all idea of change. The new leadership revived the possibility of modifying, if not actually transforming the system. This possibility was at first cautiously received, both by politicians and by public opinion, which expected nothing positive from the Soviet Union. However, as Gorbachev's words and actions filtered through to Central and Eastern Europe, these views began to shift and, over time, a growing number of people concluded that the end of immobility was in sight.

This was an important psychological shift. For half a generation perspectives and horizons had been limited by Soviet conservatism, so that the gradual acceptance of something new provided a new sense of space and even lent a degree of dynamism to those looking for reform. The intensity of this varied from country to country. In Hungary and Poland scepticism and a degree of condescension ruled until virtually the end, but in Czechoslovakia and Bulgaria some sections of the population were decidedly encouraged by Soviet developments. When Gorbachev visited Prague in 1987 he was given a very favourable popular reception, even while the party leadership was decidedly unenthusiastic about his calls for change. In Bulgaria the Zhivkov leadership had sycophantically chosen to broadcast the first channel of Moscow television on a full-time basis to Bulgarian audiences, which seemed safe enough under Brezhnev and excused the Bulgarians from having to make their own programmes, but when glasnost reached Soviet television the Bulgarians were left with a most delicate situation. The party conservatives were highly alarmed by the new and dangerous content of Soviet television, but they could hardly censor it or terminate the transmissions.

The contrary case was also observable and, in the event, was almost certainly more influential. Party reformers had been systematically undermined in their demands for change by what can be termed 'the Soviet pretext', that while reform might be very desirable, there was nothing to be done as long as the Kremlin objected. This pretext made life very easy for the Central and East European conservatives, who as a result were exempt from having to put up substantive arguments against reform. The arrival of perestroika ended this easy life, although for a while the conservative argument was sustained by the proposition that it was not worth starting anything, seeing that Gorbachev would not remain in power for long. This argument, too, decreased in effectiveness as the 1980s wore on and by 1988–9 those arguing against change were left intellectually naked.

Different Strategies for Weathering the 1980s

The 1980s were a complex decade for the Soviet-type systems of Central and Eastern Europe and while it would be nonsense to suppose that any of the ruling élites foresaw their own imminent demise, on the contrary, yet they were forced into adopting increasingly diverse strategies for their survival. The basic identity of the system was hallmarked by the formal monopoly of power and ideology; the safeguarding of this twofold monopoly represented the last line of defence. Once they were abandoned the system was doomed, as will be investigated in the next chapter. But régimes do not foresee their end and even less do they make preparations for this event; rather, they sought to shore themselves up by a variety of increasingly short-term devices. I have already described in this chapter how democratic centralism was degenerating, but this did not, of course, mean that the holders of power were ready to abandon it straightaway, however threadbare the texture of their support might have been.

In Poland, Jaruzelski proved incapable of reversing the drift that had in reality begun in 1976, when strikes showed up the emptiness of Gierek's rhetoric. The Solidarity era, from this perspective, merely intensified an already perceptible trend, showing that the aims and aspirations of the rulers were wholly at variance with those of society and no compromise was possible, thereby excluding the chance of establishing any equilibrium. State and society were locked in an awkward, actively non-consensual relationship, which eroded the leadership's ability to launch any meaningful initiatives. This state of affairs then fed back to the élite's attitude towards its own purposiveness, weakening it and locking it more tightly in confrontationalism.

The state could rule the streets and exercise some control through economic levers, but it could do nothing to restore its own authority in the face of a hostile and suspicious society, many of whose members had a fair amount of knowledge of the vastly superior economic conditions in the West. The divisions within the élite, for Jaruzelski had cobbled together a relatively unstable coalition through which to rule, were similarly unhelpful in fostering change, for some elements in the coalition would resist all attempts at reform, as these would undermine its privileges.

By the mid-1980s it was an open question as to whether the ideology of the system was still totalizing, except in the most formal sense, to which occasional reference was made but without any significance other than ritual. Certainly there was a toleration of *de facto* institutional pluralism that was unknown elsewhere, with a wide range of samizdat and non-state cultural activity involving broad swathes of society. The role played by the Church was also important, in as much as it propagated a very different system of values – one that was regarded as authentic by the great bulk of the population – and had its own network of institutions that were exempt from direct state intervention. Furthermore, the appropriation of national symbols and much of Polish history by the Church left the state in an unusually weak position when it sought to construct a secular national identity. It was a competition that the party-state simply could not win.

The coalition that Jaruzelski had put together proved, in fact, to be too diverse to be suitable for launching a strategy that might pull the country in the more consensual direction needed to revitalize the economy, the only way in which a balanced relationship between rulers and ruled could be attained. One of the key obstacles to change was that the economic and industrial bureaucracies, as in other Soviet-type countries, regarded any dilution of the *nomenklatura* system as anathema and any general opening towards society as fatal to their powers and privileges. Jaruzelski tried more than once to initiate various reform projects, but these all ran into the sand.[30]

The best illustration of this process came in 1987, when a major economic reform was trumpeted, yet again. Before its formal publication unofficial promises were made, including some to the Western press, presumably in the hope of influencing Western bankers, that the *nomenklatura* system would be dismantled in much of the economy and that technical ability would become the dominant criterion for appointment. When the actual report was published there was no trace of these promises, in other words the coalition had succeeded in sinking them. This and other weaknesses in the reform project, as well as the general disdain for the system, led Polish society to reject the now diluted reform plan in the referendum that was called, for Jaruzelski and the generals understood that, without a measure of popular support, the belt-tightening required by the scheme would not be acceptable.

The extent and depth of the gulf between rulers and ruled were shown dramatically in the spring and summer of 1988, when two waves of strikes left the authorities floundering. Indeed, what was particularly thought-provoking about the strikes was that they were in many respects aimless, anomic demonstrations of hostility to the system. It was only with difficulty that the strikers were pacified. Increasingly, the régime was forced to look at the country and to recognize that it was close to ungovernability, unless power received added infusions of legitimacy. At the deepest level it was this realization that prompted Jaruzelski to launch the contacts with the opposition that debouched into the Round Table negotiations of early 1989, probably strengthened by the fear that if underground Solidarity also lost its authority over society there would be no negotiating partner for the régime at all.

In one crucial respect Polish options were severely limited by the Solidarity experience and its aftermath. Not only was Poland saddled with a massive debt that it could never really hope to pay off, and as a result was effectively blocked from gaining substantial new loans, but equally the West made it clear that it regarded the Jaruzelski

---

[30] At the height of Poland's international isolation in the 1980s emissaries were dispatched to argue in the West in favour of economic and financial support by reference to a 'reform plan' that could only succeed with Western backing; without this benevolence the 'reform' would be undermined by 'the hardliners'. This hoary gambit found relatively little support, although there were always some takers.

régime with distaste. Whatever official Poland and its representatives might try to do, Western sympathies were with Solidarity and the declaration of martial law was regarded as somehow illegitimate. The moral support given to the opposition by the West was an added factor in bringing it home to the régime that full totalizing control could not be reimposed on society and that the undiluted Soviet-type system could not be re-established. This was something of a burden for a political order that sought its legitimation at least in part in an all-encompassing ideology.

The distaste felt for Czechoslovakia was even stronger. Indeed, the country was largely ostracized for twenty years, because the West could never fully come to terms with the forcible suppression of the Prague Spring. Unlike the régime in Poland, the Czechoslovak rulers made a virtue of a necessity. They emphasized and intensified their international isolation and used it to keep the population in a state of quiescence, insulated from the worst temptations of Western consumerism. This was coupled with a strong and constant ideological mobilization – at the verbal level only, of course – which stressed vigilance, ideological purity and undying loyalty to the Soviet Union.[31]

The reality of the strategy was somewhat different and, it must be said, not unsuccessful by the régime's criteria. The Husák régime was a coalition of ideological hard-liners and illiberal technocrats, with Husák himself more in the latter category than the former. The hard-liners, however, were more than strong enough to prevent any serious shift toward technocratic pragmatism, something that one of their number, Vasil Bilak, once described as the 'blue sky theory' that there was no danger whatever from Czechoslovakia's internal enemies, the revisionists of 1968. In effect, the experience of 1968 had become the point of reference for the Husák régime and it was used as a potent weapon by the hard-liners in blocking change, by the argument that any move towards reform, involving some dilution of party power, would automatically end up with a Prague Spring type of transformation. For twenty years the very word 'reform' was banished from the Czechoslovak political vocabulary. The different elements in the coalition kept each other in check and effectively prevented any easing of the system in politics, economics or culture.

The bases of the system were laid in the 1970s and were not changed in any meaningful way until the very end in 1989. These consisted of a pacification of Slovakia, a new upward promotion of working-class activists, rigid ideological orthodoxy and the absolute

---

[31] On Czechoslovakia see V.V. Kusín, *From Dubcek to Charter 77: Czechoslovakia 1968–1978* (1978) and Radio Free Europe Research reports, *passim.*

denial of change, together with the satisfaction of consumer demand. Husák, a Slovak himself, was able to 'normalize' – to reimpose Soviet-type norms – Slovakia quickly and efficiently in 1969. The 1968 reform had never had substantial support in Slovakia and his purge of its supporters was followed by granting the intelligentsia its place in the sun, something that the Slovaks had never enjoyed. For the first time in the history of the country large numbers of Slovaks were were given positions in the federal bureaucracy, and the maintaining of federalization as the sole relic of 1968 ensured that Slovakia would remain a loyal political base. In addition a steady and continuous transfer of resources from the Czech lands to the rather poorer eastern part of the state further satisfied its population. This dispensation removed a major source of friction that had caused Novotny not inconsiderable problems in the 1960s; the Slovaks, by being granted some satisfaction of their national aspirations, became supporters of the system.

Something analogous to this happened to the working class. The Czech working class had had a long tradition of having its economic and symbolic aspirations satisfied through communism, and in exchange gave the system a good deal of support. In the 1970s the party found itself in possession of a unique resource – patronage over around half a million jobs in the bureaucracy, these being the posts forcibly vacated by the supporters of the 1968 reforms. It used this resource to promote a new generation of working-class activists to positions of power and status. This gambit secured their loyalty to the system, not least because those newly promoted frequently knew that they were less well qualified and less competent than those whom they replaced. The remainder of the population was encouraged to satisfy itself through consumerism and to turn inwards, away from political and public consciousness.

The outcome of this political arrangement was to enable the post-1968 leadership to retain its power – it was able to shrug off the challenge from the Charter 77 opposition, for example – but at a very high cost both economically and politically. The country's economy fell steadily behind in terms of modernization and came to resemble a museum of industrial archaeology as outdated machinery and practices were never changed, infrastructure ran down inexorably, and productivity stagnated. Politically the system ensured the passivity of society, but was quite incapable of generating support. Indeed it was not designed to do so, with the result that when the Soviet Union launched perestroika, Czechoslovakia's most important external resource suddenly disappeared and domestic critics were gradually emboldened to press for change. Finally, it should be noted that the system had devastating consequences for popular attitudes in social and cultural terms. Social indicators like abortion, suicide, alcoholism all pointed downwards and the loss of any sense of purposiveness left a deep mark. In a very real sense the Husák régime abolished change and thereby stopped time; there was no sense that the 1980s were significantly different from the 1960s, social patterns, aspirations, hopes were subjected to a sense of sameness from which there was no escape. In this sense there was only a present, no past or future.[32] That in turn wrought havoc with the moral codes that underlie cultural cohesion.

The strategy adopted in Hungary, on the other hand, was widely accepted as much more successful and, indeed, it even acquired a name of its own. While no one ever seriously discussed 'Honeckerism' or 'Jaruzelskism', Kádárism became respectable both as nomenclature and as a variant of communism. In fact this was an illusion. The illusion was that reform, however defined, was still taking place, so that Hungary was a better place, with better prospects, than any other communist state in Central and Eastern Europe and would go on being so.

The key to this spell lay in what came to be known as 'negative legitimation', namely a proposition that while the existing state of affairs in Hungary might have been imperfect, it was the least bad available at that particular moment. This ingenious and disingenuous proposition was extraordinarily effective in disarming both domestic and external criticism. Potential domestic opponents of Kádárism, still traumatized by the aftermath of the failed revolution of 1956, were more than ready to go halfway to find a compromise with the régime and for all practical purposes went threequarters of the way. The régime, for its part, was similarly shell-shocked by having been swept away overnight in 1956 and understood that it would not be able to reimpose a hard-line, high mobilization system; that in order to safe-guard its monopoly of power, it would have to give society some stake in the system.

This approach to government was not developed in any conscious fashion, but evolved through trial and error; in its earliest version it was in place by the mid-1960s and then went through various modifica-tions, until by the 1980s it could be described as mature.[33] This also meant that it was increasingly running the danger of sclerosis, an

[32] The idea of time having come to a standstill is one of themes explored by Milan Kundera, in *The Unbearable Lightness of Being* (1984). In visual terms I found that the areas of Prague not visited by tourists had much the same appearance in 1991 as they had had in 1968.
[33] Bennett Kovrig, *Communism in Hungary: from Kun to Kádár* (1979).

inability to launch and absorb new initiatives, although this was far from evident except to the most perceptive of observers.

In hard political terms the Hungarian economy was gradually winding down and was less and less able to renew itself, while verbally the illusion of 'reform' was sustained with agility and intelligence. In the 1970s, in order to cushion the economy against the impact of the first oil shock, the dominant part of the élite – natural authoritarians, ouvrierists, anti-agrarians – reversed the slow trend away from subsidizing inefficient enterprises and began to take on Western credits to support their expensive habit, with far-reaching consequences for the country's indebtedness. Although attempts were made to halt the shift towards recentralization after the second oil shock of 1979, the bad habits picked up earlier in the decade were too entrenched and Kádár's own conservatism itself became an ever greater obstacle to change. For much of the 1980s the balance of negative legitimation held, but it was increasingly fragile.

Perhaps the pivotal event in the decline and fall of Kádárism occurred in 1983 when, after several years of debate and pressure, Kádár declared that there would be 'no reform of the reform', code for thoroughgoing change. The result was that the economic situation continued to deteriorate and popular acceptance of the system declined commensurately. This downward slide could be measured in terms of Kádár's own popularity, which, having reached its apogee in the early 1980s, sank noticeably as the decade wore on and was in itself a source of systemic weakness, given the anchoring function that leadership had come to play. It was in this context that the opposition's publishing of the *Social Contract* document, with its unequivocal demand for Kádár's departure, began to eat into élite self-legitimation, especially when the demands were coupled with less outspoken but equally solidly argued propositions in favour of a redistribution of power made by party reformers. The mechanism of negative legitimation ultimately broke down when growing numbers of people in the élite became convinced that the system was not the least bad that could be expected at the moment and, indeed, that without reform it would face collapse. And collapse was more than a metaphor; it was clearly identified with the situation in Romania.

The strategy pursued in Romania began from a very different set of basic assumptions and these naturally produced an utterly different outcome. This strategy only made sense in the context of Ceausescu's exclusive control over the levers of power and his mounting paranoia and isolation as the years went by. Ceausescu's objective was illusory – an illusion different in quality and nature from the one that Kádárism sought to foster – to make Romania a strong, independent state, freed of any and all threats of external intervention in its affairs. The foundations for this strategy were laid in the 1960s, but its main features were developed and intensified in the 1970s and, despite all the contra-indications, they were strengthened in the 1980s.[34]

The pillars of the strategy were Ceausescu's genuinely unique personality cult; his promotion of members of his extended family into positions of power and influence as the sole reliable instruments of his will; the promotion of massive, generally functionless, cultic projects; the deployment of Romanian nationalism and the constant rhetoric of external and internal enemies; the extraordinarily high level of mobilization sustained by terror; the creation of an élite made entirely dependent on Ceausescu through devices like continuous rotation of cadres; the inflation of party membership until it included around a fifth of the adult population; the intertwining of bureaucracies and, in the 1980s, a growing reliance on the military for non-military roles (like running the energy industry).

The Western loans taken on in the 1970s, having become due for repayment in the 1980s, suddenly came to be regarded as a source of dependence and Ceausescu insisted that every penny would be repaid, interest and capital, on the nail, which they were. The cost to the Romanian population, which had to bear the burden of this strategy in massively squeezed consumption, was discounted. According to official and, therefore, untrustworthy figures, per capita annual meat consumption fell below 28 kg by the mid-1980s. The result was a numbed, terrorized population that was quite incapable of participating in anything remotely resembling modernity and, therefore, quite incapable of dealing with modern technology.

Indeed, the Ceausescu years thoroughly destroyed a sense of community in Romania by devastating the traditional moral codes and failing to replace them with anything other than contingent, transient values. Every transaction came to be regarded as suspect, and there was no concept of fair exchange; rather the view spread that all social life was negative and resulted in negative-sum games. Atomization was near complete. The moral codes that provide the cohesiveness to hold communities together had been very largely destroyed, and the sense of good and evil, of acceptable and unacceptable, had been transformed into something wholly discretionary. Even nationhood was affected, because this was perceived as something appropriated by Ceausescu, so that all identities were affected in this negative sense.

The cultic projects, like the Danube–Black Sea canal; the bulldozing

---

[34] Trond Gilberg, *Nationalism and Communism in Romania: the Rise and Fall of Ceausescu's Personal Dictatorship* (1990).

and rebuilding of parts of Bucharest, including the unbelievable nightmare palace that Ceausescu had constructed for himself; the idea of systematization, the plan to reduce approximately 14,000 villages in the country by half and force the peasantry into soulless urban developments were all aspects of Ceausescu's megalomaniacal style and policies. They had no purpose other than to act out Ceausescu's supreme control over the country. The most extreme manifestation of this was, of course, the Ceausescu personality cult. Even allowing for the rather hyperbolic quality of Romanian public discourse, the encomia heaped on the leader surpassed all known modern equivalents, except perhaps Kim Il Sung's, which Ceausescu certainly regarded with approval. He began by signalling that he would like to be known as *conducator* meaning 'leader' and also the title assumed by Romania's wartime semi-fascist dictator Marshal Antonescu, and went on to higher things from there. Perhaps the most extraordinary expression of Ceausescu's cult was when he was declared divine on his sixty-second birthday,[35] but there was virtually no enhancing epithet that he was not awarded while in power. To Ceausescu's own cult was added the slightly lesser one of his wife Elena, who was again heaped high with all kinds of laudatory descriptions. The function of this cult was fairly straightforward, to ensure that the Romanian population understood that there really was no alternative to the ruler.

Ironically, even the ostensible aim of the strategy, to ensure that Romania would be completely independent, was undermined. As the West turned away from Romania in the 1980s, increasingly uneasy about the country's appalling human-rights record, Ceausescu found that the best market for the agricultural produce that made up the bulk of export earnings was the Soviet Union; and by the same token, a growing proportion of Romania's oil imports came from the Soviet Union too. Curiously, much of the West was reluctant to recognize this shift in Romania's foreign policy, which had been valued – possibly overvalued – in the 1960s and 1970s as a weakening of Soviet power. In consequence the United States, for example, continued to give a degree of support to Ceausescu which was quite unjustifiable in terms of either *Realpolitik* or morality and was explained by the bureaucratic culture of the State Department, where two decades of regarding Romania as an asset simply could not be sloughed off.

At the end of the day it is hard to discuss Ceausescu's Romania in terms of legitimacy at all. Ceausescu held power without any serious challenges and, precisely because so much of it was concentrated in

[35] Anneli Maier, 'Ceausescu Deified on his 62nd Birthday', *Radio Free Europe Research,* 11 February 1982.

his own hands, self-legitimation was automatic. In this context, however, it is noteworthy that when Ceausescu was publicly challenged, as he was on 22 December 1989, his self-confidence evaporated almost at once, something that was visible to television viewers of the events. It was entirely logical in the circumstances that it took a palace coup disguised as a revolution to remove him. On the other hand, it was evident that the élite which succeeded him was determined to keep power in its hands while distancing itself from its late patron as far and as fast as it could.

There were some parallels between Ceausescu's hypertrophic style and that of Zhivkov's in Bulgaria, but it should be made quite clear that the Bulgarian leader retained a sense of moderation by comparison with his Romanian counterpart. For all that, Zhivkov did seek to project himself and, as long as his daughter Lyudmila was alive, his family as well, onto the political scene.

The Zhivkovian strategy was fairly simple. It involved relying on the country's egalitarian tradition by ensuring that the gap between the highest and lowest wages did not become excessive. Support for the party was generated by high levels of nationalism, the principal targets of which were the Turkish minority and Yugoslavia, especially the claim by the Macedonians to be an independent nation. Sycophantic loyalty to the Soviet Union was practised with assidulty and relations with the West were always fairly low-key. Zhivkov's only potential problems lay in the party *apparat*, which he never fully controlled, and with the younger generation of intellectuals, who looked increasingly towards the West for their models. But in essence the country was stable for all of the 1980s and, even at the end, it looked for a while as if the communists would hold on to power in a new guise.[36]

Finally, in this brief survey, it is worth adding a short assessment of the German Democratic Republic. The GDR was unusual in the spectrum of Central and Eastern European states in that it was alone in having no underlying basis as a nation. Its existence was legitimated by its being committed to communism, and, at the moment when this was abandoned, the purposiveness and legitimation of the state, not just the system, disappeared, leaving reunification as the only alternative. Erich Honecker's strategic options were circumscribed, therefore, something that the East German leadership fully understood. It enjoyed some advantages, however, and, these cast an interesting light on possible communist survival strategies. In the first place, the existence of a viable, Western alternative acted as a constant spur to the East German party, so that it could not afford to allow itself to become

[36] John D. Bell, *The Bulgarian Communist Party from Blagoev to Zhivkov* (1986).

complacent.[37] The kind of corruption that engulfed the Polish party was always kept in check in the GDR.

Second, East German intellectuals were committed to the system, because if they were not they could generally leave for the West without too much difficulty. This was unlike, say, the position of the Poles, who knew that there was only one Poland. This meant that, throughout its existence, the East German leadership could rely on the obedience of its intellectuals to a far greater extent than its communist counterparts elsewhere. This reliability was underpinned by the in-tellectuals' attitude towards society, a relic of the 1953 uprising, which led them to the conclusion that the population of the state was untrust-worthy and would abandon communism at the first available moment. They were not far wrong, incidentally. This implied that the intellec-tuals and the régime needed each other and would go down together. Even the democratic opposition thought of itself as a part of the socialist tradition and sought to play a role as a loyal critic of the system.

Third, the East German party was also in a unique position in that 3 million of its citizens had left for the West in the 1950s; generally it is the most energetic and independent-minded who emigrate, so that those who remained were inclined to greater quiescence. Besides, this meant that the régime's access to patronage was fairly good, giving it the opportunity of rewarding its loyal supporters with jobs in the *nomenklatura*. Quiescence was also assured by a very high level of coercion or the threat of coercion. The state was enveloped by a complex series of security, educational and other bureaucracies, which supervised, indeed nannied, the population with far-reaching thoroughness, leaving little room for autonomous thinking.

Fourth, there was the generally developed state of the economy, which allowed the party to pursue a consumerist policy. In reality, as it emerged later, the economy was in a far worse state than it appeared, but for the time being, in the 1980s, there was enough slack to main-tain the strategy. In this the GDR was actively aided, even abetted, by the policies of West Germany. In the late 1960s the Bonn government formulated its policy of *Wandel durch Annäherung* or change through *rapprochement*, which was aimed at slowly humanizing the East German system by giving it a sense of security. In fact, the East German régime hardly changed, though it happily accepted the hand-

---

[37] On the GDR the following literature is relevant: David Childs, *The GDR: Moscow's German Ally* (1983); Henry Krisch, *The German Democratic Republic: the Search for Identity* (1985); and Klaus von Beyme and Hartmut Zimmermann (eds.), *Policymaking in the German Democratic Republic* (1984).

outs from Bonn. According to estimates in the mid-1980s these amounted to something like 1.5 billion dollars a year, and without them East Germany would have sunk rapidly into bankruptcy, with dire consequences for its political stability and, for that matter, viability.

Finally, from the late 1970s on, the East German régime sought to give society a separate German identity by developing its theory of a German socialist nation. This complex and contradictory set of ideas was, for the most part, eyewash and never went beyond a form of words. The basic idea was that East Germans were German, but because they were socialist, their Germany identity had nothing to do with the corrupt capitalists down the road. This attempt to square the circle was noteworthy only for the contortions used to justify it. Otherwise the project was interesting for the way in which more and more German history was unearthed and incorporated into a socialist history. Under Walther Ulbricht, Honecker's predecessor, historical figures like Martin Luther, Frederick the Great and Bismarck were condemned as proto-fascists, the precursors of Hitler, symbolizing everything that was undesirable in Germany history. Gradually, one by one, all these historical figures were given a new gloss and incorporated into the 'socialist' history of the GDR as worthy exemplars. The idea of Bismarck as a forerunner of communism has so bizarre a quality that it deserves special mention.

Thus all was changed and gradually the entire panoply of Prussian history was rehabilitated, militarism and all. While never explicitly acknowledged, this Prussian dimension had an undeniably anti-Polish and anti-Russian edge, inasmuch as it alluded tacitly to *Drang nach Osten* and the generally anti-Slav stance of Prussia. It was clearly used in this way to ward off any threat from Solidarity in 1980–1 and the sense of contempt for things Russian also had an odd, anti-Soviet twist, with significant consequences for legitimation. Shortcomings in the East German system were in effect explained away by hinting that, of course, the system as it existed had been deformed by the Russian history of the Soviet Union and that as Marx was a German anyway, the GDR would have been a much more efficient state if only it had been allowed to implement a genuinely German variant of communism. In the end, of course, none of this mattered and the East German state vanished overnight when, first, Honecker was removed under Soviet pressure and then the new leadership found itself unable to cope; the state unravelled with hardly a single hitch.

In a way the previous paragraph can be taken as a kind of epitaph for the 1980s as a whole. The Soviet-type system had run out of resources, political, economic, cultural and perhaps most important though least visible, moral. These states had lost their capacity for self-reproduction as one social group after the other abandoned its belief in the viability of the system. This assessment of the 1980s shows how and why this loss of faith happened.

9

The End of Communism in Central and Eastern Europe

Quite out of fashion, like a rusty mail
In monumental mockery.

Shakespeare, *Troilus and Cressida,*
III. iii. 152–3.

The collapse of communism and the transformation of the political systems of the countries of Central and Eastern Europe was a surprisingly rapid process.[1] It was equally surprising that the Soviet-type systems, which had once seemed so well established and firmly grounded, should have caved in as easily as they did, even if the signs of systemic decay had been visible for much of the 1980s. Decay can last a long time and most observers were mesmerized by the apparent durability of communism. The course of the events in this process was, first, the transformation of Hungary, Poland and then, more rapidly, East Germany, Czechoslovakia, Bulgaria into nascent democracies, as symbolized most spectacularly by the chipping away at the Berlin Wall after the announcement on 9 November 1989 from East Berlin that all GDR citizens were free to travel to the West. The divided halves of Europe could now begin the slow movement towards reintegration. And this was then followed by the most dramatic of all the transformations, the Romanian revolution. The collapse of communism in Albania was almost an afterthought and in Yugoslavia the process led to the bitter inter-ethnic fighting starting in 1991 that has been called the 'war of Yugoslav succession'.

In order to make sense of the collapse and to clarify the argument about it, many of the points made in previous chapters will be restated here, though without any attempt to analyse them in detail; consequently a degree of overlap is conscious and deemed methodologically useful.

It is important to be clear as to what it was that decayed and was replaced in the countries of Central and Eastern Europe. In terms of the rhetoric of legitimation it should understood that Soviet-type systems have next to nothing in common with socialism as this was defined in the West. Democratic socialism has traditionally involved commitment to equality, social justice, respect for the individual, widening choice and access to the decision-making processes that govern the life of a community.

Soviet-type systems had nothing in common with any of these ideals, but they used the slogans of socialism as one of their legitimating myths. Their connection with the socialist agenda was twofold. First, they used the state as an instrument of social engineering, which was an acceptable device to Western socialism as well, but they did this without regard to society. Second, they used the language of socialism entirely devoid of its content as a means of legitimation at home and abroad. Whereas at home this attracted very little support, especially after the 1968 invasion of Czechoslovakia had signalled that the Soviet road was mere form without real content, in the West many regarded the verbal commitment to socialism in the communist world as real and gave these slogans some credence, even while deploring some of the failures of the Soviet-type systems. This credulousness effectively prevented much of the Western left from undertaking a much-needed analysis of these systems and thereby contributed to their survival for a while.

In reality, as argued in this book, the pivot of the Soviet-type system was that it enforced the construction of a wholly politically determined future, in which all spheres – economic, social, legal, aesthetic, religious, etc. were subordinated to political criteria regardless of appropriateness in the name of an ideologically derived goal, socialism. The rulers of these systems, essentially because of their one-sided distribution of power, could never accept any significant degree of social autonomy and, indeed, consistently destroyed all manifestations of uncontrolled social thought and action, particularly in any organized form.

The initial commitment to an ideologically derived concept of the future gave these systems a degree of cohesiveness and consistency, albeit these were firmly directed against the wishes of the majority. However, once the shift towards the decomposition of ideology began in the 1970s, as seen in Gierek's Poland or Husák's Czechoslovakia, for example, the systems became increasingly arbitrary and discretionary.

---

[1] The data for this chapter, unless otherwise indicated, are derived from *Radio Free Europe Research Reports* and *Eastern Europe Newsletter*.

The language of the ideology was still deployed in public, but decisions were taken by other criteria, ranging from the pragmatic to the opportunistic, which undermined consistency and made it easier for individuals to deflect public policy to personal gain.

In the short term this pattern of development was useful for disorientating criticism from below and relativizing it. But in the medium to longer term it led the rulers into an intellectual and eventually a moral morass from which they found it impossible to escape.

However, the damage inflicted on these societies during the forty years of Soviet-type rule was far-reaching and profound, often in ways that have yet to be fully understood. Crucially, the Soviet-type revolution destroyed the civil societies that were coming into being after the Second World War. Before the communist take-overs these countries were at best semi-developed – even the Czechoslovak experiment in democracy between the wars had its shortcomings – but they were not the homogenized, simple polities that they became as a result of the Stalinist revolution. The countries of the region had embarked on their own, often rather fitful roads towards modernity, which recognized the existence of the market and the move towards greater complexity. These processes were cut short and all subsequent development took place under the aegis of the state.

In the process of collapse, six factors can be isolated as having played a role in all the countries, although in some of them the events were so telescoped that their role might have been marginal. The six factors are (1) economic decay; (2) the loss of support from pro-régime intellectuals; (3) the break in the surface unanimity of the system; (4) the growing division in the leadership; (5) the role of the crowd; and (6) the international dimension.

Economic Decay

The political system introduced by Stalinism was in many respects simple and unstructured and depended heavily on the potential or actual politicization of all transactions. Its centre was the *nomenklatura*, the arrangement by which all significant appointments were made with the acquiescence of the party and relying on political criteria. This proved to be particularly damaging in the running of the economy. Soviet-type economies were, in the final analysis, concerned not with matching supply and demand, but with administering inputs and outputs; in other words, the economy was detached from the consumer and producer and non-economic criteria were frequently used to distort economic rationality. The much-vaunted central planning system tended towards conserving a simplified industrial structure that was less and less capable of meeting the challenge of the world market. And once the Stalinist model of autarky diminished in its significance, the imperatives of the world market could no longer be fully ignored.

The unproductive and uncreative nature of the Soviet-type system was masked for a long time. It could survive by, in effect, pursuing a kind of slash-and-burn policy, in that it used up existing resources without adding enough to replace them. In the first stage it lived off the surplus labour in the countryside and the capital resources that had been amassed before communism. These were largely exhausted by the early 1960s and, indeed, the states of the area experienced a general downturn at that point, with Czechoslovakia becoming the first communist country to register a negative growth rate. In the second stage the running of the system, which was concentrated on first-generation heavy industry (coal, steel, energy generation and heavy metallurgical manufactures), was supported on the release of additional energies derived from the economic restructuring of the 1960s and the neglect of infrastructure, as well as to some extent of agriculture. In the third stage the running and expansion of heavy industry – to an extent the area underwent a second heavy industrialization in the 1970s – was financed by borrowing from the West, a resource that ran out with the Polish fiasco of 1980–1.

At this stage, the pressure to return to economic rationality became hard to fend off, but it took the best part of a decade before the rulers concluded that the political equation was in danger of coming apart. The situation was most clearly visible in Poland, where the reconstruction of a neo-Leninist, politically determined system after 1981 may have brought the semblance of a temporary and highly conditional stability, but the growing gulf between rulers and ruled was threatening to become explosive. A particular danger-point was the steady loss of authority by the rulers, which was replaced by a kind of normlessness. In essence, although the economic deterioration was the proximate cause of the crisis, this was no more than its most salient manifestation. For all practical purposes, by the end of the 1980s Soviet-type systems were no longer capable of self-reproduction.[2]

Loss of Support from Intellectuals

Not surprising, the Soviet-type systems imposed on these countries after the Second World War never gained genuine popular legitimacy;

[2] János Kornai, *Ellentmondások és dilemmák* (1983).

at best they were tolerated in periods when the going was good by the bulk of the population, as, say, in Poland in Gierek's heyday or Hungary when Kádár's régime was at its zenith. But these systems never really sought legitimacy in the Western sense of seeking continuing popular approval expressed through open elections. Rather they claimed to derive their legitimacy from the multi-tiered proposition that the party ruled because it was the legatee of a communist revolution, that it was the repository of history, that it was the most rational and efficient force in the state, that it represented the best and most progressive elements of the national tradition and, when all these claims were exposed as threadbare and no longer creditworthy, the party insisted on its monopoly rule because it held power and there was no alternative.

What was fascinating about the unravelling witnessed in 1989 was, in the first place, the fact that it took so little to launch the process and, second, that once started it happened at breathtaking speed. The reserves of the system were exhausted, reserves in this connection meaning not just the economic and material benefits that it was supposed to deliver, but its political and moral reserves as well. This raises the problem of self-legitimation. An authoritarian élite sustains itself in power not just through force and the threat of force, but more importantly because it has some vision of the future by which it can justify itself to itself. No régime can survive long without some concept of purposiveness to project its existence forward in time.

In both Poland and Hungary the vital nexus in the process of delegitimation was the loss of the support of the significant sections of the critical intellectuals and the intelligentsia. Other than in periods of high revolutionary mobilization, that is to say after routinization has overcome the initial impulsion to power, the supporting intellectuals sustain authoritarian régimes by acting as a mirror in which the rulers see themselves reflected. It is vital that this mirror reflects a picture that is positive for the rulers, hence censorship, because at the moment when some other, much more realistic picture is visible in the public sphere – and the intellectuals control the public sphere through their hegemonial control of language – the rulers become confused. This confusion is then transmitted through the hierarchy, upwards and downwards, until the ruling party loses its cohesion and becomes prey to self-doubt. Something like this was experienced in all the major crises of communism in the post-war period – in Poland and Hungary in 1956, in Czechoslovakia in 1968 and in Poland in 1980.

The next likely stage is the radicalization of at least a section of the party membership and moves towards self-preservation by the middle and upper levels of the élite. The membership is likely to demand a return to some kind of idealized vision of socialism; the upper echelons, on the other hand, will try to limit changes to the minimum in order to preserve as much of their power as is compatible with the new situation and possibly more. The pace and extent of change then depends on resistance to change by the leadership, the effectiveness of control over the media and the perception of threats from a popular upheaval.

One near standard feature of change in Soviet-type polities is their propensity to try and avoid paying the high political price that goes with the redistribution of power and to change leaders rather than policies. This was tried in Hungary with the dropping of Kádár in May 1988, in the GDR with the purging of Honecker in October 1989, and in Czechoslovakia the exchange of Husák for Jakes in December 1987. None of these devices worked, essentially because the situation was too complex for personnel changes to count as an effective reform move.

A Crack in the Surface Unanimity

Soviet-type systems relied heavily for the maintenance of power on the party's control of the language of public discourse. All ideologically derived systems place great emphasis on ideological conformity, because any deviation from that threatens one of the central legitimating myths of the system as a whole. In this context public unanimity has a multiple purpose. It serves as a means of reassurance to the élite that the system is in place and is not under threat, that the party remains in control and that opposition is being kept out of sight. Second, the continued use of the ideologically derived language, Marxist–Leninist jargon, was a constant reaffirmation that the party was still relying for some of its legitimation on the claim that it ruled by virtue of having seized power in the name of a Marxist–Leninist revolution. Third, the insistence on the use of this language had a simple censorship function. It kept unsanctioned ideas away from public opinion and prevented the expression of alternatives so that challenging ideas could not be articulated. That, in turn, helped to sustain the atomization of society on which political stability and social peace were predicated.

The loss of control over the public sphere, therefore, was a serious stage in the death of Soviet-type systems. It implied that an important aspect of power had begun to fray and that loss of support from the supporting intellectuals was gaining public notice. By the same token, it meant that alternative ideas were likely to gain wider currency, radicalizing the population and the party membership and giving them an option to reconstitute themselves as a society, as subjects, rather than as mere objects of power. This was the moment at which the now dissident intellectuals would start to give wider currency to their ideas, to generate public support for them and to signal that, maybe, the system was after all vulnerable.

This stage was reached in Hungary in late 1986 and early 1987, when several key groups of previously loyal intellectuals concluded that the Kádár régime was neither ready nor willing to engage in the far-reaching reforms they regarded as necessary, and hence that they would have to go public with their critiques. Inevitably this involved a struggle, but by this stage the contest was more even than it had been before, as the party's self-confidence was beginning to erode. In Poland this stage came less dramatically. Under martial law censorship was never as rigidly enforced as in the other countries and, in any case, it was under constant challenge from the enormous amount of samizdat that was being produced. In a very real sense the public sphere was circumscribed by secondary public opinion, or the parallel polis, to give it the name that some commentators have used.

In Czechoslovakia, on the other hand, the whole process was much more telescoped, both the second and third stages. The loss of support from sections of previously supportive intellectuals could be observed from late 1988 and early 1989 and the public sphere was increasingly witnessing bolder deviations from the officially sanctioned norm, though the surface unanimity never cracked in the sense suggested above. That took place during the 'velvet revolution' itself, after the formation of Civic Forum on 19 November 1989, when television and some of the press began to report fully on the demonstrations of that week. In both East Germany and Bulgaria the process was equally abbreviated and tended to merge together, rather than appearing as separate stages. In Romania the crack in the surface unanimity was only a brief moment in the process of collapse. The demonstrations, in Timisoara and then in Bucharest itself, against Ceausescu occurred against a background of a very rapid rise in expectations and the preparation of a palace coup.[3]

Leadership Divisions

Once the system came under challenge the communist party leaderships also began to lose their way. Essentially, they had no answers to

---

[3] Edward Behr, *'Kiss the Hand You Cannot Bite': the Rise and Fall of the Ceausescus* (1991).

their dilemmas in their storehouse of ideas. In simple terms, they could either try to contain the processes of systemic disintegration by force or they could give way more or less gracefully. The implications of such divisions were very serious, however, for hierarchically organized polities, because it meant that at every level the bureaucracy would be at a loss for instructions and the decay of the system would accelerate as a result.

This paralysis began to affect Hungary with the removal of Kádár in May 1988, after which the Politburo was deeply divided between the adherents of those who essentially took the view that Kádárism without Kádár was a viable option and those who recognized, however tentatively, that new departures were needed if the communist party was to retain any role at all. In Poland General Jaruzelski found himself under severe pressure from public opinion in 1988, through the strikes of that spring and summer, and was able to shed the sceptics from the leadership – the sceptics, in this case, being the opponents of a dialogue with Solidarity.[4]

In Czechoslovakia the division was not perceptible until after the demonstrations had begun.[5] At the Central Committee meeting of 24 November the party élite was told that the Ministry of the Interior had forces at its disposal sufficient to deal with demonstrations of up to 50,000, but could not cope with the 200,000–300,000 people who were crowding into Wenceslas Square every day. The Central Committee was then asked if it would accept the use of the armed forces, which it refused. Essentially, there was a division in the leadership over whether it was prepared to employ such a high level of force, which might well result in a blood bath. It refused, possibly mindful of the outcome in Tienanmen Square earlier that year.

In Bulgaria a group of reformers in the Politburo, who had been scandalized by Zhivkov's earlier move to expel the Turkish minority, decided that they would seek to topple him, which they did successfully. And in the GDR, after Honecker's fall, the leadership remained profoundly divided and weak, beset as it was by the repeated hammer-blows of demonstrations and pressure for emigration.

The newly promoted leaders clearly hoped that their reputations would halt the slide towards collapse and that their personalities would be more than sufficient to reinvigorate the élite. These hopes were completely confounded, largely because other factors were already at play – the impact of perestroika being the most important –

---

[4] Mauro Martini, 'La stagione del compromesso in Polonia', in Federigo Argentieri (ed.), *La fine del blocco sovietico* (1991), pp. 173–89.
[5] Judy Batt, *East Central Europe from Reform to Transformation* (1991).

which then encouraged those pushing for change to demand more. The dropping of the old leaders, instead of becoming a positive factor by becoming accepted as 'reform', as had happened so often in the past, turned out to be the necessary condition for the collapse of the system as a whole.

The speed of events certainly played a role in the second wave of countries affected – the GDR, Bulgaria and Czechoslovakia. In Hungary the leadership switch was earlier and the process could be seen in slow motion. In Poland the situation was different, with Jaruzelski actually being embedded into the new system under the Round Table Agreement as a part of the price for a redistribution of power. The problem for the new leader, however, was similar elsewhere. He was obliged to rally the faithful, to infuse the party and *apparats* with belief in the system at a time when the scent of change, probably including the redistribution of power and the redefinition of communism, were in the air. This would have required political skills of a very high order under any circumstances. The bureaucracies were already gripped by self-doubt, while the anti-reformers, well entrenched during the years of no change, were not prepared to permit initiatives of this degree of radicalism. The consequence was that the new leader tended to be hesitant, to clutch at straws, generally without any overall strategy.

The fate of the hapless Egon Krenz, who took over from Honecker in the GDR, illustrated this process vividly. Most notably, within two weeks of his succession, he was under enormous pressure to permit free travel to the West, to which he responded with evasions and prevarications, until possibly in error he created the impression that he would relent. In these circumstances lower-echelon officials were confused and, on 9 November 1989, the Berlin Wall was opened, although whether this was fully intended is open to doubt. Once the concession had been made it could not be retracted, and the system fell apart with extraordinary rapidity.

The Role of the Crowd

Soviet-type régimes spent a geat deal of time and effort in keeping societies atomized and preventing them from integrating themselves. Consequently, unauthorized and unsupervised demonstrations were a major threat to these systems, inasmuch as they called into question the power and authority of the rulers. When authoritarian régimes are faced by mass action, which they can no longer control, they tend to disintegrate very rapidly. Possibly this has been especially true of Soviet-type systems, which still hark back to the concept of revolution and proletarian action and therefore found it even more difficult to come to terms with mass action directed against them. The eroded self-legitimation of Soviet-type leaderships simply could not withstand the massive symbolic acting-out of popular disapprobation

Although the most spectacular such case was that of the crowds demonstrating night after night in Wenceslas Square in the centre of Prague, it was not the only one. The earlier demonstrations in various East German towns, especially the regular Monday evening rally in Leipzig, which for all practical purposes assumed the functions of a kind of alternative mass assembly, made an analogous impact on the East German leadership, which suddenly saw its authority and self-legitimation vanish. The removal of Zhivkov in Bulgaria was given an added fillip by the largest demonstration in Sofia since the war at the time when the anti-Zhivkov faction was ready to move. The crowds in Bucharest suddenly turned on Ceausescu, who was visibly discon-certed by this; they were playing the role of the trigger in the revolu-tion that had already been launched by the events in Timisoara earlier that week. In Timisoara a crowd had gathered to prevent the Securitate, the secret police, from evicting the ethnic Hungarian pastor, László Tökés; this seemed to have been the signal for others, including ethnic Romanians, to join in the demonstration. When the secret police fired on the crowd this did not have the expected reaction of dis-persing them, but spurred them to further action. In all these instances, then, mass action proved to be a key factor in the transformation.

However, these were not the first instances of crowd power. In October 1988, under the influence of the Serbian demagogue Slobodan Milosević, crowds chased away the provincial government in the Vojvodina and, a little later, in the republic of Montenegro. Milosević was acting to strengthen Serbian positions, but the pre-cedent was set and, no doubt, was not lost on others. In Poland the strikes of 1988 were the functional equivalent. Only in Hungary was there no serious public action at all. In all probability the Hungarian leadership felt deeply threatened by the memory of the revolution of 1956, when the demonstrating crowds had caused the collapse of the communist leadership overnight.

External Factors

The international situation had a major impact on the changes. In both the slow and the rapid transformations the process was clearly affected by the international demonstration effect. This had several aspects. In the first place, the fact that the Soviet Union was no longer a force for the *status quo* but in the vanguard of reform was significant in making it more difficult for conservatives to rely on the pretext of Soviet disapproval to keep change off the agenda. This was undoubtedly effective in Poland and Hungary from about 1987 onwards, in widening the potential agenda of change and making it possible to sketch scenarios of democratization which would have been dismissed as absurd beforehand.

From the earliest days of the imposition of communism on Central and Eastern Europe, the Soviet constraint had hemmed in the local political actors and the Brezhnev doctrine had codified this into a rigid set of rules. Before any major initiative could be expected from the Central and East Europeans the code would have to be revised substantially enough for it to be persuasive. The coming to power of Gorbachev in 1985 and the signal that change was back on the agenda was a first step, albeit Gorbachev's ascension was treated with marked scepticism in Central and Eastern Europe. They had seen too many new Soviet leaders to accept Gorbachev without very hard evidence that matters were changing. The launching of perestroika and glasnost did not in itself convince the sceptics, but gradually, between 1985 and 1988, they were increasingly persuaded by the Kremlin's apparent neutrality on reform. This neutrality certainly made life much harder for the local anti-reformers.

On the other hand, doubts were reinforced by Gorbachev's reluctance to rescind the Brezhnev doctrine and to be explicit about his aims regarding Central and Eastern Europe. The first really major, serious move was the announcement that the Soviet Union would withdraw its forces from Afganistan. The implication of this gradually filtered through and it was interpreted as a signal that the Soviet Union would no longer use force to impose its will to sustain the orthodox version of the Soviet-type system.

Equally there is reason to suppose that the Kremlin accepted the strategies of the reform communists in both these countries and encouraged them to persevere. It has been suggested that, at some stage in the autumn of 1988, Gorbachev discussed the legalization of Solidarity with Jaruzelski and indicated that there was no Soviet objection. Presumably the Soviet reasoning was that without such an opening, which would be controlled, the situation in Poland might shift towards ungovernability and thereby store up far greater trouble for the Soviet Union in the long run. In Hungary the reformers likewise received some backing, probably at the time when Alexander Yakovlev, a senior Soviet Politburo member close to Gorbachev, visited Budapest in November 1988. It was shortly after that visit that the beginnings of a multi-party system could be discerned.

Soviet intervention was much more direct in the other three countries, though not in Romania, where Moscow had little leverage anyway. When Gorbachev visited the GDR on the fortieth anniversary of the founding of the state in October 1989, it was quite evident that he voiced his disapproval of Honecker's refusal to consider change, despite mounting evidence of dissatisfaction, notably through the great wave of emigration to the West. The critique of Honecker was certainly aimed at bringing about change in East Germany and giving support to pro-reform forces; on the other hand, it is doubtful if the Kremlin anticipated the consequences of the opening of the Berlin Wall. Gorbachev, in all probability, shared the general view of the East German state, that it was sufficiently strongly grounded to survive the shifts that he wanted.

In both Bulgaria and Czechoslovakia, in November 1989, it was reported that the respective leaders, Zhivkov and Jakes, had appealed for Soviet backing and were refused it. The Warsaw Pact summit in early November in effect denied the justifiability of the 1968 invasion of Czechoslovakia, thereby undermining the Brezhnev doctrine and one of the main planks of the Jakes régime's legitimacy. When events started to move in Czechoslovakia the Soviet Union was fairly certainly involved. It was not enough to destabilize the Jakes régime by public criticism – as had been the case with Honecker – so the KGB was involved in helping to organize the early demonstrations in Wenceslas Square. Here again, as with the GDR, the question of unintended consequences surfaces: what did the Soviet Union really intend in Czechoslovakia? It seems unlikely that Gorbachev wanted the elimination of communism and it is a more plausible interpretation that the Czechoslovak régime was weaker than it appeared and control was lost at an early stage.

The Kremlin's reasoning, arguably, was based on the analogy of Poland and Hungary, where the party reformers seemed to be adequately placed in the political constellation. In Poland the communists retained the key portfolios of the interior and defence, despite the installation of the Solidarity government. If there was a Soviet strategy at all, then it seemed to have been that some kind of a formal communist presence in positions of power would be enough to guarantee Soviet interests and the presence of non-communists was needed to revitalize the countries' economies, thereby removing a burden from the Soviet Union. At the same time, accepting the redistribution of power would also be helpful to the Soviet Union's reformist alibis *vis-à-vis* the West. If Central and East Europeans could be seen as shifting towards liberal democracy, then it was a reasonable expectation that the West would pick up some of the bill for their rehabilitation. It would seem, therefore, that the crumbling of the East German and Czechoslovak régimes was not a part of Soviet calculations; on the other hand the gamble paid off in Bulgaria, certainly in the short term. In the 1990 elections the successor party to the communists, the Bulgarian Socialist Party (BSP), won an absolute majority, although the level of polarization in the country meant that no stable government was possible. After the 1991 elections the BSP emerged as the largest single party, but a right-wing coalition actually took power. It definitely looked, on the other hand, as though in Bulgaria neo-communists would retain a sizeable share of power for a good many years, although with the transformation of the Soviet Union into Russia this had become an academic issue.

Equally important in the role of the crowd was that events in the other Central and Eastern European countries became more difficult to ignore when they were no longer isolated in one country or another. It is hard to avoid the conclusion that the sight of demonstrating crowds in the GDR influenced those in Prague – accessible through West German, Austrian, Polish and Hungarian television – and that the changes in Poland, Hungary and the GDR affected events in Bulgaria. And at least some of the explanation for the Romanian revolution lay in the fact that Bulgarian television was accessible to Romanians in Bucharest, so that they were aware of what was happening in the rest of Central and Eastern Europe.

This phenomenon should also underline the significance of television and the spread of information through the modern media. It was no longer possible to seal off one country from the rest of the world, despite the best efforts of some communist leaders, at any rate in Europe. The importance of this has already been mentioned in passing, but it should additionally be noted here as a delegitimating factor. The speed of the change was undoubtedly influenced by the visual nature of information, far more vivid and digestible than the written word, to which communist censorship had no answer.

The Political Processes

In Poland, as previously mentioned, the key event in the process that debouched into the formation of a Solidarity-led government was the wave of strikes in the spring and late summer of 1988, which brought home to the rulers that the country was headed towards ungovernability, inasmuch as the strikers had ceased to be particularly concerned about material benefits and were striking for its own sake. This created a situation in which an explosion became a serious possibility. This recognition prompted a section of the élite to open negotiations with (the then) underground Solidarity in a quest for a negotiating partner that still had some authority over society. The Round Table Agreement of April 1989 was a relatively modest arrangement that provided for islands of democracy in a sea of authoritarianism, but the Agreement was simply torn up by the voters in June. That led directly to the reluctant acceptance of the first non-communist government in Central and Eastern Europe after the communist seizure of power.

In Hungary the process was not so dramatic. When stripped down to its essentials, the transformation in Hungary began in 1986 when the Kádár régime began to lose the loyalty of its supporting intellectuals, initially because Kádár refused to acknowledge that the country was in crisis and urgent reform measures were needed. This opened up the public sphere to mounting criticism, which met a ground swell of discontent from below. This spilled over into the party membership, which was sufficiently radicalized by May 1988 to remove Kádár and instal a largely new politburo. The new leadership was hesitant and low in authority, so that by the autumn of 1988 alternative political actors began to move into the resulting political vacuum.

Then, in 1989, the communist party was operating for the first time since the aftermath of the war in a competitive situation and was outmatched in political debate, making concession after concession. The role of Imre Pozsgay, who had decided that the creation of a Western-style liberal democracy was the only viable solution to Hungary's problems – valid in its own right and essential if Western support was to be forthcoming – was a vital factor in this process. By October 1989 the communist party concluded that it must undergo radical change itself if it was to survive politically and to this end it dissolved itself in order to begin a rebirth. The dissolution of the party freed both the parliament and the government from party discipline and a set of radical measures, ensuring that the bases of the communist party's power were eliminated, were enacted into law. These included the liquidation of the party's private army, the Workers' Guard; the banning of communist party cells from work places; and a public accounting by the party for all its property. Thereupon Hungary was proclaimed a liberal republic, in preparation for the elections scheduled for the spring of 1990.

The route towards democratization, starting with economic deterioration, had also affected Bulgaria and Czechoslovakia, though this was not the sole factor, as has already been seen. It was not the only instrument of transformation. In the case of Bulgaria the latter half of the 1980s saw the rise of an intellectual opposition that had grown increasingly critical of Zhivkov's refusal to contemplate change. The initial impetus to criticism was the alarming decline of the environment, but this broadened out into a general sense of dismay at the state of the country, something that was intensified by the fact that Bulgaria transmits the programmes of the first Soviet television channel on a one-to-one basis. What had originally been by intended by Zhivkov as a piece of propagandistic pro-Soviet sycophancy exploded in his face when the Soviet media became engaged in glasnost. The last straw was Zhivkov's quixotic decision to expel Bulgaria's Turkish minority. This move, taken without much consultation, angered his politburo colleagues enough to split the leadership and an anti-Zhivkov coalition came into being. The anti-Zhivkov faction in the top echelons of the party had, at the same time, become sensitized to the growing wave of intellectual criticism from below. Having established that the Soviet Union had no objection to Zhivkov's removal and having seen a major demonstration of popular dissatisfaction with the situation in early November, they finally voted to remove him and replace him with Petur Mladenov.

In Czechoslovakia the process was unbelievably compressed, in that the key events took place in a little over a week. There were preliminary elements in the process that were similar, like many years of criticism from intellectuals, like Charter 77; an economy that was declining, though not yet in the catastrophic state that characterized Poland or Hungary; and then the growing evidence of popular disaffection expressed through street demonstrations. The crowds that filled the whole of Wenceslas Square in Prague, on and after 19 November, were estimated at several hundred thousand strong; and there were demonstrations in some provincial centres as well. The fairly high level of participation in the two-hour general strike on 27 November was very bad news for the leadership indeed, because it indicated that significant sections of the industrial working class, traditionally a base of support for the party, were ready for change. Another particularly ominous sign for the leadership was when party control over the media started to crack, as several newspapers began to reject the surface unanimity essential for effective authoritarianism and carry real reports of events. This was followed by demands from television journalists to be allowed to carry full coverage of the demonstrations.

On 24 November the leadership decided to resign and try and save the situation by salvaging as much of its power as it could by appointing less exposed but equally non-reformist successors. However, this device was unacceptable to Czechoslovak opinion, especially when it emerged that there were divisions in the leadership – the prime minister, Ladislav Adamec, offered to negotiate with the newly established opposition group, Civic Forum. The pressure to transform the communist system into democracy, once initiated, seemed inexorable, as the leadership's morale crumbled and was seen to crumble by public opinion.

Last-ditch efforts by the communists to salvage their power, by refusing to accede to a non-communist majority in the government and subsequently to try to prevent the election of Václav Havel as president, also failed. Thereafter the new government acted with enormous energy to establish itself.

Special Factors in the GDR

Poland, Hungary, Czechoslovakia and Bulgaria had one enormous advantage over the GDR. Even if their communist systems were in disarray, they had other reasons for their existence. In a very real sense, the Soviet-type systems of these countries have been parasitical on nationhood, inasmuch as the central constitutive element for Poland or Hungary that has held them together as polities was their sense of purposiveness as national communities.

This did not, of course, apply to the GDR, even if East German propagandists made a brave attempt to put together an entirely spurious socialist nation that purported to be the constitutive element of the state. In reality the GDR existed overwhelmingly because it was communist, and if that ceased to be its *raison d'être* went too. The point here is that, unlike the other polities of Central and Eastern Europe, the GDR's legitimacy was weak both as a régime and as a state. Thus the exodus of large numbers of the most able and most energetic East Germans in the summer and autumn of 1989 represented a severe loss of prestige to the state and the party leadership. It was only after the disintegration of the régime that it emerged that economic decay was a factor of some importance there too, as the alarming state of the country's economic decline came to be revealed.

Hence it was more readily understandable that the régime could be knocked off its balance so easily in 1989, by an issue that prima facie looked as relatively marginal as emigration. At the same time, the impact of the enormous crowds repeatedly taking to the streets in Leipzig, East Berlin, Dresden, Halle and elsewhere in October and November evidently deeply demoralized the leadership, which had sustained itself in power by keeping all dissent out of sight. In this context it was noteworthy that, during the 1980s, the one issue on which the Jaruzelski régime was quite obdurate was its hostility to public demonstrations of dissent, even while it was prepared to live with a sea of samizdat and other opposition activity that remained out of sight. The tolerance of the GDR's non-legitimate régime for publicly expressed dissent was very low. When in October 1989, in connection with the fortieth anniversary celebrations of the communist state, the Soviet Union withdrew its moral support and then large crowds demonstrated steadily for several weeks, the leadership first sought to save itself by dumping unpopular leaders and then by making one radical concession after the other.

There were interesting parallels with events in Slovenia, where the process was less spectacular and did not involve either far-reaching economic decay or massive popular protest. The shift away from party monopoly rule was brought about by a leadership that recognized that political transformation was in its interest, by an intellectual climate that was critical of the leadership but not actually, destructive, thereby ensuring that the limits of the debate shifted gradually, and ultimately also by external pressure from Serbia that was perceived by Slovenes as illegitimate and pushed them towards seeing the changing political situation as a part of their national identity and Serbian demands as a threat to that identity.

From Erosion to Collapse

What all this added up to was that the neo-Leninist systems of Central and Eastern Europe had reached a state of affairs where only a fundamental shift in both political and economic structures could save them from collapse. That of course meant the end of communism. As has been consistently argued in this book, the agenda of socialism had become so constricted, essentially from after the suppression of the Hungarian revolution onwards, that a 'fundamental shift' – the redistribution of power and the acceptance of the market – was tantamount to terminating communism or putting it out of its misery, as some might say.

Collapse too requires some discussion. Prima facie it was no more than a metaphor, but from the mid-1980s the area had the spectacle of Romania as an awful warning of what would happen when an authoritarian leadership ignored realities. In this sense, collapse could be taken to mean an economy where society is depressed to the lowest levels of consumption of the basic necessities, like food, heat, shelter and light. Society in this state of affairs ceases to function in any communal sense and atomization to the individual level is extreme. There is deep-seated anomie and very high levels of coercion. In

Romania the population was numbed and deprived of any sense of its own future, being forced to live with futures constructed by the ruler that it neither wanted nor understood. No leadership or élite wanted to follow the Ceausescu model.

In broad terms, what these polities needed was a new set of ideas and principles – a political formula – by which to mobilize society and capture the latent energies that had been held in check by the Soviet-type system. And after forty years no society would be satisfied with anything less than a thoroughgoing clean-out of the old one. Simply to conceptualize the new political, economic, social and, indeed, moral ideas would mean a radical shift in power relations in the direction of opening up the system to new actors.

The problem of new actors, however, was not as simple as it might have appeared on the surface. The functioning of Soviet-type systems was predicated on the elimination of alternative actors, in whatever sphere. During the Stalinist period there was a massive uprooting and destruction of the interlocking network of social solidarities that go to make up a civil society. The relationship between what forms of behaviour elicited sanctions and what brought rewards had been completely altered and made arbitrary. The reconstruction of social autonomy and new social compacts was not something that could be effected overnight. This made the process of democratizing the Soviet-type dictatorships a much harder task than effecting the equivalent with the right-wing authoritarianisms of southern Europe in the 1970s, essentially because in the latter markets and social autonomies had continued to exist and could be used as a basis for later pluralism.

In Western political systems individual and group interests are primarily identified in material terms and assessed by cost-benefit criteria; and political organizations cluster around these interests. Non-material interests – national, religious, moral, aesthetic, status or gender-related ones and so on – have a real but secondary function, principally in influencing the way in which material interests are understood at any one time. All this is very different in Soviet-type systems. Crucially, these were utterly destructive of any clarity concerning the perception and articulation of interests, because of the homogenization imposed on these societies. In effect, because Soviet-type systems sought to integrate all interactions into the political sphere, they constructed an enormously reductionist order. To undo the effects of this and to create conditions for the recognition of interests would take time and required particular mechanisms.

The immediate requirement in any transition is that there should be a mechanism for the transfer of power. In the communist case a way had to be found to pass power on to some group in society that would provide a degree of continuity, abide by any bargains struck and have enough popular acceptability to provide for stability. This posed a major difficulty, seeing that the communists had spent the previous forty years in trying to prevent any kind of alternative locus of power from coming into being. The solution was pioneered in Poland, where society had the best organization and underground Solidarity had a fair claim to represent the people. Certainly in symbolic terms the Solidarity logo had been completely assumed into the Poles' visible mythopoeia and to some extent in real terms as well. The Round Table was the device that worked well in Poland and it was followed in Hungary, Czechoslovakia, East Germany and Bulgaria; different solutions were adopted in Romania.

The Round Tables were composed of members of the democratic opposition and nascent opposition groups, together with individuals whose intellectual or other qualifications made them acceptable as experts or as mediators. Round Tables came up against a number of major problems. The communists might have been willing to share power, but they were not yet ready to write themselves out of the script entirely, although the Polish precedent implied that that was exactly what the population wanted. The Polish communists, in fact, fought a sustained rearguard action and negotiated an agreement that was far more favourable to the old régime than the situation warranted. This was torn up by the voters in the elections of June 1989. In Hungary too, where the talks took place in the shadow of Polish events, the communists proved more experienced in the negotiations and not infrequently succeeded in dividing the opposition against itself, with major consequences for party formation later; in the event, the communist party self-destructed and was unable to make use of the concessions it had won.

Finally, the Round Tables had to ask themselves the question – inwardly if not overtly – what their legitimacy and status genuinely were, how far they were accepted as authentic representatives of the society in whose name they were negotiating and what kind of agreements they could or could not sign. In the light of their political inexperience and their strongly intellectual origins or, where relevant, their experiences in confronting the totalizing state in the democratic opposition, they tended to work out agreements that emphasized legality and constitutionality, strong on principles and weak on practical detail, idealistic rather than pragmatic. All the same, the model was not unsuccessful, especially as both the opposition and the communists were in uncharted waters, and while the Round Table negotiations were to influence later developments, they could be regarded as an effective way of clambering out of the totalizing system.

Conglomerate Parties

Arguably it was this need to escape from enforced homogenization that resulted in a striking phenomenon in Central and Eastern Europe – the dominant opposition to the ruling communist party emerged into the political arena with some of the same characteristics. If the communist party was a body that sought to embrace and engulf all political, economic and social interactions and absorb them, it was inevitable that the paramount opposition party would acquire similar features, though without the totalizing quality of the former.

The conversion process in Poland was effected by Solidarity, which was not a political party in the Western sense but a kind of political conglomerate, in which all political interests were submerged in the name of the higher interest of opposing the Polish party. Once the Solidarity government was in power, the conflicting interests – Solidarity as political party versus Solidarity as trade union; neo-liberal, Christian Democratic and Social Democrat elements – began to come to the fore. Something analogous to this was taking place in Hungary, where the Hungarian Democratic Forum and the Alliance of Free Democrats had increasingly assumed the role of the leading parties by early 1990. The Forum included Populist, National Radical and Christian Democratic currents and possibly others, all with different, overlapping and conflicting views of the world, while the Free Democrats stood for a centre-left strategy, a commitment to the free market, rejoining Europe and an absolute rejection of everything that communism had stood for.

However, conglomerate parties were not only the only feature of the political scene. Paradoxically, as well as conglomerates, in some countries there was also a plethora of mini-parties, small or larger groups which called themselves political parties, though some were often no more than *ad hoc* associations. Their ultimate fate would be settled through the will of the electorate, but their mushrooming was symptomatic of the confusion in societies long repressed by the Soviet-type system, which now looked to reassert themselves.

In Czechoslovakia, for example, a scattering of small groups sprang into existence within days of the beginning of the 'velvet revolution'. In the Czech lands these included the Social Democratic, Green, Agrarian and Christian Democratic parties. The Czechoslovak Democractic Initiative, which actually constituted itself before the 'velvet revolution', stood for classical liberalism; in addition, there were a number of new parties in Slovakia.

The quality of the new party system and of the new parties themselves was also determined by the way in which democratic opposi-

244 The End of Communism

tion movements had functioned before the collapse of communism. The democratic opposition had emerged in the 1970s as one of the responses to the invasion of Czechoslovakia in 1968, which had signalled that reform of the system was defined exclusively by the Soviet Union and that any ruling party going beyond a certain threshold would find itself in trouble from the Kremlin. The threshold basically started when political pluralism – challenges to the leading role of the party – came up for discussion.

This left intellectuals with the choice of remaining silent or finding an alternative basis from which to act. A minority from inside the Marxist tradition concluded that official Marxism–Leninism was dead as an ideology and moved from this to abandon their previous claim for a monopoly of Marxism. This meant that they could place democracy and human rights on an equal footing with Marxism and that, in turn, allowed them to make common cause with non-Marxists for the first time since the communist take-over. Their intellectual need was for a set of values by which they could attack the system from the outside and undermine its totalizing quality. Human rights and democracy were ideally suited to this, not least because the régimes themselves had given pro forma recognition to these ideals.

From this basis the democratic opposition developed a consistent and ultimately demoralizing critique of the régimes, by claiming to act in the name of a higher morality than the one legitimated by the Marxian utopia. The difficulty with this situation was that while morality was extremely effective as the basis for opposition to a totalizing system, it was worse than useless for open politics. Competitive politics requires not moral purity and clarity, but compromise and bargaining. This reliance on morality led the opposition to adopt positions infused by ideas of moral purity, truth, clarity and transparency. All of this proved an excellent weapon to fight systems claiming the absolute right and power to intervene potentially in all aspects of life.

But at the point when the totalizing party-state collapsed, the moral basis of the democratic opposition was actually or potentially harmful. The problem was this. While the assault on the legitimacy of the system in the name of a higher morality was essential until the end of communism, in democratic politics the use of moral categories was confusing and destructive. Morality cannot be bargained, yet politics is about compromises over the allocation of resources, it is muddy rather than clear and does not offer full satisfaction to any of the actors. Indeed, the chances are that a political solution based on the full satisfaction of one actor would result in the deep dissatisfaction of another. The carry-over from the previous state of affairs could not be eliminated overnight. The political discourse of these countries was infused by calls to morality, for moral purity and other categories inimical to political compromise. This trend affected the nascent political parties that were emerging from the democratic opposition movements and would continue to inform politics for a while.

The pull of different political imperatives – moral purity and compromise – was seen most clearly in Hungary, where the new party system was most developed. However, elements were present in the other newly emerging democracies, notably in the GDR, where part of the weakness of the opposition was that it had acted as a moral pressure group for too long to be able to make the switch easily. In Hungary the opposition split into two broad groups – the Alliance of Free Democrats and the Hungarian Democratic Forum – each the successor of a current in the old opposition. Neither party could develop readily into an organization with constituencies, but both were infused by a propensity to moralize and to spend as much time attacking each other as addressing more pressing political issues. This definitely coloured post-communist politics for some time to come and the phenomenon was not confined to Hungary.

Another group of parties that requires discussion here were those that might be termed the historic parties. These were the political parties that existed before the communist take-over, were suppressed and absorbed by the communists and then re-emerged, often led by very elderly survivors from forty years before. The historic parties, precisely because they were from the pre-communist past, could claim a degree of historic legitimacy from their potential constituencies. Their continuity could be guaranteed by elderly leaders and they could appeal to their Western counterparts.

Their success varied. In Czechoslovakia there was little evidence that historic parties were returning to the scene, other than Social Democrats, and in the GDR too the satellite parties represented the tenuous link with the past. In Poland, on the other hand, while the satellite parties could and did play a significant role, the revival of the Peasant Party was a major factor. The Peasant Party had been a considerable force in the countryside and had been a serious antagonist of the communists and thus of the satellite People's Party.

In Hungary the Social Democrats and the Smallholders, both a major force before the take-over and both with a brief flicker of existence during the 1956 revolution, revived fairly quickly, but then their fates diverged. The Social Democrats were largely caught up in their past and seemed unable to make the transition into the 1990s by coming to terms with Hungarian realities as they had come into being after forty years of communist power. They could still command the allegiance of a smallish constituency among the industrial workers, but not the mass following that might have been theirs. The Smallholders fared better, not least because their rural supporters responded more readily than was the case in the towns. The party was successful enough to gain representation in parliament, but was then torn apart by personal feuding. In Romania, the historic parties – the Liberals and the National Peasant Party – both sought to re-establish themselves and they could both claim some successes in this regard, but they were under serious pressure from the National Salvation Front from the outset.

Finally, a brief discussion of the role of satellite parties is called for in this connection. These parties had retained a shadowy existence in several communist countries – Poland, the GDR, Czechoslovakia, Bulgaria – largely as historical relics. They had no genuine function, with one marginal exception, during periods of normal communist party control. The one exception was that individuals who did not want to join the communist party, but were under pressure to do so for career reasons – their positions in the *nomenklatura* required this – could opt to join one of the satellite parties and this was accepted as a surrogate, though this course would, of course, prevent that individual from rising above a certain hierarchical level. Otherwise the satellite parties were ceremonial appendages. On the other hand, in periods of weakened party control, the satellite parties gradually began to act as if they were real organizations, to try and reconnect with their constituencies and to act effectively in the new politics. This was the evidence from Czechoslovakia during the Prague Spring and from Poland during the Solidarity period.

It was, therefore, not entirely surprising that the satellite parties found themselves endowed with a quite significant role during the transformation. Their existence was helpful as a kind of bridge between pure communist party control and the emergence of a true multi-party system. They smoothed the path in the transfer of power. This was quite evident in the case of Poland in the summer of 1989. In the elections to the Polish parliament on 4 June, Solidarity won all the seats that it could, bar one, under the terms of the 5 April Round Table Agreement, whereby it was free to contest all the seats in the new upper house, the Senate, but only one-third of the seats in the more powerful lower house, the Sejm. This meant that the communists, the Polish United Workers' Party, could still rule, but only in combination with the satellites, the People's Party and the Democratic Party. When the satellites began to hesitate after the overwhelming popular support for Solidarity and to consider their own futures separately from the communists, a Solidarity-led coalition moved into the realms of reality and was, in fact, put together by August.

In the GDR, after the destabilization of the system in October 1989, the ruling SED began to try and keep itself in power by relying on the satellite parties, which, it was thought by the SED leadership, were seen by the population as less tainted than the SED itself. Despite these efforts to boost the satellite parties, there was little evidence that the East German population placed much faith in them. Support was tending to go to the fledgling Social Democratic Party, which had been merged with the communists in 1946, precisely because it had no associations with the previous forty years.

In Czechoslovakia there were four satellite parties, two of them – the Czechoslovak People's Party (CPP) and the Czechoslovak Socialist Party (CSS) – being significant. Their influence increased as that of the communists declined, notably when the non-communist-dominated government was voted in by the National Assembly. The CPP, a historic party associated with Masaryk and Benes, stood for a Christian Democrat philosophy, while the CSS was once a liberal party.

These various factors – conglomerate parties, the problems of disaggregating material interests, above all the role of morality in politics – suggested that for some time to come the shape and tenor of Central and Eastern European politics would be informed by non-material values. The significance of this was that non-material values appealed far more directly to the affective dimension in politics – emotions – than material ones. Non-material factors tend to promote and strengthen identities and these are much more difficult and painful to bargain away. When deployed in politics non-material factors, like references to morality, to nationhood, to religion, to aesthetics and so on, tend to produce instability. Strong emotions block out reason and undermine the stabilizing factors that promote democracy. An example of this was the pattern of events in Serbia, where from 1987 onwards the Serbian party leader, Slobodan Milosević, promoted a brand of demagogic, fiery nationalism, directed against the Albanians of the Kosovo in the first place, but generally trying to place the blame for Serbia's economic, social and other problems, in no way connected with nationhood, on non-Serbs. Quiescence was extremely difficult to achieve and, without this, the bargaining needed to stabilize Yugoslavia could not take place. The other countries of Central and Eastern Europe faced analogous difficulties, in which problems of identity assumed primacy over material interests.

The central issue concerned the actual shape of the new political system, the distribution of power and the cultural context in which power would be exercised. While there was agreement on the need to move to a constitutionally based order and the rule of law, there was a near-permanent contest about the interpretation of these concepts.

The new political actors, sensing the fluidity of the situation and gaining access to power for the first time, were reluctant to accept that democracy required self-limitation and compromise. The prevalence of the politics of identity made the establishment of stable structures with genuine, authentic loyalty a fitful and contradictory process.

To this complex should be added the problem of the nature of the electorates. The political inexperience of the populations, their socialization into values that rejected complexity and bargaining, the suspicion of political power and, indeed, of politics itself, their radical expectations of sudden and dramatic economic improvement to a wholly unrealistic extent, their impatience and ignorance of political and economic interactions made them vulnerable to messianistic claims and a prey to meretricious conspiracy theories. Their vain hopes for a sudden, rapid transformation, recalling the old peasant value system, remained strong, given the unevenness of communist modernization.

Economic and Ecological Problems

To the problem of parties there should be added the clear and imminent difficulties deriving from deteriorating economies. It is far easier to achieve a major transformation in the political sphere when the economy is reasonably prosperous than when it is collapsing, though generally the pressure to change is absent when the going is good. Certainly the democratizing experiments depended on support from the West. This dependent relationship between Central and Eastern European democracy and Western money gave rise to a curious phenomenon somewhat like a cargo cult. For some of public opinion support from the West was awaited as a kind of deliverance, in a psychological state that resembled the proposition that for forty years everything was 'bad'; now, on the day after the elections, everything would be 'good'.

Besides, significant sections of opinion in various countries rejected all politics as such, democratic or communist. The problem here was one of relatively low levels of political literacy, hardly surprising after the communist experiment in long-term infantilization of society, coupled with very high expectations based on Western levels of consumption. In the GDR, for example, after the exposure of millions of East Germans to the physical evidence of Western consumer products for the first time, many people's reaction was anger, frustration and impatience that they had been deprived of this by the communists. The crude assumption that the construction of a Western-style political system would automatically bring Western prosperity was hard to dispel. There were analogous currents in the other countries. In simple terms, the communist legacy made for a very bad fit with the requirements of competitive politics and the market.

The economic problem would not find easy solutions. There were major difficulties in converting Soviet-type economies to market-based systems. Economically it was hard to see where the capital would be found to buy up state-owned industries. Throughout the area, there was considerable evidence that the existing managerial élite was busy in converting its powers derived from *nomenklatura* positions with the help of Western capital. Then, much of Central and Eastern European industry was simply uncompetitive in world market terms. For example, there was an overcapacity in steel, which was in any case produced expensively. In market terms these out-dated industries ought just to have been closed down, but the social consequences of such a move would have been horrendous, especially as these countries entirely lacked any culture of unemployment and the network of support for dealing with it. On the contrary, unemployment was seen as something that existed only in the West, so that suggestions of creating a welfare network met with suspicion and impatience.

This raised a further difficulty. The countries of Central and Eastern Europe were lagging technologically behind the West. In particular, they were a long way behind in the adoption and diffusion of information technology, overwhelmingly because the concentration of political power was inimical to the spread of the information technology revolution that would have undermined the political monopoly of the party. In addition, there was growing evidence that the gap was now so substantial that, in certain areas of Western science, development was so far ahead that it was no longer actually understood in the communist world. In this sense the Soviet-type systems succeeded in creating a new third world, one that was stuck at a certain outdated, uneconomic, wasteful, industrial and scientific base, which it lacked the resources, the human capital and the know-how to modernize. Even with Western support this gap would be extremely hard to bridge.

The final problem in this complex is the environmental one. Even if the Western record on environmental protection is spotty, at least the problem is acknowledged and some remedial steps have been taken. In the communist world the problem could not be articulated, as that would have cut across the politically determined future insisted on by the party. The party simply declared that there was no environmental problem and that was that. By the nature of the situation, the party as monopoly employer and monopoly protector of the environment could not logically attend to the needs of both and generally ended up supporting the short-term interests of the planners, with disastrous consequences. The greatest pollution black spot of Europe was the contiguous industrial area taking in Polish Silesia, northern Bohemia and the south-east of the GDR. In effect, the communist road to industrialization was cheap and ineffective in the long term, precisely because it purported to ignore long-term implications, meaning costs like ecological deterioration. The remedies would be costly and difficult.

Western Considerations

For the West the upheaval in Central and Eastern Europe meant the end of the comfortable assumptions that had governed a wide range of beliefs. Although the triumph of liberal democracy over the notionally left-wing dictatorships was in many ways a tribute to the political and economic effectiveness of the Western system, not everyone was rejoicing. In the first place, the reappraisal required an intellectual effort that was itself tiresome for those whose thought-world had been formed by the preceding forty years. No one would actually admit to being reluctant to undertake rethinking, so alternative arguments about the dangers of instability were paraded, propositions that the West had benefited greatly from the division of Europe and that it should be wary of change, that Central and Eastern Europe would be a source of new political difficulties. These were standard conservative arguments, occasionally laced with fears that the West would have to pay for the economic reconstruction of Central and Eastern Europe for no return.

Rather more serious was the argument that, at a deep and important level, Western identity had been systematically defined against the communist world and the threat of communism was the single most important factor holding the West together. When put as baldly as this the proposition is reductionist and cannot be sustained. On the other hand it contained an element of truth, inasmuch as the East-West confrontation was undoubtedly a part of the mental furniture of the West and its disappearance required new equipment. In broad political terms, of course, the collapse of communism and the commensurate expansion of room for manoeuvre for the Central and Eastern Europeans did raise questions about the nature of Europe, the process of European integration, and how Europe's identity should be defined now that it was on the road to reconnecting with the countries to the east.

Third, the democratic transformation also brought to the agenda the question of whether or not the West, and especially the Western left, acquiesced too easily in the subjugation of Central and Eastern Europe by the Soviet Union. In future years this question might well be put by those who had to live under these systems. Inasmuch as the West failed at various times to push harder against the Soviet Union and seize opportunities for an earlier transformation, it contributed – no more than that – to the survival of the Soviet-type system and thereby to the greater difficulty of democratization. For example, in 1956 the West almost certainly did not do enough to prevent the Soviet Union from reimposing its system on revolutionary Hungary. Regardless of whether such iniatives would have worked or not, the comfortable acceptance of the permanence of the East-West divide precluded any initiatives that might have reassured the Soviet Union sufficiently to consider alternatives to an invasion. Something similar and even more clear-cut took place in 1968, when the West essentially gave the Kremlin a free hand over Czechoslovakia.

The Western left was also open to charges of short-sightedness, inasmuch as it often left unexamined the alleged Marxist credentials of the Central and East European régimes. In a very general but nevertheless unmistakable way, this reluctance acted as a kind of moral support for the Soviet-type leaders and their rule, because it did nothing to challenge their ideological claims. Far too often the Western left allowed itself to be sidetracked by the unstated but psychologically real assumption that Soviet-type Marxism–Leninism was, after all, a part of its own tradition and that at some level or another it was, in the end, somehow 'progressive' and somehow about 'the general good'. In essence, this denied the Central and Eastern Europeans the right to choose the political futures that they demanded for themselves and ultimately weakened their democratic credentials. Arguments over 'peace' were analogous, for example, that Solidarity in Poland should not have Western left-wing support, for fear that if Solidarity succeeded, this might 'inevitably' provoke the Soviet Union into launching a war and that would lead to a nuclear holocaust. Another line of argument insisted that it was wrong to criticize the Soviet world when so much in the West was imperfect. This argument was a negative double standard, expecting a much higher standard of the West than of Central and Eastern Europe, and was ultimately based on the tacit assumption that these states did not have to meet a higher standard of behaviour towards their citizens.

As against these passive responses, the West did – intentionally or otherwise – launch one initiative that had a far-reaching long-term impact on the cohesiveness of the Soviet-type systems. The insistence on the introduction of human rights into the Helsinki process resulted in the slow but inexorable diffusion of the principle into Soviet-type politics and contributed qualitatively to weakening the legitimating force of Marxism–Leninism. In effect human rights transcended the universalist claims of Marxism–Leninism and provided the Central and Eastern European opposition with an intellectual basis from which to attack and thus erode the official systems. Its significance should not be underestimated.

Finally the transformation immediately brought to the surface the hidden questions of European politics – German reunification, the nature of a Western European unification process that excluded Central and Eastern Europe, and the difficulties of integrating Soviet-type countries into the matrix that had been developed by Western criteria. German reunification, furthermore, returned the national principle to the international agenda. The post-1945 political international order was completely inimical to accepting nationhood as sufficient ground for the constitution of states, and particularly for the recognition of new states which claimed statehood by this criterion. Once Germany was reunited solely because the populations of both states were German, the principle of national self-determination could no longer be marginalized. As a result a plethora of latent national questions became acute in Central and Eastern Europe and sub-acute in the West. The West was extremely cautious and acted only when there was no alternative, as was the case with the Baltic states and the ex-Yugoslav states. Besides, as far as was possible the West insisted that internal borders should remain unaltered, in order to preclude opening up impossible questions of irredentism, territorial claims and counter-claims. Nevertheless the return of national self-determination, however reluctantly it was tolerated by the international community, qualitatively changed the configuration of the political game, because it created expectations that could not be met. It added to domestic as well as international instability.

On Revolutions and the End of Communism

Two final questions deserve exploration in this chapter. The first of these is the easier of the two – when did communism end? The seemingly sophisticated answer to this is that historical processes do not have convenient beginnings, middles and ends; one period merges into another and that history is a continuity. Now this answer is, I would suggest, a little superficial in the light of the argument in this book, which has centred on the nature of power and its legitimation under communism. If it can be shown that at any one particular moment political power was, in fact, redistributed or that an alternative form of legitimation was attempted by a communist party, then that is the point at which communism can be said to have ended.

There were two such turning-points. The more obvious one centred on the redistribution of power and was, as will be evident to anyone who has read through this chapter, 5 April 1989, the signing of the Round Table Agreement in Poland. The acceptance of competing institutions with their own autonomous legitimacy, even if they were fenced in at every turn by the party, meant a qualitative change in the definition of communism as it had been understood until then. Even without the massive rejection of communist power by the Polish electorate, for the system to have functioned within the frame of its own rationality, i.e. the terms of the Agreement, would have meant major concessions by the communist party. Most notably, it would have demanded an autonomous interest aggregation and rule-making mechanism, a degree of constitutionality that would have delimited communist power and would have gone on doing so. The interface between communist power and Solidarity power would have been a source of constant friction, unless the communists were ready to go on retreating. Nor would the *nomenklatura* system have remained unscathed, as independent Solidarity would have been a source of constant pressure to trim the power and privileges of the party. Freedom of information would have had a similarly corrosive effect. The communism professed by Jaruzelski under the Round Table Agreement would have been something quite different from what had been imported by Stalin.

The other such moment occurred in Hungary. On 28 January 1989 the leading figure on the reformist wing of the Hungarian Communist Party, Imre Pozsgay, publicly announced that a historical reappraisal of the history of the postwar years in Hungary, carried out under the aegis of the party, had concluded that the events of 1956 did not, as the party had insisted until then, constitute a counter-revolution, but was in reality a popular uprising.[6] This might at first sight seem to be no more than hair-splitting, but that would be a mistaken conclusion. Pozsgay was signalling that the ark of the covenant as far as the party's legitimacy was concerned, that it had reassumed power in 1956 in the face of a reactionary attempt to undo the gains of socialism, had been abandoned. If the 1956 events were a popular uprising, then the Communist Party had been flouting the will of the people. Everyone knew this, but the admission of it amounted to a most serious breach

---

[6] The report itself was published in mid-February.

in the party's claim to be ruling in the name of the people. From that moment on the party's legitimacy was in shreds and anyone could stand up and demand by what right the party was still occupying the commanding heights of political and economic power. Many did.

The other problem posed by the events of 1989 concerns the nature of what happened. The usual way to refer to the transfer of power is to call it a 'revolution'.[7] Yet if these events did add up to a revolution, it has to be said that it was an unusual one. There was no violence, Romania excepted, and the representatives of the *ancien régime* retreated in fairly good order. Rather than a revolution, the events more closely resembled a peaceful transfer of power, a constitutional process rather than the caesura implied by the word revolution. Yet a radical rearrangement of power did take place. Not only were new élites installed in power, but the political system was fundamentally transformed, together with its legitimation. The events therefore are a puzzle. This can best be resolved by reformulating the definition of revolution. The events of 1989 resulted from a bargaining process which produced a far-reaching transfer of power and a redefinition of political legitimation. In effect, this can be termed a 'negotiated revolution', although some would claim that this is an oxymoron, doing damage to the concept of revolutions.[8] Others have demanded: if a revolution was involved, where was it? In one instance I was present at a conference in Hungary where István Csurka, a noted if not indeed notorious senior figure of the Democratic Forum, the largest party in the coalition, declared that Hungary had been cheated of its revolution and the superpowers had been responsible. It was not a coincidence, he added darkly, referring to the Bush–Gorbachev summit in December 1989, that Malta and Yalta differed by only one letter.[9] In other words, mine not Csurka's, there could be no such thing as a 'negotiated revolution'.

Yet the concept is not without value; on the contrary. There was, indeed, an élite bargain, which allowed the communists not just to escape with their lives, quite unlike the conventional image of a revolution, but to take a substantial part of their power with them. This meant that they handed over power easily and they never used their monopoly of coercion, saving many lives. However, as seen by the

---

[7] On revolutions see Jaroslav Krejci, *Great Revolutions Compared: the Search for a Theory* (1983).

[8] My various discussions with Prof. Rudolf Tökés have been very helpful in clarifying my mind on this issue.

[9] The report on this conference did not contain Csurka's alphabetical conundrum, but he certainly said it. See András Bozóki et al. (eds.), *Csendes? Forradalom? Volt?* (1991).

anti-communist politicians, they were able to retain their positions in the economy, in the bureaucracies, in the media and elsewhere. Reality was more complex; the distinction between communists as the actual holders of power and the élite that was possessed of technical skills and came into being under the aegis of the communist system was ignored in this line of argument. Consequently, the negotiated character of the transformation left numerous problems of this nature unresolved and unresolvable. These would give rise to tension and friction, as leftovers of the old system continued to function in the new, at times generating contests for power, at others conflicts of power, all of them without adequate clarity and well defined rules for their aggregation. Negotiated the revolutions may have been, but that did not mean that the post-revolutionary distribution of power was free of trouble.

10

The Condition of Post-Communism

> *Good morrow, masters; put your torches out;*
> *The wolves have prey'd; and look, the gentle day*
> *Before the wheels of Phoebus, round about*
> *Dapples the drowsy east with spots of grey.*
>
> *Shakespeare*, Much Ado about Nothing,
> *V. iii. 24–7.*

One of the major difficulties about analysing the nature of the political systems that have come into being in Central and Eastern Europe is that they have not been there long enough for any analyses to be fully convincing. If the events of 1989, the collapse of communism, deserved to be called a political revolution, which they do, the post-revolutionary system or systems took a very long time to install. This is not surprising. Communist rule was a kind of desertification. It swept away ideas, values, institutions, solidarities and people, preserving only a few of these from the previous state of affairs, so that not much of it remains. The memory of it has, of course, survived, but often in a much distorted form, seen through rose-tinted spectacles. Argument from the past, using the past as an instrument of legitimation, has become a politically important way of calling for changes in the present, that is, by pretending that these changes represent a return to a more legitimate and more desirable past. Nevertheless, the effects of the communist-imposed revolution were so far-reaching, in terms of both structures and values, that the societies of Central and Eastern Europe emerged into post-communism with very different attitudes from those with which they had entered it in 1945. Modern industrial methods, consumption patterns and work habits, communication networks and the like have combined to create a social configuration that may resemble what existed before communism, but the underlying reality points elsewhere. Naturally enough, there are continuities and historical parallels, but their extent and depth should not be exaggerated.

The task of constructing new systems was obviously going to be a long-term undertaking and the first three years of the process could be no more than a beginning.[1] The situation was, as a result, very fluid and it would be precipitate to suggest that the systems had reached even their interim shapes, let alone their final ones. What one can do, however, is to look at the legacy of the past and ask a number of questions, in the light of the leftovers of communism, in order to illuminate the constraints that exist in the condition of post-communism and chart the difficulties facing the new political actors in their avowed aim of establishing liberal democratic systems.

A further difficulty arose from the near absolute values needed to delegitimate communism. Given that the communist system of thought made absolute claims, it was understandable that equivalent ideas were needed to disperse communism, but, once that task was achieved, these absolute propositions became not merely superfluous but damaging. Concepts of honour, glory, morality have little role to play in daily politics in a functioning democracy, though they do indeed have a role in constitutional politics, the definition and re-definition of the broad framework of values and institutions within which the allocation of resources takes place. But once this has been settled, then politics is about compromise, bargaining, impersonal interactions all mediated by a large number of institutions.

Constitutional Forms

The constitutional forms that were adopted began as variants of liberal democracy, but other, rather less liberal forms came into being, with an emphasis on the nation as the key collectivity, rather than the rights of the individual articulated through civil society. In states where the initial impulse to adopt liberal democracy was strong – in Poland, Hungary, the Czech lands, Slovenia, in some respects Bulgaria – there has been pressure to shift to a more national-minded approach. Democracy, however, is accepted, at the very least in its rhetorical aspect. After living through four decades of having the technologies of politi-

[1] As in the previous chapter, the principal data base comes from the *RFE/RL Research Reports* and *Eastern Europe Newsletter;* to these sources may be added *East European Reporter* and *Uncaptive Minds.*

cal control that make up liberal democracy dismissed as class oppression, the initial reaction of the post-communists was to introduce systems said to be based on the separation of powers, the rule of law, multi-party democracy, a market economy and so on. However, the destruction of a social and political system is far easier than the construction of a new one. In particular, the post-communist reformers faced a particularly intractable dilemma. In introducing the institutions of Western democracy, they brought in forms that did not match socio-political realities. Hence their aim could only be to transform those realities gradually until the mismatch diminished.[2]

This was not necessarily an ignoble aim, but it it did raise the problem of how far these polities were to be guided by élites, enlightened or otherwise, and how far they were to respond to what the citizens demanded in the short term. Indeed, as will be argued later, there were currents in the post-communist world that were far from being sympathetic to representative democracy and looked to the immediate implementation of their desires as the definition of a democratic order. The central problem of post-communism, then, was the gap between democratic form and real substance. Democracy demands a set of values from both rulers and ruled that involve self-limitation, compromise, bargaining, reciprocity, feedback and the like, which post-communist states and societies cannot be expected to acquire overnight, for they can only result from many years of experience.

For a start, the types of parties that came into being in the post-communist world were very different from those found in the West.[3] Two stages can be identified in the formation of post-communist parties. The initial stage was that of the conglomerate party, the most characteristic political aspect of which was that it resembled a movement rather than a party, including a wide variety of different or even contradictory political currents held together by the need to eliminate the communist party. All other considerations were subordinated to this aim. The representation of economic interests remained weak, predictably so, given that the identification of interests by social groups was similarly weak. Although these conglomerate parties were widely defined as 'left-wing' and 'right-wing', left and right in Central and Eastern Europe had rather different connotations from those obtaining in the West.

[2] On constitutions see 'Toward the Rule of Law', *RFE/RL Research Report*, 1 no. 27, 3 July 1992, and Louisa Vinton, 'Polands's "Little Constitution" clarifies Walesa's Powers', ibid., 1 no. 35, 4 September 1992.
[3] I have analysed this problem in greater detail in my article 'The End of Communism in Eastern Europe', *International Affairs*, 66 no. 1 (January 1990), pp. 3–16.

The second stage was marked by the disintegration of the conglomerate and the emergence of right and left wings in their postcommunist sense. The right tended to emphasize morality, tradition, nationhood and religion, while the left – a liberal rather than a socialist left – described itself as committed to European values, market principles and individual rights. There were several dichotomies that illustrated the division between right and left. These included different emphases on the role of the state over the individual; collective interests against civil society; the right of the community to override legality and strict adherence to the rule of law; and the extent to which constitutional forms were to be derived from nationhood as against individual rights. At a deeper level, the post-communist contest was not so much about policies as about polities. The key issues centred on the nature of the constitutional order and the rules of the political game, rather than the allocation of resources that makes up the standard fare of politics in established democracies.

Thus the split in Solidarity in Poland was as much about the different styles of government favoured by Walesa as against Mazowiecki as it was about the the ostensible cause of the split, the speed of the changes. The populism espoused by Walesa was a classic appeal to non-material values and an offer of an easy solution to problems that simply do not have easy solutions. The reverberations of the statement by the Hungarian foreign minister in 1990, that the governing coalition represented the most authentic European values in parliament, was another illustration of much the same phenomenon. Ultimately, this was a rhetorical declaration without much relevance, but it was taken with deadly seriousness by the opposition, which chose to make a major issue out of it. Examples could be found in all the post-communist states. What was missing from the debates in these polities was any sense of the urgency of economic reform, the introduction of privatization and the modernization of the legal system to make investment smoother.

Another aspect of this difficulty was that the impossibility of modernization under communism had the result that both left and right were woefully unprepared for rule. The left has, in any case, suffered a massive defeat with the collapse of communism and its place has been filled by parties professing liberalism, which have a limited but authentic tradition to look back to from the democratic opposition and can refer to the practice of the Western democracies. More serious is the dilemma of the right. Because there was no opportunity to modernize conservatism under communist rule, the conservative traditions to which right-wing or 'moderate' parties hark back are those appropriate to a pre-modern polity and society, that of the 1930s, nationhood and religion. The trouble is that, in the meantime, major changes have taken place in these societies and the ideas of the 1930s are barely appropriate to the situation, while nationhood and religion have little to say about the distribution of power.

The essence of the problem was that the modernization of these societies under communism was partial and distorted, and the complexity and mutability so characteristic of Western societies had been blocked by communist power. The configuration of values and social groups remained oddly old-fashioned and static by Western criteria, something that was readily explained by the domination of the political sphere over all others and the consequent difficulty in separating economic, legal, religious, aesthetic and other interests from politics.[4] Social groups were largely isolated from one another, with communication between them difficult, and values were only secularized to a very limited extent. The relativization of values, the acceptance that there are no epistemological certainties and the privatization of moral and religious values had been impeded by communism and had had no opportunity to evolve. Consequently, the Soviet-type system had preserved a variety of pre-modern values and ideas, which were out of alignment with the true shape of these societies, but which engendered a variety of beliefs and values which were at variance with social realities.

The Role of Intellectuals

In the construction of democracy a key role was being played and would continue to be played by intellectuals. In many ways this was predictable, given the traditionally important position that intellectuals and intellectual ideas have held in Central and Eastern Europe.[5] In the light of the highly intellectual character of communism, intellectuals necessarily played a major role in the legitimation and equally the delegitimation of the old system. This left them in a unique position in the history of Central and Eastern Europe. They had direct access to power and a paramount role in legitimating the new democratic system. Events demonstrated, however, that intellectual pre-eminence was not a qualification for skilful political leadership. Intellectuals in office proved to be rather poor at the skills of compromise and coalition building, not to mention communication with public opinion;

---

[4] Jadwiga Staniszkis, 'Forms of Reasoning as Ideology', *Telos*, no. 66 (Winter 1985–6), pp. 67–80.

[5] I have explored some of these themes in greater detail in 'The Chances of Democracy in Central and Eastern Europe', in Peter Volten (ed.), *Uncertain Futures: Eastern Europe and Democracy* (1990), pp. 19–34.

they tended to start from the assumption that their proposals were self-evidently rational and they were surprised when society took a different view.

Indeed, the first two years of post-communism were marked by the rise of a current of anti-European, anti-intellectual and anti-democratic feelings. This had several sources. Economic privation and the perceived passivity of the new governments was one of them. In populations not accustomed to public debates, the sight of legislators arguing over a comma or a word in parliament appeared a useless luxury at a time of crisis; they believed that unity was the necessary watchword, not disagreement. This discredited politics as such in the eyes of many for whom not much discrediting was needed. Otherwise, intellectuals were in any case suspect for their association with the *ancien régime* and the sense that, while the population at large had suffered, they had had a relatively pampered existence. The rise of this anti-intellectual current did not discriminate between pro-régime intellectuals and the democratic opposition, but expressed a fairly general resentment. Ironically, then, anti-communism acquired an anti-European and anti-democratic twist. In a sense all intellectuals came to be identified with the previous régime, not surprisingly, given that their formation had taken place under communism. This did not mean that their qualifications as intellectuals were useless, but the distinction between a communist-trained professional and a communist was largely obscured, something that was intensified by some intellectuals, either in a direct bid for power or in order to compensate for their own rather too close relationship with the old régime; populists were particularly well placed to exploit these resentments. In this sense, quite clear anti-democratic currents could be discerned in virtually all the post-communist countries.

Some fairly persuasive answers had become available to the question of the relationship between intellectuals and society during the first three years of post-communism. Three events offered illustrations and none of them was particularly encouraging. The events of June 1990 in Bucharest, when the Jiu Valley miners were encouraged to 'restore order' in the Romanian capital, were the most extreme. Although some of the miners subsequently claimed that they had been misled and tricked into beating up anyone who looked like an intellectual, this missed the point. The issue was that they could be 'misled', they could easily be mobilized to regard anyone who dissents as a threat to democracy. In other words, from their point of view, democracy was to be understood as a highly homogeneous concept with no room for alternative views – hardly a definition of democracy that will commend itself. The situation in Romania was, of course, particularly acute, because the intellectuals had no moral capital from having opposed the Ceausescu régime and were seen as parasites. Nor was the Iliescu régime concerned; it could dispense with intellectual legitimation for democracy, because it was not really interested in introducing a system that was, in fact, democratic, but sought to preserve the power and privileges of the élites that ousted Ceausescu.

In Poland the massive vote against Mazowiecki in the first round of the presidential elections was clearly motivated by a kind of anti-intellectualism, an impatience with complex solutions and a particular style of governing that the bulk of the population disliked. The split in Solidarity into a populist and an intellectualist wing resulted in the defeat of the latter and the rise of a populist alternative, which had far-reaching consequences for both the style and the substance of Polish politics. The taxi drivers' blockade in Hungary in October 1990 likewise fell into this category, in that it represented a turning away from the issues raised by the government coalition and the opposition, which were abstract and intellectual rather than practical and empirical. Still, in the Hungarian case the outcome was nothing like as devastating, though it should certainly have served as a warning that the themes of the intellectual-dominated public discourse were of limited interest to the bulk of the population.[6]

Social Autonomies

This raises the most thorny and most problematical aspect of the post-communist condition, the state of civil society. For the best part of a decade this has been one of the more fashionable concepts in the context of Central and Eastern Europe; indeed, it was highly effective in bringing about the demise of communism. Civil society could reasonably be regarded as public enemy number one for a system that required social atomization as a necessary condition for its survival and reproduction and did virtually everything in its power to prevent the types of social-political-economic interactions that could promote individual and group autonomy. Civil society, therefore, is to be seen as the articulation of its interests by society independent of the totalizing state.

[6] I happened to be in Budapest during the blockade; I found that at every barricade an impromptu political seminar was in progress, with groups of complete strangers engaged in a thoughtful and fairly good-tempered discussion. Further, barricades were erected throughout Hungary, implying that for the population the event served as a symbolic occasion for articulating dissatisfaction with the government and possibly with the opposition as well.

This had a number of consequences, the most striking of which was that, in a paradoxical way, the definition of civil society was easier and clearer as long as it could measure itself against totalizing power, while the process became increasingly more complex, as is appropriate, once that power had disappeared. Thus self-definition and the articulation of interests had to undergo a painful process of identification and reidentification in societies which in some cases had no traditions of this or only weak ones. In any case, very few people in the 1990s had direct experience of the interwar or immediate post-war periods, when civil societies of a sort did exist. The key point of the problematic of post-communism is that it was largely unclear as to what kinds of societies did come into existence as a result of the Stalinist modernization. This was the sense in which these societies were still defining and identifying themselves, in all the various spheres of social consciousness, for they had changed thoroughly over the last forty years and the pre-communist experience was hardly an effective guide to the contemporary period.

Nevertheless, in one vital respect, the pre-communist period must be examined. Despite everything claimed by communist propagandists and their Western supporters, the polities of Central and Eastern Europe were ruled by authoritarian and not by totalizing legitimating ideologies. The old élites relied on a mixture of traditional and charismatic legitimation and they never sought to encompass all the spheres of social activity. Nor did they profess any overarching ideology, except nationalism, and nationalism left some space for social initiatives, especially in the less complex societies that existed before the communist transformation. This made it possible for a range of activities, like opposition newspapers, non-state education, nascent trade unions and opposition political parties to exist, albeit often under pressure from an expanding state.

The significance of all this for the communist period was that for at least sections of society, the totalizing ideology and practices of the communist state were alien and worked against the grain of the cultural tradition. That tradition itself may have been destroyed and distorted, but the sense that the Soviet-type system was imposed and unassimilable prevented it from becoming rooted. In this form the cultural tradition existed as an off-stage set of alternative ideas to which reference could be made. This became even more important after the communist systems of Central and Eastern Europe were exposed to the images and culture of the West, where – so it was thought – Central and Eastern Europe's own traditions were being continued with far greater success.

In this comparison the role of Austria, Finland, Greece and eventually Spain were especially noteworthy, because these were in no way countries that had been part of the developed West; on the contrary, they were seen as backward, as the Central and Eastern European countries themselves had been before communism, but they had become developed and prosperous, with access to the symbols and realities of modernity. The level of dissatisfaction, leading to a conviction that the communist experiment in constructing an alternative version of modernity had failed, undoubtedly contributed to a sense that society could and should organize itself, inasmuch as the hyper-étatist state had broken its side of the bargain and had not created a superior civilization.

From the communist period itself one could distinguish two different types of social-political expression that should be seen as the articulation of civil society. In the first place were the major upheavals causing and caused by moments of weakened party control – East Germany in 1953, Poland and Hungary in 1956, Czechoslovakia in 1968 and Poland in 1980–1 were the most obvious instances. Characteristic of all these expressions of social aspirations was that they were predicated on an assumption of homogeneity and that they were, to an extent, energized by nationalism.

Any scrutiny of the programmes of these upheavals will readily show that they were based on the assumption of a minimum of differentiation and complexity, that there were in reality only two actors, the 'evil' state and the 'good' society, this being the unavoidable consequence of taking action against a totalizing power; but equally there was more than a relic here of peasant value systems, with their suspicion of complexity and their corresponding approval of simplicity.

The bulk of those who made up the working class were either directly from the first generation off the land or were not that far removed from peasant values, above all because they not been integrated into any alternative value system that emphasized complexity, interrelationships and the counter-productive nature of simple solutions. In this sense the myth of society acquired considerable strength as a source of resistance to the state; it was far from having been dispelled under post-communism.

The other flexing of civil social muscles in the communist period came with the various forms of pluralism that evolved, particularly in the final period of Soviet-type decay in the 1980s, when the state was still strong enough to prevent society from controlling and limiting political power and the totalizing ideology, but it withdrew from certain areas, whereby society gained space for degrees of self-organization.

Although the state probably intended this as a concession that could later be retracted, a concession exercised over a period of time gradually acquires the force of custom and comes to be perceived as a right by those concerned. This could and did start a process of rooting pluralism in society, except that unfortunately the maintenance of the totalizing ideology and the exercise of arbitrary power had a negative impact on the security with which these 'customary rights' could be practised. The effect of this discretionary régime was to weaken the autonomous exercise of power by society, to create a mind-set that looked to short-term solutions and to encourage a form of negative dependence on the state, even where positive dependence did not exist. Even as people were involving themselves in the secondary economy or printing samizdat or going on pilgrimages, they were forever looking over their shoulders and calculating the political significance of what they were doing; in other words, there was a negative dependence. At the end of the day, of course, rights cannot exist in systems where the legal sphere has no autonomy.

The halting emergence of pluralism can equally be seen as a quest for representation in whatever sphere the system permitted – legal, religious, economic, political, aesthetic etc. Representations of one sphere through the medium of another, however, are bound to be imperfect and distort both to some extent. The fact that Roman Catholicism became one of the principal expressions of the aspirations of Polish society in the 1980s meant that both religion and the political aspirations expressed through it were given an awkward, intermediate expression. Neither the political nor the religious aims could be genuinely articulated. While the Roman Catholic Church may have declared itself satisfied at achieving what appeared to be the 're-Catholicization' of Polish society, with a rise in adult baptisms, church attendance, vocations, etc., it was the density of Roman Catholicism that was ultimately diluted, inasmuch as the Church was not and could not be a political institution.

The construction of an alternative cultural sphere under the aegis of the Church may at first sight be less susceptible to analysis of this kind, except for the proposition that not everything in the aesthetic sphere can or should be politicized, not every expression of opposition to the system was necessarily political, though it was frequently so interpreted. The legacy of the Polish experience of the 1980s was somewhat ambiguous for the construction of liberal democracy, because the over-politicization of a large part of the space available to Polish society meant that it could not easily be depoliticized once the totalizing power disappeared.

In Hungary the situation was a shade easier, though this was a matter of chance rather than policy. In the context of social autonomy the Kádár régime stumbled on a very particular stabilizing device, the secondary economy, which did in fact do something to encourage economic initiatives, albeit with the severe limitation that this activity could not extend beyond the framework of the family and that, in order for individuals to maintain their standard of living, they would be obliged to exploit themselves.

This signified that in reality they were offered much less freedom of choice than appeared initially, in that Hungarians really had no option but to participate in a controlled secondary economy, the legal limits and tolerance of which were blurred. Nevertheless the secondary economy allowed a very considerable number of people the experience of operating under something resembling market conditions, making the idea of a market and economic independence less alien. The secondary economy also produced a stratum of entrepreneurs, who could, in fact, constitute a bourgeoisie if they were given encouragement in the form of know-how, capital and access to technology.

In Czechoslovakia the carving out of any major social space was much more difficult, because the régime had renewed itself after 1968 through a variety of devices and was able to construct limited but authentic social bases for itself. It satisfied Slovak nationalism by retaining the federal structure, it exercised patronage over the half-million jobs of those who were purged as supporters of the Prague Spring to promote a generation of working-class activists, it offered the population a range of economic concessions and it used the threat of Soviet invasion far more directly than elsewhere in the region. Consequently the amount of space that could be established was smaller and reached out in different directions.

It was aimed at the private sphere, the possibility of individuals living relatively atomized lives untouched by the régime, to some extent through religion, through the use of state resources for private ends and the creation of an alternative culture, of which the activities of the Jazz Section were the best-known example, but extended way beyond it.[7]

Finally, civil society also received a major boost from the determination of an initially small group of intellectuals to launch themselves independently into the political sphere and to establish what became the democratic opposition. The impact of the democratic opposition varied substantially in all the countries of Central and Eastern Europe,

---

[7] H. Gordon Skilling, Samizdat *and an Independent Society in Central and Eastern Europe* (1990) provides an account of this development.

depending on local conditions. In Poland it was successful in encouraging the birth of Solidarity and in helping to maintain a large section of Polish society in a state of politicized readiness throughout the 1980s. There was an explosion of samizdat and underground organization and much of Polish society was touched by the political experience that resulted. This has left its mark on post-communist Poland and made it possible for the transfer of power to pass fairly smoothly from the communists to the post-communist order.

In Hungary the democratic opposition was overwhelmingly concerned with the creation of an alternative public opinion in the intelligentsia; there was little attempt to mobilize the wider public, although towards the end there was some interaction between the democratic opposition and the secondary economy. The legacy of this was that the transfer of power was largely restricted to élite negotiations and the emergence of political cleavages that have their origins as much in the history of the opposition as in social realities and interests.

The Czechoslovak experience was different again, in that the democratic opposition was under severe pressure throughout its existence. It had limited contact with the bulk of the population, but its resolute stand earned it much moral capital. In consequence, it had no difficulty in placing itself at the head of the revolutionary movement and taking over from the communists at the end of 1989. The East German opposition was weakened throughout its existence by its insistence that it supported the 'socialist' character of the East German state and it was very slow in coming to the conclusion that the problems it was addressing derived from the nature of the system, which had to be rejected as such. The result was that when the Soviet-type system collapsed, the opposition was badly placed to assume any leadership and was effectively swept away.

Personalities and Institutions

The role of personalities as against institutions also militates against the smooth functioning of democracy. One of the central legacies of the Soviet-type system was the atomization of society into individuals and the consequent destruction of the basic bonds of community through distrust. In particular, the relationship between the individual and the state was badly distorted in this way. Not surprisingly, the state came to be regarded as remote and abstract, beyond the will and control of the individual, and the institutions of the state as not much more than façades. The elimination of communist systems did not, in itself, change this.

As a result there was a far greater inclination to believe in persons rather than in institutions and to accept the former as the true target of political attitudes. It might be that the individual holding office had a status enhanced by that office, but for many the authenticity of the relationship was the personal one. This left institutions locked in a cycle of relative weakness, because they found it difficult to acquire their own legitimacy in competition with the real or supposed charisma of personalities.

What seemed to have happened in the early months of post-communism was that, as the communists faded away or were expelled from power, societies found themselves without a political focus with which they could feel comfortable. New parties were the relatively remote constructs of the intellectuals and the symbols of the nation were not strong guides in the circumstances. Almost hypnotically, people turned to personalities, virtually without regard to their political programmes, as a repository for society's hopes and desires in particular, because persons were felt to be more reliable, more authentic and thus more likely to embody what the individual wanted. In this way personalities were invested with what amounted to a supra-political status.

The pattern was replicated throughout the area. The November–December 1990 presidential elections in Poland confirmed the ascendancy of Walesa, almost without regard to his strategy or ideas. In a sense, the quarter of the vote that went to Tymiński underlined this. Here was another personality, with the simple message 'I'm a Pole, I'm rich, vote for me and you too will be rich' providing evidence of the same attitude, that personalities were more significant than institutions.

Václav Havel had enormous moral authority which propelled him to the Hrad in a very short space of time. Once there, he added to his authority and built up his charisma by a series of initiatives, but also through his personal charm and abilities as a communicator, so that he was effectively above criticism. In Hungary, until the end of November 1989, popular aspirations were vested in Imre Pozsgay and it was only by a tiny margin of 6000 votes that, in effect, his candidacy for the presidency was torpedoed in a referendum. There then ensued a period when no personality dominated the political scene. But after the general elections, almost with a sense of relief, the population entrusted itself to the care of József Antall, the prime minister, who as a result has established an ascendancy over politics that goes well beyond his office. Indeed, political observers in Hungary grew concerned not that there was an overmighty president, one of the fears about Pozsgay's candidacy, but that there was an overmighty prime minister, whose removal was virtually impossible. The enormous vote amassed by Iliescu in Romania in the 1990 elections and confirmed, though not quite so emphatically, two years later, spoke for itself, and so did Slobodan Milošević's success in the December 1990 elections in Serbia. Milošević, indeed, should be seen as the archetypal demagogue, who used nationalist slogans and populist simplification to project himself. Arguably, Helmut Kohl played an analogous role in the former GDR.

By way of comparison, the removal of Mrs Thatcher from office in November 1990 illustrates vividly the distinction between personality and institutions. Despite having been one of the most powerful persons ever to hold the post of prime minister in Britain, she was swept away when her tenure was felt to be counter-productive. It is hard to imagine anything analogous in the post-communist world.

The difficulty with investing persons with so much authority is that it tends to weaken the effective functioning of institutions, it allows individuals to be above criticism, to pursue personalized rather than popularly sanctioned policies and ultimately to ensure that representation is personal rather than grounded in the system. On the positive side, especially in the short term, charismatic or semi-charismatic figures can be useful as a way of channelling accumulated frustrations and uncertainties in immature political communities. The problem arises when these persons are called upon to leave the political scene. In general they are reluctant to do so and their successors will invariably be weaker, leaving a gap in the system.

Social Homogeneity

A particularly intractable problem with serious consequences for a wide range of issues is that of the blocked social mobility and homogenization imposed by communism on these societies. The argument is straightforward and has already been made, but it will be briefly summarized here.[8] Soviet-type systems went through a single experience of large-scale upward mobility with the seizure of power and the resulting one-off promotion of a generation of individuals of working-class and peasant backgrounds on the basis of political loyalty. This was paralleled by the demotion of the old élite; alternatively, the old élite was destroyed during the war and its place would in any case have been taken by persons promoted from a lower social status.

[8] Walter D. Connor, *Socialism, Politics and Equality: Hierarchy and Change in Eastern Europe and the USSR* (1979).

In all, this constituted the new class of political appointees and the new intelligentsia which filled positions in the new bureaucracies. However, upward mobility on a large scale effectively ceased with this one single act, with a few exceptions noted below, and thereafter there was an increasing trend towards the hereditary transmission of class status. The exceptions were connected with political change. In Czechoslovakia in the 1970s, as noted above, a second promotion of low-status individuals took place. In East Germany the positions of the 3 million who left for the West likewise had to be filled and to some extent social mobility in the GDR was never quite as clogged as it was elsewhere. In Poland, with every leadership change large numbers of individuals were newly promoted into the bureaucracy. But the phenomenon that was noteworthy about this last change was that many of those appointed were not so much from worker or peasant backgrounds but a younger generation of professionals.

The problem for Soviet-type systems was that upward mobility had become restricted to too few channels. Political loyalty was always a possibility, but comparatively few people could, in reality, take advantage of it in normal circumstances by joining the party. Further, the instruments of coercion provided another channel, though at a high cost in terms of social ostracism. Education, the most obvious channel, was blocked in another way. In the deal made with the 'new class' in the 1960s, the rulers accepted that the children of the intelligentsia could maintain their parents' status and tolerated the erosion of systems of preferential access for others through 'class points' at university admission. The classic channel of upward mobility through economic achievement simply did not exist, except towards the end of the system in Hungary and Yugoslavia, where the secondary economy offered individuals the economic freedom to give their children the extra coaching needed to pass university entrance requirements, but this was probably rare. Economic status – wealth – on its own was simply incompatible with the established norms of the system and the occasional campaigns equating entrepreneurs with corruption served to underline the ambiguity involved.

The outcome of all this was, for the most part, that the natural leaders of the working class were not creamed off but remained workers. The difficulty in this connection is that the status of 'worker' is a contradictory one. On one hand, workers were the nominal ruling class and this message was reinforced in a variety of symbolic ways; on the other they were as far from power as possible, except in moments of party enfeeblement. Thus in a backhanded way they were encouraged to think of themselves as special, to see themselves as separate, even while the system continuously frustrated their aspirations. Only in Poland was a section of the working class able to maintain itself with some semblance of an organization and a clear consciousness of being separate from the state in status and values.

A further complication here was the very type of working class created by communism. Communism proved to be, *inter alia*, a method for building up a nineteenth-century industry, with super-large enterprises using relatively straightforward technology. The ideal was always the male manual worker using simple technology as portrayed under Stalinism; this did not change symbolically in any major way later.[9] In this sense the working class that emerged from communism was relatively homogenized, confused and economically increasingly threatened by the collapse of these economies. It disliked differentiation, whether in material or in status terms, and was characterized by a kind of negative egalitarianism. Equally it was, with some exceptions, strongly anti-intellectual, impatient with the complex solutions offered by the new governments and politically inexperienced, making it vulnerable to demagogic manipulation.

A particularly difficult problem has arisen in connection with the antagonism exhibited by the Soviet-type system to social integration. With the elimination of mobility, the satisfaction of individual and group aspirations and the acquisition of other, wider value systems were blocked too. There was nowhere for talented individuals in the working class to go, but to remain within the class. The potential result, which became actual in Poland, was that the working class acquired a dynamism, an internal coherence, a set of values and a strong identity which either set it apart from other social groups or led it to seek to integrate the rest of society into itself.

Various kinds of integration can be conceptualized. Integration into the intelligentsia, the one reference group which the communist system did permit, was too difficult and was in any case impeded by the narrowing of educational opportunity. Under post-communism, if integration into a democratic system of values were to prove unsuccessful, only nationhood could offer the wider set of goals that could provide the intellectual instruments for the working class to construct the culture by which it could encompass politics and economics. But nationhood is ultimately incapable of providing this because this is not its function.

Again, it was absence of economic integration that explained this gulf between intellectuals and workers and, when the former sought to establish democratic systems, political communication became notably difficult. The failed relationship between the Mazowiecki gov-

[9] Gombár Csaba, *A politika parttalan világa* (1986).

ernment, the nearest to a government of philosopher kings witnessed
in Europe since the war, and the highly politicized consciousness of
Polish workers was a clear illustration of this problem. The near impossibility of Poland's existing entrepreneurs performing this integrative
function was shown by the bitter hostility towards the emergence of a
bourgeoisie based on the *nomenklatura*. Despite evidence that the
nomenklatura and those who previously constituted the state-de-
pendent private sector were virtually alone in having the know-how,
the technology and the capital to launch a private enterprise economy,
for many Poles this was quite unacceptable. Members of the former
ruling élite could not become the new ruling élite, exchanging political
for economic power, which in turn would again give rise to political
power or at least influence. Yet the extraordinary vote for Tymiński in
the presidential elections suggested that there was no hostility to
wealth as such. The contradiction here implied that there was a good
deal of confusion in much of Polish opinion.[10] The confusion seemed
to be made up of wish-fulfilment, impatience, intolerance and strong
unwillingness to accept that the reconstruction of Poland would involve years of complex effort, as a result of which there would be
major winners and losers.

An added complication in this connection was the existence of
relatively large youthful age cohorts in Poland, for which Solidarity
and martial law were the dominant, constitutive experiences and from
which they drew a set of values deeply antagonistic to existing institutions. These cohorts have been large enough to attain a critical mass
in the creation of values, to reject socialization into official value
systems; integrating them into alternative ways of viewing the world
would be problematical.

One observer, writing of the Czech working class, described it as
egalitarian in the sense that it accepted meritocratic achievement only
verbally and regarded too great a social difference as amoral; that it
believed in all work having the same value but actually arrogated a
higher status to manual labour than to intellectual; that it was anti-
intellectual and anti-élitist; that it overestimated the value of manual
labour; that it attached a high value to welfarism and social security;
that it believed in the étatistic provider state; that social life was almost
exclusively determined by economic rather than cultural considerations; and that it preferred economic rights to civil rights.[11] Analogous

[10] Michael H. Bernhard, 'Barriers to Further Political and Economic Change in
Poland', *Studies in Comparative Communism*, 22 nos 3–4 (Autumn/Winter 1990),
pp. 319–39.
[11] Miroslav Petrusek, 'A posztkommunizmus mint szociopolitikai fogalom és
probléma', in *Politikai kultúra és állam Magyarországon és Cseh-Szlovákiában*

currents could be found elsewhere in the post-communist world, notably Romania.

In Hungary it might be that this problem of a self-contained working class, resistant to integration, was not so acute. If so, then this must be ascribed in the first place to the secondary economy that evolved during the Kádár years, which offered some experience of the market to the great majority of the population. This helped to re-establish social hierarchies that society felt could be scaled and to provide a degree of openness of opportunity that is missing elsewhere in Central and Eastern Europe.[12]

It is evident from the argument above that the most effective integration into a single, more or less cohesive political community is best achieved around economics and that, in turn, demands opportunities for money-making and an acceptance of a social status to accompany economic success. Only economic integration can satisfy the aspirations of the bulk of society and these have irreversibly accepted Western levels of consumption as desirable. Alternatives like integration into political, ideological or cultural aspirations will simply not work.

From this perspective, despite the underlying hostility of the intellectuals to the nascent bourgeoisie, it is in their eventual interest to ensure that an entrepreneurial class does come into being in order to effect the necessary integration. Failure to achieve this could result in a scenario in which rather negative, introverted, working-class ideologies dominate politics and these will be maximally anti-intellectual, given that intellectuals threaten the homogenized, simplistic construction of reality by which these working classes understand the world around them. Only a polity with a strong bourgeoisie can provide the economic and political space within which intellectuals can exercise their critical function.

Besides, there is the problem of technological change. In the West the kind of manual working class that is becoming visible in the post-communist world has been disappearing as a result of the technological revolution. The transformation of Western social and economic patterns needed was far from easy, but it was made possible by the implicit promise that the shedding of outdated manual skills would be

(1990), pp. 87–105. See also Jacques Rupnik, 'The Roots of Czech Stalinism', in Raphael Samuel and Gareth Steadman Jones (eds), *Culture, Ideology and Politics* (1982), pp. 302–19.

[12] But see also Bill Lomax, 'The Rise and Fall of the Hungarian Working Class', in C. M. Hann (ed.), *Market Economy and Civil Society in Hungary* (1990), pp. 45–60 and László Kürti, 'Hierarchy and Workers' Power in a Csepel Factory', ibid., pp. 61–84.

rewarded by material and status-related gains on the part of the work-ing class. A defensive, protectionist and internally cohesive working class will not be willing to make this adjustment readily, posing the danger of major Luddite resistance, which would undoubtedly gen-erate support from a section of intellectuals who could thereby create an ideology for this attitude. The consequence could be that the technological gap between Western Europe on one hand and Central and Eastern Europe on the other will widen continuously.

The experience of the West was a clear indicator that economic integration, whatever its shortcomings, was the most effective motor of social stability, because it proved to be surprisingly even-handed in offering life chances from which the majority, though not everyone, can benefit. If the post-communist countries fail to establish chan-nels of economic integration, they will very probably be faced with rather sterile class politics that will severely weaken their democratic prospects.

The Destruction of Institutions

The greatest damage done by communism, it appeared from the experience of the first three years of post-communism, was the de-struction of institutions. The level of institutionalization, the way in which people respond to institutions and give them their trust, was very low. Under communism, official institutions were distrusted as alien and the system blocked the emergence of authentic institutions as potential challenges to the party's monopoly. Instead, persons at-tracted loyalty. The first difficulty this raised was that the codes of behaviour appropriate to persons were different from those appropri-ate to institutions.

The role of institutions in politics is not merely to represent indi-viduals, but also to provide the necessary distance between them and to establish codes of conduct and political ground rules in which there is a degree of detachment, routine and predictability. In the absence of this politics easily becomes a matter of personal passions, interactions and relations. Furthermore, institutions provide for consistency in the exercise of power and they establish the necessary distance between the individual and power. In the absence of institutions the exercise of power runs the danger of becoming arbitrary and, even if the actual exercise of power is not arbitrary, it will be widely believed that power can only be exercised in this way. In addition institutions have a valuable role in channelling and structuring information about society, politics, power and status, as well as transmitting the crucial data concerning acceptable and unacceptable forms of behaviour. The strength of the norms and the cohesiveness of society, its relationship with the underlying moral codes that are essential to define a community as a community and not an agglomeration of individuals depended on the viability of institutions and the loyalty they attract.

Then, it is through institutions that individuals attain and construct their identities in public life, especially in modern societies where family and narrow communal identities have only a secondary role. In this way the roles that people play and the meanings they attach to particular events and processes, how they respond to them and, crucially, how they evaluate their status are all intimately tied to institutions. Personal ambitions and achievement are likewise structured through institutions. What an individual attains in terms of public respect and thus self-respect is closely connected to the institutions which generate them. In the absence of an adequate institutional framework, the structuring of society will take place through other channels, like birth or religion or ascription.

The problem for the post-communist world was that the achievements of the communist period were now suspect. The collapse of communism brought into question entire personal careers and, indeed, made individuals vulnerable, because their attainments, like education, were too directly identified with the fallen order. This was exacerbated by the lack of agreed norms for the contest for power in the new situation. In the new political contest individuals felt themselves to be under attack for their entire careers, for whatever they had done, even from the best of motives, under the old régime. Significantly, their assailants made no distinction between the direct political beneficiaries of communism, like the leading members of the *nomenklatura,* and the professionals who had emerged under the old system but were not necessarily committed to it. In several of the countries of Central and Eastern Europe the communist period acted as the midwife to a Europeanized élite of professionals; under post-communism their qualifications were increasingly called into question as the unbridled contest for power gathered speed. This placed a further question mark over the operation of a Western-type democratic system.

To these factors may be added the lack of trust generated by forty years of atomization. Communist systems did what they could to prevent the coming together of individuals in institutionalized groups, but could hardly prevent personal loyalties from becoming established as a not altogether satisfactory surrogate for institutions. Thus under post-communism, thanks to the legacy of the previous period, which effectively made institutions discretionary and inauthentic, a state of affairs came into being where new institutions were unable to generate loyalty or enforce discipline, at any rate in the earliest stage.

In one other respect the communists had enjoyed a kind of windfall benefit with negative consequences for post-communism. The creation of institutions is hardest in newly modernizing societies, where the loyalties of the village community have yet to be sloughed off by the new working class. It takes at least a generation for the codes of conduct appropriate to urban life to become rooted. What the communists did, in effect, was to prevent these codes from gaining strength; they sought to keep society in a state of dependency on the system, rather than allowing it to gain the autonomy that it sought.

The Personalization of Politics

The present political system in Central and Eastern Europe should be understood as functioning in three dimensions – ideological, institutional and personal. These three overlap and interlock, and crucially the codes appropriate to one are regularly used in another context. It is important that, where the institutional level is weak, there will be a much more direct relationship between persons and ideologies, and it will be far easier for individuals to use ideology to disguise their bid for personal power or defence of a personal privilege.

In this way a personal interest may be veiled by an altogether different ideology, or the functioning of an institution may be made smoother by the deployment of personal characteristics. The example of Havel's personal authority in the Czecho-Slovak presidency has already been noted; on paper, the presidency was a relatively weak institution, but thanks to his personal qualities Havel gave it a status quite out of alignment with its formal powers. The overall difficulty with this situation is that it promotes confusion and also cynicism, because institutions will be perceived as nothing more than façades hiding different personal interests and hence nothing will be done to strengthen institutionalization.

This explains a number of features of post-communist politics. Personalization produces a rather volatile form of political activity, for it places personal loyalties above those to institutions, which leads to a low level of respect for legal, administrative and political ground rules. It explains, further, the fragmentation of political parties, for example, in Poland, where nearly thirty parties were represented in the Sejm after the elections of 1991.[13] And it also helped to illuminate the instability within political parties. The tortuous conflict within the

[13] David McQuaid, 'Poland's Parliamentary Elections: a Postmortem', RFE/RL Research Institute, *Report on Eastern Europe,* 2 no. 45, 8 November 1991.

Hungarian Smallholders' Party illustrated this very clearly. For all practical purposes this was a dispute over personal power, but it was disguised in semi-ideological terms.[14]

Behind the welter of personalized argument and, at times, abuse, there was a more serious issue. The weakness of institutionalization directly affects the distribution of power, as it enables individuals to acquire and exercise it in formally unsanctioned ways. In effect, in common with so much else, power is no more institutionalized than anything else. But because these countries do live in the European tradition and because this was one of the main criticisms of arbitrary power under the communists, it was recognized that personalization of power was unacceptable. To provide a veil for this kind of unlegitimated power, its beneficiaries cloaked their activities and aims in some other ideological guise, like nationalism or populism or clericalism or demands for accountability. All these ideologies represent a kind of political resource, which politicians were in a position to exploit.

The central difficulty, therefore, concerned power. The function of institutions in properly running democracies is to make the exercise of power equal and even-handed, even if it introduces the danger of bureaucratization and remoteness. The alternative, which could be widely seen in Central and Eastern Europe, was the personal quality of power, which was not acceptable to the bulk of the population. In addition, individuals with access to power, whether they gained this through personal or institutional channels, have a vested interest in holding on to it. That much may be accepted as part of the normal process of politics, but these individuals ignored or rejected the institutional channels and used personal ones instead. In the population this bred distrust, resentment and cynicism, and a strong sense that all politics was about personal gain and nothing else, which then led people to conclude that there was nothing to be gained from political participation and that their own fate would not be affected by what they did in the political realm. The low turnouts in Poland (42 per cent in the October 1991 general elections) and Hungary could, at least in part, be explained by this factor.

Representation

This distrust leads to the next set of problems, that of representation. It is important to ask the question: what precisely did these post-

---

[14] Judith Pataki, 'Role of Smallholders' Party in Hungary', *RFE/RL Research Report*, 1 no. 14, 3 April 1992.

communist governments seek to represent? The answer seems to be that they are in the first place interested in representing not society but the nation. The distinction is vital. Society is a complex body, involving a variety of cross-cutting and overlapping interests, articulated through numerous social, economic and political institutions. A government representing society accepts the pluralism and multifaceted character of it and equally the contradictory currents that are the norm in a democratic system. The acceptance of democratic norms also implies that the government will not understand its own position as one of being the total victor, but only as the temporary representative of society until the next elections.

On the other hand, a government that sees itself as the representative of the nation is ineluctably forced into a much less accountable position. The nation in its ethnic dimension functions in politics as a category that is connected primarily to the establishment of the state and to definitions of identity. It is not the medium through which the multiplicity of cross-cutting and contradictory interests find articulation and, it is to be hoped, aggregation. Rather, the nation is a relatively static entity, as it must be if it is to act as the foundation of the community, and one which transcends everyday politics. The nation is sacralized and cannot be the subject of the bargains and compromises needed for the smooth functioning of democracy.

Consequently a government that represents the nation and sees itself as the guarantor and embodiment of national values will be drawn towards an extra-political or supra-political attitude that has little to do with the cut and thrust of representative rule and competitive politics. A government that starts from this proposition, therefore, is deeply uneasy with the pluralism of society and, because it cannot adapt itself to the necessary complexity and change of democracy, it will do what it can to freeze society and constrain it to become as rigid and unchanging as it is itself.

However, society is generally reluctant to climb into this conceptual strait-jacket and the result is constant tension between the two. Society will resist the attempt by the government to force reality to conform to its preconceptions. The outcome is very likely to be a situation in which the government would prove more and more tempted to abandon democratic norms in favour of a 'national' policy and would become prone to see all opposition as the expression of a hostile conspiracy, which it could and, indeed, should put down with all the power available to it.

Under post-communism the salient role of nationhood was intensified by two further factors – the rise of what may be called 'chauvino-communism' and the weakness of institutions. Chauvino-communism, the use of nationalism by former communists, became an increasingly widespread phenomenon under post-communism, as members of the old *nomenklatura* sought to legitimate their continued access to power and privileges in the new order. To a considerable extent they were successful in this. Despite the theoretical incompatibility between communism and nationalism analysed extensively in previous chapters, communists found little difficulty in transferring their personal loyalties from one ideology to another; more surprisingly, perhaps, they were accepted on these terms by sections of the population. Bulgaria provides a good illustration. The Bulgarian Socialist Party, the successor to the communists, made intensive use of anti-Turkish propaganda in the parliamentary and presidential elections in 1991 and 1992 respectively. Attacks on the Turkish minority and claims to defend the Bulgarian nation were readily taken at face value, notably by the least experienced and most vulnerable sections of Bulgarian opinion.

Institutional weakness has already been discussed extensively above, but it had particular implications for the rise of nationhood. In the gulf between individuals and power it emerged fairly early that the liberal democratic ideas used to delegitimate communism would not have enough of a political basis, seeing that liberalism needed a strong civic basis for its functioning. Without this and without the corresponding values of tolerance, compromise and acceptance of conflict as normal, both rulers and ruled sought answers in the only public identity that was at their disposal, namely nationhood.[15] This mechanism gave nationalism and nationalist ideologies a prominence that proved to be highly prejudicial to the development of democratic practice, especially as questions concerning the distribution of power could not be satisfactorily answered by nationalist categories. There appeared to be no easy way out of this conceptual trap.

State Power

This meant, of course, an automatic enhancement of state power, given the role of the state in the protection of nationhood. Despite the liberal critiques of the excessive concentration of state power under communism, the temptation not to dismantle inherited structures was strong. The pretexts were manifold – the need for the state to continue

---

[15] Jirina Siklová, 'Nacionalizmus Közép- és Keleteurópában', *Valóság*, 35 no. 1 (January 1992), pp.114–16, translated from *Frankfurter Allgemeine Zeitung*, 4 September 1991.

subsidies in order to avoid unemployment, difficulties with social cohesiveness and the threat of anarchy on the part of a politically untutored population, the impossibility of deétatization in so short a period of time, etc. All these had an element of truth in them. The problem was that once the period of fluidity that follows a major upheaval is over, the structures then existing tend to crystallize, making it hard to effect change as vested interests grow around them. There was a real danger that post-communist Europe was at precisely this stage in 1993.

The state, on the other hand, was expected to play a near-impossible role. It was supposed to be both initiator and arbitrator, both the guardian of social welfare (which implies dependency) and the guarantor of freedom (which implies independence) and, over and above these requirements, the state should discharge its obligations in a neutral fashion, to avoid pursuing its own bureaucratic interests and circumscribing its autonomy over society. In the circumstances these expectations could not be fulfilled. Not only were existing tasks all but insuperable, but the entire communist and pre-communist legacy pointed in the opposite direction and, after all, the overwhelming majority of those involved in the state administration under post-communism acquired their bureaucratic habits under the culture of communism.

In particular, expectations of the role of the state in two key areas were hopelessly contradictory. The state was to be the umpire in allocating resources in the new share-out between winners and losers, like the employees of outdated industries and overstaffed bureaucracies, but this actually involved the state in shedding some of its own power and patronage, which was hard to envisage. Second, the state had a role to play in policing new abuses of power, through the newly created markets, for example; here too the temptation to bend the rules in favour of either personal or state power was very strong.

The next problem was closely related to the role of the state, that of substitution. In any political system the government and through it the state must substitute for the political, economic, social and moral aspirations of the citizens, whether they are acting in groups or as individuals. This is a necessary aspect of modern government. At the time of writing it was hard to see any sign that post-communist governments were even aware of the responsibilities that go with such substitution. Governments behaved as if they had been endowed with untrammelled power through democratic elections and paid little heed to the proposition that they were in power only because they were substituting for society which could not undertake this task, mostly because of the complexity of governance.

Substituting for society can only take place satisfactorily if the government pays careful attention to the written and unwritten rules of the political game. It must act responsively and responsibly, be prepared to listen to reasoned criticism, accept feedback from society – after all, one of the gravest weaknesses of the Soviet-type system was precisely its refusal to recognize feedback. In the event that a government chooses to ignore the wishes of the society for which it is substituting, it will very likely be turned out at the next elections. The alternative to that, of course, is the path towards authoritarianism.

The necessary responsiveness mentioned above implies a further quality that every democratic order must possess – self-limitation, the readiness to exercise a self-denying ordinance on the part of all those who exercise power, in society as well as in the state. This implies a readiness to compromise, to accept that it is not only impossible to attain one's objectives in their entirety but actually harmful, as this would inevitably give rise to resentment on the part of the loser. If a loser is consistently in this position and concludes that nothing further can be gained from the given political system, the outcome will be disaffection and worse. Self-limitation is a difficult cultural value to acquire, particularly for those coming from the cultural matrix of communism, which emphasized absolute categories, and nationalism is not significantly more helpful in this respect. Without self-limitation the variety and multi-dimensionality of social interests cannot find expression and the essential feedback between rulers and ruled will be blocked as a result.

There is considerable evidence to suggest that self-limitation is barely understood by the post-communist systems and only occasionally practised, above all where ethnic minorities are concerned. Undeniably, the relationship between ethnic majorities and minorities is one of the most sensitive in any political system, given the intimate link between the establishment and stability of the state within its existing frontiers and the real or perceived ambitions of ethnic groups to seek protection for themselves through the redrawing of those boundaries. In this respect the level of trust between majority and minority has to be high, and trust, again as a result of the communist legacy and the policies of atomization, remained low.

Citizenship

In this connection, the way in which citizenship was being defined had direct implications for the relationship between the individual and the collectivity. In liberal states the prior assumption is that the individual's rights take precedence over those of the state and that state institutions are there to serve the citizen. Under communism this was reversed and individual rights were banished from the public sphere, because an omniscient state was better able to take care of the individual than any one person could do for him- or herself. In the new situation, despite the initial rhetoric of liberalism, the emphasis in reconstructing the relationship between rulers and ruled favoured the state, albeit its role was no longer legitimated in terms of omniscience.

In part, this relationship was derived from the inherited perception of the dichotomy between public and private.[16] The totalizing state drove individuals into the private sphere and denied them any role in the public sphere other than those prescribed for them. This inevitably meant that any redefinition of these roles would pose difficulties in terms of established habits and, at the same time, give rise to a debate as to where the boundaries of private and public were now to run. In any case, there was an inherent problem in expecting the state to delimit the private sphere in anything like a sensitive fashion. The best the state could do in reality was to act as the enabling body and to exercise its pre-eminent power in a restrained way, and there was little sign of that.

The ideal-type in the liberal view is that the public sphere should find expression in civil society, through the myriad of interlocking and overlapping associations and institutions that allow the individual to transcend atomization; hence once civil society was embedded, citizenship would be established too. A strong civil society would, equally, construct a viable equilibrium between public and private by means of a clear understanding of the appropriate reciprocal rights and obligations. In this context the legacy of the past, together with the nature of the dominant political ideologies, acquired considerable relevance.

Under communism the individual was formally offered collective rights, which the state exercised in the name of the citizen;[17] they were, therefore, not rights in the liberal sense, which could be enforced through an autonomous legal system. Similarly, the ethos of nationalism, populism or religion implied the superiority of the collective over the individual and would logically result in the construction of a state–society relationship that favoured the former, albeit not to the same extent as communism had. To an extent the priority of the state

[16] This section is partly based on the argument put forward by George Kolankiewicz at a conference on the future of Central and Eastern Europe held at the Institute of Contemporary Arts, London, 13 June 1991.

[17] Discussed in Stephen White et al., *Communist and Post-Communist Political Systems*, 3rd edn (1990), chapter 1.

over the citizen was dictated by the inherited culture of state–society relationships. Under communism the individual regarded the state as hostile, state regulations as arbitrary, unpredictable and predatory and as a resource to be exploited, whether through the secondary economy or through theft. This ethos, which varied in its intensity from country to country, was expressed in poor labour morale and low levels of discipline, in considering public property as one's own, avoidance of responsibility and risk, in having little or no under-standing of the scarcity or otherwise of resources as signalled through the price mechanism, the waste and neglect of collective goods, in favouring the short term over the long term because of a weak sense of the future and in having low expectations of individual achievement.

To this list may be added the codes by which information was structured. Public information was distrusted and personal know-ledge, which might be a jumble of half-understood ideas, was given preference, coupled with a contradictory respect for the 'scientific truth'. The hierarchy of norms was received and constructed by criteria substantially different from those in the West, where on the whole the state was regarded as a relatively benign institution and its pro-nouncements were not automatically discounted.[18] Despite the strong emphasis throughout the region on the rule of law – very much in reaction to the arbitrariness of communism – there was little evidence that society recognized the implications of living under constitution-ality. On the contrary, the population had been socialized into re-garding rules as a façade, to be kept only when non-compliance would result in punishment by reason of being discovered. This gave rise to clear patterns of externalization, where norms are for for public consumption only, i.e. compliance not consent, rather than internali-zation, where rules are observed because the individual understood that both one's own and the public good were served in this way. The continued conflict over collectivist versus individualist modes of or-ganization reflected this dichotomy, for the internalization of norms is best served by regard for the individual and individual rights.

Under these conditions it was not surprising that post-communist systems had to cope with a welter of attitudes that made it hard to establish the forms and content of citizenship as understood in the West. The post-communist systems tended, on the whole, to em-phasize collective obligations rather than the rights of the individual, and to stress the community as the primary source of authority. Con-

[18] The nature of socialization in systems where the highest levels of power are distrusted by society is discussed in Elemér Hankiss, *The East European Alternative* (1990).

stitutions were inclined to encode collective rights – the Polish constitution explicitly derived authority from religion and history – and the
most effective means of overcoming atomization was seen as being
located in group rights and activity. To an extent this contradicted the
overt commitment to the market and privatization, but the implications
of that contradiction would impact only later. Furthermore, the continuing conflict over basic constitutive issues centred precisely on
collectivist versus individualist philosophies and the outcome of this
contest was far from clear.

The varying anterior experiences of the different Central and Eastern European countries obviously resulted in different debates and
different locations for the private–public boundary, but the broad
issues were similar. In Poland, where the relationship had been highly
conflict-laden and there had been a large-scale turning away from the
state, the need to re-establish respect for the public sector was regarded as vital. In Hungary, on the other hand, the relationship had
been more relaxed under late Kádárism, with the result that individualism had a better chance of gaining ground than elsewhere.
Czechoslovakia had seen a massive and conscious turning inward, so
that the nature of the public sphere was constantly under question. In
Romania the distinction between public and private was so far eroded
through the atomization imposed by Ceausescu that definitions were
inherently problematical and, indeed, the nature of citizenship, rights
and obligations was to a considerable extent fictive.

Civil Society

A great deal has already appeared in scholarly literature on civil society
and it is not proposed to rehearse it at this point. There is, however,
one aspect of the civil society debate that should be stressed. Although, in the current of analysis that dominates thinking on this topic,
civil society is generally regarded as preceding and having priority
over the state, the two are nevertheless in an organic relationship. The
nature, traditions and characteristics of a civil society influence the
nature of the state and the behaviour of the state, in turn, impacts on
civil society. The relevant feature of post-communist states was that
they had few of the qualities of modernity; consequently they could do
very little to bring into being a modern civil society.

In a way, Central and Eastern Europe was witnessing the replay of
an age-old dilemma, the problem of modernization from above. If
modernity is equated roughly with the functioning of a civil society
conscious of its autonomy *vis-à-vis* the state, then the state is hardly the

best equipped body to act as midwife. Unfortunately there is nothing else. Only the state has the resources, the knowledge and the capacity to reshape the social system in such a way as to provide space for civil society, given the weakness of the latter. For this to succeed the state would need to exercise an extraordinarily high degree of self-limitation, in effect to withdraw progressively from different areas as civil society became strong enough to take over. In practical terms this is all but inconceivable. Once the state has gained control of an area of activity, involving opportunities for power, privilege and patronage, it will not give them up without a struggle.

Equally relevant in this context is the actual functioning of the state. There is a standard assumption in much of the writing about Central and Eastern Europe that the post-communist state is both neutral and competent. Neither assumption should be taken for granted. The idea that the state is a neutral agency and functions along the legal-rational lines postulated by Weber, ready to implement the properly taken decisions of the democratic government, and do so in an even-handed way untouched by any interests other than the imperatives of implementation, has long been open to question, in the West as much as in Central and Eastern Europe.[19] In practice no bureaucracy is neutral. It always has agendas of its own and countless examples can be found of administrations that cannot deviate overtly from the formal functions and remit determined by the politicians, but which in fact operate differently, usually acting to maximize their own power and to construct a rationality which serves their own purposes without distorting too blatantly what it is genuinely supposed to do. Hence the idea of bureaucratic even-handedness cannot be an automatic premise of governance.

Matters are bound to be worse in this regard in the post-communist states for a variety of reasons. Bureaucratic distortion, the diversion of power and resources from the formal agenda to the one determined by the bureaucracy, was a normal feature of the communist system; communist parties, the supposed watchdogs, were never able to remedy this state of affairs. Thus the bureaucratic culture inherited from the past was inimical to an administrative system that was supposed to operate with a high enough degree of fairness to earn popular trust. Yet the tasks that the state was supposed to discharge were formidable and would have taxed a much more experienced and trusted machinery of administration. In the economy the state was the ultimate arbiter over the functioning of the new markets, the limits of market activity against state intervention, because the political system

---

[19] Eric A. Nordlinger, *On the Autonomy of the Democratic State* (1981).

was still too fragmented to undertake this role. By the same token absolutely fundamental issues like the definition of just and unjust profit, the delimitation of the abuse of power and the appropriate remedies, the policing of new winners and new losers, were supposedly in the care of the state, but the state machinery was not actually trusted by either the politicians or the population to achieve these objectives. To these factors should be added the legacy of the past, as discussed in previous chapters – the softness of the state and the propensity for overregulation.

The problem did not end there, however. The lack of faith in institutions was not restricted to the bulk of the population, but was shared by the new élite as well. This led to a general distrust of the professionalism of the bureaucracies inherited from communism and a predisposition to replace communist-trained bureaucrats with ones appointed by the new rulers. Quite apart from the irony of the potential revival of the *nomenklatura* system under post-communism, this attitude tended to create a new and damaging difficulty. One of the unavoidable characteristics of the new élites was their political inexperience. Their backgrounds were those of intellectuals and the intelligentsia, usually the humane rather than the scientific, with the result that they were poorly qualified in understanding the requirements of administration. In general they had little idea of management and organization and, because they distrusted the professionals, they were badly placed to learn. The consequence was that their expectations of what a bureaucracy can achieve were unrealistic and their ability to supervise the execution of policies was seldom adequate. The outcome of this state of affairs was that they tended to lose control over their bureaucracies and then blame their communist antecedents. To counteract this situation they would then politicize the bureaucracy by appointing friends and colleagues whom they trusted personally, but whose ability to manage was not necessarily proven, thereby failing to solve the problem, but intensifying the suspicion at the same time.[20] It was very difficult to see how one was to escape this vicious circle.

Nor was it easy to see how society acting through the network of intermediate institutions could do much to police state activity. Not only were these institutions weak, but they were not really trusted much either. The way in which the media operated illustrated this process clearly. It hardly needs to be stated that the sphere of public

---

[20] On the lack of adequate control over the administration in the case of Hungary see László Lengyel, 'Félúton', *2000,* 3 no. 7 (July 1991), pp. 3–14. There is no reason to suppose that the Hungarian case was in any way exceptional.

information through which political ideas are transmitted, political actions judged, models of political behaviour established and the palette of choice established is in large measure structured by the media. This was, of course, understood by the new élites and they made determined efforts to bring the press, radio and television under their supervision.[21]

The conflict over the media was exacerbated by the inexperience of politicians, particularly as regards public criticism, and of the journalists themselves. The inexperience of the latter was made worse by their reluctance to exercise self-limitation and by their failure to recognize the crucial distinction between freedom of opinion and freedom of information. Freedom of opinion is very easy to practise; all it requires is for a commentator to display his views on any and every topic; personalization ruled. Freedom of information, on the other hand, was a much more difficult matter, which necessitated deeper understanding of political processes, an ongoing reciprocal relationship between media and government and a readiness to assess information in a broad context. This latter was rare under post-communism.

The overall consequence was that officialdom did much to try and ensure that the media presented information according to its preconceptions and complained bitterly that the press was unfair when it did not do so, which was usually the case. To the above may be added the observation that the political élites in any case tended to overestimate the significance of the media and assumed that what was published was actually accepted by the consumers of the media, public opinion. This was hardly likely to be the case in the atmosphere of relative distrust between rulers and ruled, but the élites were badly placed to take this on board, because of their own overwhelmingly intellectual antecedents, which placed such a strong emphasis on the written and spoken word. The media had become the object of a major political battle and it was hard to see how a truce could be called.

The desert left by communism, therefore, consisted of ideas and values that make the smooth functioning of democracy problematical. In a very real sense, the political and economic institutions of communism made for a very bad fit with those required by democracy. The reconstruction work, therefore, meant that a great deal would have to be dismantled before it could be made to work under the new system and, because 'construction' in this context is a metaphor, it is much more difficult to achieve than on a building site. Ideas and values, a cultural matrix, cannot be transformed as easily as demolishing and rebuilding a house.

[21] Attila Ágh, 'Médiumok és politika', *Magyar Hírlap*, 21 February 1992.

Political Ideologies: Obstacles to Liberalism

The post-communist states of Central and Eastern Europe began by opting for liberal democracy as the only viable alternative to communism. While this defined their position in broad terms, it said very little about the extent to which they would shift towards liberalism in their new structures and practices. In reality there were major obstacles to the introduction of political and economic liberalism, both structural and attitudinal.

The pivotal factor conditioning the horizons of those involved in the construction of these post-communist systems was, of course, the legacy of communism. Communism could be defined as the apotheosis of étatism, as well as having other attributes. Central to communist legitimation was the proposition that the state was knowledgeable and society was ignorant, that the state embodied progress while society was an obstacle to it. This reversed the well-established Western European ideal that society was creative and the state was reactive.

The legacy of what might be termed 'hyper-étatism' is a contradictory one. On one hand there was a rejection of the centralized, command economy model, as well as the monopoly control of political power by a single party; on the other there was confusion about how far this reversal should go. Society was anxious that any radical break with the detested past would leave it worse off economically and, although it appeared to value the new-found political and economic freedoms, it remained largely uncertain of how to use them. Much the same applied to political élites. They too were uncertain about how far they should dismantle the communist-built 'hyper-state'. Indeed, the first and possibly most significant political debates of the new post-communist democracies were about the proper role of the state.

There was no one answer to this question of how far the state should exercise its regulatory and programmatic powers. The tradition in Central and Eastern Europe has been that the state played a pre-eminent role in this respect – to this extent, communism had carried a genuine pre-existing tradition to absurd lengths – but the past did not necessarily provide adequate answers for the 1990s. The communist caesura had been a real one. But legitimation of policies in the present by reference to the past was, of course, a possibility.

To restate the proposition, the pre-communist pattern of development had given rise to relatively weak and dependent societies. The communists had done little to strengthen society and encourage its autonomy, with the consequence that the new leaderships felt they were obliged to use the machinery of the state to substitute for the weaknesses of society, to help individuals and groups who were inexperienced or ignorant of the new opportunities. This was not automatically an unworthy objective, but it almost automatically led these new systems into the temptation of bureaucratic autonomy over civil society, where the state continued to exercise functions that nobody else would or could, doing so in a way congenial to the bureaucracy rather than its ostensible purpose.

This pattern created major obstacles to the emergence of civil society and liberalism, inasmuch as it re-established the state as the central and unquestioned actor, making all others dependent on it. As society gathered its strengths it would be difficult for the organs of the state to make way for it and the untried governments were unlikely to whittle down the bureaucracies either. And societies, fearful of the cold, harsh winds of competitive politics and economics, would tend to acquiesce in this, thereby helping to reproduce étatist patterns.

Part of the debate is about state regulation and equality. The communist legacy in this respect may turn out to have been highly influential. The communist use or misuse of egalitarian slogans has left much of the population suspicious, but the aspiration for equality and, just as important, hostility to differentiation made it difficult for the state to avoid playing a regulatory role in this regard. Yet the operation of the market would inevitably bring into being new winners and new losers, and state intervention to prevent this or slow it down would be counter-productive in terms of democracy and competitive politics.[22]

Something must also be said here about the nature and definition of change. Change is not universal or identical everywhere, but its nature and pace vary from society to society. Some are used to much more rapid change than others. The post-communist countries have a particular difficulty here. Communist systems were highly conservative and indeed static, so that the concept of change became more rhetorical than real. This can be seen in a wide variety of areas affecting human relations, from the family to politics. On the whole, expectations were that change would be marginal and, in general, change tended to have negative connotations, as something over which individuals have little control. This factor too was likely to strengthen the role of the state, this time as comforter.

There was a final structural factor impelling modern societies towards étatism, one that applies to all democracies.[23] Once govern-

---

[22] Witold Morawski, 'Reform Models and Systemic Change in Poland', *Studies in Comparative Communism,* 34 no. 3 (September 1991), pp. 251–94.

[23] This argument is based on William H. McNeill, *The Pursuit of Power* (1983). See also Maurice Pearton, *The Knowledgeable State* (1982).

ments entered the fields of military investment and social welfare in a significant fashion, around the turn of the century, they found themselves with no alternative but to continue. And continuing did not mean level funding or funding tapering off, but an ever-intensifying participation by the state in wider areas. When this was established the strategy in question acquired its own dynamic and became increasingly immune to the questioning. The proposition that, say, the welfare system be eliminated is generally regarded as beyond rational discourse.[24] At the same time the state builds up a substantial and growing clientele with a vested interest in the maintenance and expansion of its activity. The implication of this factor for post-communist states is that even if they attempt a radical de-étatization, this will be blocked by 'natural' barriers of the kind sketched here.

The Role of Infrastructure

The principal areas where the role of the state was bound to remain high and probably intensify were in the provision of infrastructure and industrial subsidies. The case that the state should play a major role in the provision of infrastructure does not need to be made, but how far and in what way this role should be played is another issue. Infrastructure may be broken down into four broad categories – social welfare (health, education, social support), the economy and environment, culture, and commerce and telecommunications. There could be little disagreement that the state would have to have a regulatory and strategic function in the provision of social welfare as such; the difficulty lay in the peripheral areas of provision, like food-price support, transport and housing subsidy. These could not be immediately discontinued, for fear of triggering off major social unrest, yet their maintenance was liable to become a permanent fixture. Any attempt to impose dramatic cuts in social-welfare provision would, given the low level of economic activity, immediately pauperize significant sections of the population.

As far as the economy was concerned, an immediate withdrawal by the state was impossible and debates on the pace and extent of privatization persisted without any clear outcome, except that the principle was universally supported, at any rate in theory. The environment, which was in a state of near disaster, would obviously demand far-reaching state intervention if any progress was to be made in remedying the situation. If sums of this magnitude were to be made

---

[24] Charles Murray, *Losing Ground: American Social Policy 1950–1980* (1984).

available, presumably from the West, governments would automatically be involved. Cultural subsidies would also have to continue, though maybe at a lower rate, simply to sustain activities for which there was no internal market. State prestige would dictate that drama, music and publishing would go on receiving some state support. The necessary investment in commercial infrastructure could, again, only be channelled through the state – no private entrepreneur could conceivably contemplate the modernization of the area's antiquated telephone network, for example.

One question remained open, however, and this might point in a positive direction. Given the highly distorted nature of communist modernization,[25] with its bizarre emphasis on heavy industry virtually to the exclusion of everything else, the post-communist leaderships might conclude that dismantling this sector was a high priority. If privatization plans included the heavy industrial sector, its future would be severely limited and the role of the state as patron would be restricted with it.

Ethnic homogeneity should be seen as a crucial factor in affecting the future of liberalism. Ethnically homogeneous states have an important advantage in this respect, in that ethnic heterogeneity creates almost automatic imperatives towards centralization. The function of ethnicity in politics is to satisfy the affective dimension of societies by creating identities through which individuals can define themselves against a wider community. That, in turn, promotes loyalties underpinned by a network of symbols and rituals.[26]

The problem is that these loyalties tend to transcend those of the state in multinational states and non-majority communities will inevitably be perceived as potential or actual threats to the integrity of the state simply by their very existence. The way in which the Romanian authorities used the conflict in Tîrgu-Mures in March 1990 as an excuse to strengthen the security forces is a clear illustration of this. There was little discussion of what really took place; instead it was automatically assumed that the mere existence of the Hungarian minority constituted a threat and justified stronger security measures. Examples could be multiplied from other polities. The difficulty is that, because ethnic issues appeal to the emotions, it is next to impossible to discuss them rationally, and calls for more central power will be readily heeded.

There is a final point that should be discussed in this connection –

---

[25] See chapter 4.
[26] George Schöpflin, 'The Prospects for Democracy in Central and Eastern Europe', in Peter Volten (ed.), *Uncertain Futures: Eastern Europe and Democracy* (1990).

corporatism.[27] Once an interwoven pattern of state and private enterprise activity has come into being, it becomes exceedingly difficult to
root it out. Given the nature of the communist legacy and the corresponding weakness of the market, coupled with the timidity of society,
a corporatist outcome for Central and Eastern Europe looked plausible. In this dispensation both the state and the privatized economy
would have a continuing interest in maintaining a permanent relationship, which would act as a constant factor of distortion on both political and economic transparency. The transmission of existing
enterprises into the private sector, the circumstances in which this took
place and the survival of a network of personal ties and loyalties, as
well as attitudes of mind that favoured dependence on the state for
subsidies and economic targets, were likely to provide fertile ground
for a corporatist system, which would naturally enough entrench the
state with a high-profile role. All in all the prospects for liberalism in
the post-communist world looked poor.

Political Ideologies: the Weakness of Conservatism

The difficulties faced by the emergent right had their roots in the forty
years of communism, as did so much else. The communist period
destroyed much; in this context it eliminated above all the first few
halting attempts to create a conservatism more modern than what had
existed between the wars. Such attempts were, indeed, few and not
very far-reaching, mainly because the right had been completely
discredited through its association with the authoritarianism of the
interwar period and its deliberate identification with Nazism by its left-
wing opponents. They did exist, however and, were to be found in
parties like post-war Christian Democracy. These parties were eliminated, and as history was written by the victors for forty years, their
ideas were derided. Subsequently, any idea that conservatism might
undergo a rethinking was moonshine as long as the communists were
in power.

After the collapse, as the newly dominant conglomerates divided
into left and right (in Hungary this process was avoided, as no conglomerate had come into being) and the right assumed power, these
new governments had relatively few ideas about what defined their
conservatism. The problem to which no one had applied himself was

[27] I am not referring here to fascist or fascist-type state corporatism, but to liberal
corporatism, as it exists in Austria, Sweden and elsewhere; see G. Lehmbruch and
Philip Schmitter, *Patterns of Corporatist Policy Making* (1982).

what exactly being right-wing or conservative meant under the new conditions. In this sense the newly fledged right was not only untried in terms of administrative experience, but equally had very little in the way of ideas from which to derive a strategy for how it intended to govern. This operated on two levels – the right lacked broad ideas by which to define conservatism at all and it was not well placed to formulate a specific strategy for transforming a communist order into a democratic one.

In Western Europe conservative parties had undergone an altogether different experience. They too had had the challenge of a left-wing upsurge to deal with – the construction of the post-1945 welfare-state paradigm, which won broad acceptance throughout the European liberal democracies – and more particularly they saw the opportunity for a renewed and reformulated conservatism in the growing sclerosis of welfare-state socialism turning into parasitical étatism. The shift away from the state, which found its clearest expression in Thatcherism, was by no means only a British phenomenon, though it undoubtedly had its strongest adherents there. This, in effect, left conservative parties a coalition of two broad streams – a traditionalist current, which emphasized religion, the family and tradition as its primary intellectual sources, and neo-conservatism, which was much more dynamic, and looked to free markets and individual enterprise.

Their Central and Eastern European counterparts, on the other hand, had not been able to undertake this modernization. Under communist domination this was impossible, indeed the very idea of conservative thought was inconceivable and, for that matter, ineffective politically, because only ideas which could engage in a dialogue with the rhetoric or contents of the official doctrine could offer a challenge. Conservatism by definition was well beyond the political pale. The idea of human rights, used by the democratic opposition from the mid-1970s, was much more appropriate and effective, but the conservatives had only limited resources in this contest and tended on the whole to remain outside the nascent political debates of the 1970s and 1980s, although they established a tentative political home under the aegis of the Church, especially in Poland.

Neither religion nor nationalism was effective in mobilizing opposition to the existing régimes, and neither was able to make a serious dent in the communists' self-legitimation; for the most part, the communists were successful in containing the challenge of religion. Much the same could be said for nationalism. After the initial onslaught on nationalism during the Stalinist period, when all unsanctioned ideas were under attack, and its brief, triumphant resurgence in the 1956 events in Poland and Hungary, nationalism was somewhat uneasily

294 Tbe Condition of Post-Communism

domesticated by the communists. Some forms of nationalist expression were tacitly encouraged, while others, especially anything to do with the Soviet Union, were severely suppressed. The communists could never hope to be accepted as the legitimate agents of nationhood – the communist and nationalist agendas were too far apart for this – but a sort of *modus vivendi* from which both benefited could and did come into being. In effect, therefore, two of the sources from which conservatism might have grown were diverted into less dangerous terrain by the communists.

Consequently, when the right emerged blinking into the sunlight after the collapse of communism it did so naked. In 1989–90 it proved extremely difficult to determine what being right-wing meant, except in the negative sense. Being right-wing was, evidently, anti-communist, though seeing that everyone condemned the communist period, including the newly minted socialist parties that sprang into existence on the ruins of communism, this did not mean very much. It was hard to put together a conservative agenda in any positive sense, and in this connection the lack of time did not help.

Inevitably, the right-wing packages that were offered were not very well thought out. They were – or were said to be – influenced by Christian democracy, but the right tended to be an awkward coalition between Christian democrats, radical populists, free marketeers, anti-liberal conservatives and constitutional liberals. From one particular perspective, the conservatives were in a genuine difficulty. In order to be conservative to an extent they had been forced into a paradoxical radicalism, the rejection of the previous forty years. Ideally, they would have liked to return to the pre-communist period and do away with everything that communism wrought as alien and repellent. This, of course, was an impossibility and there were aspects of the communist revolution which, however partial and distorted it might have been, did constitute a social revolution that could not and would not be undone. Some of these irreversible effects of communism included the ending of the peasant problem of rural overpopulation and low agricultural output; the corresponding rise of urbanization, the growth of an urban proletariat and the spread of industrial working methods; the demand for modern citizenship and democratic rights; the widespread acceptance of Western consumerist aspirations from Macdonalds to pop music; and the disappearance of the pre-war élites with their traditional legitimation

The unviability of this anachronistic conservatism lay in the fact that it simply sidestepped the enormous changes in social structure, political attitudes and values that had taken place since. In effect, the right was reconstructing itself on the basis of a pre-modern conservatism that was appropriate to the pre-modern semi-authoritarian system of the interwar period, but seemed incapable of coming to terms with the passage of time. The implication was that conservatism was sliding towards intellectual irrelevance at a time when new ideas were badly needed, because these parties were involved in the exercise of power.

The failure or weakness of conservatism could also be attributed to the limp response to the new situation by the intellectuals of the right. Instead of trying to assess the situation in its real terms, intellectuals of the right preferred to continue as they had always done, to refer to their mission as the spokesmen of the nation and to try to encompass what was happening by traditional, affective means, rather than modern rational ones. The weaponry of the nationalist right was fiction and poetry, rather than statistical tables; the 'true son' of the nation, it was said, could 'understand the tragedies of his people from within' and had no need of dry, academic argumentation. This reliance on the affective dimension left those with the task of governing dangerously exposed to making the decisions by no rational criteria – assuming they were listening to their intellectuals at all.

The pre-modern values articulated by the intellectuals of the right clustered around nation, religion, tradition and family, which, of course, the old right also espouses in the West, but it does so in conjunction with at least a readiness to discuss neo-conservative concepts of individualism and markets. This latter appeared to be rather weak on the right in Central and Eastern Europe. This intellectual weakness created an opportunity for the populists, which they were not slow to exploit. In summary form, populists begin from the proposition that the people, in its contemporary expression the nation, is the pivot of existence, that they constitute an organic community held together by affective bonds that are threatened by alien, modern practices. For the populists the nation is also a moral category, so that much of their discourse is couched in heavily moralizing language, which can often be highly manipulative – unavoidably so, when the affective dimension plays so salient a role in their world-view. In this perception individual choice and personal accomplishment must be subordinated to the collective good, so that consumerism is condemned as selfishness.[28]

Somewhere at the back of the populist mind-set is the ideal of the self-reliant, largely autarkic peasant family, clearly patriarchal, which is the repository of the finest values of the nation, to which the money-

---

[28] In Hungary the second issue of *Századvég* 1990 was devoted entirely to the question of populism. See in particular the article by Mária Heller, Dénes Némedi and Ágnes Rényi, 'Népesedési viták 1963-1986', pp. 69–105.

using economy is alien, and agricultural activity is patrimonial rather than orientated towards commodity production. As the peasant barely exists in contemporary Central and Eastern Europe outside Poland, the populists' ideal type has tended to focus on the stable family, with two or three children, modest aspirations, and relatively low educational levels, but superior to the underclass, either because, as in Hungary, the term 'lumpen elements' tends to be a code word for Gypsies, who, naturally, are outside the Hungarian nation, or because the lowest social strata are regarded as somehow unworthy of the nation. In effect the populists articulated the apprehensions and desires of the lower middle and upper working classes, many of whom are first generation and are fearful of the challenge of democracy and modernity.[29]

Anti-Semitism is not an automatic corollary of this set of attitudes, but the Jewish question inevitably became linked with the role of the populists because, as a result of the very particular patterns of Central European history, Jews were among the primary modernizers in the nineteenth century and came to be seen as the bearers of the alien values of modernity, albeit this was least true of the Czech lands. Some, though not by any manner of means all, of the populists brought anti-Semitism back to the political agenda, by in effect arguing that Jews could not become members of the nation, inasmuch as their ideas in politics were suspect and alien.[30] Thus there were unmistakable hints in some of these ideas that the establishment of a liberal democracy was tantamount to an attempt by Jewish liberals 'to "assimilate" the nation to its style and thinking'.[31]

In the populist thought-world, the broad strategies of politics were determined by the spokesmen of the nation, namely the populist intellectuals themselves. There was some division of opinion in this approach to the role of the state. Some populists were étatists and looked to the state to ensure that their anti-individualist, anti-consumerist, collectivist and tradition-centred ideas were properly enforced, while others distrusted the state as in itself an alien, soulless formation. It was hard to see this anti-modernist ideology as an effective repository of ideas for coalition governments that were looking for solutions for economies in crisis, involving rising inflation, growing

---

[29] Louisa Vinton, 'From Margins to the Mainstream: the Confederation for an Independent Poland', *RFE/RL Research,* 2 no. 46, 15 November 1991.

[30] For Hungary see the writings of István Csurka, *passim.* Sándor Csoóri, in many respects the most prestigious spokesman of the populists, has also implied that Jews are outside the definition (his definition) of Hungarian culture; see his 'Nappali hold (2)', *Hitel,* 3:18 (5 September 1990).

[31] Csoóri, ibid. was quite explicit on this.

unemployment and the threat of a major balance of payments deficit following the recession in the early 1990s.

While ruling right-wing coalitions, to be fair, did not fully accept the remedies of the populists, they did little to distance themselves from them either. In essence they appeared to have four major reference points in formulating a strategy. The first of these was the 'nation'. The reiteration of national goals and national endeavours might have a value as an exercise in symbolic politics by distracting attention from economic privation. Using the nation as a legitimating principle is, of course, perfectly proper, but this would involve a wide-ranging open debate about the redefinition of nationhood, its functions and its objectives in the 1990s. In Hungary, for example, the nearest the government came to this was the declaration that the prime minister of Hungary was the prime minister of all Hungarians, i.e. those living in the successor states as well as in Hungary. In political terms – and the declaration was by definition political seeing that both 'nation' and 'prime minister' are political categories – the consequences were to exacerbate relations with the successor states, whose own politicians were highly suspicious of potential Hungarian irredentism, even if there was no sign that anyone in Hungary regarded irredentism as a serious option. In Slovakia the new state was expressly defined as a national state of the Slovaks, thereby excluding Hungarians and Gypsies. The Romanian constitution stipulated that Romania was a 'national' and 'unitary' state, a provision which emphasized the community over the individual.[32]

The second reference point was religion, which had a concrete expression, for example, in the proposal to introduce compulsory religious education in schools, the banning of abortion or the return of Church property.[33] In broader terms, religion was the basis of a social protectionist attitude, that the state had far-reaching responsibilities for the welfare of the nation and that, in turn, could be utilized to legitimate an étatist, interventionist strategy.

That leads directly to the third reference point, étatism itself. To judge by the policies adopted by the governments, they were reluctant to accept the introduction of the market. Recoiling from a big bang approach to privatization, especially after its failure in Poland, policies tended to favour privatization from above, with considerable powers given to state agencies. It was inevitable that this would reproduce

[32] On Romania, see Michael Shafir, 'Romania', *RFE/RL Research Report,* Special Issue 'Toward the Rule of Law', 1 no. 27 (3 July 1992).

[33] In Poland the Senate had passed a law outlawing abortion, *The Independent,* 2 October 1990. See also Jane L. Curry, 'Poland: Are the Church and Public Opinion at Variance?', *RFE/RL Research,* 2 no. 28, 12 July 1991.

some, though not all, of the worst features of the communist party-state and would give rise to the standard problems of patron–client networks, the parasitism of the state on society, the blocking of initiatives and energies and the restriction of choice.[34]

The fourth reference point concerned the language of public discourse and the debates themselves. The coalition found itself in a difficult position as far as the media was concerned. The media were overwhelmingly populated by individuals whose thought-world and attitudes were far more open to liberal-rational ideas, rather than the 'national values' favoured by the populists. This was not necessarily because journalists and communicators were, as the right tended to believe, in the pockets of the left, but more because the views of the communicators tended to coincide with a liberal philosophy.

As a result governments came to feel that they were not treated even-handedly by the media, that the media were dominated by a liberal intellectual hegemony which excluded alternatives like their own, and hence sensitivity to media treatment grew by leaps and bounds. This was no doubt made worse by the lack of experience of the government and its ministers in criticism *per se* and the frequently personalized and moralizing tone of media comment. Demands for tighter government control of the media, with an unmistakably authoritarian flavour, began to be heard as a result, especially from among the populists.[35] This liberal hegemony in the media was a serious handicap in fostering the modernization of conservatism and promoted the emergence of a shrill populist-nationalist attitude and conspiracy-mindedness.

In conclusion, it should be understood that the collapse of the communist legitimating ideology left both élites and rulers in a state of some disorientation, and the construction of a new one would be neither easy nor rapid. This posed a certain danger in the longer term. If the right failed to cohere around a legitimating ideology and continued on its rather hesitant course, in which it was often enough hard to know whether pragmatism or opportunism was the guiding principle, it was unlikely to escape unscathed in the event of a major political crisis.

The hesitations of conservatism had a further, undoubtedly unintended consequence – to an extent its uncertainties were beginning to pull the liberal opposition onto its own ground. In part this was

---

[34] On some of the consequences of state-directed privatization, see Kámán Mizsei (ed.), *A privatizációs kihívás Közép-Kelet-Európában* (1990).

[35] In Hungary Csurka made repeated calls for government control over the electronic media.

virtually automatic, inasmuch as the government sets the agenda in all political systems and the opposition responds to it. If that agenda was primarily concerned with questions of what constituted Christian, populist and national values, then the opposition was bound to become involved.

The left was elected to parliament on individualist and free-market programmes and regarded itself as the protagonist of liberal European values. Where it was weak, however, was in formulating a conception of the role of nationhood in politics. If anything, it tended to dismiss it uneasily as an irrelevant leftover from the past, which was manifestly a mistake. The result was that the opposition parties felt vulnerable on the national issue and reacted – even overreacted – when the right made reference to it, but were incapable of formulating an alternative vision of nationhood that would be acceptable to a liberal world-view.

The long-term problem was that when a political party or government coalition relied on categories that were of limited value in drawing the cognitive map by which the real political situation could be understood, its solutions would be ineffective or counter-productive. It could then try more of the same and thereby make a bad situation worse and perhaps deploy manipulation, appeal to the affective dimension, or try scapegoating and leave the underlying problems untouched. The real threat was that this was likely to bring only short-term relief. In the medium term a major economic crisis could leave the government stripped of its legitimating ideology and find its self-legitimation undermined. It would find itself in a situation in which conservatism was afflicted with a 'scarcity of meanings', not unlike the fate of the communists in the second half of the 1980s.[36] In relatively untried democracies, the question in this scenario was whether a collapse of this kind would bring down only the government or the system as a whole.

Paralipomena

It is certainly too early to attempt anything like a conclusion, hence the title of this section. Many of the trends visible in Central and Eastern Europe after the collapse of communism were clearly negative when assessed by the criteria of promoting democracy. Indeed, the negative aspects have received a great deal of attention in this chapter, though not, I believe, too much. Nevertheless it should be stressed that the condition of post-communism is superior to that of communism in

---

[36] On legitimation crises, see Andrew C. János, *Politics and Paradigms* (1986), pp. 142–6 and the literature reviewed there.

numerous ways. The legitimacy of competitive politics and the market mean that the risk of rigidity and petrification has been much lowered. New political and economic actors can enter the stage and, in the fullness of time, lead to a release of energies that communism blocked. However primitive the culture of democracy in some areas and some sections of society, the process of learning the rules of democracy has started and sometimes its results are encouraging. The elections in Romania in October 1992 may have confirmed the strength of Romanian nationalism and the attractions of authoritarianism to the majority; all the same, the fact that the Democratic Convention could campaign on a recognizably democratic programme and gain a vote sizeable enough to dilute the overwhelming power of the National Salvation Front should not be underestimated, particularly in the light of the extremes of devastation that the country had suffered under Ceausescu.

The collapse of communism represented the best chance of establishing democracy that Central and Eastern Europe ever had. For the first time ever, popularly elected governments were in power everywhere east of the Elbe. The first three years of this experiment in democracy were bound to be fraught with difficulties, false steps and poor judgements. Nevertheless, the introduction or reintroduction of competitive politics and the market at the level of theory was a fundamental break from communism and a positive one for the widening of choice and potential for the satisfaction of individual aspirations. The speed, extent and direction of the process, on the other hand, are likely to be fitful and halting for many years to come.

Bibliography

A Magyar Szocialista Munkáspárt XI. kongresszusának jegyzökönyve, (Budapest: Kossuth, 1975), p. 134.

Aczél, Tamás and Méray, Tibor, *The Revolt of the Mind* (New York: Praeger, 1959).

Ágh, Attila, 'Médiumok és politika', *Magyar Hírlap,* 21 February 1992.

Anderson, Perry, *Lineages of the Absolutist State* (London: New Left Books, 1974).

Anonymous, *1956: A forradalom kronológiája és bibliográfiája* (Budapest: Századvég-Atlanti, 1990).

Apró, Éva, 'Mi késleltette a magyar vársosfejlödést', *Társadalmi Szemle,* 27 no. 6 (June 1972), pp. 28–38.

Argentieri, Federigo (ed.), *La fine del blocco sovietics* (Florence: Ponte alle graziet 1991).

Armstrong, John A., *Nations before Nationalism* (Chapel Hill, NC: University of North Carolina Press, 1982).

Ash, Timothy Garton, *The Polish Revolution: Solidarity 1980–1982* (London: Cape, 1983)

Avakumovic, Ivan, *History of the Communist Party of Yugoslavia* (2 vols, Aberdeen: Aberdeen University Press, 1964–7)

Balawyder, A. (ed.) *Cooperative Movements in Eastern Europe* (London: Macmillan, 1980).

Banac, Ivo (ed.), *The Effects of World War I: the Class War after the Great War: the Rise of Communist Parties in East Central Europe 1918–1921* (New York: Brooklyn College Studies, 1983).

Batt, Judy, *East Central Europe from Reform to Transformation* (London: Pinter, 1991).

Bauer, Tamás, *Tervgazdaság, beruházás, ciklusok* (Budapest: Közgazdasági és Jogi, 1981).

Bauman, Zygmunt, 'Intellectuals in East-Central Europe: Continuity and

Change', *Eastern European Politics and Societies,* 1 no. 2 (Spring 1987), pp. 162–86.

Baylis, Thomas A., *The Technical Intelligentsia and the East German Élite: Legitimacy and Social Change in Mature Communism* (Berkeley, CA; University of California Press, 1974).

Behr, Edward, *'Kiss the Hand You Cannot Bite': the Rise and Fall of the Ceausescus* (London: Penguin, 1992).

Bell, John D., *The Bulgarian Communist Party from Blagoev to Zhivkov* (Stanford, CA: Hoover Institution Press, 1986).

Bell, Peter, *Peasants in Socialist Transition: Life in a Collectivized Hungarian Village* (Berkeley, CA: University of California Press, 1984).

Berecz, János, *Ellenforradalom tollal és fegyverrel,* 2nd edn (Budapest: Kossuth, 1981).

Berglund, Sten and Dellenbrant, Jan Åke (eds), *The New Democracies in Eastern Europe: Party Systems and Political Cleavages* (Aldershot, Hants.: Edward Elgar, 1991).

Bernhard, Michael H., 'Barriers to Further Political and Economic Change in Poland', *Studies in Comparative Communism,* 23 nos 3–4 (Autumn/Winter 1990), pp. 319–39.

Beyme, Klaus von and Zimmermann, Hartmut (eds), *Policymaking in the German Democratic Republic* (Aldershot: Gower, 1984).

Bibó, István, 'Political Breviary', *Cross Currents: a Yearbook of Central European Culture,* no. 3 (1984), pp. 7–20.

—— 'Az európai társadalomfejlödés értelme', in *Összegyüjtött Munkái,* 2 (Berne: EPSzE, 1982), pp. 560–636. There is a translation of this in István Bibó, 'Reflections on the Social Development of Europe', *Democracy, Revolution, Self-Determination: Selected Writings* (New York: Social Science Monographs, 1991), pp. 421–526.

Black, Cyril E. (ed.), *Comparative Modernization: a Reader* (New York: Free Press, 1976).

Bloomfield, Jon, *Passive Revolution: Politics and the Czechoslovak Working Class, 1945–1948,* (London: Allison and Busby, 1979).

Bogár, László, *A fejlödés ára* (Budapest: Közgazdasági és Jogi, 1983).

Borbándi, Gyula, *Der ungarische Populismus* (Munich: Aurora, 1976).

Borsányi, György, 'Ezernyolcszáz kartoték a budapesti baloldalrol *Valóság,* 26:9 (1983), pp. 19–31

Boyes, Roger and Moody, John, *The Priest who had to Die: the Tragedy of Father Jerzy Popieluszko,* (London: Gollancz, 1986), pp. 142–3.

Bozóki, András, et al. (eds), *Csendes? Forraddom? Volt?* (Budapest: T-Twins, 1991).

Brecht, Bertolt, 'The Solution', *Poems 1913-1956* (London: Methuen, 1976), p. 440.

Brown, J. F., *The New Eastern Europe: the Khrushchev Era and After* (London: Praeger, 1966).

—— *Bulgaria under Communist Rule* (London: Pall Mall, 1970).

Brügel, J.W., *Czechoslovakia before Munich* (Cambridge: Cambridge

University Press, 1973) pp. 47–9.

Brzezinski, Zbigniew K., *The Soviet Bloc: Unity and Conflict*, 2nd edn (Cambridge, MA: Harvard University Press, 1967).

—— *The Grand Failure: the Birth and Death of Communism in the Twentieth Century* (New York: Scribner, 1989).

—— The Hugh Seton-Watson Memorial Lecture 1988, 'From Eastern Europe back to Central Europe', in *A Year in the Life of Glasnost* (London: Centre for Policy Studies, 1988).

Campeanu, Pavel, *The Origins of Stalinism* (White Plains, NY: M. E. Sharpe, 1986).

—— *The Genesis of the Stalinist Social Order* (White Plains, NY: M. E. Sharpe, 1988).

Checinski, Michael, *Poland: Communism, Nationalism, Anti-Semitism* (New York: Karz-Cohn, 1982).

Childs, David, *The GDR: Moscow's German Ally* (London: Allen and Unwin, 1983).

Chirot, Daniel (ed.), *The Origins of Backwardness in Eastern Europe: Economics and Politics from the Middle Ages until the Early Twentieth Century* (Berkeley, CA: University of California Press, 1989).

Clark, Katerina, 'Utopian Anthropology as a Context for Stalinist Literature', in Robert C. Tucker (ed.), *Stalinism: Essays in Historical Interpretation* (New York: Norton, 1977), pp. 180–98.

Cohen, Gary B., *The Politics of Ethnic Survival: Germans in Prague 1861–1914* (Princeton, NJ: Princeton University Press, 1981).

Connor, Walter, *Socialism, Politics and Equality: Hierarchy and Change in Eastern Europe and the USSR* (New York: Columbia University Press, 1979).

Csalog, Zsolt, *Temető Ősszel* (Budapest: Szépirodalmi, 1977).

Csoóri, Sándor, 'Nappali hold (2)', *Hitel,* 3 no. 18, 5 September 1990.

Curry, Jane L., 'Poland: Are the church and Public Opinion at Variance?', *RFE/RL Research*, 2 no. 28, 2 July 1991.

Dahrendorf, Ralf, *Reflections on the Revolution in Europe* (London: Chatto, 1991).

Deutscher, Isaac, 'The Tragedy of the Polish Communist Party', *Marxism in Our Time* (London: Cape, 1971), pp. 113–60.

Djilas, Milovan, *Conversations with Stalin* (New York: Harcourt, Brace, Jovanovich, 1962).

Douglas, Mary, 'Purity and Danger Revisited', *Times Literary Supplement,* 19 September 1980.

Drachkovitch Milorad M. and Lazitch, Branko (eds.) *The Comintern - Historical Highlights* (New York: Praeger for Hoover Institution, 1966)

Dunleavy, Patrick, and O'Leary, Brendan, *Theories of the State: the Politics of Liberal Democracy* (London: Macmillan, 1987).

Dziewanowski, M. K. *The Communist Party of Poland: an Outline of History,* 2nd edn (Cambridge, MA: Harvard University Press,1976)

Eco, Umberto, *Faith in Fakes* (London: Secker and Warburg, 1986), pp. 178ff. The paperback edition was entitled *Travels in Hyperreality.*

Eliás, Zdenek, and Netík, Jaromír, 'Czechoslovakia', in William E. Griffith (ed.), *Communism in Europe: Continuity, Change and the Sino-Soviet Dispute,* (Oxford: Pergamon, 1966), vol. 2, pp. 155–276.

Erdei, Ferenc, 'A magyar társadalom a két háború között', *Valóság,* 19 no. 4 (1974), pp. 25–53.

Erdélyi, Sándor, 'Külkereskedelem – egy beruházó mérnök szemével', *Valóság,* 19 no. 1 (January 1977), pp. 50–60.

Erényi, Tibor and Rákosi, Sándor *Legyözhetetlen erö* (Budapest: Kossuth, 1974)

Fehér, Ferenc, 'Kádárism as applied Khrushchevism', in R. F. Miller and Ferenc Fehér (eds), *Khrushchev and the Communist World* (London: Croom Helm, 1984), pp. 210–79.

Fehér, Ferenc and Heller, Ágnes, *Hungary 1956 Revisited: the Message of a Revolution a Quarter of a Century After* (London: Allen and Unwin, 1983)

Fehér, Ferenc, Heller, Ágnes and Márkus, György, *Dictatorship over Needs* (Oxford: Blackwell, 1983).

Fejtö, François, *A History of the People's Democracies: Eastern Europe since Stalin* (London: Pall Mall, 1971).

—— *Le Coup de Prague 1948* (Paris: Seuil, 1976).

Fowkes, F. B. M., 'The Origins of Czechoslovak Communism', in Ivo Banac (ed.), *The Effects of World War I: the Class War after the Great War: the Rise of Communist Parties in East Central Europe 1918–1921* (New York: Brooklyn College Studies, 1983).

Gábor, István R. and Galasi, Péter, *A "második" gazdaság* (Budapest: Közgazdasági és Jogi, 1981).

Garamvölgyi, Antal, 'Magyarország - Nógrádból nézve', *Uj Látóhatár,* 28 nos 1–2 (1975), pp. 101–8.

Gati, Charles, *Hungary and the Soviet Bloc* (Durham, NC: Duke University Press, 1986).

Gella, Alexander, *Development of Class Structure in Eastern Europe: Poland and her Southern Neighbours* (Albany, NY: State University of New York, 1989).

Gellner, Ernest, *Plough, Sword and Book* (London: Collins Harvill, 1988).

—— 'Islam and Marxism: some Comparisons', *International Affairs,* 67 no. 1 (January 1991), pp. 1–6.

Gilberg, Trond, *Nationalism and Communism in Romania: the Rise and Fall of Ceausescu's Personal Dictatorship* (Boulder, CO: Westview, 1990).

Glenny, Misha, *The Rebirth of History: Eastern Europe in the Age of Democracy* (London: Penguin, 1990).

Golan, Galia, *The Czechoslovak Reform Movement: Communism in Crisis 1962–1968* (Cambridge: Cambridge University Press, 1971)

—— *Reform Rule in Czechoslovakia: the Dubcek Era 1968–1969* (Cambridge: Cambridge University Press, 1973).

Goldfarb, Jeffrey C., *Beyond Glasnost: the Post-Totalitarian Mind* (Chicago: University of Chicago Press, 1989).

Göllner, András B., 'Foundations of Soviet Domination and Communist

Political Power in Hungary', *The Hungarian Revolution Twenty Years After,* special issue of *Canadian–American Review of Hungarian Studies,* 3 no. 2 (Fall 1976), pp. 73–106.

Gombár, Csaba, *Egy állampolgár gondolatai* (Budapest: Kossuth, 1984).

—— *A politika parttalan világa* (Budapest: Kozmosz, 1986).

Graubard, Stephen R., *Eastern Europe . . . Central Europe . . . Europe* (Boulder, CO: Westview, 1991).

Griffith, William (ed.), *Communism in Europe,* vol. 2 (London: Pergamon, 1966).

Hammond, Thomas T. (ed.), *The Anatomy of Communist Takeovers* (New Haven, CT: Yale University Press, 1975).

Hamsik, Dusan, *Writers against Rulers* (London: Hutchinson, 1971).

Hankiss, Elemér, *Társadalmi csapdák, diagnózisok,* 2nd edn (Budapest: Magvető, 1983).

—— *Diagnózisok 2* (Budapest: Magvető, 1986).

—— *The East European Alternative* (Oxford: Oxford University Press, 1990).

Hann, C. M. (ed.), *Market Economy and Civil Society in Hungary* (London: Frank Cass, 1990).

Hanson, Joanna K. M., *The Civilian Population and the Warsaw Uprising of 1944* (Cambridge: Cambridge University Press, 1982).

Hasek, Jaroslav, *The Good Soldier Svejk and his Fortunes in the World War* (London: Heinemann in association with Penguin, 1973).

—— *The Red Commissar* (London: Heinemann, 1981).

Havel, Václav, 'The Power of the Powerless' in John Keane (ed.), *The Power of the Powerless: Citizens against the State in Central-Eastern Europe* (London: Hutchinson, 1985), pp. 23–96.

—— *Disturbing the Peace* (London: Faber, 1990).

—— *Open Letters: Selected Prose* (London: Faber, 1991).

Hegedüs, András, *Élet egy eszme árnyékában* (Vienna: Zsille, 1985).

Heller, Mária, Némedi Dénes, and Rényi, Ágnes, 'Népesedési viták 1963–1986', *Századvég* no. 2, 1990, pp. 69–105.

Hirszowicz, Maria, *The Bureaucratic Leviathan: a Study in the Sociology of Communism* (Oxford: Martin Robertson, 1980).

—— *Coercion and Control in Communist Society: the Visible Hand in a Command Economy* (Brighton: Wheatsheaf, 1986).

Hosking, Geoffrey, *A History of the Soviet Union* (London: Fontana, 1985).

Hroch, Miroslav, *Social Preconditions of National Revival in Europe* (Cambridge: Cambridge University Press, 1985).

Hruby, Peter, *Fools and Heroes: the Changing Role of Communist Intellectuals in Czechoslovakia* (Oxford: Pergamon, 1980).

Huntington, Samuel P., *The Third Wave: Democratization in the Late Twentieth Century* (Norman: University of Oklahoma Press, 1991).

Ionescu, Ghita, *Communism in Rumania 1944-1962* (London: Oxford University Press for RIIA, 1964).

—— *The Politics of the European Communist States* (London: Weidenfeld and Nicolson, 1967).

James, John, *Medieval France* (London: Harrap, 1986).

János, Andrew C., *The Politics of Backwardness in Hungary 1825–1945* (Princeton, NJ: Princeton University Press, 1982).

—— *Politics and Paradigms* (Stanford, CA: Stanford University Press, 1986).

Janos, Andrew C. and Slottman, William B. (eds), *Revolution in Perspective: Essays on the Hungarian Soviet Republic* (Berkeley, CA: University of California Press, 1971).

Jowitt, Ken, *Revolutionary Breakthroughs and National Development: the Case of Romania 1944–1965* (Berkeley, CA: University of California Press, 1971).

K. N., 'How Not to Build a Foundry', *Radio Free Europe Research: Poland,* 29 May 1981.

Kaplan, Karel, *Political Persecution in Czechoslovakia 1948–1972* (Cologne: Research Project "Crises in Soviet-Type Systems", no. 3, 1983).

—— *The Short March: the Communist Takeover in Czechoslovakia 1945– 1948* (London: Hurst, 1987).

Karchmar, Lucien, 'Communism in Romania, 1918–1921', in Ivo Banac (ed.), *The Effects of World War I: the Class War after the Great War: the Rise of Communist Parties in East Central Europe 1918–1921* (Brooklyn College Studies, 1983).

—— 'Communism in Bulgaria, 1918-1921', in Ivo Banac (ed.), *The Effects of World War I: the Class War after the Great War: the Rise of Communist Parties in East Central Europe 1918–1921* (Brooklyn College Studies, 1983).

Karinthy, Ferenc, *Harmincbárom* (Budapest: Szépirodalmi, 1976).

Kemény, István, *Ouvriers hongrois 1956–1985* (Paris: L'Harmattan, 1985).

—— *Közelröl s távolból* (Budapest: Gondolat, 1991).

Kemp-Welch, Anthony (ed. and trans.), *The Birth of Solidarity: the Gdansk Negotiations,* (London: Macmillan, 1983).

Kende, Pierre, and Strmiska, Zdenek, *Equality and Inequality in Eastern Europe* (Leamington Spa: Berg, 1987), p. 144.

Kenedi, János, *Do it Yourself: Hungary's Hidden Economy* (London: Pluto, n.d., but early 1980s).

Kertzer, David I., *Ritual, Politics and Power* (New Haven, CT: Yale University Press, 1988).

King, Robert R. *History of the Romanian Communist Party* (Stanford, CA: Hoover Institution Press, 1980).

Király, Bela, 'The Aborted Soviet Military Plans against Tito', in Wayne C. Vucinich (ed.), *At the Brink of War and Peace: the Tito-Stalin Split in Historic Perspective,* (New York: Social Science Monographs, 1982), pp. 273–88.

Kis, János, *Politics in Hungary: For a Democratic Alternative* (Highland Lakes, NJ: Atlantic Research, 1989).

—— *Vannak-e emberi jogaink?* (Paris: MFK, 1987).

Kohout, Pavel, *Diary of a Counterrevolutionary* (New York: McGraw Hill, 1969).

Kolakowski, Leszek, 'Theses on Hope and Hopelessness', *Survey,* 17 no. 3 (80), (Summer 1971), pp. 37–52.

—— 'Ideology in Eastern Europe', in Milorad Drachkovitch (ed.), *East Central Europe: Yesterday≈Today≈Tomorrow* (Stanford, CA: Hoover Institution Press, 1982), pp. 43–54.

Kolankiewicz, George, 'Employee Self-Management and Socialist Trade Unionism', in Jean Woodall (ed.), *Policy and Politics in Contemporary Poland: Reform, Failure and Crisis* (London: Frances Pinter, 1982), pp. 129–47.

—— 'The Politics of "Socialist Renewal"', in Jean Woodall (ed.), *Policy and Politics in Contemporary Poland: Reform, Failure and Crisis* (London: Frances Pinter, 1982), pp. 56–75.

—— 'Changing Social Structure', in George Schöpflin (ed.), *The Soviet Union and Eastern Europe: a Handbook* (London: Muller, Blond and White, 1986), pp. 497–505.

Kolarz, Walter, *Myths and Realities in Eastern Europe* (London: Lindsay Drummond, 1946).

Konrád, György, *Antipolitics* (London: Quartet, 1984).

Konrád, György, and Szelényi, Iván, 'A késleltetett városfejlödés társadalmi konfliktusai', *Valóság,* 15 no. 12 (December 1971), pp. 19–35.

—— *The Intellectuals on the Road to Class Power* (London: Harcourt, Brace, Jovanovich, 1979).

Korbonski, Andrzej, 'Social Deviance in Poland: the Case of the Private Sector', in Ivan Volgyes (ed.), *Social Deviance in Eastern Europe* (Boulder, CO: Westview, 1978), pp. 89–111.

Kornai, János, *A hiány,* 2nd edn (Budapest: Közgazdasági és Jogi, 1982).

Kovrig, Bennet, *Communism in Hungary: from Kun to Kádár* (Stanford, CA: Hoover Institution, 1979).

Krejci, Jaroslav, *Social Change and Social Stratification in Postwar Czechoslovakia* (London: Macmillan, 1972).

—— *Great Revolutions Compared: the Search for a Theory* (Brighton: Wheatsheaf, 1983).

Krisch, Henry, *The German Democratic Republic: the Search for Identity* (Boulder, CO: Westview, 1985).

Kruszewski, Z. Anthony, *The Oder-Neisse Boundary and Poland's Modernization: the Socioeconomic and Political Impact* (London: Pall Mall, 1972).

Kuklinski, Ryszard, 'The Suppression of Solidarity', in Robert Kostrzewa (ed.), *Between East and West: Writings from Kultura* (New York: Hill and Wang, 1990), pp. 72–98.

Kundera, Milan, *The Joke* (London: Faber, 1983).

—— *The Unbearable Lightness of Being* (London: Faber, 1984).

Kuron, Jacek, 'Pour une plateforme unique de l'opposition', *Politique Aujourd'hui,* no. 3–4, 1997.

Kürti, László, 'Hierarchy and Workers' Power in a Csepel Factory', in C. M. Hann (ed.), *Market Economy and Civil Society in Hungary* (London: Frank

Cass, 1990), pp. 61–84.

Kusin, Vladimir V., *The Intellectual Origins of the Prague Spring: the Development of Reformist Ideas in Czechoslovakia* (Cambridge: Cambridge University Press, 1971).

—— *Political Grouping in the Czechoslovak Reform Movement* (London: Macmillan, 1972)

—— *From Dubcek to Charter 77: Czechoslovakia 1968–1978* (Edinburgh: Q Press, 1978).

Laky, Teréz 'A recentralizálás rejtett mechanizmusai', *Valóság*, 23 no. 2 (February 1980), pp. 31–41.

Lampe, John, and Jackson, Marvin, *Balkan Economic History 1550–1950* (Bloomington: Indiana University Press, 1982).

Lehmbruch, G. and Schmitter, Philip, *Patterns of Corporatist Policy Making* (London: Sage, 1982).

Lengyel, László, 'Félúton', *2000,* 3 no. 7 (July 1991), pp. 3–14.

Leslie, R. F., et al., *The History of Poland since 1863* (Cambridge: Cambridge University Press, 1980).

Levinson, Charles, *Vodka-Cola* (London: Gordon and Cremonesi, 1978).

Lewis, Flora, *The Polish Volcano* (London: Secker and Warburg, 1959).

Liehm, Antonin, 'The New Social Contract and the Parallel Polity', in Jane Curry (ed.), *Dissent in Eastern Europe* (New York: Praeger, 1983), pp. 173–81.

Lomax, Bill, *Budapest 1956* (London: Allison and Busby, 1976)

—— 'The Rise and Fall of the Hungarian Working Class', in C. M. Hann (ed.), *Market Economy and Civil Society in Hungary* (London: Frank Cass, 1990), pp. 45–60.

Losonczi, Ágnes *Az életmód az időben, a tárgyakban és az értékekben* (Budapest: Gondolat, 1977).

McCauley, Martin (ed.), *Communist Power in Europe 1944–1949* (London: Macmillan, 1977).

—— *The German Democratic Republic since 1945* (London: Macmillan, 1983).

M[achan], P[rokop], 'The Plague of Bureaucracy', *Radio Free Europe Research: Czechoslovakia,* 17 March 1982.

McNeill, William H., *The Pursuit of Power* (Oxford: Blackwell, 1983).

McQuaid, David, 'Poland's Parliamentary Elections: a Postmortem', RFE/RL Research Institute, *Report on Eastern Europe,* 2 no. 45, 8 November 1991.

Maier, Anneli, 'Ceausescu Deified on his 62nd Birthday', *Radio Free Europe Research,* 11 February 1982.

Mamatey, Victor S., and Luza, Radomir, *A History of the Czechoslovak Republic 1914–1948* (Princeton: Princeton University Press, 1973).

Markov, Georgi, *The Truth that Killed* (London: Weidenfeld, 1983).

Márkus, György, 'Debates and Trends in Marxist Philosophy,' in Frantisek Silnitsky et al. (eds), *Communism and Eastern Europe* (New York: Karz, 1979), pp. 104–32.

Márkus, István, *Nagykörös* (Budapest: Szépirodalmi, 1979).

Meuschel, Sigrid, *Legitimation und Parteiherrschaft in der DDR: zum Paradox und Revolution in der DDR 1945–1989* (Frankfurt/Main: Suhrkamp, 1992).

Michnik, Adam, 'Ce que nous voulons et ce que nous pouvons', *L'Alternative,* no. 8 (January–February, 1981), pp. 5–14.

—— 'The New Evolutionism', in *Letters from Prison and Other Essays* (Berkeley, CA: University of California Press, 1985), pp. 135–48.

Mićunovic, Veljko, *Moscow Diary* (London: Chatto and Windus, 1980).

Mizsei, Kálmán (ed.), *A privatizációs kihívás Közép-Kelet-Európában* (Budapest: MTA Világgazdasági Kutató Intézet, 1990).

Mlynár, Zdenek, *Nightfrost in Prague: the End of Humane Socialism* (London: Hurst, 1980).

Morawski, Witold, 'Reform Models and Systemic Change in Poland', *Studies in Comparative Communism,* 23 no. 3 (September 1991), pp. 251–94.

Mouzelis, Nicos P., 'Greek and Bulgarian Peasants: Aspects of their Socio-Political Situation during the Inter War Period', *in Modern Greece, Facets of Underdevelopment* (London: Macmillan, 1978), pp. 89–104.

Murray, Charles, *Losing Ground: American Social Policy 1950–1980* (New York: Basic Books, 1984).

Myant, Martin, *Socialism and Democracy in Czechoslovakia, 1945–1948* (Cambridge: Cambridge University Press, 1981).

Nagy, Imre, *On Communism: In Defence of the New Course* (London: Thames and Hudson, 1957).

—— 'Secret Speech', *Labour Focus on Eastern Europe,* no. 3–4 (1982), pp. 8–10.

Narkiewicz, Olga, *The Green Flag: Polish Populist Politics 1867–1970* (London: Croom Helm, 1976).

Nordlinger, Eric A., *On the Autonomy of the Democratic State* (Cambridge, MA: Harvard University Press, 1981).

Obrebski, Joseph, *The Changing Peasantry of Eastern Europe* (Cambridge, MA: Schenkman, 1976).

Olsen, Donald J., *The City as a Work of Art: London, Paris, Vienna* (New Haven, CT: Yale University Press, 1986), pp. 58–81.

Oren, Nissan, *Bulgarian Communism: the Road to Power 1934–1944* (New York: Columbia University Press, 1971).

—— *Revolution Administered: Agrarianism and Communism in Bulgaria* (Baltimore: Johns Hopkins University Press, 1973).

Paikert, G. C., *The Danube Swabians* (The Hague: Martinus Nijhoff, 1967).

Pastor, Peter, 'One Step Forward, Two Steps Back: the Rise and Fall of the First Hungarian Communist Party, 1918–1921', in Ivo Banac (ed.), *The Effects of World War I: the Class War after the Great War: the Rise of Communist Parties in East Central Europe 1918–1921* (New York: Brooklyn College Studies, 1983).

Pataki, Judith, 'Role of Smallholders' Party in Hungary', *RFE/RL Research Report,* 1 no. 14, 3 April 1992.

Pearton, Maurice, *The Knowledgeable State* (London: Burnett, 1982).

Pelikan, Jiri, *The Czechoslovak Political Trials 1950–1954* (London: Macdonald, 1971).

Pelikán, Jirí (ed.), *Socialist Opposition in Eastern Europe: the Czechoslovak Example* (London: Allison and Busby, 1976).

Petrusek, Miroslav, 'A posztkommunizmus mint szociopolitikai fogalom és probléma', in *Politicai kultúra és állam Magyarországon és Cseh-Szlovákiábán* (Budapest: Giovanni Agrelli alapitvány, 1990).

Pokol, Béla, 'Alternativ utak a politikai rendszer reformjára', *Valóság*, 29 no. 12 (December 1986), pp. 32–45.

Polonsky, Anthony, *Politics in Independent Poland 1921–1939* (Oxford: Oxford University Press, 1972).

Prins, Gwyn (ed.), *Spring in Winter: the 1989 Revolutions* (Manchester: Manchester University Press, 1990)

Puhovski, Zarko, 'The End of the Socialist Construction of Reality', unpublished MS, 1990.

Remington, Robin Alison (ed.), *Winter in Prague* (Cambridge, MA: MIT Press, 1969), pp. 88–136.

Richta, Radovan, *Civilisation at the Crossroads: Social and Human Implications of the Scientific and Technological Revolution* (White Plains, NY: International Arts and Sciences Press, 1969).

Robinson, William F., *The Pattern of Reform in Hungary: a Political, Economic and Cultural Analysis* (New York: Praeger, 1973).

Roth, Josef, *The Radetzky March* (London: Penguin, 1984).

Rothschild, Joseph, *East Central Europe between the Two World Wars* (Seattle and London: University of Washington Press, 1974).

—— *Return to Diversity: a Political History of East Central Europe since World War II* (Oxford: Oxford University Press, 1989).

Ruane, Kevin, *The Polish Challenge* (London: BBC, 1982).

Rupnik, Jacques, 'Dissent in Poland, 1968–78', in Rudolf Tökés (ed.), *Opposition in Eastern Europe* (London: Macmillan, 1979), pp. 60–112.

—— *Histoire du parti communiste tchécoslovaque: des origines à la prise du pouvoir* (Paris: Presse de la Fondation Nationale des Sciences Politiques, 1981).

—— 'The Roots of Czech Stalinism', in Raphael Samuel and Gareth Stedman Jones (eds), *Culture, Ideology and Politics* (London: Routledge, 1982), pp. 302–19.

—— *The Other Europe* (London: Weidenfeld and Nicolson, 1988).

Rusinow, Dennison, *The Yugoslav Experiment 1948–1974* (London: C. Hurst, 1977).

Sampson, Steve, 'The Informal Sector in Eastern Europe', *Telos,* no. 66 (Winter 1985–1986), pp. 44–66.

Schöpflin, George, 'The Ideology of Rumanian Nationalism', *Survey,* 20 no. 2–3 (1974) pp. 77–104.

—— 'Opposition and Para-Opposition: Critical Currents in Hungary', in Rudolf Tökés (ed.), *Opposition in Eastern Europe* (London: Macmillan, 1979), pp. 142–86.

—— 'The Political Structure of Eastern Europe as a Factor in Intra-bloc Relations', in Karen Dawisha and Philip Hanson (eds), *Soviet-East European Dilemmas: Coercion, Competition and Consent* (London: Heinemann, 1981), pp. 61–83.

—— 'Corruption, Informalism, Irregularity in Eastern Europe: a Political Analysis', *Südost-Europa, 33* no. 7–8 (July–August 1984), pp. 389–401.

—— 'The Pattern of Political Takeovers: How Eastern Europe Fell', *Encounter,* 64 no. 2 (February 1985), pp. 65–9.

—— 'Domestic Politics', in Karl-Detlev Groothusen (ed.), *Südosteuropa-Handbuch, Band V, Ungarn* (Göttingen: Vandenhoeck and Rupprecht, 1987), pp. 67–106.

—— 'Reform in Eastern Europe', *Slovo* 1 no. 1 (1988), pp. 1–5.

—— 'Central Europe: Definitions Old and New', in George Schöpflin and Nancy Wood (eds), *In Search of Central Europe* (Cambridge: Polity, 1989).

—— 'The Prospects for Democracy in Central and Eastern Europe', in Peter Volten (ed.), *Uncertain Futures: Eastern Europe and Democracy* (New York: Institute for East-West Security Studies, 1990), pp. 19–34.

Seton-Watson, Hugh, *The East European Revolution,* 3rd edn (London: Methuen, 1956).

—— *The Pattern of Communist Revolution: a History of World Communism,* 2nd edn (London: Methuen, 1960).

Shafir, Michael, *Political Culture, Intellectual Dissent and Intellectual Consent: the Case of Rumania* (Jerusalem: Hebrew University, 1978).

—— *Romania: Politics, Economics and Society: Political Stagnation and Simulated Change* (London: Frances Pinter, 1985).

—— 'Romania', *RFE/RL Research Report,* Special Issue 'Toward the Rule of Law', 1 no. 27 (3 July 1992).

Sik, Ota, *The Bureaucratic Economy* (White Plains, NY: International Arts and Sciences Press, 1972).

Siklová, Jirina, 'Nacionalizmus Közép- és Kelet-Európában', *Valóság,* 35 no. 1 (January 1992), pp. 114–16, translated from *Frankfurter Allgemeine Zeitung,* 4 September 1991.

Simecka, Milan, *The Restoration of Order: the Normalization of Czechoslovakia* (London: Verso, 1984).

Skilling, Gordon, *Czechoslovakia's Interrupted Revolution* (Princeton, NJ: Princeton University Press, 1976).

—— *Charter 77 and Human Rights in Czechoslovakia* (London: Allen and Unwin, 1981).

—— *Samizdat and an Independent Society in Central and Eastern Europe* (London: Macmillan, 1989).

Skvorecky, Josef, *The Engineer of Human Souls* (London: Faber, 1985).

Smith, Anthony D., *The Ethnic Origins of Nations* (Oxford: Blackwell, 1986).

—— *National Identity* (London: Penguin Books, 1991).

Smolar, Alexander, 'The Rich and the Powerful', in Abraham Brumberg (ed.), *Poland: Genesis of a Revolution* (New York: Vintage Books, 1983), pp. 42–53.

Sperber, Manès, 'Die legitime moralische Grenze in der Politik: ein Gespräch mit Milovan Djilas', *Kontinent,* 11 no. 3 (no. 34), (July–August–September 1985), pp. 42–51.

Staniszkis, Jadwiga, *Poland's Self-Limiting Revolution* (Princeton, NJ: Princeton University Press, 1984).

—— 'Forms of Reasoning as Ideology', *Telos,* no. 66 (Winter 1985–6), pp. 67–80.

—— *The Dynamics of the Breakthrough in Eastern Europe: the Polish Experience* (Berkeley, CA: University of California Press, 1991).

Steiner, Eugene, *The Slovak Dilemma* (Cambridge: Cambridge University Press, 1973).

Steiner, George, *In Bluebeard's Castle* (London: Faber, 1971).

Suda, Zdenek, *Zealots and Rebels: a History of the Ruling Communist Party of Czechoslovakia* (Stanford, CA: Hoover Institution, 1980).

Sugar, Peter F. (ed.) *Native Fascism in the Successor States 1918–1945* (Santa Barbara, CA: ABC–ClioPress, 1971).

—— 'An Underrated Event: the Hungarian Constitutional Crisis of 1905-06', *East European Quarterly,* 15 no. 3 (1981), pp. 281–306.

Szabó, Miklós, *Politikai kultúra Magyarországon 1898–1986* (Budapest: Medvetánc, 1989).

Szafar, Tadeusz, 'The Origins of the Communist Party in Poland, 1918–1921', in Ivo Banac (ed.), *The Effects of World War I: the Class War after the Great War: the Rise of Communist Parties in East Central Europe 1918–1921* (New York: Brooklyn College Studies, 1983).

Szalai, Júlia, 'A szociálpolitika nyelve – amit kifejez és amit eltakar', *Medvetánc,* no. 4, 1984–no. 1, 1985, pp. 105–19.

Szczepanski, Jan, 'A munkásosztály összetételének változása', *A szociológus szemével* (Budapest: Gondolat, 1977), p. 19.

Sztompka, Piotr, 'The Intangibles and Imponderables of the Transition to Democracy', *Studies in Comparative Communism,* 24 no. 3 (September 1991), pp. 295–311.

Szücs, Jenö, *Vázlat Európa három történeti régiójáról* (Budapest: Magvetö, 1983); a translation 'Three Historical Regions of Europe', is in John Keane (ed.), *Civil Society and the State* (London: Verso, 1988), pp. 291–332.

Tigrid, Pavel, *Amère Révolution* (Paris: Albin Michel, 1977).

Tökés, Rudolf L., 'Hungary's New Political Élite: Adaptation and Change 1989-1990', *Problems of Communism,* 39 no. 6 (November–December 1990), pp. 45–65.

Tomasevich, Jozo, *Peasants, Politics and Economic Change in Yugoslavia* (Stanford, CA: Stanford University Press, 1955).

Torańska, Teresa, *Oni: Stalin's Polish Puppets* (London: Collins Harvill, 1987).

Triska, Jan and Gati, Charles (ed.) *Blue-Collar Workers in Eastern Europe* (London: Allen and Unwin, 1981).

Turner, Victor, *Dramas, Fields and Metaphors: Symbolic Action in Human Society* (Ithaca, NY: Cornell University Press, 1974).

Vajda, Mihály, *Fascism as a Mass Movement* (London: Allison and Busby,

1976).

Vale, Michael (ed.), *Poland: the State of the Republic – Two Reports by the Experience and Future Discussion Group (DiP) Warsaw* (London: Pluto, 1981).

Vámos, Tibor, 'Iparpolitika és gazdaság: eredmények, gondok, távlatok', *Valóság,* 28 no. 6 (June 1985), pp. 25–38.

Vass, Henrik (ed.), *Studies on the History of the Hungarian Working Class Movement 1867–1966* (Budapest: Akadémiai, 1975).

Vinton, Louisa, 'From Margins to the Mainstream: the Confederation for an Independent Poland', *RFE/RL Research,* 2 no. 46, 15 November 1991.

Völgyes, Iván (ed.), *Hungary in Revolution 1918–1919: Nine Essays,* (Lincoln: University of Nebraska Press, 1971).

Vukmanović-Tempo, Svetozar, *Revolucija koja teče,* vol. II (Belgrade: Komunist, 1971), p. 233.

Wallerstein, Immanuel, *The Modern World System* (2 vols, London: Academic Press, 1974–80).

Wedel, Janine, *The Private Poland: an Anthropologist's Look at Everyday Life* (New York: Facts on File, 1986).

Weydenthal, Jan B. de, *The Communists of Poland: an Historical Outline* (Stanford: Hoover Institution Press, 1978).

White, Stephen, et al., *Communist and Post-Communist Political Systems,* 3rd edn (London: Macmillan, 1990).

Wirpsza, Witold, *Pole, wer bist du?* (Lucerne: C. J. Bucher, 1972).

Zinner, Paul E., *Communist Strategy and Tactics in Czechoslovakia 1918–1948* (London: Pall Mall, 1963).

Index

Action Programme (1968) 155
Aczél, György 191n
Aczél, Tamás 120n
Adamec, Ladislav 239
Afghanistan 234
Ágh, Attila 287n
Agrarian Radicals 59, 65
Agrarian Union 46
agriculture, Stalinist strategy
    100–1
Albania: collapse of
    communism 224; party
    system 88; tribal structures
    20
Anderson, Perry 11n
Antall, József 268
anti-Semitism 12n, 42–3, 296
Antonescu, Ion 62, 219
Apró, Éva 171n
Arab world 9
Armenians 32
Armstrong, John A. 10n, 17n
Ash, Timothy Garton 184n
atomization 169–71
Austria:
    economy 189, 263–4;
    Soviet policy 64

Austria-Hungary 41–2
    bureaucracy 15; declaration of
    war (1914) 12; Social
    Democrats 41
Austrian State Treaty 113–14
autonomy, social 202–6
Avakumovic, Ivan 45n, 55n

Balawyder, A. 91n
Balkans: bourgeoisie 32; Social
    Democrats 41; wars 38;
    working class 33, 34
Baltic states 252
Batt, Judy 231n
Bauer, Tamás 127n, 138
Bauman, Zygmunt 29n, 147n,
    260n
Baylis, Thomas A. 147n
Behr, Edward 230n
Belgrade Declaration 111
Bell, John D. 220n
Bell, Peter 206n
Beneš, Eduard 62, 247
Berecz, János 99n, 101n
Beria, Lavrenti P. 106, 108, 110,
    112, 118